Community-of-Interests as a Theory of International Water Law

International Water Law Series

VOLUME 14

The titles published in this series are listed at *brill.com/iwl*

Community-of-Interests as a Theory of International Water Law

Normative Elements, Functions and Status

By

Flavia Rocha Loures

BRILL | NIJHOFF

ISSN 2351-9606
ISBN 978-90-04-74952-8
ISBN 978-90-04-50703-6 (PDF)
DOI https://doi.org/10.1163/9789004507036

Library of Congress Control Number: 2025038198

Brill Nijhoff and Koninklijke Brill BV are part of De Gruyter Brill.
www.degruyterbrill.com

Questions about General Product Safety Regulation: productsafety@degruyterbrill.com.

For my parents, Celia and Reinaldo Rocha Loures. You are the strength that pushes me forward and the kindness that drives my commitment to building a better world. To my sister, Marcela, my best friend and an inspirational light of heartfulness and professionalism. To my godson, Lucas "Anjo" R.L.S., and my niece, Fernanda Prestes. What I do is for you and your children in the eternity of my love for you both.

Contents

Acknowledgements

The author would like thank Xiamen University for the incredible and stimulating opportunity to study in China. The thesis on which this book is based could not have been envisioned and written anywhere else, as it carries with it so much of my experiences in the country and with the professors, colleagues, and friends who have been part of this journey. A special word of gratitude goes to my supervisor, Prof. Chen Huiping.

The author also thanks the visiting scholars and colleagues who provided invaluable guidance and shared with the students hours of relaxation and informal debate.

Outside school, an amazing community of friends opened opportunities to get to know Xiamen and Chinese culture better, walking alongside the author in fun, solidarity, and poetry.

Immense gratitude is owed to my family, whose unconditional love and encouragement have made it possible finally getting to this day. When determination to complete the task faltered, my parents' voices telling me to persevere kept me going. When I needed a break and laughter, my sister, her partner, Fernando Prestes, and our friends never let me down. When I needed to be reminded of why this work matters, my nephew and niece smiling at me always did the trick.

Acronyms

AEC	African Economic Community
AfDB	African Development Bank
AMCOW	African Ministers' Council on Water
ASEAN	Association of Southeast Asian Nations
AU	African Union
CARU	River Uruguay Executive Commission (*Comisión Administradora del Rio Uruguay*)
CBD	Convention on Biological Diversity
CBDR	Common But Differentiated Responsibilities
CEN-SAD	Community of Sahel-Saharan States
CFA	Nile Basin Cooperative Framework Agreement
COMESA	Common Market for Eastern and Southern Africa
EAC	East African Community
ECCAS	Economic Community of Central African States
ECE	UN Economic Commission for Europe
ECEWC	UNECE Convention on the Protection and Use of Transboundary Watercourses and International Lakes
EIA	Environmental Impact Assessment
EU	European Union
GEF	Global Environment Facility
GWP	Global Water Partnership
HLPF	High-Level Political Forum on Sustainable Development
IBWC	International Boundary and Water Commission
ICJ	International Court of Justice
ICPR	International Commission for the Protection of the Rhine
ICWE	International Conference on Water and the Environment
IGAD	Intergovernmental Authority on Development
IIL	Institute of International Law
IISD	International Institute for Sustainable Development
ILA	International Law Association
ILC	International Law Commission
IRBM	Integrated River Basin Management
IWMI	International Water Management Institute
IWRA	International Water Resources Association
IWRM	Integrated water resources management
IWT	Indus Water Treaty
LVBC	Lake Victoria Basin Commission

MERCOSUL	Southern Common Market
NBI	Nile Basin Initiative
NGO(s)	Nongovernmental Organization(s)
OAS	Organization of American States
OAU	Organization of African Unity
OMVS	Senegal River Basin Development Organization
OMVS PWC	OMVS Permanent Water Commission
PCA	Permanent Court of Arbitration
PCIJ	Permanent Court of International Justice
PIC	Permanent Indus Commission
PTA	Preferential Trade Area for Eastern and Southern Africa
REC	Regional Economic Community
SAARC	South Asian Association for Regional Cooperation
SADC	Southern African Development Community
SADC WSCU	SADC Water Sector Coordinating Unit
SADC WRTC	Water Resources Technical Committee
SADC CWSO	Committee of Water Senior Officials
SDG(s)	Sustainable Development Goal(s)
SIWI	Stockholm International Water Institute
S2S	Source-to-Sea
UN	United Nations
UNCED	UN Conference on Environment and Development
UN DESA	UN Department of Economic and Social Affairs
UNEA	UN Environmental Assembly
UNECA	UN Economic Commission for Africa
UNEP	UN Environment Program
UNESCO	UN Educational, Scientific and Cultural Organization
UNESCO IHP	UNESCO International Hydrological Program
UNFCCC	UN Framework Convention on Climate Change
UNGA	UN General Assembly
UNSG	UN Secretary-General
UN Water	UN Water
UNW-DPAC	UN-Water Decade Program on Advocacy and Communication
UNWC	UN Convention on the Law of Non-Navigational Uses of International Watercourses
ZAMCOM	Zambezi Watercourse Commission
WMO	World Meteorological Organization

Cases

Permanent Court of International Justice (PCIJ)

Case Concerning the Territorial Jurisdiction of the International Commission of the River Oder, Denmark-Czechoslovakia-France-Germany-Sweden-UK *v.* Poland, Judgment of 16 Sep 1929 ('River Oder Case').

The Diversion of Water from the Meuse, Netherlands *v.* Belgium, Judgment of 28 June 1937, Series A/B, Judgments, Orders and Advisory Opinions, Fascicule 70 (1937) ('Meuse Diversion Case').

International Court of Justice (ICJ)

Corfu Channel Case (UK *v.* Albania), Judgment of 9 Apr 1949, ICJ Reports 4 (1949).

Reparation for Injuries Suffered in the Service of the United Nations, Advisory Opinion of 11 Apr 1949, ICJ Reports 1949, p. 174.

Cases Concerning the North Sea Continental Shelf (Germany *v.* Denmark & Germany *v.* Netherlands), Judgment of 20 Feb 1969, ICJ Reports 3 (1969) ('North Sea Continental Shelf Cases').

Fisheries Jurisdiction (UK *v.* Iceland), Merits, Judgment of 25 July 1974, ICJ Reports 3 (1974) ('Fisheries Jurisdiction Case').

Fisheries Jurisdiction Case, *Declaration*, Judge Ignacio-Pinto.

Passage through the Great Belt (Finland *v.* Denmark), Provisional Measures, Order of 29 July 1991, ICJ Reports 12 (1991) ('Great Belt Case').

Legality of the Use by a State of Nuclear Weapons in Armed Conflict, Advisory Opinion of 8 July 1996, ICJ Reports 66 (1996) ('Nuclear Weapons Use in Armed Conflict AO').

Legality of the Threat or Use of Nuclear Weapons, Advisory Opinion of 8 July 1996, ICJ Reports 226 (1996) ('Nuclear Weapons Threat or Use AO').

Case Concerning the Gabčíkovo-Nagymaros Project (Hungary *v.* Slovakia), Judgment of 25 Sep 1997, ICJ Reports 1997, p. 7 ('Gabčíkovo Case').

Gabčíkovo Case, *Separate Opinion*, M. Bedjaoui.

Case Concerning Pulp Mills on the River Uruguay (Argentina *v.* Uruguay), Judgment of 20 Apr 2010, ICJ Reports 1 (2010) ('Pulp Mills Case').

Pulp Mills Case, *Request for the Indication of Provisional Measures*, Order of 13 July 2006, ICJ Reports 113 (2006) ('Pulp Mills 2006 Provisional Measures').

Dispute over the Status and Use of the Waters of the Silala (Chile *v.* Bolivia), Judgment of 1 Dec 2022, ICJ Reports 2022, p. 614 ('Silala Case').

Permanent Court of Arbitration (PCA)

Case Concerning the Auditing of Accounts between the Kingdom of The Netherlands and the French Republic pursuant to the Additional Protocol of 25 Sep 1991 to the Convention on the Protection of the Rhine Against Pollution by Chlorides of 3 Dec 1976, (Netherlands *v.* France), Arbitral Award of 12 March 2004 (Unofficial English Translation) (on file) ('Chlorides Case').

Ad Hoc Arbitral Tribunals

Arbitral Tribunal, *Affaire du Lac Lanoux* ('Case Concerning the Lake Lanoux') (Spain *v.* France), Award of 16 Nov 1957 ('Lake Lanoux Case').

ICJ, Kasikili/Sedudu Island (Botswana *v.* Namibia), Judgment (13 Dec 1999), 1999 ICJ Report 1045 ('Kasikili Case').

Kasikili Case, *Separate Opinion*, Judge Kooijmans.

Kasikili Case, *Declaration*, Judge Ranjeva.

US Supreme Court

State of New Jersey *v.* State of New York, 283 US 336 (1931).

Introduction: The Duty to Cooperate from the Universal to the Basin Level

> *Water is humanity's lifeblood. From the food we eat. To the ecosystems and biodiversity that enrich our world. To the prosperity that sustains nations. To the economic engines of agriculture, manufacturing and energy generation. To our health, hygiene and survival itself.*[1]

International law has historically played a key role in regulating and guiding interactions between co-riparian states, alongside other enablers of cooperation, such as funding availability, data generation, exchanges between subnational political units, and capacity building. International law has contributed to bringing co-basin states together to exchange information, consult and negotiate with one another on planned measures, settle their disagreements peacefully, and jointly protect the ecosystems of shared waters.[2]

Legal clarity and common understanding of the theoretical bases of international water law and their progressive development are fundamental for the rule of law to continue to facilitate transboundary water cooperation in a meaningful and positive manner. This book is thus motivated by the deepening interdependencies among the states sharing freshwaters and the potential role for the *Community-of-Interests Theory* (hereinafter, *Community-of-Interests* or *the Theory*) in this context.

Community-of-Interests is one of four theoretical bases for international water law that different scholars have identified in state discourse and practice over the years. *Absolute Territorial Integrity* and *Absolute Territorial Sover-*

1 A. Guterres, *Secretary-General's Remarks at the UN Water Conference* (22 Mar 2023), at https://www.un.org/sg/en/content/sg/speeches/2023-03-22/secretary-generals-remarks-the-united-nations-water-conference.

2 On the value of international water law, *see*, e.g., Government of Tajikistan, High Level International Conference on the International Decade for Action, Water for Sustainable Development, 2018–2028 (Dushanbe, 20–22 June 2018) ('2018 Dushanbe Conference'), *Co-Chairs' Summary*, at https://wsdconf2018.org/wp-content/uploads/2017/05/Dushanbe-Water-Summary-fin.pdf, p. 7.

 | HTTPS://DOI.ORG/10.1163/9789004507036-002

eignty – both of which aim to justify claims of absolute control over the resource, have been largely discredited: states accept that shared freshwaters are subject to international law, which establishes rights and obligations in connection with their use, management, and protection; and so, that sovereign rights over these resources are not absolute and must be exercised within the limitations and according to the requirements imposed by the rule of law.

Interstate cooperation over water resources, even where superficial, has tempered extreme sovereignty assertions. *Limited Territorial Sovereignty* is widely accepted as the dominant theory underlying current international water law, and which recognizes the need for equitably balancing state interests and for preventing transboundary harm. *Community-of-Interests* serves as a basis for stronger, more systematic and basin-wide cooperation.

Viewing a transboundary basin as a biogeographic unit, the foundational purpose of the Theory is to advance the common interests that co-riparian states come together to safeguard and promote. With the duty to cooperate at its core, the normative significance of Community-of-Interests finds expression in the numerous implicit or explicit references made thereto in judicial precedents,[3] water agreements,[4] and renowned scholarship.[5] At the same time, questions remain as to what, specifically, Community-of-Interests

3 *See* Permanent Court of International Justice (PCIJ), *Case Concerning the Territorial Jurisdiction of the International Commission of the River Oder* (Denmark-Czechoslovakia-France-Germany-Sweden-UK *v.* Poland), Judgment of 16 Sep 1929 ('River Oder Case'); International Court of Justice (ICJ), *Case Concerning the Gabčíkovo-Nagymaros Project* (Hungary *v.* Slovakia), Judgment of 25 Sep 1997 ('Gabčíkovo Case'); ICJ, *Case Concerning Pulp Mills on the River Uruguay* (Argentina *v.* Uruguay), Judgment of 20 Apr 2010 ('Pulp Mills Case'); Permanent Court of Arbitration (PCA), *Case Concerning the Auditing of Accounts between the Kingdom of The Netherlands and the French Republic pursuant to the Additional Protocol of 25 Sep 1991 to the Convention on the Protection of the Rhine Against Pollution by Chlorides of 3 Dec 1976* (Netherlands *v.* France), Arbitral Award of 12 Mar 2004 (Unofficial English Translation) ('Chlorides Case'); ICJ, *Dispute over the Status and Use of the Waters of the Silala* (Chile *v.* Bolivia), Judgment of 1 Dec 2022, ICJ Reports 2022, p. 614 ('Silala Case').

4 *See Protocol for Sustainable Development of Lake Victoria Basin* (Arusha, 29 Nov 2003) (in force 1 Dec 2004), Burundi-Kenya-Rwanda-Tanzania-Uganda, Art.4(2)(i) ('Lake Victoria Protocol'); *Charte des Eaux du Fleuve Sénégal* ('Charter of the Senegal River Waters') (Nouakchott, 28 May 2002), Guinea-Mali-Mauritania-Senegal, Preamble, ¶17 ('Senegal Basin Charter'); *Protocol on Shared Watercourse Systems in the Southern African Development Community* (SADC) (Johannesburg, 28 Aug 1995) (in force 29 Sep 1998), Angola-Botswana-Lesotho-Malawi-Mozambique-Namibia-South Africa-Swaziland-Tanzania-Zambia-Zimbabwe ('1995 SADC Protocol'); *Acuerdo que Establece la Comisión Binacional para la Gestión Integrada de los Recursos Hídricos de las Cuencas Hidrográficas Transfronterizas*, Ecuador-Peru (Trujillo, 20 Oct 2017) ('Ecuador-Peru Agreement').

5 *See*, e.g., S.C. McCaffrey, *The Law of International Watercourses*, 3rd ed (Oxford 2019), p. 219–37.

means or entails under the law of transboundary basins; or what legal concepts characterize interstate water interactions thereunder.

Looking at the Theory's composite terms offers a general direction to follow in our investigation. The *Merriam-Webster Dictionary Online* defines a *community* as "the people with *common interests* living in a *particular area*";[6] or else, "a *body of … nations* having a common history or *common* social, economic, and political *interests*".[7] The Cambridge Dictionary also captures the spatial component of the definition, adding the notion of "people who are considered as *a unit* because of their common interests".[8] In Law, the term *community* may refer to "the people who live in a *particular place or region* and usually are *linked* by some *common interests*";[9] or, similarly, "a neighborhood, vicinity, or locality [or] a society or group of people with similar rights or interests".[10]

As defined by Simma, a *community* is "a 'higher unity', as it were, the representation and *priorization of common interests*",[11] as opposed to a mere *society*, which "does not presuppose more than factual contacts among a number of individuals".[12]

As the second composite term of the Theory, McCaffrey interprets *interests* as representing those interests delimited around a state's "present and prospective uses of the watercourse as well as its concern for the health of the watercourse ecosystem", the latter concern being shared among all co-riparian countries. In this sense, whether the interests of co-riparians are common and/or unilateral, all such interests "are in one and the same watercourse system".[13]

In line with the above definitions, Community-of-Interests is founded on the hydrological, geological, and ecological unity of the drainage basin and on the multidimensional interdependencies among co-riparian states that arise from that factual unity. As viewed under Community-of-Interests, catchment-based ecological, social, cultural, and economic interstate connections moti-

---

6 Merriam-Webster Dictionary Online: *Community*, at http://www.merriam-webster.com/dictionary/community (emphasis added).

7 *Ibid* (emphasis added).

8 English Cambridge Dictionary: *Community*, at https://dictionary.cambridge.org/us/dictionary/english/community (emphasis added).

9 Merriam-Webster Legal Dictionary Online: *Community*, at https://www.merriam-webster.com/dictionary/community#legalDictionary (emphasis added).

10 B.A. Garner ed, *Black's Law Dictionary*, 9th ed (Thomson Reuters 2009), p. 317.

11 B. Simma, *From Bilateralism to Community Interest in International Law*, 250 Recueil des Cours 217 (1994), p. 245 (emphasis added).

12 *Ibid.*

13 McCaffrey (2019), *supra*, p. 232.

vate the countries within that common space to work closely together towards shared goals, while reconciling differences peacefully.[14] Acting within the Theory's framework allows riparian states to profit from *interdependence*, i.e., "the reliance of countries on each other to ensure their mutual subsistence and advancement."[15] Importantly, focusing in on priority common goals does not mean ignoring vital individual interests, but rather realizing the former while considering and balancing the latter as necessary to preserve the cooperation regime and respect the rights of its members.

Our journey towards unpacking Community-of-Interests builds on analogy, but not analogy as a "special type of legal reasoning [for] the application of a rule which covers a particular case to another case which is similar to the first but itself not regulated by the rule".[16] Analogy is used here as a heuristic tool for aiding in the discovery of state practice on close cooperation in relation to common interests at different levels. We "explore fluid and creative applications of analogy to shape concepts on the frontlines of scientific research"[17] – like the elements of Community-of-Interests. The pathway chosen is to start by considering the core meaning of the duty to cooperate, as practiced on a global scale based on general international law. We then bring the still vague cooperation duty to the context of interactions between states at the regional level. Finally, the book applies, tests, and adjusts elements of cooperative state practice for common interests from the global to the regional and to the scale of transboundary basins. Through this comparative exercise, we unpack the Theory's normative content.

As its main contribution, the book presents the *elements, functions, and status* of *Community-of-Interests* as a *Theory* that frames the set of norms governing the use, management, and protection of transboundary waters. The normative elements, as identified and unpacked herein, are the legal concepts and approaches that flow from state practice on transboundary water cooperation framed by Community-of-Interests; and upon which we build the Legal Analytical Framework that supports the analysis of the Theory's functions and status. Through these elements, Community-of-Interests operates as a principle influencing the applicability of existing or possibly emerging rules of interna-

14 *See*, e.g., O. McIntyre, *Environmental Protection of International Watercourses under International Law* (Ashgate 2007), p. 39.

15 Garner ed, *supra*, p. 884.

16 S. Vöneky, *Analogy in International Law*, in MPEPIL, p. 2 (2008).

17 *Analogy and Analogical Reasoning* (25 Jan 2019), Stanford Encyclopedia of Philosophy, at https://plato.stanford.edu/entries/reasoning-analogy/#ConChaTheDev.

tional law in this field. In the light of the Theory's functions and elements, we determine its status as a distinct theoretical basis for international water law.

The Theory has underlined state practice in this field without displacing collaborative efforts framed by Limited Territorial Sovereignty. The Theory's uptake might accelerate in the face of a mounting global water crisis and in an increasingly interdependent world, as states advance in their understanding of shared benefits, costs, risks, challenges, and opportunities and the value of closer cooperation. In this process, states would need to overcome unilateralism instincts and prioritize strong engagement and long-term commitment to dialogue and common basin planning and associated shared benefits.

1 Terminology

> *Transboundary water cooperation is an act of empowerment, of trust, and of hope in the face of increasing uncertainty.*[18]

Scholars have referenced Community-of-Interests using a variety of terms. This reflects, at the same time that it contributes to, the lack of clarity regarding the Theory's normative character. Convinced that Community-of-Interests is a theoretical framework under international water law, we refer to our central subject matter, throughout this book, as the *Theory of Community-of-Interests* – or simply *Community-of-Interests* or the *Theory*.

As employed herein, the expression *common interests* is used interchangeably with *common, shared, agreed, or joint interests, goals, concerns, or priorities.*

The expressions *international water law, the law of international watercourses,* or the *law of transboundary basins* refer interchangeably to the set of norms that govern the protection, management and development of all transboundary freshwaters.

The terms *transboundary, shared,* or *international,* accompanying the words *water*[*s*], *freshwater*[*s*], *freshwater system*[*s*], *watercourse*[*s*], *watercourse system*[*s*], *aquifer*[*s*], *aquifer system*[*s*], *basin*[*s*], *drainage basin*[*s*], *catchment*[*s*] *or watershed*[*a*] are all used herein to refer to the shared natural resources that are governed under international water law. The terms [*co-*]*basin,* [*co-*]*ripar-*

18 Tatiana Molcean, Executive Secretary, UNECE and UN Under-Secretary-General, *in* IISD, *Summary of the 10th Meeting of the Parties to the UN Water Convention: 23–25 October 2024*, Water Convention Bulletin (28 Oct 2024), p. 7.

ian, watercourse or *aquifer state*[*s*] refer to the states physically sharing those resources.[19]

The book coins and uses the expressions *communities-of-basin-interests*, *communities-of-interests* or *Community-of-Interests regimes* in reference to specific groupings of states that share water and thus have catchment interests in common, and which interact on the basis of the Theory.

Our *Legal Analytical Framework* identifies the four primary and the three secondary normative elements of Community-of-Interests. The through-line across all such elements is the drainage basin: the factual basis of Community-of-Interests and the foundational biogeographic scope of the shared concerns at stake.

While each element is later analyzed in detail, we present here the expressions coined for each, together with brief explanations, so the readers have a general understanding of the Theory from the outset.

The *Community-of-Interests Drainage Basin Scope* ('Basin Scope') expresses the basin-level biogeographic ambit of Community-of-Interests and aligns with the so-called *drainage basin approach*, introduced into international law discourse via Article II of the Helsinki Rules. Basin-level cooperation, or cooperation with a Basin Scope, means considering, as appropriate, the drainage basin (or a sub-basin) as the basic (though not necessarily exclusive) biogeographic unit for the planning and management of shared waters and their ecosystems. Herein, the Basin Scope is examined through the water-system concept, including the latter's applicability under agreements not involving all states within the catchment, and that concept's relationship to the drainage basin; as well as regarding possible future legal developments on freshwater-marine interlinkages.

---

19 As legal bases for some of these terms, *see* United Nations (UN), *Convention on the Law of Non-Navigational Uses of International Watercourses* (New York City, 21 May 1997) (in force 17 Aug 2014), 36 ILM 700 (1997) ('UNWC'), Art.2(a)-(c); *Draft Articles on the Law of the Non-Navigational Uses of International Watercourses and Commentaries thereto and Resolution on Transboundary Confined Groundwater* ('ILC Draft Articles (1994)'), *in* ILC Report, 46th Session (2 May-22 July 1994), UN Doc A/49/10 ('ILC (1994)'); UN Economic Commission for Europe (ECE), *Convention on the Protection and Use of Transboundary Watercourses and International Lakes* (Helsinki, 17 Mar 1992) (in force 6 Oct 1996), 31 ILM 1312 ('ECEWC'), Art.1(1) & (4); International Law Commission (ILC), *Draft Articles on the Law of Transboundary Aquifers, with Commentaries* (2008) ('ILC Draft Articles (2008)'), Art.2(a)-(d), *in* ILC Report, 60th Session (NYC, 5 May-6 June & 7 July-8 Aug 2008), UN Doc A/63/10(SUPP); International Law Association (ILA), *Helsinki Rules on the Uses of the Waters of International Rivers* ('Helsinki Rules'), Art.II, *in* ILA Report, 52nd Session (Helsinki, 16 Aug 1966), Uses of Waters of International Rivers, p. 447–533 ('ILA (1966)').

The *Community-of-Interests Drainage Basin Treaty* ('Basin Treaty') is a particular kind of transboundary water agreement that, being framed by the Theory, formalizes, regulates, and institutionalizes communities-of-interests. Given the specificities of each basin and sub-basin, co-riparian states around the world have adopted agreements and arrangements applying and adjusting basic principles and rules of international water law to a local context. The Basin Treaty is a subset of context-specific treaties or, to use terminology from the UN Watercourses Convention (UNWC), *watercourse agreements*. The Basin Treaty displays the following characteristic features that go beyond balancing unilateral concerns, interests, and rights for peaceful coexistence: specification of priority common interests, risks, and opportunities; definition of states' mutual relations and relevant conduct in the pursuit of those shared interests, founded on Close Drainage Basin Cooperation, as defined below; and establishment of the Community-of-Interests Drainage Basin Body.[20] The book explores this normative element of the Theory by highlighting its legal significance for Community-of-Interests regimes and its core purposes, its geographic scope, and how the Basin Treaty compares to a nonbinding basin arrangement.

The *Community-of-Interests Drainage Basin Body* ('Basin Body') is a basin organization not only established "to facilitate cooperation on relevant measures and procedures",[21] but specifically designed to house individual communities-of-interests. The Basin Body is established by the Basin Treaty and is principally structured to facilitate the achievement of shared goals. Safeguarding peaceful interstate relations is a subsidiary objective of the Basin Body. Both objectives are principally pursued through Close Drainage Basin Cooperation and with a Basin Scope. In unpacking this normative element, we demonstrate the legal significance of the Basin Body and its core function and address jurisdictional questions. We also elucidate the legal nature of the Basin Body *vis-à-vis* institutional mechanisms established by nonbinding arrangements.

Close Drainage Basin Cooperation ('Close Basin Cooperation') refers to interstate interactions framed by the Theory. Whereas cooperation informed by Limited Territorial Sovereignty is characterized by unilateral restraint and mostly *ad hoc* interactions for peaceful coexistence, Close Basin Cooperation centers on securing common interests in the protection, management, and development of the international watercourse. To safeguard those interests

20 *See* UNWC, *supra*, Art.3(3) & ECEWC, *supra*, Art.9(1) – both of which inform the characterization of the Basin Treaty.

21 UNWC, *supra*, Art.8(2).

effectively, Close Basin Cooperation is long-term, ongoing, systematic, and so more advanced than relations under Limited Territorial Sovereignty. As a residual goal, Close Basin Cooperation also aims to balance unilateral state concerns and to prevent and swiftly resolve disputes. Close Basin Cooperation involves any kind of engagement by co-basin states on shared interests and may thus assume different modalities – from domestic measures through coordination to joint or common action.[22] Yet, in the framework of Close Basin Cooperation, joint action prevails over, being supplemented by, other modalities of state engagement. Close Basin Cooperation does not imply endorsement of the notions of common property and mutual consent.

Further, Close Basin Cooperation requires political will, commitment, and accountability for maximizing benefits from cooperation *vis-à-vis* eventual risks and potential short-term advantages linked to non-cooperation; necessitates legal-institutional frameworks that set out guiding goals and norms for law-based, stable, mutually beneficial, and peaceful interstate collaboration; entails planning and management that consider interdependencies; implies joint responsibility for the protection of water bodies, their catchments, and ecosystems; and calls for stakeholder participation and due consideration of their concerns.[23]

Close Basin Cooperation is a specific manifestation of *Close Cooperation* between states, a form of cooperation that happens across levels and branches of international law when common interests are at stake and are prioritized by the states concerned. This includes Close Regional Cooperation through Regional Integration Organizations.

Among the secondary elements of Community-of-Interests, *Coherence* characterizes external or interinstitutional relations, i.e., the mutually reinforcing and harmonized relationships between an individual community-of-sub-basin-interests and related broader, narrower, or parallel water and related cooperation regimes. Coherence may apply as between communities-of-sub-basin-interests within the same catchment; between basin-wide

---

22 In this same sense, see J.G. Howden, *The Community of Interest Approach in International Water Law: A Legal Framework for Common Management of International Watercourses*, Thesis submitted for Degree of Philosophiae Doctor, University of Bergen (2019), p. 26–6 (emphasis added), p. 237, affirming "a broad understanding of the obligation to cooperate, from unilateral acts to joint management".

23 *See* J.M. Unturbe, *A 10 Year Story: The Water for Life Decade 2005–2015 and Beyond* (UN Office to Support the International Decade for Action 'Water for Life' (2005–2015) ('UN Office') & UN Water Decade Program on Advocacy and Communication ('UNW-DPAC') (2015), p. 38–42, describing these characteristics, though not specifically in the context of Close Basin Cooperation.

communities-of-interests and water cooperation regimes formed at the sub-basin level; and between communities-of-sub-basin-interests in different catchments but under an overarching umbrella regime, whether governing regional interests and/or various transboundary basins.

Solidarity characterizes intra-institutional relationships, i.e., those relations among the states within a certain drainage basin. The book unpacks Solidarity in general international law, as regards the hydrosolidarity policy paradigm, and as an element of the Theory.

Social Basin Engagement reflects the finding that communities-of-basin-interests tend to integrate into the cooperation process the stakeholders operating within their respective areas of jurisdiction. Social Basin Engagement can be understood from the perspective of international democratic governance and in light of Community-of-Interests state practice on relations with interested actors.

The above normative elements form a set of interlinked legal concepts that gain unique characteristics when applied in the context of Community-of-Interests, and through which the Theory gains concrete expression.

2 Water and Cooperation for Sustainability

Understanding Community-of-Interests requires setting its investigation within the wider context of modern environmental challenges and the vulnerabilities and attributes that are unique to water as a fluid natural resource essential for all life. Freshwater lies at the center of socioeconomic progress, planetary health, and international relations, but has been overlooked and is under major pressures from human development and climate change. Freshwater ecosystems are the most affected by biodiversity loss – more than terrestrial and marine. Water builds interdependencies and shared interests as the ultimate connector of humans, economies, and nature, especially at the basin level.

2.1 *The Global Water Crisis*

> *Billions of people worldwide are still living without access to safely managed drinking water and sanitation services. Water pollution levels are alarmingly high. Inefficient water use practices are common. Water scarcity is a growing problem. Degradation of water-related ecosystems con-*

> *tinues unabated. Governance and transboundary cooperation on water resources are too weak.*[24]

The *2030 Agenda for Sustainable Development* includes a dedicated Sustainable Development Goal (SDG) to "ensure availability and sustainable management of water and sanitation for all"[25] (SDG-6). With an all-encompassing and integrative approach, the Agenda implicitly recognizes the cross-cutting nature of that vital resource;[26] and reflects the complexity of today's world and the difficulties rapid environmental change and globalization pose, through water, to the attainment of sustainability objectives.

These difficulties become apparent from recent UN accounts for the degree of implementation of SDG 6.5, on sustainable water resources management at all levels. The Target is measured through four dimensions: *enabling environment* (laws, policies, and plans); *institutions and public participation*; *management instruments*; and *financing*. The assessment is based on national reports submitted by 191 countries up to 2023 for SDG Indicator 6.5.1, on degree of implementation of integrated water resources management at the national level. There have been improvements in most countries, progress remains offtrack, with varying advancements across regions. Only 47 of reporting countries should soon reach or have reached advanced stages of implementation; and 73 countries remain at low or medium-low levels. The global average in degree of implementation is at 57%, representing a small increase from 54% in 2020. At this rate, sustainable water management globally will not materialize until at least 2049.[27] In fact, according to UN-Water, not only for SDG 6.5, but generally for the global water agenda, progress is offtrack.[28]

Simply put, implementation status and speed of global commitments remain insufficient to meaningfully address the global water crisis as emi-

---

24 A. Lario, in United Nations Environment Program (UNEP), *Progress on Implementation of Integrated Water Resources Management. Mid-Term Status of SDG Indicator 6.5.1 and Acceleration Needs, with a Special Focus on Climate Change* (UN 2024) ('UNEP (2024)'), p. vi.

25 UN General Assembly (UNGA), *Transforming our World: The 2030 Agenda for Sustainable Development*, Res 70/1 (25 Sep 2015), UN Doc A/RES/70/1 (21 Oct 2015) ('2030 Agenda'), SDG-6, p. 35.

26 Stockholm International Water Institute (SIWI), Policy Brief – *Water: The Path to Agenda 2030 Implementation* (2018) ('SIWI (2018a)'), p. 1.

27 UNEP (2024), *supra*, p. viii, x, 10.

28 UN, *Blueprint for Acceleration: Sustainable Development Goal 6: Synthesis Report on Water and Sanitation* (UN 2023), p. 17.

nently *a crisis of governance* – a crisis of governance in the sense that, in many countries, mechanisms for interinstitutional and cross-sectoral coordination, stakeholder participation, monitoring and data management, and performance evaluation, transparency, and accountability require improvements. Legislation, water management plans, or other long-term strategic planning instruments may be lacking, are outdated in relation to contemporary water management principles, or are poorly implemented and enforced. Economic regulation, availability of funds, levels of investments and enabling conditions for revenue raising are inadequate. Institutions lack capacity or are not in place at all appropriate levels, including for basins that cross domestic or international political borders. Institutional mandates are often unclear, overlapping, or fragmented; and horizontal and vertical policy coherence is not always ensured. Other common reported challenges include addressing the water-climate nexus and raising the level of political commitment to sustainable water management to the highest level.[29]

Development trials linked to water resources, such as their sustainable and equitable allocation within and across borders and sectors, are not new. Such trials emerge when water is too polluted or too scarce; when water is not available where and when it is most needed; or simply if there is too much water at a given place and time. These situations are associated with storms and floods; snowmelt and glacial lake outbursts; rising sea-levels and saltwater intrusion into coastal aquifers and deltas; overuse, water scarcity, drought and desertification; lack of or poorly managed infrastructure; or polluted runoff from urban drainage and untreated wastewaters. Water may then become insufficient or inadequate to support various human needs, socioeconomic activities, and ecological health, such as when rivers fail to reach the sea or resource quality conditions no longer support wildlife.

Inadequate governance and management can also lead to conflict among water users and across political borders; loss of life and property; damage to infrastructure; impacts on water-dependent industrial activities; disrupted energy generation, agricultural production, and water supply and wastewater

29 UN Environment Program (UNEP), *Progress on Integrated Water Resources Management: Global Indicator 6.5.1 Updates and Acceleration Needs* (UN 2021), p. 16–17, 23–24, 27, 36, 53; UN Water (2023), *supra*, p. 51; UNEP (2024), *supra*, p. xi. *See also* UNEP (2024), *supra*, p. xiii-xv, unpacking concrete recommendations to accelerate progress sustainable water management through addressing the finance gap, on coordinating climate and water action, and on raising the profile of water as a benefit multiplier across sustainability goals.

management services; human populations displacement and forced migration; polluted water sources and waterborne diseases; land degradation, sedimentation, and riverbank erosion; as well as landslides and mudslides.

The water crisis is unfolding rapidly and at multiple levels, so that only local water management cannot ensure water security. Associated trials have grown and become more intricate in recent history and continue to worsen. Population and poorly planned economic growth and rapid urbanization affect water quality, demand, and availability through overexploitation and river diversions; and thus, aggravate the challenge of distributing the resource among users. The unprecedent levels of water pollution worldwide are a major threat to human health and to ecological systems. Climate change and variability add to the challenges posed by good-quality water's uneven distribution in space and time by accelerating the hydrological cycle, disrupting precipitation patterns and water bodies' temperatures, and increasing the frequency and potency of extreme events.

For a more concrete picture of the water challenge, consider that 90% of natural disasters happening worldwide are water-related. Catchments where water use exceeds recharge are home to over 1.7 billion people and 1/5 of the world's river basins are experiencing rapid changes in surface water. Water scarcity affects approximately 700 million people across 43 countries and about 2.4 billion people live in water-stressed nations, but 3.6 billion already face severe water scarcity at least one month of the year. By 2030, water scarcity might have displaced millions in arid and semiarid regions. By 2050, over ¾ of the world's population will be suffering from drought, 2.7 to 3.2 billion living in potential severely water-scarce areas, and up to 1.6 billion at risk of floods.[30]

The cross-cutting nature of water also entails major economic risks, as water is indispensable to support industrial and agricultural activities and as input to energy production. Maintaining current levels of pressure on water resources will, by 2050 and on a global scale, threaten 45% of gross domestic product, 52% of the population, and 40% of grain production. The UN estimates a 70% growth in global food demand by 2050, translating into at least a

30 S. Moore, *How to Solve the Global Water Crisis: The Real Challenges Are Not Technical, but Political* (20 Mar 2018), Council on Foreign Relations, Foreign Affairs, at https://www.foreignaffairs.com/articles/world/2018-03-20/how-solve-global-water-crisis; J.M. Unturbe, *supra*, p. 32–3, 81; Y. Min (UNDESA), *in* IISD, *Summary of the 2018 Meeting of the High-level Political Forum on Sustainable Development: 9–18 July 2018*, 33:45 Earth Negotiations Bulletin 1–17 (21 July 2018) ('IISD (2018a)'), p. 5; UN (2023), *supra*, p. 34, 74; UNCCD, *Drought in Numbers 2022: Restoration for Readiness and Resilience* (UNCCD 2022), p. 18, 37; J. Luterbacher *et al*, *United in Science 2020* (WMO 2020), p. 14.

19% increase in the sector's consumption of water resources; and that is assuming significantly improved productivity levels. Similarly, the share in global water demand from the industry and energy sectors is expected to grow to 24% by 2050. For energy, in particular, global water withdrawals will increase by less than 2% by 2040, yet consumption will grow by nearly 60%. According to the UN as well, water-related losses across dependent sectors could lead to growth rates in some regions declining by as much as 6% of GDP by 2050.[31]

The water-biodiversity relationship is mutually reinforcing: the health of both terrestrial and aquatic ecosystems depends on the availability of water at the right time and place, and of adequate quality and in sufficient quantity; conversely, various ecosystem types are crucial in regulating and maintaining water supplies for multiple uses. As noted by the President of the General Assembly, reporting on outcomes of the 2023 UN Water Conference: "The global water cycle is now out of balance; the water crisis is interacting with the twin crises of climate change and the loss of biodiversity in ways that exacerbate all three."[32]

Freshwater ecosystems cover less than 1% of the Earth's surface and yet wetlands are home to 40% of the worlds' biodiversity. The last 40 years have seen a decline of 85% in freshwater species populations, steeper than for all other biomes, and a loss of 40% of the world's wetlands. Going back to 1700, this wetland loss is of 87%, a rate three times faster than that for natural forests. Estimates are that the remaining global wetland area is of only 10–12 million km^2. Almost 2/3 of the world's large rivers have been dammed, with significant impacts on basin connectivity and natural flows. Between 1990 and 2010, increasing wastewater loads into freshwaters have aggravated pollution across the developing world; and, in the 102 countries for which data is available, the provision of wastewater services is still absent for 2/3 of the popula-

---

31 UN Water Decade Program on Advocacy and Communication (UNW-DPAC), International Annual UN-Water Zaragoza Conference 2012/2013: Preparing for the 2013 International Year – Water Cooperation: Making it Happen (Zaragoza, 8–10 Jan 2012), *Conference Report – Water Cooperation in Action: Approaches, Tools and Processes* (UN Water 2013) ('UNW-DPAC'), p. 10; UN Water, *Sustainable Development Goal 6 Synthesis Report 2018 on Water and Sanitation* (UN Water 2018) ('UN Water (2018)'), p. 25; *United Nations World Water Development Report 2020: Water and Climate Change* (UNESCO & UN-Water 2020), p. 97, 162.

32 UNGA President, UN Conference on the Midterm Comprehensive Review of the Implementation of the Objectives of the International Decade for Action 'Water for Sustainable Development', 2018–2028 (New York City, 22–24 Mar 2023), *Summary of Proceedings*, at https://digitallibrary.un.org/record/4012972?ln=en&v=pdf ('UNWC 2023 Summary'), p. 19.

tion. Elsewhere, exact estimates of water pollution are not possible, due to limited water quality monitoring. Globally, 42% of household wastewater does not receive proper treatment.[33]

Progress on SDG Target 6.6 – "protect and restore water-related ecosystems, including mountains, forests, wetlands, rivers, aquifers and lakes" – is also offtrack.[34] Here, again, the element of governance is central, as evidenced by UNEP's recommendation for countries to "accelerate the development and implementation of national-and basin-level policies, laws and practices to better protect freshwater ecosystem integrity; and, as necessary, undertake wide-scale restoration of degraded ecosystems".[35]

In view of the above realities, states and other global actors have become more aware of water as a vital resource that is "finite and irreplaceable".[36] The international community has started to pay more attention to the global water challenge and to how it is worsening over time, in the face of related risks and possibly increased competition within and between states. With this awareness has come a greater concern with sustainable water management, good governance of shared natural resources, and coordination across sectoral and political boundaries.[37] Among companies, "water has risen from obscurity and neglect to a key issue and priority".[38] In the Pact for the Future, UN member states decide to "address and promote the prevention of water scarcity and build resilience to drought to achieve a world in which water is a sustainable

33 UN (2023), *supra*, p. 35, 74; UN-Water (2018), *supra*, p. 56, 59, 63, 87; Unturbe, *supra*, p. 36; M.R. Urrego, quoted *in* Ramsar Convention Secretariat, *Ramsar Convention at the High-level Political Forum on Sustainable Development* (18 July 2018), Ramsar Convention webpage, News, at https://www.ramsar.org/news/ramsar-convention-at-the-high-level-political-forum-on-sustainable-development; J. Barzdo, quoted *in* Ramsar Convention Secretariat, *Ramsar Convention at the 6th GEF Assembly* (6 July 2018), on *Ibid*, at https://www.ramsar.org/news/ramsar-convention-at-the-sixth-gef-assembly; M. Finer & C.N. Jenkins, *Proliferation of Hydroelectric Dams in the Andean Amazon and Implications for Andes-Amazon Connectivity*, 7:4 PLoS ONE 1–9 (2012), p. 1; Almond, R.E.A., Grooten, M., Juffe Bignoli, D. & Petersen, T. eds, *Living Planet Report 2022, Building a Nature Positive Society* (WWF 2022); *The WWF (2024) Living Planet Report 2024 – A System in Peril.* WWF, Gland, Switzerland, p.7. *Global Wetland Outlook: Special Edition 2021* (Ramsar Convention on Wetlands 2021).

34 UNEP (2021), *supra*, p. 1.

35 *Id*, p. 48.

36 Unturbe, *supra*, p. 32.

37 Unturbe, p. 33; SIWI *et al*, *Building a Resilient Future through Water: An Open Letter to the High-Level Political Forum for Sustainable Development from Multistakeholder Representatives of the Water and Development Community* (Apr 2018), p. 2.

38 Unturbe, *supra*, p. 47. *See also* IISD (2018a), *supra*, p. 10, where Colombia notes efforts to reduce by 1/5 the water consumption of the country's businesses.

resource and ensure the availability and sustainable management of clean and safe water, sanitation and hygiene for all".[39]

In transboundary basins, "[u]nequal power dynamics, national interests and lack of trust [may] influence efforts to share data and establish institutional and legal frameworks to promote cooperation and avoid conflict".[40] At the same time, as interdependencies emerge, so do common interests. In other words, the presence of more than one sovereign compounds governance and management challenges, along with cooperation opportunities. Going forward, climatic and related changes are expected to aggravate problems faced by riparian states, as users and nations exhaust domestic supplies and find themselves more reliant on shared resources.

2.2 *Freshwater Transcends Political Boundaries*

> *Water more often unites than divides peoples and societies ... as riparian states recognize that they must safeguard their greater common interests.*[41]

In this century, the good governance of peaceful, equitable, and sustainable water allocation, ecosystem protection, and basin management "is one of the great challenges facing international law and institutions".[42] Towards improving transboundary water governance, UN Water underscores, *inter alia*, the imperative of "creating clear agreements to manage these basins, resolve disputes and promote cooperation",[43] thus reaffirming the importance of international law in this context.

Freshwater systems that cross international political borders are the rule, not the exception, being present in 153 countries. There are 468 transboundary aquifer systems that have been inventoried and an estimated 313 shared lakes and rivers, with the latter accounting for 60% of the world's freshwater flows. Transboundary river and lake basins are home to more than three billion people.[44]

---

39 UNGA, 79th Session, *The Pact for the Future*, Res 79/1 (22 Sep 2024), UN Doc A/Res/79/1 (22 Sep 2024), 25(f) ('The Pact for the Future').

40 UN Water (2023), *supra*, p. 52.

41 UNW-DPAC, *supra*, p. 5, 10.

42 McCaffrey (2019), *supra*, p. 143.

43 UN Water (2023), *supra*, p. 53.

44 UNECE, UNESCO, UN-Water, *Progress on Transboundary Water Cooperation: Mid-Term Status of SDG Indicator 6.5.2, with a Special Focus on Climate Change* (UN & UNESCO 2024), p. xix.

Recognizing that international catchments merit great attention, the UN celebrated 2013 as the *International Year of Water Cooperation* (IYWC).[45]

Following suit, the extensive multistakeholder dialogue during the consultations leading up to the 2030 Agenda ensured that the already-mentioned SDG-6 captured the transboundary dimension of water management. Target 6.5 calls for the integrated management of water resources "at all levels, including through *transboundary cooperation* as appropriate". This SDG Target is groundbreaking. Only three years earlier, the outcome document of Rio+20 had failed to mention transboundary water cooperation for lack of state support.

Rieu-Clarke and this author explain that governments at Rio+20 were reluctant to discuss their obligations as co-riparians. A toxic atmosphere eventually trickled down to influence the text of the outcome document, whose section on water and sanitation ignores the complexities of transboundary basins by assuming that national action would suffice to secure sustainable management.[46] Rio+20 reminds us of how important it is for states and stakeholders to reinforce the duty to cooperate by widely supporting international water law, including, where appropriate, within the Theory's framework. With a stable legal environment, states "have less room to maneuver for downplaying [cooperation requirements], leaving more time for discussions on substantive issues",[47] such as the importance of Close Basin Cooperation in today's world.

A decade into the implementation process of Agenda 2030, most states are unlikely to question the value of transboundary water cooperation. Yet, since what governments say is not always reflected on how they behave, unilateralism still may trump cooperation on the ground. When this happens, the health of freshwater systems is often compromised, with negative consequences for people, nature, and the economy in the countries involved.

45 UNGA, *International Year of Water Cooperation: 2013*, UNGA Res 65/154 (20 Dec 2010), UN Doc A/RES/65/154 (11 Feb 2011). The UN has declared special *international years* since 1959, with a view to highlighting key global concerns and mobilizing action thereon. UNW-DPAC, *supra*, p. 5. The IYWC meant to position cooperation as a cornerstone for the achievement of water security and sustainability and to characterize water resources as "the foundation for developing stronger ties between nations, states and communities." *Ibid.*

46 A. Rieu-Clarke & F. Rocha Loures, *Should we Care whether the UN Watercourses Convention Enters into Force?* – Chapter 2 (22 July 2012), International Water Law Project Blog, at https://www.internationalwaterlaw.org/blog/2012/07/22/should-we-care-whether-the-un-watercourses-convention-enters-into-force-part-ii/. *Ibid.*

47 *Ibid.*

Consider the Incomati Basin: reduced river flows caused by dams unilaterally implemented in South Africa have led to the estuary's salinization and, consequently, to the extinction of native flora and fauna not adapted to the new environment – important species on which local livelihoods within Mozambique depended. In the lower Nile, the lower Jordan, and the tributaries of the Aral Sea, certain ecosystems have mostly disappeared, in part because of uncoordinated unilateral water resources developments across those basins. Unilateralism might lead to unforeseen geopolitical impacts on the country of origin itself, as in the Ganges: India's dam at Farakka has caused major detrimental impacts to Bangladesh, like depleted water reserves, salinization, and damaged fisheries, with grave consequences for public health, navigation, and local economies. These outcomes are deemed to have contributed to major migration movements, including into India.[48]

Noncooperation may thus pose significant social, economic, and environmental risks and severely constrain the pursuit of optimal water management. The dangers of noncooperation are of greater concern in this time of rapid and significant global change, materializing across various scales and multiple dimensions and so demanding "a coherent approach, focused upon common priorities that should guide decisions on development alternatives."[49]

Limited cooperation on freshwater protection, management, and use, albeit better than absolute unilateralism, may still prove insufficient if implemented without a concern for long-term changes and basin-wide sustainability. Even where treaties are present, they may not yet reflect a progressive and adaptive cooperation mindset that goes beyond fixed volumetric water allocations, unilateral restraint, and interstate consultations on the potential transboundary impacts of individual projects. Treaties with such traits lack flexibility and are hardly suited to respond to climate change and variability, which demand resilient regimes as enablers of joint management.[50]

Strengthened interstate cooperation is thus probable and, most likely, desirable, if not essential, where the countries sharing this resource mean to exercise their rights effectively.[51] In practice, water's fluidity pushes riparian states to collaborate to varying degrees, as a "powerful incentive … com-

48 A. Kramer *et al*, *The Key to Managing Conflict and Cooperation over Water*, 11:1 A World of Science 4–12 (Jan-Mar 2013), p. 5, 7, 9.

49 SIWI *et al*, *supra*, p. 1.

50 A.D. Tarlock, *Four Challenges for International Water Law*, 23 Tul. Envtl. L.J. 369–408 (2010), p. 384–5.

51 Kramer *et al*, *supra*, p. 4; Unturbe, *supra*, p. 86; UNW-DPAC, *supra*, p. 10.

pelling stakeholders to reconcile even the most divergent views".[52] Kramer *et al*, for example, based on a historical screening of relations between co-basin states, draw attention to a significant prevalence of cooperation over conflict; thousands of existing watercourse agreements; evolving treaty content, from mostly navigation to broader water management; an increase in the number of water and related treaties adopted in recent years; eventual disputes getting settled, including in least likely scenarios of enmity and persistent conflict on other issues; and resilience of basin organizations, in general and through periods of interstate tensions.[53]

The Theory's present and future relevance in shaping interstate water relations must be placed against the context presented above and the questions one must raise about the status and efficacy of international water law. Going forward, Community-of-Interests may prove crucial and gain in normative persuasion as a theoretical framework that enables states to "cooperate closely",[54] including across sectors and in all their shared basins – the kind of cooperation required as water availability becomes more unpredictable; ecosystems, increasingly vulnerable to mounting threats; and, co-basin countries, more interdependent, with deepening shared priorities, opportunities, and risks, alongside conflicting interests that can only be solved through continued engagement within the framework of Close Basin Cooperation.

Of course, cooperation is not an absolute requirement, whether under Limited Territorial Sovereignty or Community-of-Interests. Because international law does not deal in absolutes, the applicability of Community-of-Interests to a concrete situation is tied to context, i.e., the Theory mostly applies *where appropriate*, as necessary to safeguard common interests, while balancing individual state concerns. Legal frameworks, institutional arrangements, and cooperation modalities framed by Community-of-Interests are not ends in themselves but means that states employ to pursue jointly agreed priorities, while taking account of their own interests and the basin as a whole. At the same time, *where-appropriate situations* that call for the Theory's application are becoming more easily detectable and increasingly frequent in a world of rapid environmental, climatic, geopolitical, and related change. As a result, cooperating within the Theory's framework is turning into an imperative for states in the pursuit of shared water security for sustainable development.

---

52 UNW-DPAC, *supra*, p. 5, 10.

53 Kramer *et al*, *supra*, p. 4, 6–7. *See also* UNW-DPAC, *supra*, p. 10, on interstate water cooperation and conflict statistics since 1948, with 37 incidents involving violence *versus* 295 watercourse agreements signed.

54 McCaffrey (2019), *supra*, p. 77.

3 Overview of Community-of-Interests

> *We are at a time of profound global transformation. We are confronted by rising catastrophic and existential risks ... Yet this is also ... a chance for renewal and progress grounded in our common humanity. ... This will require a recommitment to international cooperation based on respect for international law, without which we can neither manage the risks nor seize the opportunities ... Our challenges are deeply interconnected and far exceed the capacity of any single state alone. They can only be addressed collectively, through strong and sustained international cooperation guided by trust and solidarity for the benefit of all.*[55]

Greater clarity and fresh findings about Community-of-Interests will contribute to a better understanding of the law of transboundary basins. In relation to international water law, generally, and Community-of-Interests, specifically, this improved understanding will advance the effective application, progressive development, and continued positive influence of the law on the sustainable management, use, and protection of basins shared by increasingly interdependent riparian states in a rapidly changing world and in the face of growing water challenges.

The book builds on existing literature and relevant legal sources to assess the progressive evolution and status of the Theory in light of modern legal developments. These include the 2014 entry into force of the UNWC, the 2016 full global opening of the ECEWC, and the recent adoption and entry into force of another basin agreement explicitly referring to the Theory. In terms of case law, recent judicial or arbitral precedents also reference Community-of-Interests and thus merit a closer analysis.

Taken as the starting point for the research undertaken, the already cited 2019 edition of McCaffrey's seminal book contains a thorough literature review on Community-of-Interests and is probably the most authoritative and complete doctrinal source in that respect. He offers a detailed account of the Theory's historical origins and introduces relevant agreements, decisions, and the opinions of other writers. In this Chapter, we refer back to McCaffrey's work, supplementing it with other important opinions, presenting ongoing debates, and introducing relevant legal developments.

There is a scarcity of recent and thorough legal analyses on the topic.[56] Many relevant writings date back to the early and mid-20th Century and

55 The Pact for the Future, *supra*, 2–3, 5.

56 Howden, *supra*, p. 13–15.

thus predate fresh developments in international water treaty and case law. Such early scholarship provides valuable insights into the Theory's general contours, its legal antecedents, and its evolution in international law from navigation to multiple uses; pinpoints where the Theory has been explicitly or, in their view, implicitly, referenced in early treaty and case law; and feeds into the debate regarding the Theory's status and elements.[57] Yet, existing writings remain insufficient for painting a complete and current picture of Community-of-Interests, on the basis of well-delineated elements which allow for the Theory's functions and status to be assessed.

Further, there is scholarly dissent on the distinction and relationship between Limited Territorial Sovereignty and Community-of-Interests, as well as on the Theory's precise legal implications for the non-navigational uses of international watercourses.[58] This book takes an informed stand in relation to both scholarly debates. We also expand on the scholarly basis to give more precision to the scope of Community-of-Interests and to the special features of the treaties, bodies, and cooperation modalities characteristic of the Theory.

Community-of-Interests and Limited Territorial Sovereignty: Beyond general premises, existing scholarship does not offer clear, thorough, and well-founded answers on the relationship between the two theories.

To illustrate, Sievers opines that Limited Territorial Sovereignty and Community-of-Interests are "often consonant, but *ultimately dissimilar*".[59] For Leb, Community-of-Interests emerges as "an *alternative*"[60] to other theories of international water law. Further, Sievers considers Limited Territorial Sovereignty to be the *more conservative*[61] and Leb refers to Community-of-Interests as being *more cooperative*.[62] Together, the two authors point us in the right direction, but their focus is on delineating a sharp distinction rather than uncovering the relationship between the two theories. Howden, similarly, notes that Limited Territorial Sovereignty and Community-of-Interests, along with the other two proposed theories of the law of transboundary

---

57 *See*, e.g., H.A. Smith, *The Economic Uses of International Rivers* (P.S. King & Sons 1931); J. Lipper, *Equitable Utilization*, *in* A.H. Garretson, R.D. Hayton & C.J. Olmstead eds, *The Law of International Drainage Basins* (Oceana 1967).

58 *See* McCaffrey (2019), *supra*, p. 231.

59 E.W. Sievers, *Transboundary Jurisdiction and Watercourse Law: China, Kazakhstan, and the Irtysh*, 37 Tex. Int'l L.J. 1 (2002), p. 16 (emphasis added).

60 C. Leb, *Cooperation in the Law of Transboundary Water Resources* (Cambridge University 2013), p. 52 (emphasis added).

61 Sievers, *supra*, p. 15.

62 Leb (2013), *supra*, p. 56.

basins, each "indicate four different collections of general ideas and principles covering four different directions that exist – or have existed – in international water law, each focusing on *different fundamental understandings of the principle of territorial sovereignty* and its application".[63] Sievers, Leb, and Howden all suggest that Community-of-Interests is something other than Limited Territorial Sovereignty.

When unpacking the Theory, however, the Oder Case Decision links the natural unity of a watercourse to justice and utility and thus, to equity; and sees in that same unity the Theory's factual basis.[64] Along these lines, Dellapenna considers that Limited Territorial Sovereignty (or, in his vocabulary, *restricted sovereignty*) is based on an international drainage basin as a coherent juridical and managerial unit.[65] In his turn, McIntyre connects equitable and reasonable use, a hallmark of Limited Territorial Sovereignty, to the "notion that international watercourses are shared resources in which there exists a community-of-interest among all co-basin states".[66]

Hence, the watershed's physical and hydrological unity and equity considerations underlie both Limited Territorial Sovereignty and Community-of-Interests. In other words, the elements of Limited Territorial Sovereignty and the Theory have the same foundations, and are necessary to ensure and sustain Close Basin Cooperation. In specific communities-of-interests, rules under each theory play different and yet complementary roles. On the one hand, Community-of-Interests "reinforces"[67] Limited Territorial Sovereignty by being "conducive, if not essential, to the ongoing development and elaboration"[68] of equitable and reasonable use. On the other, a stable community-of-interests "requires a 'reasonable and equitable' balancing of state interests which accommodates the needs and uses of each state".[69]

As such, Limited Territorial Sovereignty is not separate from, or an alternative to, but a facet of, cooperation informed by Community-of-Interests. Limited Territorial Sovereignty is part and parcel of Close Basin Cooperation under Community-of-Interests. As the same time, the greater relevance and applicability of norms framed by Limited Territorial Sovereignty or by Community-of-Interests, respectively, for a given interest or regime depend on

63 Howden, *supra*, p. 26–7 (emphasis added).

64 River Oder Case, *supra*, p. 27.

65 J.W. Dellapenna, *Rivers as Legal Structures: The Examples of the Jordan and the Nile*, 36 Natural Resources Journal 217–250 (1996), p. 230.

66 McIntyre, *supra*, p. 23.

67 McCaffrey (2019), supra, p. 235.

68 McIntyre, *supra*, p. 28.

69 Id, p. 23.

how close the physical and associated interdependency of states has become. State interests – common or unilateral, combined or on their own – may call for varying modalities or degrees of interstate interaction and cooperation. Under treaties framed by Community-of-Interests, however, norms for cooperation on common goals consistently prevail over those regulating unilateral restraint. That does not mean that the Theory ignores the interests of individual states, but merely that Community-of-Interests shifts the primary focus of cooperation from unilateral to common interests.

Sievers further opines that, if Community-of-Interests entails "consideration of the best use of the entire basin [and] efficiency as a starting point",[70] Limited Territorial Sovereignty "does not burden states with any substantive obligation to maximize"[71] efficient water use. The latter point on Limited Territorial Sovereignty may be true, but not the former on the Theory. Community-of-Interests centers, not on efficiency, but on broadly conceptualized common interests, as agreed upon and refined among co-basin states. In a specific basin, efficiency may be potentially identified as one such interest, though not necessarily the only one. In other catchments, perhaps efficiency is not a common priority at all, and other shared challenges are the motivating factors for cooperation, like combatting pollution, for example.

Another helpful insight comes from McCaffrey, according to whom Limited Territorial Sovereignty "merely connotes unilateral restraint";[72] whereas the Theory "evokes *shared governance, joint action* [and] a regime of *joint institutional management*",[73] in view of the interest that the riparian countries have in the same watercourse. The concepts italicized are embedded in the treaties known to reflect the Theory, whereas unilateral restraint is indeed characteristic of Limited Territorial Sovereignty.

Normative Content of Community-of-Interests: Recent research tends to stay within the bounds of generalizations and suppositions on what Community-of-Interests is and entails, going no further than hinting at the Theory's normative elements through references to the *unity of the basin, agreements, bodies,* and *common management.*

Leb, for example, draws attention to how the Theory has resurfaced in recent watercourse agreements,[74] but does not take the next step of developing a detailed analysis of such agreements to verify whether they may contrib-

70 Sievers, *supra*, p. 16.

71 *Ibid.*

72 McCaffrey (2019), *supra*, p. 236.

73 *Ibid* (emphasis added).

74 Leb (2013), *supra*, p. 55.

ute to a deeper, better grounded, and more refined understanding of Community-of-Interests.

Teclaff and Utton also stress common action when arguing that Community-of-Interests "is most conductive to international cooperation and to joint or integrated development"[75] of transboundary waters. Along these lines, McIntyre unpacks the concept of *international drainage basin* and equates Community-of-Interests to *common management*, i.e., an *approach* to managing water challenges that regards the drainage basin as an integrated whole and an economic unit.[76] Yet, the status of Community-of-Interests as a theory of international water law does not correspond to the nature of common management, a mere approach which remains vague and ill-defined. McIntyre also emphasizes the centrality of *bodies*, as established by *treaties*, in the administration of common management regimes for the design of *common policies.* His analysis leaves open questions regarding the precise contours of treaties and bodies framed by the Theory and of cooperation practices reflective of common management.

McCaffrey sees Community-of-Interests reflected in those watercourse agreements that contemplate the creation of *joint bodies* with functions linked to *joint planning* and, sometimes, *joint implementation.*[77] When outlining the foregoing italicized concepts, McCaffrey does not do so on the basis of the treaties and jurisprudence known to reflect the Theory; neither does he investigate the features of legal-institutional regimes framed by Community-of-Interests; nor unveils the centrality and full meaning of joint action for such regimes or the tools through which this modality of cooperation materializes. By thoroughly unpacking the normative content of the Theory's elements, the book addresses these gaps.

Community-of-Interests, Common Property, and Veto Power: The Theory has been equated with, or considered as being embedded into, notions of *common, joint,* or *shared property* or *ownership*; and *veto rights*, which translate into a *requirement of mutual consent or agreement* before planned measures can advance. Common property reflects the notion that an international watercourse is owned jointly by the co-riparian states. In its turn, the veto power, a prolongation of the joint-ownership concept, erases a state's sover-

75 Teclaff & Utton, *supra*, p. 51.

76 McIntyre, *supra*, p. 28. *See also* L.A. Teclaff & A.E. Utton, *International Groundwater Law* (Oceana 1981), p. 51, who, having written before McIntyre, already considered that Community-of-Interests sees the basin as an *economic unit* that transcends artificial borders.

77 McCaffrey (2019), *supra*, p. 224–5.

eign right to unilaterally develop the watercourse. The reasoning to connect those concepts with the Theory is that treaties using expressions like *shared or common waters* reflect Community-of-Interests and that those expressions imply that the states concerned recognize those resources as being their joint property and, accordingly, subject to the mutual-consent requirement.

Common property, along with correlated veto rights, deserve careful consideration given the confusion they engender. While scholarship tends to deny a place for joint ownership in customary law, in light of overwhelming state rejection thereof, disagreement among authors remains as to the concept's connection to Community-of-Interests.

McCaffrey presents the views of publicists on the Theory and of its "*equivalent* notion that an international watercourse is the common property of the riparian states."[78] Later in his analysis, however, he rebuffs common property and veto power as elements of Community-of-Interests.[79]

McIntyre reviews treaties implying or embracing joint ownership of shared resources when exploring the common management approach,[80] thereby implicitly interconnecting the two concepts. Like McIntyre, Kaya conflates common management with Community-of-Interests, but also with *res communis*, rejecting all three.[81] Benvenisti alludes to *community-in-waters* as the approach capturing the notion of shared property.[82] Bouchez suggests that, under Community-of-Interests, co-riparian countries "have to determine in *common agreement* the purposes for which the drainage basin is to be used".[83] Sievers considers that Community-of-Interests "*requires* that decision-making be undertaken collectively".[84] Upon connecting the veto power with Community-of-Interests, Salman dismisses state support for the Theory; and opines that Community-of-Interests is but "an ideal principle that overlooks sovereignty and nationalism, and the competing demands of the different riparians".[85]

---

78 *Id*, p. 226 (emphasis added).

79 *Id*, p. 233–7.

80 McIntyre, *supra*, p. 31–2.

81 I. Kaya, *Equitable Utilization: The Law of the Non-Navigational Uses of International Watercourses* (Ashgate 2003), p. 85–86, 88.

82 E. Benvenisti, *Collective Action in the Utilization of Shared Freshwater: The Challenges of International Water Resources Law*, 90 Am. J. Int'l L. 384–415 (1996), p. 399, FN79.

83 *In* ILA (1966), *supra*, p. 454 (emphasis added).

84 Sievers, *supra*, p. 16 (emphasis added).

85 S.M.A. Salman, *The Helsinki Rules, the UN Watercourses Convention and the Berlin Rules: Perspectives on International Water Law*, 23:4 J. Water Resources Dev. 625–40 (2007), p. 628.

In contrast, Lammers warns that the Theory "must not be associated with concepts such as *co-imperium* or *condominium*". He explains that transboundary waters are "merely 'common' in a physical and perhaps also socioeconomic sense."[86] Howden recalls how the Gabčikovo and Pulp Mills Decisions nowhere imply or mention joint ownership and never suggest a connection between the condominium concept and Community-of-Interests, concluding that support for this connection is not significant.[87]

The above contradictory opinions among writers contribute to the overall state of uncertainty surrounding Community-of-Interests. Although both joint ownership and veto rights may be reflected in treaties based on the Theory, neither concept is a necessary or inherent element of Community-of-Interests.

Moreover, treaties referring to resources that are shared or are of common interest do not necessarily endorse joint ownership and its correlated mutual-consent requirement. Yet, such treaties may be seen as indications of the endorsement of Community-of-Interests by their parties since they hint at the unity of the catchment from which the Theory derives.

From these premises, this book attempts to go further than existing writings in analyzing the meaning of common property, including in the context of Community-of-Interests. This work does so when presenting Close Basin Cooperation as the umbrella of various modalities of state engagement under Community-of-Interests. We then show how common property has rarely come into the picture within the Theory's framework.

Functions of Community-of-Interests: McCaffrey recognizes that the Theory may operate "*as a principle* that informs *concrete obligations* of riparian states".[88] He does so *en passant,* building on the above-cited Gabčikovo Case.

Community-of-Interests may indeed function as a principle, and it is already doing so concretely. Such is the case when the Theory reframes the codification, clarification, interpretation, application, and progressive development of existing or emerging rules in the field, and then may lead to deeper cooperation requirements than those under Limited Territorial Sovereignty; to the creation of specific joint-action obligations that are accessory to the effective implementation of an accepted customary rule; and, perhaps, to the gradual emergence of new norms in the law of transboundary basins.

86 J.G. Lammers, *Pollution of International Watercourses: A Search for Substantive Rules and Principles of Law* (Martinus Nijhoff 1984), p. 507.

87 Howden, *supra*, p. 220.

88 McCaffrey (2019), *supra*, p. 221 (emphasis added).

Status of Community-of-Interests in international law: A chapter in McCaffrey's seminal book is titled '*The Theoretical Bases of International Watercourse Law: An Examination of the Four Principal Theories*', namely: Absolute Territorial Integrity, Absolute Territorial Sovereignty, Limited Territorial Sovereignty, and Community-of-Interests. McCaffrey rejects Absolute Territorial Integrity and Absolute Territorial Sovereignty, and then examines Limited Territorial Sovereignty, followed by Community-of-Interests. In so doing, McCaffrey *implicitly* places Community-of-Interests alongside Limited Territorial Sovereignty, thus viewing both as valid theoretical bases for the law in the field.

Similarly, Sievers explains that both Limited Territorial Sovereignty and the Theory find support in scholarship and state practice; and explicitly considers Community-of-Interests to be a *theory* of international water law that stands on its own.

For McCaffrey, Limited Territorial Sovereignty remains prevalent for now, but Community-of-Interests will "probably ... come to be recognized as not only the optimal, but also the necessary approach to dealing with future water problems".[89] Already, Community-of-Interests might be signalizing the path of evolution of international water law and practice.[90] His assumption that the Theory is likely to be further embraced in state practice going forward is probably correct, as co-basin states grow more interdependent. Sievers endorses McCaffrey's points about the current dominance of Limited Territorial Sovereignty over Community-of-Interests and notes the rapidly growing uptake of the latter.[91] This trend detected by McCaffrey and Sievers must be kept in mind when reflecting about the status of Community-of-Interests.

Attributing normative value to Community-of-Interests as an independent Theory also finds support in Lammers. He develops his opinion based on the above-cited River Oder Judgment, where Community-of-Interests is invoked alongside the well-known and accepted *right-of-passage*. Accordingly, in Lammers' view, "it may be assumed that [Community-of-Interests] was also to be considered as a legal, i.e., *normative concept*."[92]

The contrasting opinion of McIntyre is that Community-of-Interests has not "evolved, [nor] is likely soon to evolve, into a requirement of general or

89 Id, p. 185.
90 *Ibid.*
91 Sievers, *supra*, p. 15.
92 Lammers, *supra*, p. 507 (emphasis added).

customary international law".[93] Tarlock considers Community-of-Interests, to which he also refers as *shared management*, to be no more than an "aspirational principle".[94] For Hunter *et al*, Community-of-Interests – or, as they call it, *joint integrated management* – represents a "preferred approach"[95] as to how transboundary waters should be administered, rather than a legal requirement.[96]

Leb shows caution when considering the status of Community-of-Interests in international law. But her thinking also takes us back to McCaffrey's. Like him, she approaches the question from the perspective of the four theories of the law of transboundary basins. Then she asks if, in customary law, Community-of-Interests already stands on its own in relation to Limited Territorial Sovereignty and outside specific agreements. She concludes that Community-of-Interests is not yet consolidated as "a legal concept that exists independently of treaties";[97] and that it remains unclear if the law in this field will develop towards the endorsement of Community-of-Interests as a "distinct legal theory".[98] Jurisprudence, in Leb's opinion, does not unequivocally identify Community-of-Interests as a normative concept, going only as far as "confirming the factual existence of such a community based on a treaty".[99]

However, a Basin Treaty does not constitute a given community-of-basin-interests, but rather formalizes, regulates, and institutionalizes cooperation framed by the Theory. Community-of-Interests emerges from the interdependencies among states that may exist to varying degrees within individual basins. As states' common interests become more evident, with individual interests harder to reconcile, agreements may be put in place to better enable Close Basin Cooperation and, at the same time, assure compliance with the rules that characterize Limited Territorial Sovereignty.

Taking a more extreme view than the previous authors, Magsig interprets Community-of-Interests to imply a complete removal of basin states' sovereignty, with supposed unclear legal implications, deadlocks in its future devel-

---

93 McIntyre, *supra*, p. 33.

94 Tarlock, *supra*, p. 404.

95 D. Hunter, J. Salzman, D. Zaelke, *International Environmental Law and Policy*, 5th ed (Foundation Press 2015), p. 884.

96 Id, p. 892.

97 Leb (2013), *supra*, p. 53.

98 Id, p. 56.

99 Id, p. 53–54.

opment, and questionable widespread support. Consequently, Magsig outright dismisses the Theory's usefulness for transboundary water management.[100]

The teachings of McCaffrey, Lammers and Sievers are more closely aligned with this author's views regarding the status of Community-of-Interests as a practiced, independent, and accepted theory of international water law, alongside and inclusive of Limited Territorial Sovereignty. Community-of-Interests is more than aspirational and more than an approach to, or trend in, transboundary water management. The Theory has functioned as a principle underlying cooperative relations between basin states in concrete treaty and case law. Community-of-Interests may still be evolving and, perhaps, its reach is not as extensive as that of Limited Territorial Sovereignty, but the Theory is probably more widespread than normally assumed. Community-of-Interests is not contrary to state sovereignty. In fact, the Theory operates as an enabler of the effective exercise of states' rights in transboundary basins.

Our contributions: Existing scholarship has not given proper weight to the numerous references to the Theory in treaty and case law and lack of consensus and analytical gaps remain. This has created an opportunity for us to develop, as introduced above, our own opinions and findings on the normative elements, functions, and status of Community-of-Interests. The book advances on existing work by offering contextualized, well-delimited, and innovative approaches for the examination of the Theory. Our analytical journey leads to a more precise understanding of the applicability and normative value of Community-of-Interests when the multiple uses of transboundary waters are at stake.

Community-of-Interests cannot be placed at either end of the spectrum of international law standards: the Theory is neither an autonomous and binding rule, on the one hand, nor simply a moral ideal, lacking in normativity, or a good practice approach to water management, on the other. It is rather a legal theory, not a principle, but which has operated as a principle of international water law. For Fitzmaurice, a principle and a rule are different standards, with the former illuminating the *raisons d'être* of, and expressing itself through, the latter: "A rule answers the question 'what'; a principle … *the question 'why'*."[101]

100 B.O. Magsig, *International Water Law and the Quest for Common Security* (Earthscan 2015), p. 129–30.

101 G. Fitzmaurice, *The General Principles of International Law Considered from the Standpoint of the Rule of Law*, 92 RCADI (1957), p. 7 (emphasis added).

Community-of-Interests plays this function in relation to existing or possibly emerging rules governing shared basins.

4 Book Outline

The analysis unfolds in six main steps, each with its dedicated Part. Part I anchors the Theory in international law and relations and their evolution towards closer global cooperation on shared concerns. This exercise allows us to draw parallels between the development of general international law and international water law. We also devote space to elucidating the differences and similarities among global community interests, common regional water interests, and Community-of-Interests, with a view to well-delimiting the context of applicability of the Theory.

Part II analyzes the Founding Charters and related legal instruments of select Regional Integration Organizations to understand how these bodies have been empowered to act in the pursuit of their members' shared interests. State practice under regional integration regimes, i.e., those founded on common interests and Close Regional Cooperation, is analogous to that under communities-of-interests. In both contexts, countries within a given geographical space cooperate closely in the name of shared goals. We thus identify the fundamental concepts that have served common regional interests, some of which, with the appropriate adjustments, have been employed to advance common basin interests as well. This approach has not yet been taken in scholarship on Community-of-Interests and leads to a preliminary analytical framework through which to unpack the Theory into its normative elements.

Parts III and IV transpose the findings about regional integration regimes to the context of communities-of-basin-interests. We conduct an in-depth investigation of a package of primary and secondary legal sources identified by scholars and jurisprudence as reflecting Community-of-Interests, namely:

a) The UNWC and the ECEWC – the former deemed by the ICJ to be an expression of the Theory and, the latter, displaying a rich common-interests content.
b) The four legal instruments in the field that refer expressly to the Theory, three adopted among African countries and one in effect in Latin America.
c) Other watercourse agreements from which Community-of-Interests may be inferred.

d) The four decisions that invoke and develop the Theory when ruling on disputes between co-basin states.

The value and authority of the global Conventions are widely recognized. As recently as 2023, stakeholders reiterated how essential the UNWC and the ECEWC are as legal bases for cooperation and recalled recent accessions, recommending that more countries follow suit.[102] In case law, the UNWC is cited in both the Gabčíkovo and Silala Decisions.[103] Many UNWC provisions are geared towards "common management through a holistic perspective on the watercourse and the strong cooperative commitment that this perspective requires".[104] The ECEWC is seen as an even stronger basis for "common management and for close cooperation between states based on shared interests of protecting and preserving shared basins".[105]

The global Conventions offer the general contours of Community-of-Interests. The watercourse agreements and decisions in question demonstrate how the Theory has been put into practice.

Parts III and IV substantiate the design of the final Legal Analytical Framework at the heart of this book, through which we determine the Theory's functions and status, as a theoretical basis for international water law. The Framework is structured upon the primary and secondary normative elements of Community-of-Interests. These elements show how well-known legal concepts in transboundary water management – namely, the drainage basin approach, treaties, bodies, and the duty to cooperate – gain particular characteristics when framed by Community-of-Interests; and how communities-of-basin-interests conduct their internal and external relations with other states and intergovernmental organizations and how they engage stakeholders.

Part V applies the Legal Analytical Framework as a lens to determine the functions of Community-of-Interests in international water law. These functions relate to the Theory underpinning the codification and clarification, interpretation and application, and possibly progressive development of the law of transboundary basins.

---

102 *See*, e.g., UNWC 2023 Summary, *supra*, p. 17–18.

103 Gabčíkovo Case, *supra*, p. 56; Silala Case, *supra*, p. 32. In the latter case, the UNWC is invoked by both parties to the dispute in support of their positions, with those states deeming various UNWC provisions to reflect customary law. This is despite neither state being a party to the Convention. Silala Case, *supra*, p. 31.

104 Howden, *supra*, p. 80

105 Id, p. 87.

Part VI begins the investigation of the status of Community-of-Interests by presenting the different standards that have been identified under international law and policy. We then consider the language used by the texts of relevant treaties and decisions when referring to the Theory. But this literal analysis does not provide us with a satisfactory response. We thus recall the functions of Community-of-Interests to demonstrate we are before an autonomous Theory that may *operate as* a legal principle through its primary normative elements by framing international water law rules.

Further research, however, will be necessary to ascertain if, more than a theoretical framework, Community-of-Interests is a legal principle of international water law. To that end, this same Part VI presents two case studies testing the Legal Analytical Framework as a tool to examine other water agreements and assess whether they reflect Community-of-Interests. Uncovering the actual uptake of Community-of-Interests in water treaties would further advance the debate around the Theory's status.

PART I

Contextualization and Delimitation of Community-of-Interests in International Law

> *[O]nly through the pursuit of collective interests may the right of each individual be secured.*[1]

Sovereignty is the foundational principle of international law, positioned at the center of the relations between independent states.[2] Notwithstanding its emotional undertones in political discourse, sovereignty has been evolving with the movement of the international legal order towards institutionalization, and from coexistence through cooperation and in the direction of co-progressiveness. In the law of transboundary basins, a parallel movement may be detected from theories of absolute control through Limited Territorial Sovereignty and towards Community-of-Interests.

In this sense, both general international law and its specific field of international water law have been reacting to geopolitical changes that demand ever closer interstate cooperation on common interests. As the multidimensional challenges facing humanity grow more complex and pervasive, a fertile ground expands for cooperation to permeate sovereignty and, within transboundary basins, for Community-of-Interests to gain strength as a legal theory.

Outside the Theory's remit and beyond individual shared catchments, water interconnects states, economies and societies across sectors and borders and on global and regional scales. Common *basin* interests, as pursued through the Theory, are different from *global* community interests in a balanced *hydrological cycle* and from *regional water* interests that may emerge *between basin and non-basin states*. These distinctions cement Community-of-Interests as *a theory specific to the field of international water law*, while recalling that water links

1 P. Magalhães, *The Earth Condominium: From Climate Change to a New Legal Concept for the Planet* (Almedina 2007), p. 142.

2 ICJ, *Corfu Channel Case* (UK *v.* Albania), Judgment of 9 Apr 1949, ICJ Reports 4 (1949), p. 35.

 | HTTPS://DOI.ORG/10.1163/9789004507036-003

states with one another at different levels and broader shared environmental interests connect the international community as a whole.

1 Friendly Relations and Cooperation among States

> *It is in the darkest moments that we must ask the hardest questions and peer through the gloom in an attempt to see the light. … [F]or there to be evolution, there needs first to be vision – a vision that lifts the gaze beyond tomorrow or the day after or the year after that, to the longer-term.*[3]

There is a danger that certain basin states may dismiss Community-of-Interests in view of its very title, before taking a closer look at its elements and their respective places in state practice. At the same time, understanding opportunities and challenges across international law more broadly and within specific closely related fields provides insights as to the Theory's current and future status.

This Chapter thus reaffirms the true *legal* meaning of "the sacrosanct principle"[4] of state sovereignty and its compatibility with the Theory. As a functional concept, sovereignty encompasses both state rights and obligations – towards one another and *vis-à-vis* the wider international community. In a world of growing interdependence, states are unable to rely on unilateralism alone to realize their interests and perform their responsibilities.[5] States, therefore, "have a responsibility to cooperate in order to fulfil their function."[6]

Connected to these wider state interdependencies and the resulting Close Cooperation imperative, historical trends in international law inform and advance similarly progressive developments in the rules of transboundary basins. A larger application of Community-of-Interests may tap on the same opportunities and trends and face the same challenges as other areas of international law, such as on the environment, in the quest for deeper interstate cooperation.

---

3 Sir D. Bethlehem, *Project 2100 – Is the International Legal Order Fit for Purpose?* (29 Nov 2022), *in* EJIL: Talk!, at https://www.ejiltalk.org/project-2100-is-the-international-legal-order-fit-for-purpose/?utm_source=mailpoet&utm_medium=email&utm_campaign=ejil-talk-newsletter-post-title_2.

4 UNGA, 51st Session, 99th Plenary Meeting (NYC, 21 May 1997), UN Doc A/51/PV.99, p. 12 ('UNWC Voting Records').

5 Howden, *supra*, p. 217.

6 *Id*, p. 240.

In the field of international organizations law, for example, before the 1900s, "the degree of development of interstates' relations made it impossible to conceive further institutionalization (until the legal personification level)."[7] Now, international organizations endowed with legal personality abound. Similarly, with greater interdependence, more basin states may come to view cooperation framed by the Theory as a necessity for the effective exercise of their sovereign rights.

1.1 *Sovereignty and the Organization of the International Legal Order*

Understanding the root of sovereignty in human nature, as a reflection of people's instinctive want for connecting to a delimited geographic space, helps to clarify the politics of shared natural resources, such as water. As Magalhães explains, this *territoriality* underlies most interstates disputes and plays various *social* roles: "defense, physical space, possession, exclusive use, signs, personalization, identity, power, control, safety, vigilance, privacy, affection, symbology, ideology, culture, politics and economics."[8]

Territoriality explains the progressive formation and proliferation of separate political units claiming absolute sovereignty and control over the portions of the planet they had each claimed and artificially delimited as their own. The origins of this process date back to the early stages of agricultural development and population settlement, when the conquering and defense of a fixed territory by force became the means to ensure a community's survival.[9] This initial conception of territorial sovereignty as supreme assumes multiple sovereign powers acting mostly in isolation from one another. In Yee's words: "each actor [as] a separate, independent and sovereign entity and a self-contained system on its own".[10] If this scenario of almost total state autonomy once prevailed, it was never pervasive and has been progressively overtaken by a world of intricate and expanded interdependencies among sovereign states.

Towards safeguarding humanity against the critical global threats that thus emerge, the Law has sought to reimagine the international order through strengthened *institutionalization* or *organization*.[11] Creating the UN was an

7 M.C. Runavot, *The Intergovernmental Organization and the Institutionalization of International Relations: The Modelling of International Organization at Stake*, in Virzo & Ingravallo eds, Evolutions in the Law of International Organizations, Series 'Legal Aspects of International Organizations', Vol.54 (Brill Nijhoff 2015), p. 17–43, 19.

8 Magalhães, *supra*, p. 40.

9 *Id*, p. 39–41.

10 S. Yee, *Towards an International Law of Co-Progressiveness* (Martinus Nijhoff 2004), p. 5.

11 *See*, e.g., Simma, *supra*, p. 235.

attempt to better address international society's disorganization in the aftermath of two world wars and the identified shortcoming of the League of Nations. Both those wars were caused by states opting to realize unilateral interests through confrontation and on the basis of absolute notions of sovereignty, fueled by the primitive human desire for consolidated and expanded territoriality. Simma interprets the UN Charter[12] as having codified and institutionalized community interests. In his mind, the Charter serves as the *constitution* of the international community, setting out "its structure, organization and allocation of competences";[13] as well as the "institutions, principles and rules through which commitment to the interests common to humankind can be activated".[14]

Since the creation of the UN, efforts at international organization have been possible because, as a matter of law, states have generally accepted that territorial sovereignty, while central for interstate relations, is not absolute.

Still, there are instances where states revert to an absolute sovereignty discourse as part of a political strategy, and some act upon it.[15] In the last few years, in particular, fears have been expressed that sovereignty's emotional undertones might be back at play to challenge the international legal order. These fears may seem justified in a world marred in intra- and interstate conflicts, anti-globalization movements, over-politicization of the legal system, absolute sovereignty claims, economic slowdown and trade wars, backsliding democracies, human rights violations, and attacks on multilateralism.

Responding to how Western countries have reacted differently to the wars in Ukraine and Gaza, Zarbiyev remarks: "one of the most essential tenets of the rule of law in international affairs – even-handed application of law – is nothing but a myth [if] not all human lives are worth protecting in the eyes of [the] powerful".[16] Lately, in Zarbiyev's eyes, "the rule of law in international affairs increasingly looks like humbug".[17] Before thus concluding, however, he

12 *Charter of the United Nations and Statute of the International Court of Justice* (San Francisco, 26 June 1945) ('UN Charter').

13 Simma, *supra*, p. 259, paraphrasing A. Verdross, *Die Verfassung der Volkerrechtsgemeinschaft* (Springer, 1926).

14 *Id*, p. 248.

15 Magalhães, *supra*, p. 78, 100.

16 F. Zarbiyev, *Damaged Beyond Repair? International Law after Gaza* (26 Mar 2024), EJIL: Talk!, at https://www.ejiltalk.org/damaged-beyond-repair-international-law-after-gaza/?utm_source=mailpoet&utm_medium=email&utm_campaign=ejil-talk-newsletter-post-title_2.

17 *Ibid.*

invokes "the power of the idea of international law, making a distinction between individual breaches of *rules of law* and what undermines *the rule of law*."[18] This brings us to the more recent comments by Istrefi and Pasquet. They highlight "a growing tendency [among superpowers] towards disregarding the international legal system in its entirety",[19] failing to even bother "to justify [their] actions in terms of international law … [and this] brings a new and unprecedented challenge to the world legal order".[20]

The above precedents are dangerous: "Every breach of international law by a government solely interested in some immediate gratification is a loaded weapon ready for use by any other government interested in doing the same."[21] Indeed, in the Pact for the Future, UN member states themselves express their concerns with "the increasing and diverse threats to international peace and security",[22] contrary to the purposes and principles of the UN Charter.

But Zarbiyev reminds us of how international law "may well be an ideological tool in the hands of powerful states, but that does not prevent it from being a tool in the service of more broadly valued purposes".[23] As pointed out by a former British Army Officer, "all legal rules express deeper power structures [and so] to refer to the international order as being rules-based does not entail commitment to a utopia of rules unmoored from the realities of power".[24] Yee further explains that, while claims of absolute sovereignty and resistance to multilateralism arise from time to time, international law violations must be viewed not in isolation but within a larger historical and geopolitical context.[25] Only then can we assess the real impact of such behaviors on the rules-based global order.

Even, therefore, if certain states sometimes disregard international law and impose their will with power, truth remains, for now, to Henkin's widely

---

18 *Ibid.*

19 K. Istrefi & L. Pasquet, *Mind Your Attitude: The Erosion of International Law?* (3 Mar 2025), EJIL: Talk, at https://www.ejiltalk.org/mind-your-attitude-the-erosion-of-international-law/?utm_source=mailpoet&utm_medium=email&utm_campaign=ejil-talk-newsletter-post-title_2.

20 *Ibid.*

21 Zarbiyev, *supra.*

22 The Pact for the Future, *supra*, ¶32.

23 Zarbiyev, *supra.*

24 E. Simpson, *There's Nothing Wrong with the Liberal Order that Can't Be Fixed by What's Right with it: Realists Need to Get a lot more Realistic about the Global Legal System*, Foreign Policy, Voice (7 Aug 2018), at https://foreignpolicy.com/2018/08/07/theres-nothing-wrong-with-the-liberal-order-that-cant-be-fixed-by-whats-right-with-it/.

25 Yee, *supra*, p. 14.

quoted remark: "almost all nations observe almost all principles of international law and almost all of their obligations almost all of the time."[26] While international law violations have thus occurred, perhaps more frequently in recent times, they still represent the exception not the rule;[27] and, as Yee maintains, "the tenor of international relations seems to have been progressive".[28]

Yet, we must remain committed and vigilant, at the same time that we reflect on the suitability of our rules and institutions. As foundations for the renewal of a commitment to multilateralism and international cooperation, the Pact for the Future invokes "the principles of trust, equity, solidarity and universality".[29] On those bases, what can be done so that violations do not become a regressive trend in the evolution of international law towards organization and the joint protection of common interests?

The Pact for the Future devotes Section V entirely to outlining steps aimed at the transformation of global governance. There, UN member states declare: "we are not complacent about the future of our international order, and we know that it cannot stand still".[30] For Sir Bethlehem, "we are patching and re-engineering and re-upholstering a heavily worn vehicle rather than asking ourselves whether we need a more fundamental overhaul for the next leg of the journey."[31] Moving forward, Sir Bethlehem ponders, another layer of governance must be added to multilateralism: "a workable model of variable geometry where we do multilaterally what can be done multilaterally but are also prepared – proactively, not simply as a last resort – to do regionally or bilaterally or thematically or sectorally what can be done by such means, even if the effect of such action may only be to move the issue partway forward."[32]

From the perspective of community interests, organization, as now structured, aims to balance equal sovereign powers and their individual interests,

26 L. Henkin, *How Nations Behave*, 2nd ed (1979), p. 47.

27 Simpson, *supra. See also* By O.A. Hathaway, *War Unbound Gaza, Ukraine, and the Breakdown of International Law* (23 Apr 2024), at https://www.foreignaffairs.com/ukraine/war-unbound-gaza-hathaway?check_logged_in=1, noting: "even a hobbled system of international humanitarian law … has provided continuous pressure on belligerents to limit civilian casualties, provide safe zones for noncombatants, and allow for humanitarian access – knowing they will face international consequences when they do not".

28 Yee, *supra*, p. 14.

29 The Pact for the Future, *supra*, ¶65.

30 *Id*, ¶64, p. 28.

31 Bethlehem, *supra*.

32 *Ibid*.

while protecting the sphere of interests shared by all peoples. Balancing interests remains the foundational purpose of international law, whereas deepening interdependence demands proactive cooperation driven mostly by common rather than unilateral interests, which does not mean the latter are to be overlooked or superseded.

The above reflections are just as valid within the specific legal field of transboundary waters. The pertinent question is whether the current state of world affairs might deny the premise of a modern international legal system concerned with common interests as a fertile ground for the Theory to take root. In the words of Sir Bethlehem: "The international legal system has struggled to cope with [climate change, a pandemic, food security, and other global] challenges";[33] and yet: "We continue to turn to multilateral rules and institutions in our search for solutions to these challenges. And we must, because it is in such rules and institutions – shared endeavors – that lie our only hope of enduring and effective solutions."[34] As thus recognized by UN member states and other actors gathered under the UNGA in 2018, "the sheer scale of global connectivity and global challenges made multilateralism essential".[35]

For water resources, in particular, a recent interministerial declaration emphasizes "inclusive coordination and collaboration among governments and water-related stakeholders at all levels",[36] while explicitly encouraging transboundary cooperation – calling, in both contexts, for cooperation to be "in accordance with applicable international law, including international instruments countries are parties to".[37]

To further illustrate how co-basin states interlink international law and cooperation, consider the explicit references to *sovereignty* in the ILC Draft Articles on Transboundary Aquifers;[38] and in Article 2 of the Guarani Aquifer Agreement, which affirms: "Each Party exercises sovereign territorial control

33 *Ibid.*

34 *Ibid.*

35 UNGA Presidency, 72nd Session, *Letter to Permanent Representatives and Observers, Informal Discussions Summary* (14 Mar 2018), Morning Dialogues 5–7: Multilateralism under Fire? (NYC, 15 & 23 Feb, 9 Mar 2018), at https://www.un.org/pga/72/wp-content/uploads/sites/51/2018/03/Morning-dialogue-23-March.pdf.

36 10th World Water Forum (Bali, 20–21 May 2024), *Ministerial Declaration on "Water for Shared Prosperity"*, at https://worldwaterforum.org/outcomes.

37 *Ibid.*

38 ILC Draft Articles (2008), *supra*, Art.2.

over their respective [aquifer] portions".[39] For their apparent emphasis on sovereignty, these references deserve a closer look as to their meaning and significance for the status of international water law.

The Guarani Aquifer Agreement is modeled on the ILC Draft Articles on Transboundary Aquifers and both instruments, in their Preambles, invoke UNGA Resolution 1803 (XVII), on the permanent sovereignty of states over natural resources within their territories. When adopted, however, said Resolution was not meant to estipulate a claim of exclusive and absolute control of the resource by one basin state to the detriment of another sharing the same water body. Rather, the Resolution was about boosting the decolonization process and reaffirming developing countries' territorial sovereignty and independence,[40] including in relation to sovereign rights over natural resources and possible foreign intervention under the guise of environmental protection. Along the lines of the above Resolution, the Guarani Aquifer Agreement aims for the collective protection of the interests of the four co-aquifer states against external meddling, while safeguarding the aquifer itself through its sustainable management. This is evident in the ratification process by Uruguay. On the basis of the document presented before the Senate to introduce the Agreement, in 2011, Sindico *et al* explain Uruguay's goal to ensure "the defense of its own natural resources vis-à-vis the interference of developed nations"[41] as the reason for including an explicit reference to sovereignty in the treaty.

In both the Draft Articles and the Guarani Aquifer Agreement, the references to sovereignty are immediately followed by a legal caveat: that, in the exercise of such sovereign rights, states remain bound by international law. Moreover, other provisions in each instrument establish specific requirements for cooperation and coordination.

39 *Guarani Aquifer Agreement* (San Juan, 2 Aug 2010) (in force 26 Nov 2020), Argentina-Brazil-Paraguay-Uruguay, on International Water Law Project, at https://www.internationalwaterlaw.org/documents/regionaldocs/Guarani_Aquifer_Agreement-Portuguese.pdf.

40 H. Elver, *Peaceful Uses of International Rivers: The Euphrates and Tigris Rivers Dispute* (Transnational Publishers 2002), p. 116.

41 F. Sindico, R. Hirata, A. Manganelli, *The Guarani Aquifer System: From a Beacon of Hope to a Question Mark in the Governance of Transboundary Aquifers*, 20 Journal of Hydrology: Regional Studies 49–59 (2018), p. 54. *See also* World Bank, *Environmental Protection and Sustainable Development of the Guarani Aquifer System Project: Implementation Completion and Results* (TF-50950 TF-51223), Report ICR00001198 (2009), p. 23, noting that the four aquifer countries had to show their citizens they held sovereign rights over the resource.

While, therefore, the international order may be showing signs of its "fragility and limitations",[42] the value of such an order and the validity of the international rule of law underlying it stand even more firmly in an increasingly interdependent and multipolar world. The truth remains: "All states ... have interests that they cannot achieve on their own and so need to develop rules for working together."[43] In the context of transboundary basins, "riparian states appear as participants in a shared resource, the best use and protection of which is an interest that they have in common and that they can effectively pursue through cooperation and joint action".[44]

Acknowledging that such rules, as currently devised, are imperfect in an evolving context of intertwined global and transboundary waters interests, we must pause to consider larger trends in legal progression, at the same time that thoughts around reimagining general international law begin to take shape. We must also take a closer look at the progressive development of international water law to ask: Is this field evolving from Limited Territorial Sovereignty towards Community-of-Interests?

In order to do so, and to contextualize Community-of-Interests for the purpose of this book, we must first paint a clearer picture of the development of general international law and of the law of transboundary basins and the similarities in their respective paths through history in the face of changing interstate relationships.

1.2 *Coexistence and Cooperation in the Development of International Law*

The contextualization of regional integration and Community-of-Interests, and how these levels of state interaction present similarities and are interlinked, must happen through the lens of the *Declaration on Principles of International Law Concerning Friendly Relations and Cooperation among States*, seen as representing "a landmark in the development of international law and of relations among states".[45]

The Declaration incorporates seven Principles. Good-faith compliance with international obligations is transversal to all other six. There are five that

42 Simpson, *supra*.

43 *Ibid.*

44 A. Tanzi & M. Arcari, *The United Nations Convention on the Law of International Watercourses: A Framework for Sharing* (Kluwer 2001), p. 23.

45 UNGA, 25th Session, Res 2625 (24 Oct 1970), Annex, Declaration on Principles of International Law Concerning Friendly Relations and Cooperation among States in accordance with the Charter of the United Nations, UN Doc A/RES/2625(XXV) ('Friendly Relations Declaration').

relate largely to ensuring states can coexist in peace, namely: refraining from the threat or use of force; peaceful settlement of disputes; non-intervention; equal rights and self-determination of peoples; and sovereign equality, including territorial integrity. In contrast, the *duty to cooperate* is more directed at common goals and entails cooperation "in the various spheres of international relations", including for economic development, the nations' general welfare, and respect for human rights. The duty to cooperate includes both joint and separate action. The Declaration thus integrates principles of coexistence and cooperation as mutually reinforcing requirements for states in their relationships.

Building on the Declaration, the teachings of Friedmann and Yee help us to tell the story of how international law has been evolving and how the duty to cooperate has been applied at different levels. Friedmann's *law of coexistence* and *law of cooperation* and Yee's *law of co-progressiveness* frame the analysis of the parallel developments in the law of transboundary basins, with most countries having relinquished absolute control claims to embrace Limited Territorial Sovereignty and many, possibly, taking steps towards or embracing Community-of-Interests.

General international law and, like other specialized legal fields, the law of transboundary basins have gained shape as the world's nations and peoples become increasingly interdependent across multiple material dimensions and governance levels. On the wheels of globalization, the international legal order has expanded and deepened, bringing states and peoples closer together to face challenges no one nation or region could handle alone.

In the international water law arena, placed in the bosom of general international law, legal principles and rules have been reacting "to the emergence of inherently transboundary issues";[46] and the Theory has surfaced and has been progressing as a guiding framework for closer cooperative relations between co-riparian states. At the same time, developments in the field of the law of international watercourses have influenced wider legal progress. Shared watercourses "were perhaps the genesis of [a] move toward cooperation"[47] and organization in general international law, through the early establishment of watercourse commissions, which, in their turn, play a central role under the Theory.

---

46 J. Taylor, *Unravelling Cooperation: The Role and Limits of Cooperation in the Governance of International Watercourses in Customary International Law,* Research Paper 15–05, submitted for Honors Thesis, ANU College of Law, The Australian National University (2014), p. 21.

47 *Ibid.*

In his influential book, Friedmann traces the evolution of international law over the years – from one primarily of coexistence to one centered strongly, albeit not exclusively, on cooperation. As he explains, in its origins, international law was primarily concerned with diplomatic relations and "did not purport to penetrate … into the economic and social aspects of the polities that dealt with each other as units."[48] The law of coexistence shaped up amidst the rise of absolutist states and their expanding interactions dominated by confrontation and competition. This scenario required basic rules to enable those states to attempt to reconcile conflicting interests, mostly at the bilateral level, and thus coexist peacefully as much as possible. As then conceived, state *dominium* comes within an international legal framework designed for states largely self-sufficient to solve domestic challenges, acting within their respective territories in opposition and with autonomy in relation to one another.[49] In other words, the *law of coexistence* provides for "a *minimal* international order, primarily out of necessity",[50] in a time of scarce cooperation and absolute conceptions of sovereignty. For Yee, "this was a picture of international law for *isolated, uncoordinated action*."[51]

Nowadays, the territoriality imperative that marked the birth of the modern state still informs interstate relations, and international law remains state-centric and, to some extent, disorganized. But the space for nonstate actors continues to grow and intergovernmental institutions and Close Cooperation frameworks have proliferated worldwide. The law of coexistence now serves to balance state interests and to address exceptional instances of recalcitrant behavior and abuse of power, as nations "deal with each other in continuous attempts to adjust their respective national interests short of war."[52] Coexistence also plays a role in situations where interstate relations are limited in nature, extent, or scope due to residual tensions – for example, where border disputes have yet to be resolved.

At the same time, nations have come to realize that many challenges, including some traditionally viewed as essentially domestic, trigger the emergence of common interests in their resolution through cooperation and organization; and that the law of coexistence is not designed to safeguard shared concerns,[53] whether such concerns exist among basin states, across a region or

48 W. Friedmann, *The Changing Structure of International Law* (Stevens & Sons 1964), p. 5.

49 Magalhães, *supra*, p. 43–4.

50 Yee, *supra*, p. 6 (emphasis added).

51 *Ibid* (emphasis added).

52 Friedmann, *supra*, p. 16.

53 *Ibid.*

the entire world. An international law that allows states to coexist remains necessary, but its persistent prevalence may not be conducive to meeting the needs of the international community in the 21st Century.

Under Friedmann's *law of cooperation*, therefore, common action and collective enforcement gain prominence, and "the growth of international obligations and rules result in a 'community interest' in the smooth functioning of the international system".[54] The law of cooperation is "defined by rules of abstention to preserve the coexistence of sovereign states [*and* by] rules of positive conduct [on] a range of issues with transboundary effect",[55] across all relevant scales and legal fields. Similarly, rules of Close Basin Cooperation prevail in the Basin Treaty, supported by norms ensuring sustained coexistence. As such, the law of cooperation represents a second stage in the evolution of the international legal order, which contemplates, *inter alia*, "*joint* political planning and *action* [within] a *joint organization* of those linked by *common interests*, goals and traditions."[56] More parallels between Community-of-Interests and Friedmann's law of cooperation thus become apparent, with joint action, joint organizations, and common interests at the heart of both.

In his turn, Yee splits the evolution of international law into three phases: coexistence, aligned with Friedman's coexistence law; and then *coordination*, followed by *co-progressiveness*. Yee's law of coordination entails less ambitious *coordinated* efforts rather than joint action. Coordination would have characterized the period of détente in the early 1960s, when the US and the USSR started engaging in exchanges to address strained relations. Such efforts initially focused on disarmament and later extended to cover economic, cultural, and environmental matters, and to inspire other countries to follow suit. It was then recognized that each state's own political, social, and economic system should not stop nations from coexisting peacefully and cooperating. Amidst the outspreading spirit of cooperation of the times, acceptance of international law's compulsory nature also became prevalent, and apparent violators themselves attempted to justify potentially questionable behavior invoking the relevant rules. Yee thinks of coordination as a basis for both state cooperation and coexistence: a means to produce efficiency in international relations.[57]

54 Yee, *supra*, p. 10.
55 Taylor, *supra*, p. 22.
56 Friedmann, *supra*, p. 35 (emphasis added).
57 Yee, *supra*, p. 6–7, 11–12.

Yee argues that international law has now entered a third stage in its structural evolution: that of co-progressiveness, under which the overarching and universal interest of states in a stable and effective international legal order, as had already been identified by Friedmann, gains strength and a broadened scope. The law of co-progressiveness goes beyond coordinated cooperation, and its making and application involve the international community of non-state actors. Whereas the law of coexistence has a limited number of states as its main subjects, and the law of coordination sees an increase in the number of states and in the types of international law stakeholders, the law of co-progressiveness places the rights and participation of individuals and nonstate groups at its center.[58] Yee's age of co-progressiveness portrays modern international law as "all-encompassing (hence 'co'), preoccupied with advancements in moral and ethical terms … and [with] *human flourishing* as its ultimate goal (hence 'progressiveness')".[59]

Going back decades, though ever more relevant, the UN Charter makes clear the centrality of human beings for the international legal order already in its Preamble by referring to the "peoples"; fundamental human rights; each individual's "dignity and worth"; socioeconomic advancement; enhanced life standards "in larger freedom"; and the employment of international machinery to achieve these goals. In addition, Article 1(1)(3) affirms the promotion and encouragement of respect for human rights.

The Corfu Channel Case reflects this process of international law humanization, which has since intensified. The case involves harm suffered by the UK and its nationals as a result of Albania's failure to inform and warn approaching ships about a minefield within its territorial waters. The Court declares Albania's conduct to be unlawful by invoking "*certain general and well-recognized principles*, [like] *elementary considerations of humanity*, even more exacting in peace than in war".[60]

This focus on human flourishing takes us back to Kofi Annan's remarks about the reconceptualization of state sovereignty in today's world in relation to the individual: "*States* are now widely understood to be *instruments at the service of their peoples*";[61] and, the UN Charter, as meant "to protect individual

58 *Id*, p. 4, 7, 14, 20.

59 *Id*, p. 3 (emphasis added).

60 Corfu Channel Case, *supra*, p. 22 (emphasis added).

61 K. Annan, Two concepts of sovereignty (18 Sep 1999), on United Nations, at https://www.un.org/sg/en/content/sg/articles/1999-09-18/two-concepts-sovereignty (emphasis added).

human beings, not to protect those who abuse them."[62] Similarly, Simma sees international law evolving to become "more socially conscious".[63] Under international water law, specifically, one of the Theory's secondary elements has to do with Social Basin Engagement, as later explored.

Yee associates co-progressiveness with the "concretization of grand ideas in international law [aimed at] building a better international society",[64] both economically and ethically, and in key areas such as the environment and sustainable development, as well as democracy and good governance. States cooperating under the law of co-progressiveness are aware of their interdependence and how that affects their individual interests. Such states demonstrate concern "with vindicating their existence as members in good standing of the international system",[65] *inter alia*, by joining international organizations.

Finally, Yee highlights transition and blurriness in the evolution of international law. He explains that coordination was also present in coexistence and that both the former and the latter remain in use in the age of co-progressiveness. To illustrate, treaty-based coordination and economic integration emerge under coexistence, even if not greatly successful. The period of détente reflects predominantly coordination and exceptional instances of violations and abuses still occur. Under co-progressiveness, states may interact within the framework of coexistence and not go beyond coordination in certain aspects of their relations, but the general state of affairs would be one of cooperation for human flourishing.[66]

For the law governing transboundary waters, this blurriness means that, even as Community-of-Interests becomes more widespread among certain countries, not all states may yet be ready to engage in Close Basin Cooperation. Moreover, operating within the framework of Community-of-Interests, Limited Territorial Sovereignty ensures that any disputes that do arise can be resolved efficiently. In this world of asymmetries, both Community-of-Interests and Limited Territorial Sovereignty have important roles to play in relation, respectively, to unilateral interests and shared concerns, whether under regimes founded primarily on one or the other theory.

In a time, however, of accelerated global change and growing interdependence among states, organization in international law and relations, Close

62 *Ibid.*

63 Simma, *supra*, p. 234.

64 Yee, *supra*, p. 16.

65 *Id*, p. 21.

66 *Id*, p. 2, 6, 12.

Basin Cooperation, and an accelerated transition towards co-progressiveness are more needed than ever, as enablers of the identification of shared priorities and the collective actions required to realize them.

In relation to the use of force in the common interest, for example, the former UN Secretary-General has asked: "But what is the common interest? How shall we define it? Who will defend it? Under whose authority? And with what means of intervention?"[67] Only by coming together can states seek answers here. The same questions are valid in the case of transboundary basins and illustrate the importance of the Theory, also founded on common interests, as a legal theoretical framing for interstate relations on the topic.

1.3 *From Absolute Control Claims to Community-of-Interests*

Friedmann and Yee provide an understanding of the overall direction and stages in the evolution of *general* international law. We can see a similar pattern in international *water* law in its movement from a principal focus on unilateral restraint based on Limited Territorial Sovereignty to a stronger attention to common interests through Close Basin Cooperation, on the basis of the notions of coexistence and cooperation, as well as of the laws of coordination and co-progressiveness.

This comparative exercise must bear in mind two different contexts: on the one hand, a prevailing scenario of isolated and autonomous entities in the early stages of international law; and, on the other, the reality that co-basin states have always been interdependent to some degree, given water's interconnecting and fluid properties. To be sure, the international law of transboundary basins is an inherently collaborative field, in which absolute sovereignty claims have never been given much credence and the governance of transboundary catchments could never be framed purely by coexistence. Hence, while there are parallels, the specificities of the context where international water law applies and evolves must be kept in mind and the lessons of Friedmann and Yee can only be employed with adjustments for the purpose of contextualizing Community-of-Interests.

Limited Territorial Sovereignty would be a hybrid of Friedmann's law of coexistence and Yee's law of coordination. With its widely accepted and core rules of equitable and reasonable use[68] and harm prevention,[69] Limited Ter-

---

67 Annan, *supra*.

68 *See*, e.g., UNWC, *supra*, Art.5; A.C. Kiss & D. Shelton, *International Environmental Law*, 3rd ed (Foundation Press 2004), p. 181; Hunter *et al* (2015), *supra*, p. 886.

69 Harm prevention is cemented as a rule of not only international water law, but also under general international law and international environmental law. *See*, e.g., Corfu

ritorial Sovereignty aims mostly at enabling peaceful *coexistence* through *coordination* in the promotion of equitable and reasonable use and prevention of significant transboundary harm. Those two binding rules may be seen as the minimum set of cooperation standards between riparian countries, demanding basic levels of coordination needed to govern international watercourses so that interstate disputes are avoided as much as possible or, at least, peacefully resolved. In so doing, states may, progressively, create an enabling environment for closer cooperation on common interests.

This view of Limited Territorial Sovereignty as a parallel development in international water law that mixes characteristics of Friedmann's law of coexistence and Yee's law of coordination is well expressed in the *Charter of Economic Rights and Duties of States*. When dealing with *shared natural resources*, Article 3 requires coordination for coexistence, i.e., cooperation "on the basis of a system of information and prior consultations in order to achieve the optimum use of such resources without causing damage to the legitimate interest of others."[70]

In its turn, Community-of-Interests goes beyond the basic rules of abstention and minimum coordination characteristic of coexistence and Limited Territorial Sovereignty. Community-of-Interests gains value as riparian states embrace organization, resembling an amalgamation of Friedmann's law of cooperation and Yee's law of co-progressiveness. The Theory's focus on close, positive, and institutionalized cooperation for common interests embeds the links made by Friedmann between his law of cooperation and the notion of common goals and traditions, the establishment of international organizations, and state engagement through joint action. The elevation of nonstate actors is present under both the law of co-progressiveness and Community-of-Interests. The treaties that reflect Community-of-Interests, examined here, to varying degrees, reveal a concern with human flourishing, while broadening the set of actors involved in international relations.

Similar parallels may be traced with the development of international environmental law – a legal field closely related to the rules governing transboundary waters. Like general international law and the law of transboundary basins, international environmental law has gradually progressed towards

---

Channel Case, *supra*, p. 22; ICJ, *Legality of the Threat or Use of Nuclear Weapons*, Advisory Opinion of 8 July 1996, ICJ Reports 226 (1996) ('Nuclear Weapons Threat or Use AO'), p. 242; UNWC, *supra*, Art.7; ECEWC, *supra*, across various provisions; ILC (1994), *supra*, p. 103–4.

70 UNGA, 29th Session, *Charter of Economic Rights and Duties of States*, Res 3281 (XXIX) (12 Dec 1974), resolutions adopted on the Reports of the 2nd Committee.

greater organization, deeper cooperation, and stronger engagement of non-state actors.

The early stages of international environmental law are largely not informed by an awareness of the potential for long-range transboundary impacts from human activities and thus by notions of globally shared interests and values. The rules governing environmental protection are then mainly reactive and bilateral in scope, focusing on state actions or omissions with cross-border effects within immediately neighboring states,[71] much like the field of international water law.

Principle 21 of the Stockholm Declaration reflects this initial limited and localized focus of international environmental law, with its references to sovereign use rights, the supremacy of national policies, and the harm prevention rule.[72] Yet, the same Declaration signalizes an emerging international environmental law of cooperation, when Principle 24 references the importance of a "cooperative spirit by all countries". Recall here Yee's clarification about transition and blurriness between legal evolutionary stages. Looking forward 20 years, Principle 7 of the Rio Declaration invokes a "spirit of *global* partnership" that must inspire international environmental cooperation.[73]

Like the rules governing transboundary waters, international environmental law has always been "marked by a concern for common objectives".[74] At first, this concern is mostly expressed in the no-harm rule in relation to neighboring states and the coordinated actions necessary to abide by that rule, as in the Stockholm Declaration. Later, the Law evolves to encompass a broader focus on common environmental interests at various levels and, accordingly, the higher degree of cooperation and stakeholder engagement required to safeguard those interests.

As the transboundary dimensions of the environmental challenge gain global and regional scale, and greater complexity, a broader law of positive and multilateral cooperation develops. This process mirrors the emergence

---

71 Magalhães, *supra*, p. 45–6.

72 UN, *Declaration* ('Stockholm Declaration'), *in* Report, UN Conference on the Human Environment (Stockholm, 5–16 June 1972), UN Doc A/CONF.48/14/Rev.1 (UN 1973); Simma, *supra*, p. 238.

73 UN, *Rio Declaration on Environment and Development*, *in* Report of the UN Conference on Environment and Development ('UNCED Report'), Vol.I, Annex I (Rio de Janeiro, 3–14 June 1992), UN Doc A/CONF.151/26 (12 Aug 1992).

74 H.P. Hestermeyer, *Reality or Aspiration? Solidarity in International Environmental and World Trade Law*, Outcome Paper 2/2012, Otto-Hahn-Gruppe, Diversität und Homogenität, (Max-Planck-Institut für Ausländisches Öffentliches Recht und Völkerrecht 2012), p. 9.

and growth of Community-of-Interests in the field of transboundary basin cooperation. The illusion of unlimited control and strict unilateralism being viable in the fields of environment and shared waters has been broken, burying the theories of absolute territorial sovereignty and integrity in the law of transboundary basins.

2 Community-of-Interests and Common Water Interests

As humanity's most precious global common good, water unites us all.[75]

Community-of-Interests is not encompassing of just any kind of common water interest a given group of states might share. The Theory's foundation lies on the interdependencies of co-riparian states within a unitary freshwater system and is thus concerned, specifically, with the interests of the countries sharing a given basin and which may arise in connection with each such basin; and not with water concerns unrelated to, or outside of, that same transboundary catchment.

However, the special characteristics of water – a fluid resource that no one or nothing can do without, make it the ultimate connector – not only within individual transboundary catchments, but also across sectors and borders on global and regional scales. The water crisis unfolds at multiple levels, which means shared state interests in freshwater do so as well; and, accordingly, instances abound of global-to-local water cooperation and related policy developments.

The Theory has thus a narrower ambit than water cooperation broadly considered, i.e., cooperation that may be driven by a range of water-related challenges and common interests, whether in national or international catchments, between local communities across political borders, or in the hydrosphere as a whole. In this wider sense, water cooperation may be global; continental and intercontinental; regional, interregional, and subregional; and national or subnational.

Notwithstanding the distinction between state engagement framed by the Theory and other interstate water-related interactions, exploring cooperation linked to the *global* hydrological cycle and under certain *regional* agreements and arrangements offers lessons on how countries may pursue together shared water interests at any level.

---

75 Guterres, *supra.*

2.1 *Community Interests in the Hydrosphere*

The hydrological cycle operates as Earth's "bloodstream"[76] – flowing in the air, on land, underground, in aquatic environments, and even within each individual – "from the planetary scale down to the cell scale".[77] Earth's water molecules have been constant and the same from the beginning, circulating in different states, across the planet and within living organisms, countless times.[78]

The emergence of universal concerns with the state of water resources and dependent ecosystems is thus not surprising, and we ponder over the imperative of governing and managing water as a global resource. A world environment interconnected through water flows speaks to interdependencies, common challenges and vulnerabilities, and shared opportunities, on scales far beyond any one individual basin. These are interests the entire human family shares in common, raising questions about the efficacy of only managing water at the local or basin levels, as has been common practice.

Scientific findings about the so-called *sky rivers*, for example, illustrate long-range water-based linkages in the form of the ecological services performed by forests as their roots absorb soil humidity and water vapor comes out of their foliage into the atmosphere. The mega clouds and rainfall that result from evapotranspiration in large tropical forests, like the Amazon and Congo, travel great distances to support agricultural productivity in the US, India, and China. Conversely, extensive deforestation may negatively affect the global hydrological cycle. Yet, the sky-rivers phenomenon lacks dedicated governance mechanisms and tailored international law norms.[79] Customary international law has not evolved in tandem with the science behind universal water interests; and there is no conventional precedent expressing a global human interest in a balanced hydrological cycle.

In the face of the unifying traits of the hydrological cycle, arguments for water as a global public good have been made. Magalhães, for example, focuses on the entire hydrosphere as representing, together with the atmosphere, "global diffuse interests".[80] He draws from Lovelock's demonstrated

76 M. Falkenmark, *Forward to the Future: A Conceptual Framework for Water Dependence* (Volvo Environment Prize Lecture 1998), 28:4 Ambio 356–61 (1999), p. 356.

77 *Id*, p. 357.

78 Magalhães, *supra*, p. 107.

79 F. Pearce, *Rivers in the Sky: How Deforestation Is Affecting Global Water Cycles* (24 July 2018), on Yale Environment 360 at https://e360.yale.edu/features/how-deforestation-affecting-global-water-cycles-climate-change. *See also* UN Water (2018), *supra*, p. 142, on airborne water pollution carried by winds.

80 Magalhães, *supra*, p. 104.

Gaia Theory about planetary connections[81] and proposes to organize the Earth as a *global condominium*, i.e., a unitary whole which "divide[s] what may be subject to individual sovereignty and maintain[s] what is necessarily collective and cannot be reduced to the dimension of state organization as a common thing".[82]

In domestic law, the concept of condominium results from a reshaping of traditional property notions to respond to the once new situation presented by buildings, where private and common interests must be reconciled and safeguarded. A building is a spatial unit inhabited by multiple persons, where each inhabitant enjoys exclusive rights over its respective fraction; and, together, all residents share rights over, and are responsible for, the common parts and the building as a whole.[83] As such, the condominium serves as an appropriate conceptual legal frame for "understand[ing] and organiz[ing] the use and the ownership of a good which maintains the unitarian and materially undivided structure, such as the Planet Earth, by a plurality of sovereign states".[84]

Thus modeled, the Earth Condominium would inform the global administration of the Planet in a manner that accounts for its unity, while respecting territorial sovereignty; it would maintain the legal fiction of political borders and enable the continued exercise of sovereign powers dependent on a healthy planet, while adjusting global environmental management to physical reality.

In organizing the Earth Condominium, Magalhães deems the lithosphere "sufficiently stable and firm"[85] to be categorized as a state fraction. In contrast, he classifies the hydrosphere and the atmosphere as necessarily collective parts – fluid elements that blanket and penetrate the lithosphere; interlink and flow universally across ecological systems and nations; and move in cycles interacting with one another constantly. Hence, the utilization of the hydrosphere and the atmosphere may lead to impacts across borders and farther away, on state fractions and on common parts, and possibly with long-lasting or irreversible negative effects. These collective parts of Magalhães' Earth Condominium are essential for securing a healthy planet and safeguarding nature and people, now and in the future.[86]

---

81 *Id*, p. 54–58.
82 *Id*, p. 97.
83 *Id*, p. 80, 84–85.
84 *Id*, p. 80.
85 *Id*, p. 102.
86 *Id*, p. 103–108.

Water is not only shared between states drained by the same water bodies, but also regionally and globally, thus transcending the realm of the law of transboundary basins. Hydrosphere-atmosphere interlinkages give rise to a global human interest in preserving the balance of the entire hydrological cycle. For the most part, "each participant's selfish interests in community life are only feasible with the accomplishment and the pursuit of the common interests".[87] This is true on a planetary scale and within communities-of-basin -interests.

The Earth Condominium would be founded on exclusive, supreme, and independent sovereignty over individualized fractions within each state's territory, and shared sovereignty regarding the hydrosphere and the atmosphere. This complex-sovereignty structure, Magalhães argues, is fit for a globalized world, whose functionality is ultimately contingent upon the joint conservation and use of universally shared resources.[88]

The Earth Condominium would be formalized through a Constitutive Convention setting out agreed norms and designing a specialized and dedicated global institution – much like a Basin Treaty does. This institution, composed of all states, would determine, for example, "the way in which to choose the [Earth Condominium's] administrator and the powers he may exercise while administering the common parts".[89] Among other functions, this Administrator would "promote projects for the conservation and improvement of the common parts".[90] Here, similarities with the Basin Body exist.

The Constitutive Convention would also provide for the contributions of states in the upkeeping of the common parts, through a benefit and cost-sharing system. Contributions by each political unit in the management of common parts would be proportional to how much a state benefits from their utilization and how much it provides for their conservation. In other words, states that conserve common parts would be compensated and countries that degrade such parts would respond for related costs. Resources generated through the development of common parts would be invested back in their maintenance. Magalhães uses the scenario of a country considering a project capable of irreversibly harming a wetland. This country would face the choice between holding on to the income it receives for protecting such wetland or foregoing those resources and shouldering the costs associated

87 *Id*, p. 80.
88 *Id*, p. 88, 91.
89 *Id*, p. 137.
90 *Id*, p. 144.

with the loss of ecosystem services.[91] Magalhães' benefit and cost-sharing system aligns with the spirit of Close Basin Cooperation as expressed through equitable and reasonable Participation in the use, management and protection of shared basins, as codified in Article 5(2) of the UNWC.

Therefore, some of Magalhães' ideas for how the Law may deal with natural resources shared among sovereign states, such as a transboundary basin, hint at the normative content of Community-of-Interests, even if international law has not reached a stage in which the hydrological cycle is globally governed.

In international policy discourse, already back in 1992, the water community, gathered at a major international conference,[92] concluded that the water crisis had implications reaching beyond the local level; placed this natural element at the center of the global ecological and climate systems; and, accordingly, called for the development of international governance and management mechanisms, such as policies, monitoring, and coordinating institutions. On this same occasion, the water community discussed and identified priority objectives for a future global water governance framework, in support of multilevel and multistakeholder dialogue. These objectives included keeping the topic high in the global policy agenda for sustained commitment; fostering debate, experience exchange, and the formulation of advice; enabling the review of progress towards agreed goals; and, on transboundary waters, bringing together co-riparian states to build cooperation and mutual confidence.[93]

The Dublin Statement was then unanimously endorsed, with participants commending it to world leaders for follow-up action. The Statement points to the global dimensions of the water crisis then emerging, and which demand "a greater recognition of the interdependence of all peoples, and of their place in the natural world".[94] UN-Water refers to the Statement as "the foundation for an integrated approach to managing water resources".[95]

---

91 *Id*, p. 125–26, 131, 134.

92 Moving away from a sectoral mindset, the *International Conference on Water and the Environment* (ICWE) "was the first major meeting of world experts to focus on the holistic management of water in its proper context, that is, in the integrated spectrum of human and environmental uses and needs". UN Administrative Committee on Coordination Inter-Secretariat Group for Water Resources (ACC/ISGWR), Report, *International Conference on Water and the Environment* (ICWE): *Development Issues for the 21st Century* (Dublin, 26–31 Jan 1992) (ICWE Steering Committee 1992) ('ICWE Report'), p. 12.

93 *Id*, p. 40–1.

94 *Dublin Statement on Water and Sustainable Development*, Introduction (31 Jan 1992) ('Dublin Statement'), *in* ICWE Report, *supra*, p. 3.

95 UN Water (2018), *supra*, p. 104.

Since then, there has been a proliferation of water conferences, campaigns and initiatives, dedicated organizations and coalitions, and other global water-related activities undertaken by various state and nonstate actors.[96]

At the 5th World Water Forum, in 2009, high-level participants framed water as an interconnecting element across the social, cultural, and economic spheres, capable of generating vital benefits for people and nature and, yet, vulnerable to global shifts. Promoting innovative approaches that would enable stakeholder engagement, cross-sectoral action, and interdisciplinary thinking, state participants underscored the value of a dedicated, globally agreed-upon common vision and framework for water.[97]

In 2015, the UN highlighted the importance of thinking of water as a universal matter for the achievement of relevant international policy goals.[98] Adopted in that same year, Agenda 2030 comes to reinforce that thinking with the inclusion of a Goal dedicated to water, namely, SDG-6.

These trends are strengthened by the recent calls to view all public environmental goods as Earth-wide and all peoples' concerns.[99] A key message arising from the 2023 Water Conference, as highlighted by the General Assembly President, is that the "global water cycle is a global common good"[100] and must be treated as such and protected collectively for all communities and nations.[101] Integrated management of water and related resources should be promoted to "address the whole hydrological cycle".[102] As a follow-up to the

96 A.K. Gerlak *et al*, *Hydrosolidarity and International Water Governance*, 14 International Negotiation 311–28 (2009), p. 312.

97 World Water Council (WWC), 5th World Water Forum (Istanbul, 16–22 Mar 2009) ('WWC (2009)'), *Istanbul Declaration* (16 Mar 2009). The *World Water Forum* is a large, dedicated water conference that happens every three years, gathering multiple stakeholders, including high-level government representatives, with each resulting in declarations and ministerial statements.

98 Unturbe, *supra*, p. 4.

99 L. Movilla, *Towards Globalization of Earth Jurisprudence* (23 Apr 2018), UN Harmony with Nature, 8th Interactive Dialogue of the General Assembly on Harmony with Nature, at http://www.harmonywithnatureun.org/dialogue/LYezQHBEJqbu9RKc9hzp6Kpd28074Qe3L5Z3QdOJjWC8y1fGgRWFbNsjD2pI9uZuVQf9Ctk!buwmSbHIYKd1Sw==.

100 UNWC 2023 Summary, *supra*, p. 1.

101 *Id*, p. 19.

102 *Id*, p. 14, 19.

Conference, in 2024, the UN adopted its first System-wide Strategy for Water and Sanitation[103] and the UNSG appointed a Special Envoy on Water.[104]

The desired formation of international rules and policies for all freshwaters, not just for transboundary basins, must be placed in the broader context of viewing the environment itself, not just climate change or biodiversity, as representing a global common interest, of which water is an element. In this respect, Simma devises the concept of *community interests* in connection with the "needs, hopes and fears"[105] of all states and, ultimately, the entire human family. For Simma, community interests embed themselves into international law as it becomes more aware of global interdependencies and universally recognized common concerns. The environment is at the center of these progressions. Threats to a healthy Planet can seldom be solved without universal cooperation that transcends bilateralism.[106] Nature, after all, operates as a universal unity, as a vital priority for all states and peoples.

Reflecting a community interest in certain elements of a healthy environment, the Conventions on Biodiversity[107] and Climate Change[108] introduce in international law the notion of *common concern of humankind*, which has since been evolving. In relation to the environment beyond national jurisdictions, some goods have been considered to be a *common heritage of mankind*.[109] Neither notion has been formally applied to the global hydrological cycle.

Adopted in 2000, the Earth Charter aligns concepts of cultural and biological diversity with visions of a *common destiny* for *one human family* and *one Earth community*; the global environment as all people's *common concern*; and a *global partnership* caring for the Planet and for humanity.[110]

---

103 *UN System-wide Strategy for Water and Sanitation* (UN 2024), at https://www.unwater.org/publications/united-nations-system-wide-strategy-water-and-sanitation.

104 IISD, SDG Knowledge Hub, *UN Secretary-General Appoints Special Envoy on Water* (18 Sep 2024), at https://sdg.iisd.org/news/un-secretary-general-appoints-special-envoy-on-water/.

105 Simma, *supra*, p. 244.

106 *Id*, p. 234, 239.

107 UN, *Convention on Biological Diversity* (CBD) (Nairobi, 22 May 1992) (in force 29 Dec 1993) 1760 UNTS 30619 (1992), Preamble.

108 UN, *Framework Convention on Climate Change* (FCCC) (New York City, 9 May 1992) (in force 21 Mar 1994), 1771 UNTS 30822 (1992), Preamble.

109 *See*, e.g., UN, *Convention on the Law of the Sea* (UNCLOS) (Montego Bay, 10 Dec 1982) (in force 16 Nov 1994), art.136.

110 Earth Charter Initiative, *Earth Charter* (Hague, 29 June 2000), Preamble, at https://earthcharter.org/wp-content/uploads/2020/06/Booklet-Earth-Charter-52-FINAL.pdf, p. 5–6 (expression in italics are direct quotes). The Charter results from the work of an inde-

Over two decades later, the knowledge and awareness of ecosystemic and even planetary interconnections has outspread, reaffirming the inadequacy of a geographically limited and inherently reactive neighborhood law, no longer just for climate or biodiversity, or for goods beyond national jurisdiction, but for the Planet itself. As Simma remarks, environmentally "harmful or dangerous conduct ... threatens the natural basis of the life of all states and all human beings."[111] Accordingly, the object of international environmental law must be to secure the ecological balance of the entire planetary system – a task that represents a "truly communal responsibility".[112]

Simma does not explicitly qualify freshwater as a community interest, focusing instead on resources beyond national jurisdiction or problems easily qualified as global in scope, like climate change. Yet, when the Earth system is viewed as a community interest, as Simma does, all environmental resources, taken as a unitary whole on a planetary scale, merit the status of global public goods. This includes water – a natural element that interconnects all others.

Simma highlights two pillars necessary to materialize community interests: *norms* that prevail, postulate and govern an international community shaped around recognized shared goals; and *institutions* representing a high degree of international organization, and which promote and protect those interests.[113]

Like Magalhães, therefore, when discussing common environmental interests, Simma identifies the key legal mechanisms which states may employ when they come together to tackle common interests, at whatever level said interests may be shared. Analogously, a community-of-basin-interests requires the Basin Treaty as its constitution to regulate the Regime's internal functioning and structure; and the Basin Body to act in the promotion of agreed-upon common interests. Both authors also make the case that joint governance regimes are not incompatible with, and may indeed be necessary for, the sustained exercise of state sovereignty.

Yet, this comparison between global environmental interests and common basin interests must be taken with the caveat that, under international law, the respective riparian countries hold exclusive rights to access, explore and

---

pendent Commission, which, during almost a decade, consulted extensively with stakeholders. Since its adoption, over 6000 organizations have endorsed the Charter. On those bases, it has been argued that the Charter has become a soft law instrument. Earth Charter Initiative webpage, *What is the Charter?*, at http://earthcharter.org/discover/what-is-the-earth-charter/.

111 Simma, *supra*, p. 239.

112 *Ibid.*

113 *Id*, p. 285.

make decisions about their shared catchment, unless they all agree otherwise. Conversely, all such states together bear the responsibility for conserving the environment of the basin.[114] International law does not authorize states outside the basin to make claims or take legal action in defense of a supposed global interest in the protection of the hydrosphere. The latter interest is not within the scope of international law as currently structured or of Community-of-Interests.

2.2 *Common Basin Interests* versus *Regional Water Interests*

Water, as a natural resource, may itself be the specific object of interstate cooperation, as a common interest shared at the regional level. Whereas regional water cooperation takes place among neighboring countries that may or may not be co-riparians, cooperation founded on the Theory occurs at the basin level among the states that share a watercourse. Yet, it is possible to build on lessons from regional water cooperation given that water interconnects those countries within a region facing common water-related challenges, and which so choose to explore solutions in a collaborative manner within the framework of international law and policy.

International law does not mandate states to engage in regional water cooperation focused on common interests. Where countries do so, it is for practical reasons linked to optimal resource use. Water cooperation among states within a region, and across basins and aquifers, may expand the basket of resulting benefits. By placing water in the context of wider regional cooperation and integration to assess water interests at scale, states might be better-positioned to address cross-sectoral challenges such as those involving water, food, and energy security; and to consider optimal resource management opportunities through, e.g., regional energy planning and integration of power grids, or more rational trade in agricultural products.

In this sense, various country groupings collaborate at the policy level to address common freshwater and related interests and regionally shared risks. The *African Ministers Council on Water* (AMCOW) is a specialized technical committee of the African Union. Meeting periodically, AMCOW coordinates, monitors, and reports on measures taken by states, individually or in cooperation, in the pursuit of agreed continental water priorities and related high-level commitments.

---

114 J.W. Dellapenna, *Treaties as Instruments for Managing Internationally-Shared Water Resources: Restricted Sovereignty vs. Community of Property*, 26:1 Case W. Res. J. Int'l L 27–56 (1994), p. 35.

The AMCOW Strategy 2018–2030 identifies Strategic Priorities and Actions on four areas, namely: *water security for human and ecosystem use*, which includes, *inter alia*, promoting and supporting the design of water resources management and development plans at national and regional levels and, in this context, integrating water resources into development and ecosystem protection plans; *safely managed sanitation and hygiene*, including through the development of model comprehensive sanitation guidelines and policies, plans and regulations for states to adapt to their needs; *good water governance and transboundary water cooperation*, e.g., by contributing to increased water storage capacity and enhanced disaster risk-management capabilities through natural and built infrastructure; and a dedicated action area focused on enhancing *AMCOW's governance and operational effectiveness*. These priorities are further supported by four Cross-Cutting strategies, targeting, respectively, climate resilience of water resources and infrastructure; financing; monitoring, evaluation and knowledge management; and gender equality and youth empowerment.[115]

A few take-home lessons: the attention to the development of regional planning and model policy instruments illustrates joint action as a modality of cooperation for common interests – the one that prevails under the Theory; a focus on AMCOW's own strengthening points to the institution's centrality for regional water cooperation, which is true also for the Basin Body; and the 'gender and youth' strategy invokes the element of Social Basin Engagement within communities-of-basin-interests. The Strategy also refers to the *African Water Facility*, which is an AMCOW initiative directed at financing water resource development across the Continent. The Facility exemplifies joint action in the form of pooled funds for common goals – a form of joint action we also see in regimes framed by Community-of-Interests.

In its turn, the *Union for the Mediterranean* (UfM) promotes *interregional* cooperation between European and African countries around the Mediterranean Sea.[116] The Union targets various common-interest matters, including water, its sustainable use, and multisectoral dimensions and related issues that reflect the region's particular and major traits, needs, challenges, and vulnerabilities, like resource scarcity, extreme events, land degradation, and desertification.

---

115 AMCOW, Strategy 2018–2030 (2018).

116 Euro-Mediterranean Heads of States and Government, *Joint Declaration of the Paris Summit for the Mediterranean* (Paris, 13 July 2008), at https://ufmsecretariat.org/wp-content/uploads/2012/09/ufm_paris_declaration1.pdf.

The UfM Water Agenda comprises the *Financial Strategy for Water* and the *Policy Framework for Actions 2030*.[117] The Agenda recognizes and elevates the role of stakeholders in the cooperation process, centering on four priority areas connected to water: energy, food, and ecosystems; employment and migration; access to water, sanitation and hygiene; and climate change. While focusing on Mediterranean concerns, the UfM remains committed to global goals as evidenced by the multiple references to the SDGs in both the Framework and the Strategy. The UfM *Malta Declaration* introduces a new element of cooperation for common interests when referring to the *Water Strategy in the Western Mediterranean* – a precedent for subregional water cooperation.[118] The Declaration here hints at the notion of coherent cooperation regimes across global, regional, subregional, and even basin scales. *Coherence* across related regimes operating at different levels is a secondary element of Community-of-Interests.

States have also come together to collaborate on other regional issues that have close ties to sustainable water management. In the Americas, a regional action plan informs the concerted pursuit and monitoring of global disaster risk reduction targets and related regional priorities and associated regional, national, and local initiatives.[119] The Plan is founded on a whole-of-society approach that builds on government leadership and presupposes the engagement of all relevant actors, in line with their respective mandates, priorities, needs, capacities, and contexts. The Plan so notes its underlying premise: "Only together can the countries and people of the region be truly resilient".[120]

A 2024 ASEAN Statement reaffirms the commitment of member states to pursuing in concert global biodiversity and sustainable development goals. These joint efforts are facilitated by the *ASEAN Centre for Biodiversity* and

117 A. Abadi & R. M. Hurtado, UfM *Financial Strategy for Water*, v.2 (UfM 2020), at FS-WEB-EN.pdf; Water, Environment & Blue Economy Division, *UfM Water Policy Framework for Actions 2030: Water Agenda Booklet* (UfM 2022), at PolicyF-2023-EN-Web-2.pdf.

118 UfM, Water Ministers Meeting (Malta, 27 Apr 2017), *Declaration on the UfM Water Agenda* (03 Apr 2017) ('Malta Declaration').

119 *Regional Action Plan for the implementation of the Sendai Framework for Disaster Risk Reduction 2015–2030 in the Americas and the Caribbean* (3 Nov 2021), VII Regional Platform for Disaster Risk Reduction in the Americas and the Caribbean: Building Resilient Economies in the Americas and the Caribbean (1–4 Nov 2021, Virtual Event), at https://rp-americas.undrr.org/sites/default/files/inline-files/Regional%20Action%20Plan_EN.pdf?startDownload=true.

120 *Id*, p. 8.

include the adoption of a dedicated regional biodiversity strategy and action plan implemented with resources from the *ASEAN Biodiversity Fund*.[121]

The above examples show how countries within a given region may take steps to advance common water and other environmental interests on a broader scale. To recap, this may include nonbinding instruments that set regional goals; dedicated institutions as regional platforms for dialogue, coordination, and the monitoring of progress; stakeholder engagement; calls for cooperation on funding and financing matters; and linkages to global policy processes for coherence across cooperation levels.

Comparatively, under the Theory, the Basin Treaty identifies, refines, and prioritizes common interests. The Basin Body facilitates and coordinates cooperation on shared concerns and balances unilateral interests and may pool funds for Close Basin Cooperation. Individual communities-of-interests remain connected and committed to international processes and tend to integrate nonstate actors into the cooperation process under the Basin Treaty and Body.

While global and regional cooperation is common, however, only the riparian states have rights to their shared watercourse. The starting point for discussions on regional projects must be the basin and involve all the riparian states potentially affected. Otherwise, the planning riparian state, acting in partnership with a non-riparian, must, in accordance with international customary law, notify and consult with co-basin nations that might suffer significant harm resulting from the project in question.[122] This may be done on the basis of an existing watercourse agreement or using the provisions in Chapter 3 of the UNWC as guidance.

2.3 *Community-of-Interests and the Law of Transboundary Basins*

Community-of-Interests, as a theory of international water law, applies as between the states that are co-riparians in a watercourse system. Third countries are, in principle, excluded from the cooperation process.

This scope of the Theory, however, as under international water law, generally, is without prejudice to the obligations co-riparians may owe, individually or collectively, to third states. Article 28 of the UNWC, for example, deals with emergency situations and safeguards third states that might be affected by

121 Association of Southeast Asian Nations (ASEAN), *Joint Statement on Biodiversity to the 16th Meeting of Conference of the Parties to the Convention on Biological Diversity*, 44th and 45th ASEAN Summits (Vientiane, 9 Oct 2024), at 19-Final_AJS-on-Biodiversity-to-the-CBD-COP-16.pdf.

122 Silala Case, *supra*, p. 36.

changes in the condition of an international watercourse. This provision refers to *other potentially affected states*, instead of *watercourse states*. Riparian parties thus bear duties in relation to third nations potentially impacted by emergency situations. Under the ECEWC, parties undertake more broadly to protect the environment as an obligation owed *erga omnes partes*.[123] Therefore, non-riparian nations retain the right not to suffer harm in connection with the watercourse, in accordance with the general principle of international law under which states must take all measures to prevent environmental impact on other states.[124]

Otherwise, when formalizing their respective communities-of-interests with the adoption of a Basin Treaty and the establishment of a Basin Body, co-riparian countries do so among themselves, to the exclusion of others. Basin states retain the prerogative to decide whether, and the extent to which, to integrate third countries into their community-of-basin-interests but must do so as appropriate to comply with relevant obligations under international law.

In the context of navigation, Article 108 of the Vienna General Act makes clear that its relevant provisions apply among those riparian countries "separated or crossed by the same navigable river". On scope *ratione personae*, therefore, all co-riparian states, and only those states, have navigation and related management rights thereunder.[125]

For a scenario of multiple water uses and shared interests, Article 2(c) of the UNWC defines a *watercourse state* as a party thereto "in whose territory part of an international watercourse is situated". The 8th Preambular Paragraph of the ECEWC refers to "agreements between countries bordering the same waters". Article 2(1) of the 1995 SADC Protocol and Article 3(2) of the Revised SADC Protocol[126] restrict access to the uses of each shared watercourse to the respective riparian states.

---

123 *Guide to Implementing the Water Convention*, UN Doc ECE/MP.WAT/39 (UN 2013) ('ECEWC Guide'), p. 16.

124 *See*, e.g., Nuclear Weapons Threat or Use AO, *supra*, p. 242.

125 *See also* Vitanyi, *supra*, p. 33.

126 *Revised Protocol on Shared Watercourses in the Southern African Development Community* (Windhoek, 7 Aug 2000) (in force 22 Sep 2003) ('Revised SADC Protocol').

3 History of Community-of-Interests in International Water Law

> *[S]tates cannot escape their membership in the community of riparian states because it is established by the nature of their territories, ... interconnected through a shared hydrologic system.*[127]

The Theory finds its origins in the law of the navigational uses of international watercourses. Progressively, Community-of-Interests transcends its applicability to navigation to embrace all uses of international watercourses, together with their protection and sustainable management. A historical perspective[128] is essential to understand how the treaties and cases we present in this Chapter – and which, together, serve as this book's principal sources – have contributed to constructing and continuously developing Community-of-Interests as a theoretical basis for international water law.

3.1 *Origins of Community-of-Interests in Inland Water Navigation*

In its early stages, interstate water relations – and thus international fluvial law – centered on inland water transport on border or transboundary rivers. Navigation once received priority over other water uses and remained prevalent until the late 19th and early 20th Centuries, as then reflected in treaty practice.[129]

The legal origins of Community-of-Interests, therefore, are in the long-standing and generally accepted basic norms governing international navigation and the reality that no one country could exercise that activity without affecting the rights and interests of its counterparts along the watercourse and without relying on cooperation from others to achieve optimal use. The full exercise of navigation rights requires not only unilateral restraint (Limited Territorial Sovereignty), but also positive collective duties, certain uniform rules, and consideration of the watercourse system in its entire mainstem, inclusive of all navigable tributaries (Community-of-Interests).[130]

---

127 Leb (2013), *supra*, p. 52.

128 *See*, e.g., McCaffrey (2019), *supra*, p. 184 & Leb, *supra*, p. 43 *et seq*, both applying a historical approach to the analysis of Community-of-Interests.

129 McCaffrey (2019), *supra*, p. 142; B. Vitanyi, *The International Regime of River Navigation* (Sijthoff & Noordhoff 1979), p. 1. *See*, e.g., *Treaty of Peace with Germany*, Allied and Associated Powers-Germany (Versailles, 28 June 1919) (in force 10 Jan 1920) ('Treaty of Versailles'), Art.337, requiring the consent of all the states concerned for the priority accorded to navigation in relation to other uses of international watercourses to be displaced.

130 ILA (1966), *supra*, p. 468–9.

In the name of commerce and communication, states have long abandoned claims of absolute control over international watercourses, recognizing that the benefits of free navigation outweigh concerns with cooperation requirements for the exercise of sovereign rights. As Vitanyi explains, citing Grotius: "The right of riparians to possess the river does not mean … the recognition of the right to dispose of them in an absolute way."[131] Communities-of-navigation-interests have so flourished around the world, leading to a well-developed *corpus* of international law in the field, whose antecedents go back to ancient times.

Roman Law approaches streams as *rei publicae jure gentium*. This means universal navigation freedom, as opposed to access restricted to riparian states. The introduction of the so-called *principle of freedom of innocent passage* came in the 16th Century through Grotius,[132] according to whom, as paraphrased by Caponera, "rivers should be open for transit for legitimate purposes".[133] Granting navigation freedom to parties, numerous bilateral agreements were adopted between the 1600s and 1800s. In 1815, the Congress of Vienna culminated in the adoption of the Vienna General Act, which spells out two recognized principles of international law: regulation by *common agreement* (Article 108) and *freedom of navigation and commerce* (Article 109).[134] Over a century later, both principles are reaffirmed in the Treaty of Versailles, and still reflect Community-of-Interests as applied to inland water transport.[135]

While the Vienna General Act has European scope, the Treaty of Versailles involves a wider set of countries. Interpreting both such treaties early in the 20th Century, the PCIJ issues the River Oder Decision, the first jurisprudential precedent referring to and discussing Community-of-Interests, albeit with a principal focus on international navigation. Unpacking the relevant provisions of the Vienna General Act and the Treaty of Versailles elucidates the normative elements of Community-of-Interests in inland water transport,

---

131 Vitanyi, *supra*, p. 21.

132 H. Grotius, *De Jure Belli ac Pacis*, Libri Tres, in Quibus Jus Naturae et Gentium, Item Juris Publici Praecipua Explicantur, Book 2, Cap. 2–3 (1625).

133 D.A. Caponera, *Principles of Water Law and Administration: National and International*, 3rd ed, revised & updated by M. Nanni (Taylor & Francis 2019), p. 269.

134 *General Treaty*, Austria-France-Portugal-Prussia-Russias-Spain-Sweden-Norway-UK (Vienna, 9 June 1815) ('Vienna General Act'), *reproduced in* Translation of the General Treaty, signed in Congress at Vienna, June 9, 1815, with the Acts thereunto Annexed, Presented to both Houses of Parliament, by Command of His Royal Highness, The Prince Regent (London Gazette Office 1816).

135 Caponera, *supra*, p. 269–271.

which can then be transferred to scenarios of multiple water uses. In particular, the exercise reveals the geographic scope of communities-of-navigation-interests; contributes to unpacking the Theory into some of its other elements; introduces the concepts of common consent and joint ownership; and helps to delineate the relationship of Community-of-Interests with equitable and reasonable utilization and with equitable and reasonable Participation.

Basin Scope: The first sentence of Article 109 of the Vienna General Act affirms free navigation on international rivers "along their whole course, … from the point where each of them becomes navigable, to its mouth". Supplementing the former provision, Article 110 governs the duties and police systems, which extend beyond the watercourse mainstream along or across the border to encompass "branches and junctions, which, in their navigable course, separate or traverse different states". Read together, Articles 109 and 110 suggest that a community-of-navigation-interests extends along the entire watercourse where navigation is viable, i.e., the navigable international watercourse mainstem and its boundary or transboundary navigable tributaries.

Based on those same provisions, as framed by Community-of-Interests, the PCIJ considers Article 331 of the Treaty of Versailles to represent the law governing the questions put before it.[136] Article 331 declares the Oder, along with other watercourses, to be international rivers, including "all navigable parts of these river systems which naturally provide more than one state with access to the sea", as well as connected canals and channels built to enhance navigation conditions. The focus on the shared navigable portions of the watercourse system shows how the Theory safeguards common state interests in light of each fluvial system's particular political and hydrological realities and natural or artificial connections – in this case, as those might be relevant specifically for navigational uses.

The above treaty provisions delimit the ambit of communities-of-navigation-interests from the point where an international watercourse becomes navigable throughout its navigable course, inclusive of its shared tributaries where transport may still occur. In its origins in international navigation law, therefore, already the Theory displays an inherently systemic ambit, congruent with water's fluid and unifying power along a given river system. Albeit systemic, the scope of Community-of-Interests under the Vienna General Act and the Treaty of Versailles remains limited to navigable parts, as required by the common interest at stake.

---

136 River Oder Case, *supra*, p. 31.

Comparably, the application of a basin-wide approach to cooperation holds great significance for the protection of common interests when other uses, in addition to navigation, come into play, at which point a limited legal framing of the Theory's scope, even if systemic in nature, becomes problematic. Managing multiple water uses is often more complex, with greater likelihood of conflicting interests and potential for negative environmental impacts, possibly with ripple effects across the basin. Accordingly, domestic water bodies connected to transboundary basins come within the scope of both Global Water Conventions. This is clear from how Article 2(1) of the UNWC delimits the term *watercourse*; and from the definition of *transboundary waters* in Article 1(1) of the ECEWC.

In short, the scope of communities-of-navigation-interests only partially fulfills the needs of communities-of-basin-interests, which often display an *expanded* systemic ambit – one that considers the basin as a unitary whole, inclusive of domestic and non-navigable connected water bodies, on the surface and underground.

Basin Treaty: The importance of watercourse-specific treaties to implement general norms is affirmed in Article 116 of the Vienna General Act, which calls for the adoption of arrangements giving "due regard to circumstances and locality". This provision suggests that a tailored legal instrument is a primary element of Community-of-Interests as the overarching governing legal framework for transboundary basin cooperation.

Comparable examples of Basin Treaties that serve as context-specific governing frameworks for individual communities-of-interests are the Lake Victoria Protocol and the Senegal Basin Charter.

Basin Body: Article 108 of the Vienna General Act envisions the designation by each co-riparian state of national commissioners, empowered to work together as an *international body*, including by drafting joint regulations.

The institutional arrangements for river management here imagined take on a primitive form, comprising the joint work of government representatives, as opposed to a permanent binational or multinational body endowed with legal personality. Taking a step towards further institutionalization, the articles annexed to the Vienna General Act, and which deal with Rhine navigation, call for the establishment of a central commission to promote compliance with the applicable regulations, offer a platform for interstate exchanges, and regularly report back to members. As part of the commission's structure, inspectors are to be designated to perform monitoring and reporting functions.[137]

Conversely, Basin Bodies, i.e., the intergovernmental bodies in place to facilitate transboundary cooperation on multiple uses, as framed by Community-of-Interests, assume a diversity of shapes, with some more developed and empowered than others, according to the specific circumstances of each watershed and the needs of its riparian states.

Close Basin Cooperation: Per Article 108 of the Vienna General Act, states undertake to set up a common system of duties and police. In addition, Article 113 envisions joint regulations to define the Participation of each co-riparian state in maintenance works on river channels, which includes undertakings by each party within its territory – all to ensure the absence of barriers so as to safeguard a common interest in navigation.[138]

Joint regulation is an expression of joint action, whereas certain duties linked to the maintenance of works may be delivered domestically. Hence, joint action is the prevalent, but not the only, modality of state engagement under Community-of-Interests.

By referring to Participation, Article 113 also implies that belonging to a community-of-interests in shared waters entails positive cooperation, which may be performed domestically (e.g., works carried out by a state in its own territory), through coordination (e.g., coordinated releases from a cascade of dams along the river), or through joint action (e.g., commonly agreed regulations), as appropriate. Codified in Article 5(2) of the UNWC, Participation was thus already present in the Theory's early contours; and now Participation applies to all state interests in the watercourse, not only navigation; and to the entire system, not just navigable internationally shared rivers.

Mutual Consent and Joint Ownership: Article 108 of the Vienna General Act uses the expression *common consent* in relation to the design, adoption, and revision of regulations. The same expression appears in Articles 111 and 116. The former determines that, once tariffs are settled, any increase thereof requires the common consent of the co-riparian states; and that no other duties may be imposed beyond those established by said regulations. Under

137 Vienna General Act, *supra*, Annexes, Act XVI – Regulations for the Free Navigation of Rivers, *Articles Concerning the Navigation of the Rhine* ('Rhine Articles'), Arts.X & XVI.

138 *See also* Treaty of Versailles, *supra*, Art.336.

Article 116, common consent by all co-riparian states is required for future amendments to special river arrangements in place.

The above provisions raise the question of the extent to which a mutual-consent requirement exists in the case of Community-of-Interests centered on navigation. As there employed, common consent applies only to the adoption or amendment of specific regulations that states are encouraged to adopt with a view to better enabling free navigation for all. Nowhere in Article 108, nor in any other provision of the Act, is it implied that the exercise of navigational rights by a riparian state depends on prior consent by its neighbors or on the prior adoption of the appropriate regulations. As used in Articles 111 and 116, common consent seems to reflect the principle of *pacta sunt servanda*, so that established regulations are complied with and only amended if all parties thus agree, rather than a restriction imposed on future unilateral developments.

Similarly, communities-of-basin-interests are not governed by a mutual-consent requirement, although they *may* be – by prior agreement among the states concerned, as is the case in the Senegal basin.

On joint ownership, Article 25 of the Vienna General Act outlines demarcation arrangements in relation to specified *boundary* rivers, which, per the provision, *belong in common* to co-riparian states. This sentence deals with a specific border situation as between only the parties concerned; and, as such, suggests that states may, by agreement, decide to consider their frontier waters as jointly owned. In their turn, Articles 108 and 109 of the Act, deemed to reflect the Theory by the PCIJ in the River Oder case, make no reference to the concept of joint ownership or to the just-referenced sentence in Article 25.

Coherence: Article 108 of the Vienna General Act envisions general or umbrella norms as the basis for the joint drafting of more detailed regulations on the collective use of the river for transport. The provision hints at Coherence, a secondary element of the Theory. Coherence is here expressed by a framework convention codifying basic rules and procedures as guidance for a watercourse-specific treaty then governing the concrete and harmonious exercise of navigation.

Beyond navigation, such framework treaties are here represented by the UNWC, the ECEWC, and the two SADC Protocols.

Equitable and Reasonable Use: Article 25 of the Vienna General Act governs boundary issues on the Rhine, between Luxembourg and The Netherlands. The provision foresees the establishment of a joint commission to regulate water infrastructure development – "in the most equitable manner, and conformably to the mutual interests" of the states concerned. This provision places equitable and reasonable use under the Theory's umbrella, which is consistent with state practice on Community-of-Interests beyond navigation.

Community-of-Interests in Navigation and Beyond: For navigation, interdependence and thus the emergence of common or conflicting state interests are inevitable on account of the hydrological and other interconnections that exist along a shared watercourse system; and those interests must be properly managed for common benefit and peaceful relations.

Communities-of-navigation-interests have a systemic geographic scope, which corresponds to the common interest at stake; emphasize legal arrangements and management institutions; build on joint action obligations, but do not go as far as to endorse the concept of joint ownership and the mutual-consent requirement as general rules; and place equitable and reasonable use and Participation within the framework of Community-of-Interests.

When non-navigational uses come into the picture, the reality of interdependence becomes more salient, and international water law evolves to respond accordingly. With deeper interdependence comes greater complexity in the needs of riparians to advance and balance the multiple uses, management, and protection of transboundary basins and their ecosystems. Compared to communities-of-interests centered on navigation, communities-of-*basin*-interests presuppose even closer cooperation. The normative elements of Community-of-Interests in its origins remain generally applicable in this evolving reality but are adjusted to respond to a multiplicity of interests in the watercourse.

3.2 *Community-of-Interests and Other Theoretical Bases of International Law for the Multiple Uses of Transboundary Basins*

Transport remained predominant as a mode of watercourse use up to the late 1800s and early 1990s. Halfway through the 19th Century, this began to change, with accelerated technological and economic development enabling and pushing non-navigational water uses to grow exponentially.[139]

At the early stages of this transition process, state practice beyond navigation, in which to anchor emerging rules of international law, was scarce. In time, more states became engaged in water negotiations, and disagreements over unilateral projects proliferated across regions. In this context of changing water uses and evolving state practice, the broader law of transboundary basins progressively developed[140] – as appropriate, applying, adjusting, and

139 ILA (1966), *supra*, p. 491.

140 Vitanyi, *supra*, p. 1.

innovating in relation to its antecedents in navigation. On the one hand, state practice has demonstrated the usefulness of joint bodies for administering cooperation on all types of water uses, inland water transport or otherwise. On the other, managing multiple water uses requires a more encompassing geographical outlook of the watercourse system than a narrow focus on navigable rivers and tributaries.

Keeping pace with these legal and factual developments, four theories were eventually formulated as possibly underlying the rules on the non-navigational uses of international watercourses. Community-of-interests is among such foundational theories. The other three are *Absolute Territorial Sovereignty*, *Absolute Territorial Integrity*, and *Limited Territorial Sovereignty*. To examine each, we build on the discussion in Chapter 1 around parallel progressions in general international law and in international water law.

Absolute Territorial Sovereignty and Absolute Territorial Integrity: Both theories have been "abandoned as rules of decision";[141] and are here considered only to show how international water law beyond navigation has progressed from absolute claims of territorial sovereignty and integrity to the more cooperative frameworks of Limited Territorial Sovereignty and Community-of-Interests.

Also referred to as the *Harmon Doctrine*, Absolute Territorial Sovereignty conceives that a state would hold complete control over natural resources within its territory; and be free to decide on the uses of such resources, regardless of any impact that might result within neighboring nations.

The Harmon Doctrine is first formulated by the US in an 1890s dispute with Mexico. The US Attorney-General Opinion asserts his country's absolute sovereignty over resources within its territory and so its right to proceed with a proposed river diversion, regardless of potential detrimental effects on irrigation needs in Mexico.[142] Despite the extreme position then expressed by the US Government, the two countries eventually negotiated a treaty to settle their differences in an equitable manner. It is believed that the US never really endorsed that theory. Most likely, when faced with Mexico's protests, the US resorted to Absolute Territorial Sovereignty as a political strategy to pressure its neighbor into an agreement as favorable as possible for the US.[143]

---

141 Hunter *et al* (2015), *supra*, p. 884.

142 *See* N. Islam, *The Law of Non-Navigational Uses of International Watercourses: Options for Regional Regime-Building in Asia* (Wolters Kluwer 2010), p. 102.

143 McCaffrey (2019), *supra*, p. 187–8.

More recently, the Chinese Government Statement on the occasion of the UNWC's adoption may seem to imply, at a first glance, a claim of absolute control to justify China's negative vote. The Statement questions the absence from the Draft Convention of an explicit reference to territorial sovereignty; and suggests that this "basic international law principle"[144] gives riparian states absolute control over the portions of shared watercourses within their respective territories. In the same Statement, however, China affirms its right to deal with the multiple uses of international watercourses "in a fair and reasonable manner and in accordance with relevant international practice and with bilateral watercourse agreements",[145] invoking concepts that may be associated with both Limited Territorial Sovereignty and Community-of-Interests. Concretely, China has watercourse and related agreements with some co-riparian states, which implies its acceptance that sovereign rights over shared waters are not absolute.[146]

Beyond the above examples, upper riparians have mentioned Absolute Territorial Sovereignty in unilateral statements – in essence, like the US, to strengthen their negotiating positions in the context of specific disputes.[147] Like the US, as well, states that raise Absolute Territorial Sovereignty tend to settle disagreements eventually through specific treaties.[148]

Otherwise, it is generally agreed that Absolute Territorial Sovereignty has long been rejected in state practice for disregarding the interests of some riparian states to the unproportionate benefit of others, thus being incapable of equitably solving disputes over shared freshwaters.[149]

In its turn, Absolute Territorial Integrity translates into an extreme no-harm claim, under which a state would be entitled to the full integrity of its territory, inclusive of the natural volume and quality of the waters flowing through it. The notion presupposes the existence of a supreme, unlimited, and unconditional duty of riparian states not to cause negative transboundary impacts through an international watercourse, in particular in relation to existing uses.

---

144 UNWC Voting Records, *supra*, p. 6.

145 *Id*, p. 7.

146 *See*, e.g., F. Rocha Loures, *The Dragon as Part of Transboundary Basin 'Villages': Community-of-Interests and International Law in China*, 24 Water Law 220–38 (2015), for a study of China's agreements with co-riparian countries through the lens of Community-of-Interests and advances in the country's foreign policy.

147 Hunter *et al* (2015), *supra*, p. 884.

148 ILC (1994), *supra*, p. 99.

149 *See*, e.g., ILA (1966), supra, p. 486–7; McCaffrey (2019), *supra*, p. 199; S. Bogdanović, *The International Law Association Helsinki Rules: Contribution to International Water Law* (Brill 2019), p. 37.

In the case of unilaterally planned measures, Absolute Territorial Integrity implies the mutual-consent requirement. On occasion, some lower riparian states have referred to the no-harm rule in its extreme form to question upstream state behavior. Yet, Absolute Territorial Integrity is not a part of international law.[150]

International water law thus rejects absolutist views that imply total freedom of action or prohibit all transboundary impact in relation to watercourses shared between different political units. Historically, the theories of Absolute Territorial Sovereignty and Absolute Territorial Integrity have been invoked by only a small number of states and never really applied beyond rhetoric or to solve concrete interstate disputes.[151] As put by McCaffrey, absolute claims in transboundary water relations "may be useful as tools of advocacy, but they afford little assistance in the resolution of concrete controversies."[152]

A good illustration here comes from a US Supreme Court decision on water allocation between New York and New Jersey. On the one hand, it is unlawful for New York, in taking advantage of its upper riparian position, to pursue a river diversion project completely blocking water flows into New Jersey; on the other hand, New Jersey has no claim to the river's full natural flow, in a way that would deprive New York of its own right to use the transboundary resource. In short: "Both states have real and substantial interests in the river that must be reconciled".[153]

With the widespread realization of the inadequacy of the two radical claims of absolute control over an international watercourse, Limited Territorial Sovereignty and Community-of-Interest emerge as possible theoretical bases of international water law. Both theories entail *compromises* and *cooperation*, ever more required as interdependencies between states increase, caused but the displacement of navigation as a principal water use, and reinforced by accelerating global environmental change.

Limited Territorial Sovereignty: This theory underlies the international law constraints placed "upon a [riparian] state's freedom of action";[154] and, accordingly, determines that "each state must respect the rights of the other".[155]

150 *See* McCaffrey (2019), *supra*, p. 200–205, 207–208, presenting precedents of lower riparians invoking the theory and discussing the implications of Absolute Territorial Integrity in terms of freezing the development of the watercourse.

151 Islam, *supra*, p. 114.

152 McCaffrey (2019), *supra*, p. 202.

153 US Supreme Court, State of New Jersey *v.* State of New York, 283 US 336 (1931), p. 342.

154 McCaffrey (2019), *supra*, p. 215.

155 *Id*, p. 209.

Limited Territorial Sovereignty is widely reflected in treaties, state practice and *opinio juris*, actual or proposed codifications, and jurisprudence; and has permeated the application, interpretation, codification, clarification and development of international water law as its generally accepted and principal theoretical basis.[156]

Limited Territorial Sovereignty encompasses the due diligence duty to prevent transboundary harm and is the "theoretical precursor"[157] of the principle of equitable and reasonable use.[158] As such, Limited Territorial Sovereignty is a theory of international water law expressed fundamentally through the customary rules of *equitable and reasonable use* and *harm prevention*.[159]

Equitable and reasonable use is for the first time formulated and enunciated in the Helsinki Rules, in the following terms: "each basin state is entitled, within its territory, to a reasonable and equitable share in the beneficial uses of the waters of an international drainage basin".[160] Equitable use does not mean equal rights for each basin country. Rather, the norm aims to balance the needs and interests of riparians within an international watercourse and requires that a dynamic condition of interstate fairness be maintained by means of ongoing and reasonable assessments of, and adjustments to, changing social, economic, environmental, and other relevant factors, on a case-by-case basis.[161]

Harm Prevention is also a binding customary norm, finding expression, *inter alia*, in Article 7 of the UNWC. The rule is a widely accepted due diligence obligation, i.e., an obligation of conduct, not of result. Harm prevention translates into the duty of a riparian state to take all appropriate measures for avoiding significant transboundary harm when utilizing an international watercourse.[162] Albeit often associated with Limited Territorial Sovereignty, the harm-prevention rule is present in Community-of-Interests regimes alongside equitable and reasonable use.

---

156 *See*, e.g., Taylor, *supra*, p. 27; McCaffrey (2019), *supra*, p. 135, 218–9; Islam, *supra*, p. 114.

157 McCaffrey (2019), *supra*, p. 208.

158 *Ibid.*

159 *But see*, e.g, Hunter *et al* (2015), *supra*, p. 884, approaching equitable and reasonable use as a theory that informs most international water law codifications; Teclaff and Utton, *supra*, p. 51, viewing Limited Territorial Sovereignty as a rule of international customary law; and Sievers, *supra*, p. 15, seeing equitable and reasonable use as the "shifting middle ground" between Limited Territorial Sovereignty and Community-of-Interests.

160 Helsinki Rules, *supra*, Art.IV.

161 Hunter *et al* (2015), *supra*, p. 886–87; Kiss & Shelton, *supra*, p. 886.

162 *See*, e.g., Pulp Mills Case, *supra*, p. 38.

Community-of-Interests: The Theory has long been embraced in navigation law; and, more recently, Community-of-Interests has expanded to encompass multiple water uses, as well as the protection and management of transboundary freshwaters and associated ecosystems.

Now, as before, interstate relations framed by the Theory treat the shared basin as the physical unity it is and unfold through Close Basin Cooperation, so that common state interests may be met. At its core, Community-of-Interests facilitates the joint pursuit of the optimal and sustainable development, management, and protection of the catchment as an integrated whole.

In broad strokes, the normative content of Community-of-Interests, when multiple uses are at stake, may be illustrated by a passage in the ILC Commentaries to its 1994 Draft Articles. While not explicitly referring to the Theory, the Commission cites contemporary treaties that provide for the integrated management of the watercourse and aim to achieve optimal socioeconomic use and environmental protection and associated benefits, all under the auspices of joint organizations with basin-wide jurisdiction.[163] The ILC invokes here the Basin Scope; refers to cooperation regimes that could be viewed, at a glimpse, as reflecting the Theory; and even illustrates the notion of common interest in integrated catchment planning.

While the elements of Community-of-Interests may be progressive, the attention to water's unifying capacity, and which gives birth to the Theory, is not new in the history of water law. The notion of a community formed among those sharing a water body comes from Roman times, as expressed in the writings of Plato, Ovid, and Virgil.[164] Dellapenna and Gupta revisit the earliest water statutes across regions and find the prevalence of "a process of communal management".[165] Writing in the 1660s, Grotius, referenced by McCaffrey, explains that a river, "viewed as running water, has remained common property, so that anyone may drink or draw water from it".[166]

When classified as *res communis* in the domestic legal plane, water is not subject to private appropriation or free disposition. This understanding is in consonance, for example, with the Brazilian Constitution, which determines that all inland waters are public property, and considers the ecologically bal-

163 ILC (1994), *supra*, p. 98.

164 McCaffrey (2019), *supra*, p. 219.

165 J.W. Dellapenna & J. Gupta, *The Evolution of Water Law Through 4,000 Years*, Villanova University School of Law, Public Law and Legal Theory, Working Paper 2013–3041 (2013), p. 8–9.

166 McCaffrey (2019), *supra*, p. 219.

anced environment to be an asset of common use held in trust by the government and society for present and future generations.[167]

In the international sphere, *res communis* invokes physical interdependence and connected political, cultural, social, and economic interests that co-basin states share in relation to an international watercourse, without necessarily implying common property. To act on those common interests, co-basin states may rely on a variety of tools that give practical expression to the Theory and enable common action thereunder. Riparian countries states *may* decide among themselves to regulate a shared watercourse as joint property, but Community-of-Interests does not presuppose that they do so. As McCaffrey explains, communities-of-basin-interests are "created by the natural, physical unity of a watercourse",[168] but "a 'community' based upon possible interdependence falls far short of co-ownership."[169]

Both Community-of-Interests and Limited Territorial Sovereignty challenge claims of absolute state control over transboundary waters and impose limits in the form of cooperation requirements on the sovereign rights of basin states. Moreover, the two theories are mutually interdependent and inherently interlinked, as reflected in the spectrum of cooperation interests and degrees captured in a treaty. Each theory thus underlies different and yet interconnected purposes of the same cooperation regime, i.e., balancing unilateral interests through mostly unilateral restraint and safeguarding common concerns largely through joint action. The latter purpose prevails in cooperation regimes framed by Community-of-Interests.

In this sense, comparing the two theories is more about gradation than distinction. Perspectives contraposing Limited Territorial Sovereignty and Community-of-Interests miss the reality of state practice, in which pure regimes, guided exclusively by one or the other theory, are probably rare. In the cases studied in this book, Limited Territorial Sovereignty comes under the umbrella of Community-of-Interests to prevent and settle disputes, which emerge even under Close Basin Cooperation. While, therefore, Community-of -Interests centers largely on the joint pursuit of shared goals, regimes founded on the Theory include mechanisms aimed at balancing potentially conflicting individual priorities.

By emphasizing interdependencies and shared concerns within the basin, Community-of-Interests promotes Close Basin Cooperation for shared aspira-

---

167 *Constituição da República Federativa do Brasil* ('Brazilian Constitution') (1988), Arts.20 (III), 26(1), 225.

168 McCaffrey (2019), *supra*, p. 219

169 *Id*, p. 234.

tions, going beyond a dominant focus on water allocation and the aim of balancing rights between riparian states through *ad hoc* exchanges, as under Limited Territorial Sovereignty. As such, the regimes primarily framed by the Theory are better suited to simultaneously achieve the twin purposes of promoting mutual benefits through long-term basin management and of preempting and resolving disputes.

Take data management as an example. Riparian states tend to perceive differently the science underlying disputed facts, the extent of their rights, and the manner of allocating costs equitably to fund possible solutions. Differences in perspectives point to the need for baseline information upon which all parties agree as a starting point for negotiations. In any context, the good governance and sustainable management of water and related resources rest upon an accurate picture of the basin, i.e., "a foundation of credible, timely, and relevant information."[170] In the case of transboundary waters, information must not only be obtained but also *shared*.

Under Limited Territorial Sovereignty, data is mostly generated domestically, and exchanges occur on a case-by-case basis, such as in reaction to a unilateral project proposal; or else data management involves some degree of coordination when exchanges occur on a regular basis and the information collected by each state, individually, is processed, so as to become accessible and understandable by all.[171]

Under Community-of-Interests, domestic data management is supplemented by joint efforts at information gathering, analysis, processing, and storing, often under the umbrella of the Basin Body and in accordance with jointly agreed parameters, methodologies, and reporting templates. Where establishment of a shared data management system cannot be immediately realized due to financial and/or technical constraints, communities-of-basin-interests at least agree to work towards that goal.

Case Study 1: Zambezi Cooperation on Data Management

The Zambezi basin countries cooperate under the umbrella of the *Zambezi Watercourse Commission* (ZAMCOM). Adopted five years after the entry into force of the respective Agreement, the *Rules and Procedures for Sharing of Data and Information related to the Management and Development of the Zambezi Watercourse* foresee a joint data manage-

170 Secretariat of the 3rd World Water Forum, Virtual Water Forum, *Final Report* (2003), p. 75 ('VWF Report'); Kramer *et al, supra*, p. 10.

171 UNWC, *supra*, Art.9.

ment system and establish advanced data-sharing obligations and procedures among co-basin states.[172]

Cooperation based on Community-of-Interests thus empowers riparian states to develop and keep up-to-date a shared understanding of the rules and facts at stake (e.g., the basin's uses, conditions, vulnerabilities, and dependent populations and ecosystems), in particular of the challenges they must face together, interests to be reconciled, corresponding solutions, and win-win opportunities. Such a shared understanding enables common trust and informs the identification, refinement, and ongoing pursuit of common goals as well as collective decision-making on tradeoffs and the balancing of eventual conflicting interests through informed dispute prevention and resolution.

Community-of-Interests reflects good management practices, as emphasized by experts and practitioners: joint monitoring, research, and development systems; studies conducted on the basis of common or comparable parameters; joint assessments as the basis for long-term joint action; pooling of resources, capacities, and information into a jointly established and maintained database; financial sustainability so that data management is assured in the long-term; data quality control; joint bodies as neutral parties to conduct technical studies; integration between transboundary and national monitoring programs; and standardized reporting. The foregoing elements of a joint framework for data management allow for faster and more efficient information processing and for improved data reliability, accuracy, and completeness than in the case of national systems not linked to one another or, more broadly, of related efforts limited to a basic degree of coordination.[173]

Planned measures may also illustrate a movement from Limited Territorial Sovereignty towards Community-of-Interests. In early or less developed stages of transboundary relations, states utilize the watercourse unilaterally, hoping to avoid transactional costs; and only worry about cooperation when a dispute arises. Instances of unilateral action occur often and are lawful if compliant with basic rules of prior notification, consultations and negotiations, and equitable and reasonable use and harm prevention.

---

172 *Agreement on the Establishment of the Zambezi Watercourse Commission* (ZAMCOM) (Kasane, 13 July 2004) (in force June 2011), Angola-Botswana-Malawi-Mozambique-Namibia-Tanzania-Zambia-Zimbabwe ('ZAMCOM Agreement'); ZAMCOM, *Rules and Procedures for Sharing of Data and Information related to the Management and Development of the Zambezi Watercourse*, ZAMCOM Council (25 Feb 2016) (in effect 26 Mar 2016).

173 *See*, e.g., Leb (2013), *supra*, p. 160; UNW-DPAC, *supra*, p. 16–7.

Lawful unilateralism, however, as the dominant approach under Limited Territorial Sovereignty, may pose a challenge to the goals of sustainable water management and stable riparian relations in an increasingly interdependent world. Tarlock observes that the unilateral building of river infrastructure has been historically a problem in many places.[174] The limited degree of cooperation that takes place in such contexts is likely to lead to tensions, prolonged disagreements, and unmitigated transboundary impacts. These risks are heightened in the absence of some form of institutional mechanism to promote ongoing interstate dialogue, while preventing and resolving disputes. As conflicts linger, the environment and dependent populations are placed in jeopardy, at times to an irreversible degree. At the same time, anxieties and mistrust intensify, further preventing the states concerned from coming to the negotiating table in good faith, thereby reinforcing a cycle of noncooperation and inequity. Kramer *et al*, for example, note how "mistrust and tensions can hamper regional development by impeding joint projects and mutually beneficial infrastructure."[175]

When states move together in the direction of Community-of-Interests, they formulate, under the Basin Treaty, specific requirements, including in the form of joint action, in that regard; and prioritize joint planning as much as possible across the basin. The Theory then transcends *ad hoc* efforts aimed at peaceful coexistence, such as occasional interstate coordination on planned measures between an implementing country and potentially affected co-basin states. Under the Theory, unilateralism becomes the exception rather than the rule, as states' attentions shift from national to common interests – these now being the principal motivation for continued, systematic, and close interstate engagement. Joint management then unfolds in parallel to, or even ahead of, unilateral development measures; and, in the latter case, Close Basin Cooperation allows for potential impacts to be jointly identified and addressed at the catchment level.

3.3 *Historical Account of Treaty and Case Law on Community-of-Interests*

The treaty and case law introduced chronologically in this Subchapter forms our core legal reference package on transboundary basin cooperation framed by Community-of-Interests. For the most part, these materials have been reviewed only superficially, if at all, in literature with the specific intent to unpack the Theory's normative content.

---

174 Tarlock, *supra*, p. 372, 374, 377.

175 Kramer *et al*, *supra*, p. 7.

These sources are singled out here because they *unequivocally* reflect Community-of-Interests. The treaties in question either refer to the Theory directly or are deemed by the courts to be informed by Community-of-Interests. These agreements apply globally, regionally or at the basin or sub-basin levels, and illustrate experiences from Africa, Europe and Latin America. Although the select treaties represent a fraction of the watercourse agreements in existence and do not cover all regions where transboundary cooperation has unfolded, such instruments, collectively, offer a foundation to pinpoint the Theory's normative elements where Community-of-Interests is clearly at play. The case law examined consists of jurisprudence grounded on the Theory, going back to the early 20th Century up to recent years. While focused on specific treaties, these cases have legal implications for international water law in general.

The Theory is for the first time named and endorsed in 1929, in the River Oder Ruling. The Case consists of a dispute between Poland – the uppermost riparian, and six neighboring countries downstream. The PCIJ is seized to clarify – in relation to the stretches within Poland of two Oder tributaries – the geographic extent of the other riparian states' navigation rights, as expressed through the jurisdiction of the *International Commission of the River Oder* ('River Oder Commission').

Specifically, the PCIJ is asked to indicate the legal principle to be applied in the delimitation of the Commission's jurisdiction.[176] The Court notes that the questions posed by the parties to the dispute "must be solved solely on the basis of the Treaty of Versailles",[177] but a firm conclusion cannot be reached from a "purely grammatical [text] analysis".[178] Recalling that several interpretation methods exist, the Court invokes "the principles governing *international fluvial law in general*";[179] and applies Community-of-Interests, as one such principle, to the interpretation of the disputed Treaty and, ultimately, to formulate its Decision. The Court deems Community-of-Interests, as reflected in the Vienna General Act and, subsequently, applied and developed by the Treaty of Versailles, among other agreements, to be the basis of international law in this field.[180]

176 River Oder Case, *supra*, p. 6, quoting from the Special Agreement by means of which the parties submitted their dispute to the PCIJ.

177 *Id*, p. 22.

178 *Id*, p. 26.

179 *Ibid*, (emphasis added).

180 *Id*, p. 27.

The Decision is about navigation but must be approached within the broader context set out by the Court. Reviewing the case, McCaffrey points out that nowhere does the PCIJ suggest that Community-of-Interests, as a principle of international fluvial law, is restricted to navigation.[181] Bruhács, similarly, notes that the PCIJ Decision, when searching for international water law principles, does not distinguish between navigation and other watercourse uses.[182] On this basis, McCaffrey sees the precedent as evidence of the applicability of Community-of-Interests across the entire field of the law of transboundary basins.[183] The Decision is thus an authoritative source for the identification of the normative elements of Community-of-Interests as a theoretical framework for international water law as a whole.

The next step scholarship detects in the development of Community-of-Interests comes many years later, in 1992, when the members of the *Economic Commission for Europe* (ECE) adopt the ECEWC. This Convention rests on three main pillars: prevention, control, and reduction of transboundary impacts; equitable and reasonable use of shared waters; and cooperative catchment management.[184] In 2003, its parties decided to amend their Convention, opening it to accession by all UN member states.[185] These amendments have since entered into force and become fully operational.[186] The Convention's global status boosts its normative authority. While most of its parties still come from Europe and Central Asia, over 15 come Africa, Central America, Asia and the Middle-East.

While the ECEWC does not make an explicit reference to the Theory, there is robust evidence that its parties consider their Convention to reflect Community-of-Interests, viewing the environment as the central shared concern to be protected thereunder. The ECEWC Guide – an official document adopted by the Meeting of the Parties (MoP) to guide implementation[187] – alludes to or mentions Community-of-Interests several times. Such is the case where the

181 McCaffrey (2019), *supra*, p. 220–21.

182 J. Bruhács, *The Law of Non-Navigational Uses of International Watercourses* (Translation by M. Zehery) (Martinus Nijhoff 1992), p. 30. *See also* Lammers, *supra*, p. 507.

183 McCaffrey (2019), *supra*, p. 221.

184 *See* ECEWC, *supra*, Articles 1–2, 6.

185 ECEWC, Meeting of the Parties (MoP), 3rd Session (Madrid, 26–28 Nov 2003), Decision III/1 (28 Nov 2003) (in force 6 Feb 2013).

186 *See* ECEWC, MoP, 6th Session (Rome, 28–30 Nov 2012), Decision VI/3 (30 Nov 2012), ¶4.

187 *See Vienna Convention on the Law of Treaties* (Vienna, 23 May 1969) (in force 27 Jan 1980), 1155 UNTS 331 ('VCLT'), Art.31(3)(b), considering subsequent treaty application practices agreed among parties to be valid tools of interpretation.

Guide underscores the common interest of parties in environmental preservation[188] and in its commentary about the duty to cooperate as formulated in Article 2(6). According to the Guide, the duty to cooperate "reflects the *interdependence* between riparian parties and also recognizes their Community-of-Interests in transboundary waters."[189]

Hence, the ECEWC transcends the focus of Limited Territorial Sovereignty on respect for correlative rights through unilateral restraint and minimum engagement. Cooperation based on this Convention is not *ad hoc*, but continued and systematic. State interactions here rest on advanced and detailed joint proactive measures, as specified across various ECEWC provisions, including those that stress the centrality of agreements and bodies in transboundary water management. This author's opinion that Community-of-Interests underlies the ECEWC is shared with Sievers, who compares the Convention with the UNWC to affirm that the former *more fully embraces*[190] the Theory.

The ECEWC's evolution from a regional into a universal legal framework represents a significant development in international water law, which scholarship has yet to consider in the study of Community-of-Interests. The Convention has served as an effective treaty governing and informing cooperation on the waters shared among ECE states and beyond. The ECEWC has been applied within diverse contexts and in response to varying circumstances:[191] its 57 state parties include water-rich and water-scarce countries; developed and developing states and others with economies in transition; and upper, middle and lower riparians. The Convention's implementation process is cutting-edge, dynamic, embedded with flexibility and facilitated by its bodies, taking account of each party's capabilities, resources, and specific challenges, while remaining attentive to emerging problems and trends.[192]

The current Program of Work includes specific activities to increase awareness of the Convention and galvanize accessions thereto, as well as to support implementation by new parties, drawing on the benefits of cooperation.[193] The Convention's global status has attracted attention among stakeholders worldwide. In 2024, the Meeting of the Parties gathered more than 500 partic-

188 ECEWC Guide, *supra*, p. iii, 16, 22–4, 32–4.

189 *Id*, p. 33.

190 Sievers, *supra*, p. 24.

191 UNW-DPAC, *supra*, p. 14

192 *Ibid.*

193 ECEWC, MoP, 10th Session (Ljubljana, 23–25 Oct 2024), *Draft Program of Work for 2025–2027*, UN Doc ECE/MP.WAT/2024/2 (14 Aug 2024), at https://unece.org/sites/default/files/2024-09/ECE_MP.WAT_2024_2_draft_POW_2025-2027_ENG.pdf.

ipants from 100 countries among parties, non-parties, UN agencies, research organizations, multilateral development agencies, the private sector, and civil society.[194] Non-ECE parties are now Bangladesh, Cameroon, Chad, Gambia, Ghana, Guinea Bissau, Iraq, Ivory Coast, Namibia, Nigeria, Panama, Senegal, Sierra Leone, Togo, Zambia, and Zimbabwe.[195]

The ECEWC gains further authoritative status as it expands membership across regions. In parallel, we may assume that its implementation by more and more states results in increasing levels of the Theory's uptake.

Three years after the ECEWE is signed, the members of the Southern African Development Community (SADC) adopt the Protocol on Shared Water Courses ('1995 SADC Protocol'), as their own regional legal instrument on the law of transboundary basins. As a framework agreement, the Protocol codifies, adjusts, and develops basic principles and rules of international water law for tailored application to the region. The Protocol is the first treaty to reference the Theory explicitly. Under Article 2(2), parties undertake to respect and abide by the "principles of Community-of-Interests" in the equitable use of shared watercourse systems. McCaffrey considers this provision "remarkable [and] an important and forward-looking statement".[196]

The UNWC comes into being in 1997, under the umbrella of the UNGA, with affirmative votes from a vast majority of member states, to become a widely accepted framework of the law of the non-navigational uses of international watercourses.[197] Having entered into force in 2014 and counting now 41 contracting states, the UNWC represents a milestone in the evolution of international law, serving as a "constitution"[198] for the governance of transboundary water relations.

The UNWC is the product of governments and renowned legal experts coming together around the recognition that the world's transboundary basins were poorly governed; and riparian states generally did not have a clear understanding of the applicable norms in the field. This recognition eventually trig-

194 IISD (2024), *supra*, p. 2.

195 *See* UN, *Status of Treaties*: *ECEWC*, as of 14 May 2025, Treaty Collection, at https://treaties.un.org/Pages/ViewDetails.aspx?src=TREATY&mtdsg_no=XXVII-5&chapter=27&clang=_en.

196 McCaffrey (2019), *supra*, p. 224.

197 *See, e.g.*, S.C. McCaffrey, *The Convention Enters into Force*, 44:4 Envtl. Pol'y & L. 351–6 (2014), p. 354–5; F. Rocha Loures *et al*, *The Authority and Function of the UN Watercourses Convention*, *in* F. Rocha Loures & A. Rieu-Clarke, The UN Watercourses Convention in Force: Strengthening International Law for Transboundary Water Management (Routledge 2013), p. 49–66, 49–51.

198 McCaffrey (2014), *supra*, p. 356.

gered the drafting process of the UNWC, so that customary law would no longer be the only legal source governing transboundary waters in the absence of watercourse agreements. Customary norms tend to be vague, unclear, and contested, while lacking a neutral enforcement mechanism. Unpacking international custom is a complex endeavor, "requiring research into the proffered reasons for a practice in what often are obscure and inconclusive sources";[199] and even successful efforts tend to retain gaps and ambiguities.[200] Customary law is thus unfit, on its own, to tackle the transboundary water challenge.

In contrast, the UNWC "offers a universal common ground arrived at after exhaustive discussions and which makes all watercourse states aware of their minimum rights and duties"[201] at the outset of negotiations. This same motivation for developing the UNWC underlies de importance of the Basin Treaty as the normative foundation for an individual community-of-basin-interests, and which provides legal clarity and stability for interstate relations. As stated in the 5th Preambular Paragraph of the UNWC, the states which voted in favor of its adoption were convinced that an umbrella legal instrument, authoritative and globally endorsed, would secure and enable the sustainable use, protection, and management of the world's international watercourses.

Globally, the ECEWC and the UNWC may be viewed as a legal package codifying, clarifying, and developing the principles and rules on the non-navigational uses of international watercourses. The ECEWC generally contains stricter, more detailed provisions than the UNWC. Still, certain aspects of the UNWC supplement the ECEWC, such as the former's well-developed articles on equitable and reasonable use, planned measures, and dispute settlement. The two Conventions are highly authoritative and have inspired regional and basin agreements and arrangements around the world. Both, therefore, serve as central treaty sources to inform the search for the elements, functions, and status of Community-of-Interests.

Soon after the UNWC's adoption, still in 1997, the ICJ grounds a second ruling on Community-of-Interests and does so building on the River Oder Decision and on the basis of the Convention itself. The Gabčíkovo Case concerns a joint project on the Danube River, as governed by a treaty between Hungary and Slovakia.[202] The dispute arises as major environmental risks

199 J.W. Dellapenna, *International Water Law in a Climate of Disruption*, 17:1 Mich. J. Int'l L 43–94 (2007), p. 66.

200 *Ibid.*

201 F. Rocha Loures *et al*, *supra*, p. 52.

202 *Treaty on the Construction and Operation of the Gabčíkovo-Nagymaros Barrage System* (Budapest, 16 Sep 1977) (in force 30 June 1978), Hungary-Slovakia ('1977 Treaty'). This

posed by the project come to light, and Hungary and Slovakia disagree as to the appropriate way to proceed. The dispute is made worse by each party's resort to unilateral measures – with Hungary suspending implementation activities; and Slovakia initiating the construction of its own river damming and diversion works to replace project components for which Hungary was originally responsible.[203] After various attempts at negotiations failing, the parties decide to bring their dispute before the ICJ. In their Special Agreement, the parties request the Court to base its decision on their 1977 Treaty and, also, on the relevant principles and rules of general international law.[204]

In its ruling, the Court interprets both the UNWC and the Treaty in question as expressions of Community-of-Interests. The Court invokes the Convention as evidence of the extended applicability of Community-of-Interests to transboundary water uses other than navigation.[205] The Gabčíkovo Case reinforces the authority of the UNWC and, importantly, establishes the connection between the Convention and Community-of-Interests. The Case also advances a better understanding of the Theory by emphasizing the interdependencies between the two riparian states, as created by the Danube; considering the environment as a common interest; placing equitable and reasonable use under the umbrella of Community-of-Interests; and illustrating how the Theory may govern and inform specific joint river development projects under a Basin Treaty.

Building further on the above jurisprudence, a thread interlinking Community-of-Interests, the Oder and Gabčíkovo precedents, and the UNWC comes up in a separate opinion in the Kasikili Case. The Opinion references the Theory as part of observations aimed at providing further guidance and a wider context for relations between parties going forward. The Opinion highlights equitable and reasonable use, applicability of the UNWC to both navigational

---

Treaty was originally signed between Hungary and Czechoslovakia. Yet, the dispute was brought to the ICJ after Slovakia had gained independence, in 1993. Hence, the corresponding *compromis* is between Hungary and Slovakia, the latter being the successor to the 1977 Treaty. For simplicity, all references in the book to Slovakia in the context of the Gabčíkovo Case encompass Slovakia itself, after the new state was formed, and Czechoslovakia, in relation to events preceding its breakup.

203 Gabčíkovo Case, *supra*, p. 7, 25, 27.

204 *Special Agreement*, Hungary-Slovakia (Brussels, 7 Apr 1993) (in force 28 June 1993), Art.2(1).

205 Gabčíkovo Case, *supra*, p. 56.

and non-navigational uses, and the consideration of the Chobe River as a unitary whole, regardless of where the boundary, then in dispute, is placed.[206]

The UNWC's adoption motivates a decision by the SADC member states to align regional state practice with the Convention, which they do by endorsing the Revised Protocol of 2000.[207] Through transboundary water cooperation, the new Protocol aims to give effect to the SADC agenda of regional integration and poverty alleviation.

The Revised SADC Protocol does not reiterate an express reference to Community-of-Interests. Yet, via the Protocol's relationship to the UNWC, the Theory remains entrenched therein, influencing existing and future basin-specific agreements adopted in the region. The intent to align entails importing Community-of-Interests, as an underlying theoretical framework, into the new Protocol.

We find evidence of this intent in the 1st Preambular Paragraph, per which SADC members "bear in mind" the UNWC's adoption. The Revised Protocol then largely *applies* – though, on few occasions, *adjusts* – the UNWC normative framework to the regional context, leaving small differences between the texts of the two instruments. A thorough study of the practical implications of such differences finds that there is no outright contradiction between the new Protocol and the UNWC.[208] The latter adds value to the former by addressing ambiguities and filling gaps, on topics such as the relationship between equitable and reasonable use and harm prevention; the centrality of vital human needs in the allocation process; and the importance of joint contingency plans to prevent emergencies in connection with shared watercourses.

Moreover, Article 2, *caput*, indicates that the Protocol's objective is to foster "closer" cooperation. Article 3(1) innovates in relation to its 1995 counterpart by referring to the "principle of the unity and coherence" of shared watercourses, under which states commit to harmonizing their respective water uses, consistent with regional and basin objectives of sustainable develop-

---

206 ICJ, Kasikili/Sedudu Island (Botswana *v.* Namibia), Judgment (13 Dec 1999), 1999 ICJ Report 1045 ('Kasikili Case'), *Separate Opinion*, Judge Kooijmans, p. 110.

207 *See* M. Kgomongoe & R. Meissner, *The Revised Protocol on Shared Watercourses and the Management of Water Resources in SADC*, SA Yearbook of International Affairs, 2003104, p. 351–59. The same article recalls a SADC-commissioned report containing a comparative analysis of the UNWC and the 1995 Protocol as a basis for future alignment. *Ibid*, p. 354.

208 D. Malzbender & A. Earle, *The Impact and Implications of the Adoption of the 1997 UN Watercourse Convention for Countries in Southern Africa* (WWF) (undated), International Water Law Project, at https://www.internationalwaterlaw.org/bibliography/WWF/RA_SADC_states.pdf.

ment and integration. Community-of-Interests is embedded in that provision, through the Theory's first and most essential normative element: the Basin Scope. Once again, Community-of-Interests surfaces from the unity of the catchment, and the common interests that thus emerge.

In 2002, the adoption of the Senegal Basin Charter brings about the second precedent of treaty law expressly codifying Community-of-Interests, in its 17th Preambular Paragraph. In addition, the Charter's 14th Preambular Paragraph invokes the general principles and customary norms of international law governing international watercourses – in particular, those captured by the UNWC. This direct reference to the UNWC in an instrument expressly codifying Community-of-Interests shows how a Basin Treaty that significantly draws inspiration from the UNWC, beyond just individual provisions, is likely to be framed by Community-of-Interests.

The Senegal Basin drains the territories of Guinea, Mali, Mauritania, and Senegal, in West Africa, and it is an outstanding case study of progressive transboundary water cooperation in its own right. The Charter's adoption marks yet another milestone in the long history of interstate engagement in basin management, as framed by Community-of-Interests, through successive legal instruments that either supersede or strengthen their earlier counterparts. Taken together, those instruments require and presuppose advanced stages of Close Basin Cooperation. This applies, *inter alia*, to the joint planning, construction, operation, and ownership of water infrastructure.

The Basin Body, the Senegal River Basin Development Organization (OMVS), has broad decision-making powers and, under its auspices, member states have equitably shared measurable and mutual gains. Cooperation has not always been smooth, "often due to 'micro-nationalisms' and the desire of some parties to act independently".[209] Yet, even in periods of suspended diplomatic relations between members, the organization remained operational, serving then as those countries' only communication channel.[210] The benefits of joint financing and fundraising and other advantages have kept countries engaged, with cooperation thus enduring and progressively deepening.[211]

The following year, a different set of African co-basin countries adopt the third legal instrument known to reference Community-of-Interests explicitly. Article 4(2)(k) of the Lake Victoria Protocol cites the Theory among the principles guiding the management of the basin. The Theory thus serves as a foundational pillar for the entire Protocol. The framing of the Protocol by Commu-

209 UNW-DPAC, *supra*, p. 33.

210 UN Water (2018), *supra*, p. 153.

211 UNW-DPAC, *supra*, p. 33.

nity-of-Interests is reinforced in the instrument's own terminology, which refers throughout its text not to parties but to *partner* states.

The Lake Victoria Community-of-Interests has unfolded within the framework of the *East African Community* (EAC) – like the SADC, a regional integration regime. The Protocol underscores the commitment by members to supplement their wider collaboration process with actions at the catchment level. Along with the Protocol, other EAC legal frameworks have been endorsed for diverse thematic areas.

In 2004, Community-of-Interests receives attention in an Arbitral Award. The Chlorides Case settles a dispute between The Netherlands and France in connection with the implementation of jointly agreed measures against pollution of the Rhine River. The case centers on the correct interpretation of the applicable treaties – successive stages in the parties' technical attempts to deal jointly with their common water quality problem[212] – as regards the allocation of implementation costs.[213]

The Award innovates in relation to previous cases on the Theory by building on the Solidarity that exists between co-basin states within a community-of-basin-interests. The Award also views the Theory as being entrenched in the treaties then under dispute, thereby supplying the book with a European set of primary sources. The cooperative efforts enabled by this package of Rhine legal instruments, as interpreted by the Award, illustrate the concrete and successful application of Community-of-Interest towards realizing shared goals: joint actions "initially focused on assessing the extent of pollution were converted to cooperation measures that eventually led to effective improvements in water quality."[214]

The next time the ICJ invokes Community-of-Interests and explores its elements is in 2010, when deciding on a dispute between Argentina and Uruguay. The Pulp Mills Case is triggered by Argentina claiming a breach on the part of

---

212 *See* L. Boisson de Chazournes, *The Rhine Chlorides Arbitration Concerning the Auditing of Accounts (Netherlands-France): Its Contribution to International Law*, in B. McMahon ed, The Rhine Chlorides Arbitration Concerning the Auditing of Accounts (Netherlands-France), Award of 2004 (TMC Asser Press 2008), p. 1–2.

213 *Convention on the Protection of the Rhine against Pollution from Chlorides* (as amended with annexes and exchanges of letters constituting an amendment) (Bonn, 3 Dec 1976), France-Germany-Luxembourg-Netherlands-Switzerland, 1404 UNTS 91 (1985) ('Rhine Chlorides Convention'); *Additional Protocol to the Rhine Chlorides Convention*, (Brussels, 25 Sep 1991) (in force 1 Nov 1994), France-Germany-Luxembourg-Netherlands-Switzerland, 1840 UNTS 423 (1994) ('Rhine Chlorides Protocol').

214 Leb (2013), *supra*, p. 155.

Uruguay of obligations under the Uruguay River Statute[215] – the agreement applicable to the part of the watercourse forming the border between them, along with its surrounding environment. The alleged violations relate to Uruguay's authorization of the construction of two pulp mills on the riverbank, with potential detrimental effects on water quality and other environmental values.

When interpreting the Statute, the Court recognizes the Community-of-Interests that exists between the co-riparians Argentina and Uruguay;[216] and refers to the Statute's "common-interest dimension"[217] regarding sustainable river development. Being framed by the Theory, as recognized by the Court, the Statute is a longstanding and comprehensive Basin Treaty for close and institutionalized binational cooperation.

The Theory appears once again in treaty law in 2017. The Agreement in question, adopted between Ecuador and Peru, governs the transboundary basins shared between the two countries. To the author's knowledge, this Basin Treaty has not yet been examined by other writers in connection with Community-of-Interests. The 13th Preambular Paragraph recognizes the Community-of-Interests that unites the two states in the management of those basins.

Finally, as recently as 2022, Community-of-Interests receives attention in the Silala Case. The ICJ remarks that "an international watercourse constitutes a shared resource over which riparian states have a common right";[218] and recalls the River Oder and Gabčíkovo Cases.[219] Unfortunately, the Court does not go any further in unpacking the Theory's normative content.

4 Conclusions

Community-of-Interests lies within the broader framework of general international law. The law of transboundary basins has been evolving from Limited Territorial Sovereignty towards the Theory in tandem with the institutionalization of the international legal order, through coordination and cooperation and towards organization and co-progressiveness.

215 *Statute of the River Uruguay* (Salto, 26 Feb 1975) (in force 18 Sep 1976), Argentina-Uruguay, 1295 UNTS 340 (1982) ('River Uruguay Statute').

216 Pulp Mills case, *supra*, p. 9, 79.

217 *Id*, p. 55 (emphasis added).

218 Silala Case, *supra*, p. 32.

219 *Ibid.*

Beyond the level of a transboundary basin, water policy and cooperation have pragmatically unfolded at the global and regional levels as well, in light of the multilevel and multidimensional interdependencies created by this resource. Globally, a wider community interest exists in the preservation of the hydrological cycle. Water ultimately interconnects all places and peoples, thereby requiring some degree of universal cooperation towards addressing related risks and opportunities. Building on science, the ideal of a well-structured and effective regime for global water governance has policy traction; and such an ideal has not gone unnoticed by stakeholders and decision-makers, nor by expert literature. Even so, acceptance of the hydrological cycle as a global public good has yet to penetrate international law.

At the regional level, water cooperation takes place between neighboring states not necessarily sharing a particular catchment, but with broader common interests in integration through sectors dependent on water, such as food and energy security.

Based on lessons from global and regional Close Cooperation on common state interests, the mechanisms that countries may employ in this context include *tailored legal or policy instruments* as the bases for the cooperation process; *dedicated bodies* that facilitate cooperation; and *collaborative, especially joint, measures* for safeguarding unilateral interests and promoting common goals. Similar mechanisms are present in cooperation regimes known to reflect the Theory.

Community-of-Interests is founded on the shared goals of each grouping of states within individual basins; and the catchment is the point of departure for further unpacking the Theory's normative content. As a legal theory guiding transboundary water cooperation, Community-of-Interests applies among the respective co-riparians, except where their actions may affect third states. This delimitation of the applicability of Community-of-Interests should not stop us from building on comparable instances of Close Cooperation, as above-described.

The origins of the Theory are in navigation. Since the River Oder Case, Community-of-Interests has evolved to also inform international norms governing the multiple uses of international watercourses, as well as their management and protection. With this extended scope, Community-of-Interests builds on Limited Territorial Sovereignty to advance the degree of cooperation in ways that account for interconnections and interdependencies across the watershed as an integrated whole and across sectors, and which favor close, systematic, and long-term governance and management, with stakeholder engagement.

Limited Territorial Sovereignty and Community-of-Interests are not mutually exclusive. In fact, regimes framed by the Theory retain obligations reflective of coexistence to sustain peaceful relations when disputes arise. Communities-of-basin-interests require principles and rules across the spectrum of interstate engagement; and even the most limited cooperation arrangement may entail minimum joint action.

This will all be shown in Parts III and IV, where we examine in detail the sources of international law that form the basis of our Legal Analytical Frame-Work structured upon the primary and secondary elements of Community-of-Interests.

Supplementing these sources that come from the field of international water law, Part II discusses regional integration regimes – comparable instances of Close Cooperation founded on common interests and through which we identify a set of normative patterns later found to be also present, with the appropriate adjustments, within regimes informed by the Theory.

PART II

Close Regional Cooperation: Analogy as a Heuristic Tool to Identify the Elements of Community-of-Interests

> *The growing realization of the insufficiency of the national state … has [led to] closer political and legal integration between … states linked by closer ties of common interests, values and purposes.*[1]

⁘

Cooperation between co-basin countries bears resemblance with that among states within a specific region in advanced stages of integration. As international law phenomena, both processes are founded on deep bonds and shared purposes among a subset of the world's countries located in physical proximity to one another – be it at the basin or regional level. In other words, regional integration regimes, being informed by common interests, and basin cooperation informed by Community-of-Interests involve close relationships among neighboring states.

The resemblance between Community-of-Interests and regional integration regimes becomes clear in what motivates states to establish international organizations, i.e., the perceived need for "the management of interdependence, in the [members'] common interest".[2] To illustrate, ASEAN seeks to strengthen cooperation on *mutual interests* and *common problems*; and to set out a *firm foundation for common action* and a *prosperous and peaceful community*, in a *spirit of partnership*. ASEAN is viewed as representing member states' *collective will* to *bind themselves together in friendship*. The *ASEAN identity* builds on historical and cultural ties, on *unity in diversity*, i.e., *common values* and a blend of diverse cultures, languages and religions.[3]

---

1 Friedmann, *supra*, p. 18 (emphasis added).

2 N. Blokker, *General Introduction, in* Virzo & Ingravallo eds, *supra*, p. 1–13, 2.

3 SEAN, *Declaration* (Bangkok, 8 Aug 1967), Indonesia-Malaysia-Singapore-Philippines-Thailand ('ASEAN Bangkok Declaration'), Preamble, ¶¶1–3, Body, ¶¶2(1), 5; *Charter of the Association of Southeast Asian Nations* (ASEAN) (Singapore, 20 Nov 2007) (in force 15 Dec

 | HTTPS://DOI.ORG/10.1163/9789004507036-004

Similarly, Article 1 of the EU Treaty refers to the role of the Union in the pursuit of "objectives [parties] have in common".[4] The 2nd Preambular Paragraph of the EAC Treaty, the Founding Charter of the *East Africa Community*, recalls the successive joint organizations established "to control and administer certain matters of common interest" through Close Regional Cooperation.[5] At the country level, Senegal links the ratification of the new Charter[6] of the *Community of Sahel-Saharan States* (CEN-SAD), of which it is a member, to its awareness of the *communauté d'intérêts* among the region's countries.[7]

The governance tools and institutional relationships detected across various regional integration regimes form the contours of what is consolidated in this Part into our preliminary analytical framework. In broad strokes, cooperation regimes for regional common interests are delimited by the scope of the common interests at stake; are governed under the umbrella of tailored context-specific treaties and dedicated institutions; display joint and positive action as the prevalent modality of state engagement; and include provisions guiding internal and external interstate and interinstitutional relationships. Similar features appear in cooperation regimes informed by the Theory.

Evidence of state practice under the umbrella of Regional Integration Organizations, as ruled by their Founding Charters, is abundant. Including this evidence in the book is consistent with the contextualization of the Theory in general international law and, in particular, in trends towards institutionalization. Interdependence and common interests form the factual and pragmatic roots of Community-of-Interests, Close Regional Cooperation, and the institutionalization of the international legal order.

In fact, scholarship often cites the *Central Commission for the Navigation of the Rhine* as the world's first international organization, established in 1815.

2008), Brunei-Cambodia-Indonesia-Lao PDR-Malaysia-Myanmar-Philippines-Singapore-Thailand-Viet Nam, *reproduced in* ASEAN Secretariat, The ASEAN Charter (2015) ('ASEAN Charter'), Preamble & Art.2(2)(l) (italicized parts of the text are direct quotes from the two legal documents cited).

4 *Treaty on European Union* (Maastricht, 7 Feb 1992) (Consolidated Version 2016) (2016/C 202/01), OJ C 202 (7 June 2016) ('EU Treaty').

5 *Treaty for the Establishment of the East African Community* (EAC), as amended (Arusha, 30 Nov 1999) (in force 7 July 2000), Burundi-Kenya-Rwanda-South Sudan-Tanzania-Uganda ('EAC Treaty').

6 Summit of Heads of State, *Revised Treaty of the Community of Sahel-Saharan States* (CEN-SAD) (Ndjamena, 16 Feb 2013), Benin-Burkina Faso-Chad-Djibouti-Eritrea-Guinea-Ivory Coast-Mali-Morocco-Niger-Sudan-Senegal-Togo ('Revised CEN-SAD Treaty').

7 Senegal, Decree 2016–1494: *A Bill to Authorize Ratification of the Revised* CEN-SAD *Treaty* (26 Sep 2016), p. 2.

The Rhine Commission and other early international organizations, the UN itself, global and regional intergovernmental institutions, and the numerous transboundary basin bodies that now exist are all manifestations of states responding to their own perceived needs, rather than attempts to infringe upon territorial sovereignty. Riparian states, in particular, come together to constitute the Basin Body when unilateral regulation and some degree of coordination of water uses become insufficient to address shared concerns, from which arises a common interest in formalizing, institutionalizing, and deepening the cooperation process.[8] In each interstate organization, the common interests at stake may be different, but the legal tools employed by countries in Close Regional Cooperation regimes and in communities-of-basin-interests are similar.

The selection for the book of precedents of Close Regional Cooperation – or, interchangeably, regional integration regimes – aims to keep the work manageable, while targeting examples that resemble communities-of-interests. The goal is to sustain the validity of findings by means of a representative sample of institutions across continents and regions. Like the Community-of-Interests regimes later examined, the regional integration regimes considered here are founded on treaties – or *Founding Charters*, which define the origins, competences, and status of the respective institutional frameworks – herein, *Regional Integration Organizations*. The latter are personalized entities, i.e., 'hard' or intergovernmental organizations. As explained by Runavot, by definition, an *intergovernmental organization* is always treaty-based, whereas an *international organization* may be more flexible in terms of constitution and governance.[9] Regional Integration Organizations have at their core the pursuit of the common social, economic, environmental and other interests of their members and their peoples.

1 Scope of Common Interests under Close Regional Cooperation

The interests that the states within a given region may share originate from their geographic proximity and physical interdependence as the principal (albeit not necessarily only) motivations for Close Cooperation. From there, those interests may expand and deepen over time. Conflicting interests needing peaceful management may emerge as those countries sharing a given

8 Blokker, *supra*, p. 1, 4–5.

9 Runavot, *supra*, p. 32–3.

space and related resources become ever more integrated. In this sense, the geographic scope of those interests is regional.

To illustrate, under the *Treaty Establishing the African Economic Community* (AEC), North, West, Central, East, and Southern Africa are each considered *regions* of the African Union in the context of parallel and complementary regional integration and cooperation regimes; and a *subregion* includes at least three states of one or more regions.[10] This is a political division, but it reflects how countries across the Continent have come to organically organize themselves based on more closely shared interests.

The focus here is on select individual regions, with clear and deep geographic ties, and where states are cooperating closely under the umbrella of Regional Integration Organizations. These institutions emerge from palpable physical realities that unite neighboring nations, giving origin to shared interests, values, and challenges that may be addressed, at least in part, at the regional level. It is that geographic regional scope which is invoked as underlying the formation, development and continued operation of effective regional integration regimes.

Within this geographic ambit, regional integration regimes go beyond the establishment of common markets to cover other cooperation areas, in order to respond effectively to the range of interests member states share. In Europe, for example, the Preamble of the EU Treaty codifies the *principle of sustainable development*, alongside environmental protection, as bases for socioeconomic development that advances economic integration, while promoting parallel progress in other fields.

Accordingly, the analysis excludes universal organizations, whose underlying foundations gain expression in Simma's community interests. This is not to deny the existence of universal interests that demand treaty-based, institutionalized, and Close Cooperation, in view of the "necessities of life in our growing global village".[11] However, the diversity of interests at the global level makes organizations existing on that scale more distant in conception from communities-of-basin-interests. A regional, geographic basis for cooperation, involving a smaller number of members, is more compelling than globally shared interests to motivate Close Cooperation.

Excluded, also, are intergovernmental organizations formed principally in reaction to common bonds of language, culture, or religion – without, there-

---

10 *Treaty Establishing the African Economic Community* (Abuja, 3 June 1991) ('AEC Treaty'), Art.1(d)–(e).

11 Blokker, *supra*, p. 6–7.

fore, a geographic regional scope. In such cases, political or social connections are at the heart of the regime, as opposed to physical realities.

The most well-developed regional integration regime is that under the umbrella of the European Union, as established and regulated by the EU Treaty and the EU Functioning Treaty,[12] together with annexes and protocols.

Like the EU, the *African Union* (AU) aims for continent-wide integration. With 55 member states, the AU serves as a *continental* umbrella for interregional, regional and subregional intergovernmental organizations. Its members' overarching common interest consists in addressing "the multifaceted challenges that confront [the African] continent and peoples".[13] This entails moving towards free trade and movement, while promoting peace, security, stability, development, and progressive integration across the economic, social, and cultural arenas.[14]

The *Common Market for Eastern and Southern Africa* (COMESA)[15] and CEN-SAD are *interregional* pillars of African integration, with memberships that overlap with other regional African organizations. CEN-SAD, for example, groups together over 20 states across West, North, and East Africa. In

---

12 *Treaty on the Functioning of the European Union* (Rome, 25 Mar 1957) (Consolidated Version 2016) (2016/C 202/01), OJ C 202 (7 June 2016) ('EU Functioning Treaty').

13 Assembly of African Heads of State and Government, 36th Ordinary Session (Lomé, 7 Nov 2000), *Constitutive Act of the African Union* (in force 25 May 2001), as amended (Assembly, 1st Extraordinary Session (Addis Ababa, 3 Feb 2003); 2nd Ordinary Session (Maputo, 11 July 2003) ('AU Act'), Preamble, ¶5. *See id* Art.29, restricting AU membership to African states. On legal personality, it is generally agreed that member states had intended to attribute it to the Union, despite the absence of an explicit Treaty provision on the matter. *See* H. Wubie & Z. Tsegaw, *Legal Personality of the African Union* (29 Feb 2012), *Abyssinia Law*, at https://www.abyssinialaw.com/about-us/item/380-legal-personality-of-the-african-union, on the concept of *functional personality*.

14 *See* AU Act, e.g., Art.3(k)-(l), (n)-(o), on objectives pertaining to sustainable development, living standards, science and technology, and good health; Art.4(l) & (n), on gender equality and social justice.

15 *Revised Treaty Establishing the Common Market for Eastern and Southern Africa* (COMESA) (2009), Angola-Burundi-Comoros-Djibouti-DRC-Egypt-Eritrea-Ethiopia-Eswatini-Kenya-Libya-Madagascar-Malawi-Mauritius-Rwanda-Seychelles-Somalia-Sudan-Tunisia-Uganda-Zambia-Zimbabwe ('Revised COMESA Treaty'). *See ibid*, Art.52(2)(a), mandating members to enact legislation endowing COMESA with legal personality as required for the performance of its functions; Art.2(2) & (4), listing the Eastern and Southern African countries that may join the Common Market; and permitting accession by other states (e.g, Libya and Tunisia) that fulfill certain conditions, including immediately neighboring an existing member; Art.1, thus defining *region*: "the geographical area covered by the Common Market".

2013, CEN-SAD received a boost with the adoption of the Revised Treaty, under which the two overarching common interests consist of sustainable development and regional security.[16] The Revised Treaty symbolizes CEN-SAD's rebirth, and the Organization has since grown as a player in African integration.[17]

At the African regional level, Preambular Paragraph 11 of the EAC Treaty articulates the parties' broad policy goal: "realizing a fast and balanced regional development". Members share an interest in ensuring development occurs in ways that, per Article 5(3), are sustainable, balanced, and harmonious, and consistent with the protection of the environment. To that end, Article 5(1) of the Treaty envisions policy and program development towards wider, deeper, and mutually beneficial cooperation among partner states across the political, economic, social, cultural, juridical, defense and security, and research and technology spheres.[18]

Other important African Regional Integration Organizations include the *Economic Community of West African States* (ECOWAS); and the *Southern Africa Development Community* (SADC), under the auspices of which the two above-referenced Protocols on shared watercourses reflecting Community-of-Interests were adopted.

In the Americas, the *Common Market of the Southern Cone* (MERCOSUR), created under the Treaty of Asuncion,[19] has Argentina, Brazil, Paraguay, and Uruguay among its founding members. The establishment of the Market is seen as a step towards deeper integration among its parties, building on a history of cooperation among a wider set of countries in Latin America under

16 *See* Revised CEN-SAD Treaty, *supra*, Arts.2 & 53, restricting membership to the states within and around the Sahel-Saharan zone, and which are members of the UN, accept Community objectives and have joined the Revised Treaty; Art.3, on objectives; Art.7, on the Community's legal personality.

17 A. Traore, *Sommet Extraordinaire de la CEN-SAD à N'Djamena: L'Ère du Renouveau* (17 Feb 2013), Lefaso.Net, at http://lefaso.net/spip.php?article52854.

18 *See* EAC Treaty, *supra*, Art.3, on application for, and negotiations on, EAC membership or association, or participation in its activities, and referring to the criterium of "geographical proximity to and interdependence between it and the partner states"; Art.138(1), on legal personality.

19 *Treaty Establishing a Common Market* (MERCOSUR) (Asuncion, 26 Mar 1991), Argentina-Brazil-Paraguay-Uruguay-Venezuela ('Treaty of Asuncion'), Preamble. *See also ibid*, Art.20, allowing accession by ALADI members; *Additional Protocol to the Treaty of Asuncion on the Institutional Structure of the MERCOSUL*, Art.34, giving the Organization legal personality ('Protocolo Adicional ao Tratado de Assunção sobre a Estrutura Institucional do MERCOSUL') (Ouro Preto, 17 Dec 1994), Argentina-Brazil-Paraguay-Uruguay-Venezuela ('Ouro Preto Protocol').

the auspices of the *Latin American Integration Association* (ALADI). The regime's overarching goal is that of economic development with social justice, which requires, *inter alia*, preserving the environment and improving physical links. In pursuit of that goal, the Preamble of the Treaty of Asuncion affirms the parties' will to promote "increasingly close ties" between their peoples. Although the MERCOSUL started off with a narrow focus on economic integration, it has since expanded its focus to more directly address topics such as the environment and human rights, including through dedicated bodies created and agreements adopted under the auspices of the Organization.

In Asia, the *Association of Southeast Asian Nations* (ASEAN) exists to respond effectively to shared challenges and opportunities associated with the member states' multidimensional and evolving interdependencies.[20] This shared goal and its pursuit gain specificity in two provisions of the ASEAN Charter: Article 1(2), on "regional resilience [through] greater political, security, economic and social-cultural cooperation"; and Article 2(2), on a "shared commitment and collective responsibility" to regional peace, security and prosperity, and to "enhanced consultations on matters seriously affecting the common interest".

Like its counterparts in other regions, the *South Asian Association for Regional Cooperation* (SAARC) has a broad remit, including tourism; agriculture; environment, natural disasters, and biotechnology; poverty alleviation; energy, transport, science and technology; and education, security, and culture – all of which can be assumed as making up the core common interests being pursued under the Association's umbrella.[21]

We draw from the Founding Charters and derivative agreements of the above organizations to identify the elements of *governance* and *institutional relationships* that characterize Close Regional Cooperation – i.e., regional-level cooperation centered on common interests. Some of those elements form a preliminary basis to unpack the normative content of Community-of-Interests.

---

20 *See* ASEAN Charter, *supra*, Art.3, conferring legal personality upon ASEAN; Art.6(2)(a), listing "location in the recognized geographical region of Southeast Asia" as a membership criterium.

21 *Charter of the South Asian Association for Regional Cooperation* (Dhaka, 8 Dec 1985), Afghanistan-Bangladesh-Bhutan-India-Maldives-Nepal-Pakistan-Sri Lanka ('SAARC Charter'). Among SAARC members, Bangladesh, Bhutan, India, and Nepal share the Ganges basin. While falling outside of this book's scope, it would be interesting to assess whether SAARC has devoted attention to shared water resources in the context of regional cooperation.

2 Governance of Regional Cooperation on Common Interests

The governance elements of regional integration regimes are three:

a) *Founding Charter*, which formalizes interstate relations and provides a solid legal basis for Close Regional Cooperation as the enabler for the achievement of regional interests.
b) *Regional Integration Organization*, placed at the heart of treaty implementation and regional integration and tailored to pursue regional common interests.
c) *Close Regional Cooperation*, i.e., regional cooperation centered on common interests, under which joint action prevails, supported by other modalities of collaborative measures and by domestic undertakings, all of which advance shared concerns and balance unilateral interests.

2.1 *Founding Charter*

The Founding Charter lies at the core of the formalization and progressive development of Close Regional Cooperation and the integration process.

Preexisting Bonds: The roots of cooperation for common regional interests are found, not in treaty adoption, but in geographic ties among neighboring countries, from which may derive associated historic, cultural, religious, and/or linguistic bonds. The Preamble of the EAC Treaty, for example, emphasizes the "historical, commercial, industrial, cultural and other ties" that parties have enjoyed.

Across various Founding Charters, there is language recalling regional cooperation that preexists their adoption and/or the establishment of organizations; and pointing out to interdependence, shared bonds and correlated common problems, interests, and aspirations as triggers for region-based interstate collaboration. As interdependence deepens and shared interests expand, Founding Charters come, not to originate, but to promote Close Regional Cooperation by formalizing, regulating and institutionalizing preexisting regional interactions among neighboring nations.

The Preamble of the EU Treaty, for example, underscores the "European identity" and invokes the parties' resolve to "mark a new stage in the process of European integration", with the Union's creation reflecting the steps required to achieve that goal. Article 2 also invokes values that are "common to the member states"; and Article 3 refers to "Europe's cultural heritage".

In the case of ASEAN, the Preamble views the Charter as the culmination of milestones aimed at "intensifying community-building through enhanced regional cooperation and integration". The Preamble reinforces the original triggers of Close Regional Cooperation in the form of peoples' and states' "*bound by geography*, common objectives and a shared destiny"; "mutual interests and interdependence"; "a common desire and collective will to live in ... shared prosperity"; and "the need to strengthen *existing bonds* ... to effectively respond to current and future challenges and opportunities". The SAARC Charter similarly points to factors that already tied together members even before its adoption. The Preamble recalls how members "are bound by ties of history and culture"; and, as such, share "common problems, interests and aspirations"; and recognizes the importance of "increased cooperation, contacts and exchanges", which the Charter aims to enable.

In Africa, the Preamble of the AEC Treaty notes: "the efforts already made in subregional and regional sectoral economic cooperation ... justify a *larger and fuller* economic integration". The African Union builds upon a preexisting "common identity" shared across the Continent, as affirmed in the Preamble of the AU Act. According to the Preamble and Article 3(c) of the AEC Treaty, that common identity is guided by a shared vision of regional unification. The aim is to establish a stronger framework for collective action and fast-tracked integration across the political and socioeconomic spheres.

Treaties as tools to boost preexisting ties towards Close Regional Cooperation have marked international organizations from the beginning. The creation of the first permanent international bodies builds on the experience of years of *ad hoc* diplomatic conferences.[22] Having engaged in longstanding informal cooperation in certain fields, states would eventually decide to step up collaborative efforts within the framework of formal legal-institutional regimes specifically designed for the pursuit of shared goals. At that point, states had begun to view nonbinding rules and soft organizations as unsatisfactory to meet the "need for permanent and structured international cooperation".[23] The rationale behind modern international organizations focused on common interests remains the same.

The Founding Charter: The Charters examined create the necessary legal basis upon which the cooperation process may evolve and deepen. These treaties do so by identifying priority areas of common interests. To illustrate, the EAC Treaty connects Community objectives with the development of "policies and programs aimed at widening and deepening cooperation among the partner states in political, economic, social and cultural fields, research and technology, defense, security and legal and judicial affairs, for their mutual

22 Blokker, *supra*, p. 2.

23 *Id*, p. 12.

benefit". In addition, Founding Charters outline the principles, rules, institutional mandates, tools, and state engagement modalities deemed appropriate to enable the pursuit of those interests.

The integration and Close Regional Cooperation processes of the regions here considered have all been governed by treaties. In the case of ASEAN, the original framework for cooperation was the Bangkok Declaration. Foreseeing the ASEAN Charter, ultimately adopted at the Association's 40th Anniversary, the Declaration's Preamble states the vision of a "firm foundation for common action".

The ASEAN example also illustrates that a Charter may not only represent the culmination of negotiations on a binding instrument but also result from an evolution of a prior nonbinding arrangement. The ASEAN Charter thus embraces, reinforces, and develops the Declaration's precepts and concepts and broadens and refines the Association's purposes. The environment, for example, is not addressed in the Declaration, but receives prominent attention in the Charter. According to Article 1(8)–(9), a formalized ASEAN endorses the *principle of comprehensive security*, being concerned with transboundary challenges of all kinds, including sustainable development, natural resources and cultural heritage protection, and life quality. In other fields, whereas the Bangkok Declaration generally identifies regional peace and security as a priority, Article 1(3) of the ASEAN Charter provides specificity to cooperation on that area with the goal of a nuclear-free region. On economic integration, a vision of intraregional trade expansion in the Bangkok Declaration evolves into one of a single market in Article 1(5) of the ASEAN Charter.

A Charter may establish a Regional Integration Organization where no prior institutional arrangement existed or formalize a preexisting soft organization by granting it legal personality, as is the case with ASEAN, established originally under the Bangkok Declaration and, years later, granted personality by the Charter.

The ASEAN precedent suggests that, while a nonbinding legal instrument and a soft organization may be appropriate for the early stages of regional cooperation centered on common interests, informal or *ad hoc* arrangements no longer suffice when the intent is to evolve towards Close Regional Cooperation. Having cooperated within the framework of a political document, states eventually agree on the need for deeper and more systematic collaboration on the basis of binding rules and under an empowered and personalized institution. This point has implications for our later discussion on the role of binding agreements *versus* nonbinding arrangements and of hard *versus* soft organizations under the Theory.

A Charter may stand on its own, but often these treaties contain clauses for additional instruments to be adopted in succession so that Close Regional Cooperation may continue to expand, deepen, and gain strength in pace with evolving common state interests. Successive treaties may amend and expand upon earlier instruments, with a view to progressively stepping up regional cooperation.

Examples here include the thematic side agreements supplementing the ASEAN Charter. Under the AU umbrella, members have adopted a series of legal instruments over time, including various agreements and conventions in areas such as nature and natural resources, rights of persons with disabilities, the African Continental Free Trade Area, and maritime security; statutes for new bodies under the Union, like the African Minerals Development Center, as a specialized agency, and the AU International Law Commission, as an independent advisory organ; and protocols operationalizing the African Court of Justice and Human Rights and the Pan-African Parliament.[24] In the case of COMESA, progressive cooperation through the adoption of successive agreements is reflected in the gradual establishment of an economic community among Eastern and Southern African states. The seeds of the Common Market are found in an earlier treaty establishing the *Preferential Trade Area for Eastern and Southern Africa* (PTA), itself a steppingstone in the economic integration process, followed by the creation of COMESA.[25]

The original Founding Charters themselves may be amended or overhauled when the common interests at stake change or call for even closer cooperation. The 6th Preambular Paragraph of the Revised COMESA Treaty proclaims the parties' determination "to mark a new stage in the process of economic integration"; and Article 3(b) spells out the Common Market's objective to "foster closer relations" among members, hinting at the significance of treaties to deepen cooperation.

In the case of CEN-SAD, the final Preambular Paragraph of the Revised Treaty states the parties' determination to build on the results achieved under the previous regime and to reaffirm and deepen the Organization's achievements.[26] The motivations among member states in negotiating and adopting the new Treaty are to deepen economic, social, and cultural bonds and enable closer collaboration through a strengthened institutional framework and refocused cooperation efforts; as well as to reposition CEN-SAD as

24 *See* here for a list of OAU/AU treaties, conventions, protocols and charters: https://au.int/en/treaties.

25 Revised COMESA Treaty, *supra*, Preamble & Art.177.

26 Decree 2016–1494, *supra*, p. 2–3.

a central organization of action and state interaction in the Sahel-Saharan region.

Common ties and shared interests, therefore, tend to naturally exist among neighboring countries within a region, independently from the adoption of formal or informal legal instruments. In the context of regional integration, the Founding Charter does not give rise to but may deepen shared bonds and goals. Expressing states' commitment to regional integration, the Founding Charter builds upon preexisting interlinkages to establish, strengthen or further develop the legal-institutional machinery for Close Regional Cooperation. Nonbinding legal instruments may suffice in the earlier stages of common interest-based regional cooperation but are expected eventually to be replaced or supplemented by treaties.

2.2 *Regional Integration Organization*

The criticality of institutionalized cooperation in the pursuit of regional common interests is apparent across the various Founding Charters studied, all placing the Organization at the center of interstate collaborative relations.

The Preamble of the AU Act affirms the members' determination to strengthen, empower, and resource "common institutions" to perform their competences in an effective manner. Article 5 the EAC Treaty creates an institutional mandate for actions aimed at strengthening, widening, deepening and consolidating cooperation for the members' mutual benefit. In Asia, the Preamble of the SAARC Charter reaffirms the parties' commitment to boost "cooperation within an institutional framework".

The Founding Charter strives to tailor the institutional design of the Regional Integration Organization for the effective pursuit of shared concerns prioritized by member states and, where necessary, for the balancing of individual interests, e.g, through assisted dispute resolution. The Founding Charter shapes the Regional Integration Organization to go beyond treaty implementation so as to focus also on the continuous and progressive strengthening of cooperation. Close Regional Cooperation is dynamic, facilitated and pushed forward by member states and the institutional machinery itself.

The Regional Integration Organization follows a hierarchical structure, with mechanisms for intra-institutional coordination and exchanges, such as reporting and oversight of higher bodies over lower-level organs, for ensuring policy coherence and efficiency. Regular meetings of the Organization's organs sustain interstate dialogue. As designed by the respective treaties, the internal architecture varies across Organizations, mainly as to their degree of development, with some more complex and comprehensive than others. But some commonalities can be found, even if bodies with similar functions receive a variety of titles under each regime. Some of these functions may also be found within communities-of-basin-interests. Recognizing this may be an imperfect classification, with mandates that may appear to overlap, such functions generally include:

a) The **Highest Bodies** are composed of heads of state and government to provide general policy directions, recommendations and opinions, and to issue regulations, directives, and decisions. These may be binding on members, organs and persons, and intend to steer, supervise, and control the cooperation process, including through guidance for national policy: e.g., AU *Assembly*; COMESA *Authority*; CEN-SAD *Conference*; EAC *Summit*; ASEAN *Summit*; SAARC *Meeting*.
b) **Policy Organs** consist of sectoral or foreign affairs ministerial representatives, holding advisory and policy formulation powers for promoting, coordinating, monitoring and reviewing treaty implementation; overseeing the Organization's operation and evolution, for example, to embrace new cooperation areas; and coordinating and deciding on common-interest policies within their respective mandates, possibly water: e.g., AU *Executive Council*, CEN-SAD *Executive Council*; EAC *Council*, ASEAN *Coordinating Council* and *Sectoral Ministerial Bodies*; SAARC *Council of Ministers*.
c) **Technical Bodies** gather qualified government officials to promote implementation of common policies, including by preparing, coordinating and harmonizing programs, plans, and projects across sectors, and making recommendations on cost-sharing: e.g., AU *Specialized Technical Committees*; COMESA *Intergovernmental Committee of Experts* and its other technical committees, such as on environment, tourism, wildlife, and agriculture; EAC *Sectoral Committees*; SAARC *Technical Committees* and *Action Committees* (the latter implement projects involving more than two, but not all, members); MERCOSUL *Commerce Commission*.
d) **Implementation Committees** report and advise on treaty implementation; propose draft decisions for higher-level bodies and ensure their implementation; mobilize resources; and may negotiate agreements with third countries or organizations: e.g., EAC *Coordination Committee*; SAARC *Standing Committee*; MERCOSUL *Common Market Group*.
e) **Specialized Bodies** coordinate and support the pursuit of sectoral objectives and the Organization's thematic pillars; implement relevant actions and programs; and articulate with one another on crosscutting issues: e.g. COMESA *Committee of Governors of Central Banks*; CEN-SAD *Permanent Councils of Peace and Security* and of *Sustainable Development*, respectively, and the *Economic, Social and Cultural Council* (ESCC), as a

consultative body; EAC *Lake Victoria Fisheries Organization*; ASEAN *Political-Security, Economic, and Sociocultural Community Councils*, respectively, and its dedicated environmental bodies: e.g., ASEAN's *Mekong Basin Development Cooperation, Ministerial Meeting on the Environment, Conference of the Parties to the Agreement on Transboundary Haze Pollution, Center for Biodiversity*.

f) **Permanent Executive Bodies/Secretariats** and their Heads, whose functions may include to implement high-level decisions and projects; monitor and report on treaty implementation; propose norms to be considered for adoption by the Organization; assist other organs and organize meetings; generate knowledge, translate decisions, and store, manage and disseminate information and updates on national implementation, including data the members are required to share with one another: e.g., AU *Commission*, COMESA and EAC *Secretariats*.

g) **Stakeholder Engagement Bodies:** e.g., MERCOSUL *Economic and Social Consultative Council*, organ of representation of social and economic interests.

h) **Courts** established to settle disputes and contribute to treaty effectiveness.

i) **Parliamentarian Organs** congregate representatives from national parliaments: e.g., MERCOSUL *Joint Parliamentarian Commission*, which works to accelerate the internalization of norms adopted by the Organization, to promote harmonization of national laws, and to consider priority topics as mandated by the highest body.

j) **National Focal Points:** e.g., the National Secretariats within each member responsible, among other things, for promoting ASEAN identity and community-building.

Decisions at higher levels are usually taken by consensus or, if not feasible, in the case of the AU, for example, by a two-thirds majority – and tend to be binding on member states and other organs.

Founding Charters often include detailed provisions on the international, technical, and neutral character of the secretariat, and related parties' obligations when appointing qualified staff and interacting therewith. Such obligations may relate to an equitable distribution of positions among member states' nationals; include cooperating with the secretariat in the performance of its functions; and entail refraining from attempting to unduly influence secretariat officers. Executive bodies, in turn, being responsible only to the Organization, are expected not to seek or receive instructions from member states or external actors. These and other provisions express the parties' commitment to enable the bodies of the Regional Integration Organization to function effectively and, in so doing, to assure the fulfillment of common interests and agreed goals.

The Regional Integration Organization represents "a *personified* mode of institutionalizing international relations".[27] *Institutionalization* describes a gradual process that "does not necessarily imply a legal personality"[28] or an expansive or cross-sectoral mandate from the outset, and which progresses in response to the evolution of the common interests at stake. As with ASEAN, these bodies may be preceded by soft institutional arrangements, and/or receive upgrades overtime, as with CEN-SAD. The changes brought about by the Revised Treaty to CEN-SAD's original structure reveal the members' intent to strengthen the Organization; to make CEN-SAD more effective and adaptive to evolving sociopolitical contexts and better equipped to advance regional security and sustainable development – the priority common interests identified by the members.[29]

The EAC represents yet another example of intended progressive institutionalization: from a regional intergovernmental organization to a customs union and common market and, eventually, to a monetary union and then a political federation, through the adoption of successive treaties and other measures. This gradual institutional integration reflects a collective interest among the states concerned to deepen and better govern their multidimensional and cross-sectoral ties; and to do so through an evolving joint legal-institutional framework for cooperation on regional interests.

Like the Founding Charter, the Regional Integration Organization is created and its progressive strengthening realized when and as necessary for addressing effectively targeted shared concerns through formal, deepened, and systemic integration. The Regional Integration Organization plays a prominent role in treaty implementation and progressive development.

3 Close Regional Cooperation

> *Men work together,' I told him from the heart, / 'Whether they work together or apart.*
>
> R. FROST, The Tuft of Flowers

27 Runavot, *supra*, p. 18.

28 *Ibid.*

29 Traore, *supra*.

The primordial *raison d'être* of the Regional Integration Organization is the pursuit of common interests. To enable this overarching purpose, the Founding Charter is built on Close Regional Cooperation, as framed by the laws of cooperation and co-progressiveness. Friedmann's and Yee's teachings, therefore, offer theoretical bases for the Regional Integration Organization to thrive.

Commitments to Close Regional Cooperation may appear, implicitly or explicitly, in the preamble of the Founding Charter, in general or specific substantive and procedural norms, and in institutional mandates, all then combining to form the pattern of state engagement dedicated to the pursuit of common interests.

The Preamble of the AU Act emphasizes cooperation, which thus permeates its entire text. Per Article 3(l), the Union aims to "promote cooperation in all fields of human activity". Similarly, Article 3(c) of the AEC Treaty identifies interstate cooperation as a fundamental principle to which member states adhere; and Article 4 underscores close relations among members. The Preamble of the Revised CEN-SAD Treaty expresses the parties' resolve to achieve among them economic, political, cultural, and social integration. The Preamble of the SAARC Charter calls for "meaningful" and "enhanced" cooperation to secure common goals (peace, freedom, social justice, and economic prosperity) and address shared problems, interests, and aspirations, while accounting for national political and economic systems and cultural traditions.

In order to sustain long-term stable and peaceful relations, an objective of Close Regional Cooperation, the Regional Integration Organization is also guided by the law of coexistence. Hence, the Founding Charter contains provisions balancing unilateral and potentially conflicting interests; preventing and mitigating disagreements; ensuring the swift and equitable resolution of eventual disputes; and handling instances of noncompliance through specific enforcement mechanisms. Here, too, cooperation is indispensable. Per Article 163 of the Revised COMESA Treaty, parties are "to foster and maintain an atmosphere ... conducive to peace and security through cooperation and consultations", with the objectives to prevent, better manage, and resolve conflicts within or between members.

The Founding Charter thus views both cooperation and coexistence as "prerequisites to social and economic development and vital to the achievement of regional economic integration";[30] and both notions inform how mem-

30 Revised COMESA Treaty, *supra*, Art.163(1).

ber states regard one another when engaging in different modalities of collaborative action to realize joint goals and to reconcile unilateral interests.

Collaborative state engagement for common interests within the Regional Integration Organization, on the one hand, and mechanisms for conflict management and enforcement, on the other, reflect how the laws of cooperation/co-progressiveness and coexistence/coordination, as theoretical underpinnings for interstate relations, interact with one another, both being consistent with the principle of sovereignty and expressing two sides of Close Basin Cooperation. In this sense, the formalization and institutionalization of regional cooperation are manifestations of state sovereignty being exercised through the pursuit of regional common goals.

To be sure, both cooperation and coexistence are also likely to permeate state interactions under any intergovernmental bodies, more generally. Yet, what characterizes regional integration regimes aligns with how Friedmann views "international law and authority from the standpoint of 'enlightened national interest' [in] ensuring national survival."[31] Cooperation for regional integration is envisioned and legally and institutionally enabled by the Founding Charter to stay in the foreground while coexistence is meant to operate as a backup mechanism to deal with subsisting conflicting interests. This structure ultimately serves the common and self-interest of members in the long-term stability of the regional regime. The focus is on Close Cooperation for joint goals while reaffirming and safeguarding member states' independence and own interests and ensuring the continuity of the cooperation process when disagreements or violations occur.

As explained in the *Terminology* Chapter in the Introduction, *cooperation* is understood here as an umbrella term for specific modalities of close state engagement that may be appropriate to advance the objectives of regimes focused on common interests in relation to specific areas or circumstances. To illustrate, Article 1 of EAC Treaty defines cooperation to encompass coordinated and joint action; and Article 2 of the Revised COMESA Treaty applies the term, somewhat redundantly, to state activities undertaken "in common, jointly or in concert".

The examples that follow illustrate how cooperation modalities under Close Cooperation range from domestic (or national) to collective (or interna-

31 Friedmann, *supra*, p. 48.

tional); coordination to joint or common action; passive to active; *ad hoc* to ongoing; and hybrid.

a) *Domestic* versus *Collective*

Domestic action may qualify as cooperative state engagement within the framework of Close Cooperation when aimed at contributing to regional goals.

Article 5 of the EAC Treaty imposes framework duties that each member must fulfill within its own territory, such as creating favorable conditions for the pursuit of common interests; refraining from acting unilaterally in ways that may hinder said pursuit; and taking the appropriate measures to enact implementing legislation.

National action requirements may also apply to specific cooperation areas. Under Article 51(1) of the AEC Treaty, member states employ and strengthen science and technology, and relevant research institutions, to achieve environmental goals.

Collective: all other modalities of state engagement implying some form or degree of interstate interaction and combined efforts.

Collective is the broadest category of state engagement within Regional Integration Organizations, encompassing all of the subcategories examined next: joint action and coordination, *ad hoc* and ongoing; passive and active; and elements of hybrid.

b) *Joint Action* versus *Coordination*

Joint or Common Action is exemplified by instances where states establish a unified database maintained by the Organization, adopt a joint action plan, or design common projects, programs, and strategies, and may entail member engagement that is:

> *Direct* or *interstate*, i.e., actions under the auspices of, and facilitated by, the Organization, executed jointly by countries. The expression *direct cooperation* appears in Article 6 of the Revised COMESA Treaty.

> *Indirect* or *institutional*, i.e., measures *through* the Regional Integration Organization, taken by its organs in the performance of their functions.

This state-engagement modality prevails over others. In the *joint action* process, member states engage with the institution and interact with one another under or through its organs.

As an example, various Founding Charters foresee the joint handling of budgetary, fundraising and financing matters. Similar requirements in relation to the Basin Body would reflect joint Participation in the use, management, and protection of transboundary waters, under which states must contribute their due share to the advancement of common interests.

***Coordination* Encompasses**

Consultations, e.g., on specific projects or agenda-setting.

Negotiations on joint rulemaking or in the context of dispute settlement, among others.

Exchanges of information, data, knowledge, experiences, etc.

Coordination may serve as a precursor to more a complex regime where Close Cooperation for common interests is at the center of members' intent.

c) *Passive* versus *Active*

Passive, when a state awaits another's request, if and when one arises, to cooperate on a given issue – e.g., under Article 66(4) of the Revised COMESA Treaty, parties must take certain measures in response to requests by other members concerning customs offences, such as producing and sharing evidence.

Active or Positive, when countries take a positive collaborative stance – e.g., Article 6 of the Revised COMESA Treaty and Article 3(f) of the EAC Treaty refer to *active cooperation*, comparable to Participation under international water law.

Not all proactive behavior is necessarily carried out jointly and thus may involve domestic or coordinated behavior; but all joint measures, by their very nature, require some degree of active cooperation.

d) Ad Hoc versus *Ongoing*

Ad hoc cooperation: sporadic contacts on a case-by-case or project-by-project basis – for example, where states interact, prior to and/or during project implementation, to exchange information on potential significant transboundary impacts; and, thereafter, go back to acting mostly unilaterally.

Ongoing: consistent interactions focused on long-term goals, required for safeguarding common interests.

e) **Hybrid:** e.g., the combination of state engagement modalities needed to promote harmonization of laws, policies, programs, or other tools.

Close Cooperation is majorly characterized by joint, ongoing and active state engagement. Joint action is often supplemented by coordination, unilateral and blended measures, and harmonization, as envisioned by the Founding Charter and so, not all state engagement to realize shared priorities is performed through joint action, and specific objectives, principles, commitments, and obligations may entail different state engagement modalities, or a combination thereof.

Some Charter provisions specify the engagement modality required, i.e., unilateral action, coordination, joint action, or a combination thereof; in others, the reference is simply to *cooperation* or *to cooperate*. Article 46(1) of the AEC Treaty mandates countries to cooperate on agriculture, forestry, livestock, and fisheries, including within river and lake basins, and on the protection of plant and animal species. In such cases, Close Regional Cooperation may involve any collaborative measure deemed appropriate to serve or balance the interests in question. Then, under Article 73(1), on health, AEC members "agree to promote *and increase* cooperation among themselves". Here we presume the desire to move from basic towards Close Regional Cooperation in that area.

3.1 *Centrality of Joint Action*

In a regime centered on common interests, all of the above cooperation modalities come under the umbrella of Close Regional Cooperation. Yet, the Charters examined place emphasis on joint action, as the core strategy for treaty implementation and development. In specific provisions, joint action may appear on its own or combined with other modalities of state engagement. The Preamble of the Revised CEN-SAD Treaty, for example, expresses the parties' conviction that common action in complementarity is the best avenue for integration of its member states and peoples.

Specific Commitments or Requirements: The EAC Treaty illustrates both direct and indirect joint action on financing and fundraising. On the former,

Article 87 codifies the partner states' commitment to common action for financing projects in each other's territory and for mobilizing foreign capital for both domestic and joint measures. On the latter, Article 71 empowers the Secretariat to mobilize funds from development partners and other sources and to prepare the EAC budget for Council review.

CEN-SAD's financial regime includes rules and procedures governing the joint formulation, adoption, and execution of its budget; joint design of related regulations; and the Organization's joint financing in the form of the annual contributions made by each party and calculated on the basis of a formula jointly established by the Conference, upon a proposal by the Executive Council. Similarly, under Articles 42 and 166 of the Revised COMESA Treaty, the Council defines annual member contributions based on an agreed-upon formula to jointly maintain the Court of Justice and the Secretariat.

Article 168 of the Revised COMESA Treaty takes the concept of shared institutional funding further when envisioning the establishment of a Common Market levy to generate resources for joint activities. The levy's corresponding source, level, and application conditions are determined by the Council.

Regional Policies and Common Regulations: Joint action may be embedded in provisions foreseeing the design of regional policies across cooperation areas. Articles 3 and 4 of the AU Act, respectively, view the adoption and promotion of common trade policies as an objective, and the development of a common defense policy as a principle. Specifically, Article 6 makes clear that sectoral common policies are needed for the *African Common Market*, such as on quality assurance of goods and services. The 6th Preambular Paragraph and Article 3 of the Revised COMESA Treaty, respectively, refer to common policies on sustainable development and macroeconomics.

On joint regulations or common standards, Article 49(m) of AEC Treaty envisions their adoption in the context of industrial cooperation and integration. Article 4 of the Revised COMESA Treaty refers to common measurements systems that would apply to goods produced and traded within the Common Market. In the social and cultural fields, the EAC Council exercises joint regulatory powers under Article 143(3), to "adopt a social charter, programs and regulations" towards the achievement of related objectives; per Article 170, to issue financial regulations; and, according to Articles 14 and 16, to issue regulations, directives, and decisions that are binding for the persons they address, for member states, and for subsidiary bodies.

Joint Planning and Implementation: The Founding Charters often refer to common strategies, plans, programs, and projects, which are jointly designed and, sometimes, jointly executed, and aim to coordinate and optimize overall treaty implementation. Articles 48 and 49 of the AEC Treaty envision the development of African industrial multinational enterprises and industries through the formulation of regional master plans and through jointly designed and financed projects. Article 80 of the EAC Treaty foresees the development of the *East African Industrial Development Strategy.*

Article 173 of the Revised COMESA Treaty envisions the joint adoption, monitoring, and evaluation of a dedicated implementation plan. To that end, the Secretary-General proposes a draft plan for the Council's consideration, following the applicable guidance; the Secretariat prepares periodical reports on progress; and the *Intergovernmental Committee* advises on transitions between implementation stages and the achievement of the corresponding objectives.

Joint Management of Information, Knowledge, Science and Technology: Article 42 of the AEC Treaty foresees "an intra-community trade information network" connecting relevant national and regional information systems; and, Article 49, "a data and statistical information base to serve industrial development at the regional and continental levels". For COMESA, Article 3 of the Treaty includes among its aims and objectives the "*joint* promotion of research and adaptation of science and technology", as part of efforts to create an enabling environment for investment.

Catchall Provisions: Reinforcing the centrality of joint action, some Charters contain catchall provisions that anticipate the need for Close Regional Cooperation in fields other than those specified therein. Article 4 of the AEC Treaty encourages all activities that members may undertake jointly for realizing common interests. Under Article 77, states may engage, through the Regional Integration Organization, in mutual consultations regarding policy harmonization; and, under Article 131, following interstate consultations through the competent bodies, parties may decide to take in common other cooperation steps they deem appropriate.

Joint Regime Development: More fundamental to the above examples of Close Regional Cooperation is the signing of the Founding Charter itself and, possibly, its later revision; and the adoption of subsequent legal instruments to cover specific cooperation areas and to contemplate, like each Founding Charter, the joint performance of relevant obligations and the shared pursuit of common interests.

For example, deeper cooperation through joint action is seen as having been elevated with the adoption of the Revised COMESA Treaty. Similarly, specific AEC protocols are foreseen, for example, on natural resources, energy, and tourism. Article 90 of the EAC Treaty mandates parties to join and implement relevant treaties in the area of road transport; and Article 151 serves as a catchall provision broadly foreseeing the conclusion of protocols for specific focal areas, with "the objectives and scope of, and institutional mechanisms for, cooperation and integration". On the *Executive Council*'s recommendation, the CEN-SAD *Conference* may adopt protocols as side agreements to the main Treaty, which supplement and clarify its provisions. ASEAN member states have adopted agreements across various cooperation areas, such as disaster management, and the Charter envisions a central role for ASEAN organs in that respect: the *Coordinating Council* administers implementation; the sectoral ministerial bodies are responsible for side agreements within their respective spheres of competence; and the Secretary-General facilitates and monitors progress and reports back to the Summit.

3.2 *Other Modalities of State Engagement*

The above Treaty provisions demonstrate how joint action is prevalent across the Founding Charters examined. As already noted, however, the pursuit of common interests entails other modalities of state engagement as well, either because such other modalities supplement shared efforts or stand as the most appropriate avenue in a particular focal area or circumstance to achieve the goals of the Regional Integration Organization.

Coordination: the AEC Treaty implicitly requires *consultations*, through the Executive Council, on environmental protection, energy, minerals, and water policies; and explicitly mandates direct interstate consultations prior to the election of the Assembly Chairman. Coordination may also take the form of exchanges of information, knowledge, experiences, good practices, technologies, among others.

Under the AEC Treaty, states commit to collecting, disseminating, and exchanging meteorological data on a continental scale, particularly to feed into early warning systems, enable disaster prevention, and ensure navigation safety, including on watercourses. The Treaty also foresees exchanges of information on water resources, a knowhow transfer system, as well as scientific, technical, and economic data-sharing. The EAC Treaty mandates partner states to coordinate with each other through experience and information sharing about the common problems they face on road transport. The Revised COMESA Treaty requires states to share information on changes in customs legislation and policies, including on measures to prevent, investigate and suppress offences. The same Treaty foresees negotiations, another element of coordination, on the possibility of third countries associating with COMESA.

Domestic Action: Close Regional Cooperation depends on *national efforts*, where the obligation aimed at promoting common interests may or can only or be better fulfilled through a parties' action within its territory.

Language on general undertakings, i.e., a broadly formulated duty for each state to perform domestically tasks required to advance common goals, is often included in Charters. Article 5(1) of the Revised COMESA Treaty requires members to "make every effort to plan and direct their development policies" towards enabling effective treaty implementation, while refraining "from any measures likely to jeopardize" said implementation process. Other general commitments under the Treaty include enacting implementing legislation, including the internalization of the decisions adopted by high-level bodies; and supplying relevant information to one another when so required by the Treaty, with copies to be sent to the Secretariat. Another form of domestic undertaking, found in various provisions of the Revised COMESA Treaty, is the requirement for members to accede to relevant international agreements (e.g., on energy), where relevant to advance common objectives.

In terms of specific requirements for domestic action, obligations of EAC members on a topic closely related to communities-of-basin-interests are illustrative. Article 94 of the Treaty governs "common navigable inland waterways". Obligations to be performed by each party in this respect include providing one another space for goods on board vessels on a nondiscriminatory basis; facilitating vessel and equipment deployment for efficient conveyance of all classes of traffic; and supplying vessels with adequate meteorological, communication, and safety equipment.

Hybrid Cooperation: Advancing certain cooperation areas may require a blend of state engagement modalities, albeit still with an emphasis on joint action. This form of state engagement is exemplified by harmonization requirements, which demand a combination of domestic, coordinated, and joint measures. Articles 3 and 4 of the AEC Treaty codify national policy harmonization and programmatic integration across fields as a principle and an objective. Under these umbrella provisions, member states have agreed to aligning their policies, programs, and/or regulations on agricultural development; environmental protection; industrialization; and air, maritime and inland water transport, among others.

Within COMESA, Article 71(2) of the Revised Treaty unpacks the harmonization process by calling for the "simplification, harmonization and standardization of customs regulations, documents and procedures and their computerization". The *Regional Automated System for Customs Data Centre* at the COMESA Headquarters – itself, a joint facility – is meant to aid cooperation in this regard. Within the East Africa Community, Article 80 of the EAC Treaty mandates parties to harmonize and rationalize incentives, in order to promote the EAC as a single investment area.

Hybrid cooperation also exists when a Founding Charter calls for various cooperation modalities in relation to a given sector. Article 51 of the AEC Treaty requires states generally to "cooperate in the development, acquisition and dissemination of appropriate technologies". Articles 49, 51 and 52 specify the scope of cooperation on the topic. *Domestically*, each member must adjust its relevant training programs to the African context. *Harmonization* commitments apply to domestic regulations on industrial property and technology transfer. Per Article 51(2)(b), countries are expected to "*coordinate* their programs in applied research, research for development, and scientific and technological services". *Exchange requirements* apply to relevant information and documentation, and experience on industrial technology; and exchanges between researchers and specialists of the different members are envisioned. Finally, states undertake to *act jointly* in establishing and maintaining databanks, training programs, scientific research and technological development.

The same is true with the way the AEC Treaty deals with energy resources. Article 54(2)(a) and (c) requires each member within its territory to ensure the effective development of energy resources, including by promoting new and renewable energy. States agree to harmonize national energy development plans, to establish a mechanism enabling concerted and coordinated action towards improving energy access, and to design jointly a common energy policy. Under Article 58 (1), states also "undertake to promote a healthy environment"; and, to that end, to "adopt national, regional and continental policies, strategies and programs and establish appropriate institutions".

On freshwater, Article 109 of the EAC Treaty envisions "concerted efforts to expand agricultural land through irrigation and water catchment strategies". Mandated cooperative steps extend to joint irrigation programs and the protection of traditional irrigation systems. At the same time, each state must improve catchment management, rainwater harvesting, environmentally safe land use methods, and aquaculture and fish farming.

Under the EAC Treaty, moreover, Articles 89 *et seq.* establish a series of policies on transport infrastructure, both generally applicable and sector-specific, and which entail joint use of training facilities, programs and institutions; harmonization of laws, regulations, practices, standards; and information exchange on technological developments. At the domestic level, countries undertake to build, maintain, integrate, upgrade, rehabilitate and redesign infrastructure, as appropriate; and to issue regulations for transport systems' responsiveness to regional interests in terms of efficiency, competitiveness, cost-effectiveness, security, and protection. On inland navigation, specifically, EAC members must harmonize relevant national policies, rules, regulations, administrative procedures, and tariff structures; coordinate safety measures; and integrate efforts to control and eradicate aquatic invasive species.

Reinforced by the foregoing obligations, joint action commitments in the context of inland water transport are otherwise predominant in the EAC Treaty, and may involve, *inter alia* and as appropriate, joint use of maintenance facilities; common rules for packaging, marking and loading procedures; joint ventures, including joint shipping services; joint search and rescue operations; joint studies on the use and management of inland waterways; regional training and research facilities; joint surveying and mapping, and development of navigational charts; and joint action on water pollution. In relation to the installation and maintenance of cargo handling equipment and storage facilities, domestic action is envisioned, but preference is given to joint action.

3.3 *Norms for Coexistence among Member States*

The law of coexistence and correlated norms also inform cooperation within Regional Integration Organizations and are consistent with Close Regional Cooperation, thus influencing Charter provisions and state engagement modalities. As Vöneky explains, "the underlying rationale of some rules is to solve conflicting interests; in other cases, it may be the promotion of a certain common good or common concern".[32]

As captured in the Friendly Relations Declaration,[33] the law of coexistence can be seen in general statements regarding ideals, principles, objectives, and legal concepts, as well as in the rules on dispute settlement and enforcement mechanisms, supplementing duties and commitments focused on common interests.

---

32 Vöneky, *supra*, p. 6.

33 *See* P.M. Dupuy, *International Law as a Common Heritage of Mankind* (21 Mar 2025), EJIL: Talk!, Blog of the European Journal of International Law, at https://www.ejiltalk.org/international-law-as-a-common-heritage-of-mankind/?utm_source=mailpoet&utm_medium=email&utm_campaign=ejil-talk-newsletter-post-title_2.

General Statements: Preambular references to sovereignty invoke coexistence and remind us that, when states join together to formalize a legal-institutional regime, they remain sovereign entities. When interests diverge within a Regional Integration Organization, member states resort to the law of coexistence to safeguard the integrity of the regime. The establishment of a treaty-based organization is an exercise in sovereignty motivated by common interests that, pragmatically, demand states to reach beyond coexistence towards more cooperation. Hence, coexistence and cooperation simultaneously characterize interactions among member states within a Regional Integration Organization.

In the AU Act, the Preamble and Article 3 place side by side implicit references to coexistence (*sovereignty, territorial integrity, nonintervention, sovereign equality, political independence*) and to cooperation (*interdependence, African unity, collective action*). The revised treaties of COMESA and CEN-SAD reproduce this pattern. The AU Act also affirms *regional peace, security, and stability* as members' rights and as preconditions for continental development and integration; and the Revised COMESA Treaty mentions those three terms as objectives contingent upon respect for nonaggression and good neighborliness. The AU, COMESA and CEN-SAD Treaties all codify the principle of peaceful dispute settlement.

As an exceptionally progressive provision, Article 4(h) of the AU Act empowers the organization "to intervene in a member state … in respect of grave circumstances" for restoring peace and stability. Here, the law of coexistence comes under the umbrella of institutionalized Close Regional Cooperation, since only the AU, at its highest level, may yield this power, never the member states individually.

In Asia, the Preamble and Article II of the SAARC Charter link strict adherence to coexistence principles, including peaceful dispute settlement, as well as the pursuit of regional peace and stability and regional amity and progress. A connection is also made between coexistence and mutually beneficial cooperation under the Association's umbrella. The principles of independence, sovereignty, equality, territorial integrity, national identity, and non-interference appear in Article 2 of the ASEAN Charter.

Dispute Settlement and Compliance: Cooperation for coexistence is embedded in well-developed conflict resolution systems for disagreements about the interpretation and application of Founding Charters and derivative instruments, as well as in mandates and mechanisms to handle noncompliance.

Provisions on dispute settlement tend to emphasize direct negotiations, but then also offer a variety of mechanisms for dealing with disagreements.

There is arguably an implicit recognition here that negotiations may not always succeed, while tensions linger, thereby threatening the integrity of the regime. This approach aligns with common ideals of nonconfrontation and friendly relations, while reinforcing a sense of community. On compliance, dedicated courts or other bodies under the Organization may be empowered to consider disputes and alleged treaty violations, advise members on the matter, and apply sanctions on nonconforming states.

Articles 22 and 23 of the ASEAN Charter promote peaceful and timely dispute resolution through dialogue, consultations, and negotiations; as well as, when so agreed between the members concerned, through resort to time-bound conciliation, mediation, or the good offices of the Chairman or the Secretary-General. Tailored conflict resolution rules and procedures may be established for specific cooperation areas. Disputes that remain unresolved after application of Chapter VIII-mechanisms shall be referred to the Summit for a decision. The Summit is also competent to decide on cases referred thereto by a member affected by another's noncompliance.

In the MERCOSUL, Article 4 of the Olivos Protocol requires states to start with negotiations, which, per Article 5(1), shall not exceed 15 days. Unless states agree otherwise, either party may resort to the options foreseen in subsequent provisions. These include a joint submission to the Common Market Group for consideration and recommendations. Alternatively, an *Ad Hoc* Arbitral Tribunal may be constituted and, to challenge the latter's award, a recourse may be presented before the Permanent Revision Tribunal. Under Article 33, parties recognize *a priori* the jurisdiction of those tribunals, thus without the need for special agreements.[34]

A dedicated Court is an avenue chosen by the AU. Article 18 of the Act foresees the establishment of a court of justice, as part of the Organization's institutional architecture, with its statute, composition and functions having been outlined in a specific protocol.[35] The Court may consider cases submitted not only by state parties to the Protocol, but also by AU organs and third parties. Cases may relate to the interpretation of the Act and other AU instruments; any international law questions; acts adopted by AU organs; facts associated with a potential breach; nature and extent of reparations; or other matters as provided for by an Assembly decision or other agreements.[36]

---

34 *Protocol for the Resolution of Controversies in the MERCOSUL*, Argentina-Brazil-Paraguay-Uruguay (Olivos, 18 Feb 2002) ('Olivos Protocol').

35 AU Assembly, 2nd Ordinary Session, *Protocol of the Court of Justice of the African Union* (Maputo, 11 July 2003).

36 *Id*, Arts.18–19.

In the case of COMESA, the Court serves as a fallback mechanism for unresolved interstate disputes and noncompliant behavior. The Treaty contains provisions to ensure the aptitude, impartiality, and independence of persons composing the Court; the effectiveness of Court procedures and judgements; and clarity about the relationship between the Court and national judicial systems. The Court's core mandate is to support treaty interpretation and application in accordance with the relevant law. To that end, the Authority, the Council and member states may request from the Court advisory opinions on questions of law. Members may submit to the Court the disputes between them pursuant to a special agreement; directly refer to the Court suspected instances of unlawful actions or omissions; and approach the Court to determine the legality of Council actions. The Secretary-General, if specified prerequisites are met, may refer to the Court cases of noncompliance.

The Revised CEN-SAD Treaty does not create a dedicated judicial body but determines that all disputes not resolved amicably are to be submitted to the Conference for consideration, thus placing the Regional Integration Organization at the center of conflict resolution and the maintenance of peaceful relations.

The ASEAN Charter foresees alternatives even outside the Regime. Parties may resort to other international legal instruments binding upon them; and, for disagreements unrelated to ASEAN, they must turn to the mechanisms under the *Treaty of Amity and Cooperation in Southeast Asia*.[37]

On sanctions, Article 23 of the AU Act governs their application on member states that default on the payment of contributions to the African Union budget, or which become noncompliant in relation to AU decisions and policies. In the first case, sanctions may affect the rights of members to speak and to vote at meetings; to present candidates for AU staff positions; or to enjoy other benefits linked to Union activities or commitments. In the latter situation, on top of those sanctions already stated, the AU Assembly may impose the denial of transport and communications links and other political or economic measures.

The COMESA Authority may sanction noncompliance, generally, but also behavior detrimental to regional objectives or to the Common Market's existence, by suspending membership or related rights and privileges, imposing financial penalties, or determining a member's expulsion. In line with the general prevalence of the law of cooperation, an expelled member may apply for readmission.

---

37 *Treaty of Amity and Cooperation in Southeast Asia* (Denpasar, 24 Feb 1976).

Under the Revised CEN-SAD Treaty, the highest body is competent to discuss serious treaty breaches and decide on an appropriate course of action. The suspension of membership rights is foreseen specifically for states that fall considerably behind in the payment of required budget contributions.

Article 27 of the ASEAN Charter establishes a connection between dispute settlement and enforcement. The provision mandates the Secretary-General to monitor compliance with findings, recommendations or decisions that emerge from dispute resolution proceedings and to report back to the Summit.

4 External Relations of the Regional Integration Organization

> *In its relations with the wider world, the Union shall ... contribute to peace, security, the sustainable development of the Earth, solidarity and mutual respect among peoples, free and fair trade, eradication of poverty and the protection of human rights, ... as well as to the strict observance and the development of international law, including respect for the principles of the [UN] Charter.*[38]

Coherence and *Cohesion* inform the relations of Regional Integration Organizations with "the rest of the world",[39] i.e., subregional and continental entities, other regional bodies, the family of nations as a whole, and third states.

4.1 *Coherence*

This book coins the term *Coherence* building on the ICJ advisory opinion that describes interactions among the various international organizations, across levels and topics, which make up the international cooperation system. According to the Court, the UN Charter sets out "the basis of a 'system' designed to organize international cooperation in a *coherent* fashion by bringing the [*UN*], invested with powers of *general scope*, into relationship with various autonomous and *complementary organizations*, invested with sectorial powers".[40]

---

38 EU Treaty, *supra*, Art.3(5).

39 Expression used in the Revised COMESA Treaty, *supra*, Art.3(e).

40 ICJ, *Legality of the Use by a State of Nuclear Weapons in Armed Conflict*, Advisory Opinion of 8 July 1996, ICJ Reports 66 (1996) ('Nuclear Weapons Use in Armed Conflict AO'), p. 80 (emphasis added).

Coherence finds inspiration in the "sense of universal responsibility",[41] as proclaimed in the Preamble of the Earth Charter, based on the multilevel environmental, social, cultural, economic, and other interdependencies that interconnect all beings across all nations; local communities and ecosystems back to our planetary home; and all cooperation regimes to the entire international community.

In this sense, Coherence means a general commitment to consistency on the part of countries belonging to a Regional Integration Organization – consistency with broader international legal obligations and with the common interests protected by the regime when member states enter into relations with each other on matters falling outside the main regime; when members or the Organization interact with external bodies or with non-members; and when a member state is also a member of another regional organization, whether focused or not on geographic integration.

Article 93(1) of the AEC Treaty, for example, allows parties to engage with other AU members, third countries or any international, regional, or subregional organization by entering into side agreements on economic, technical, or cultural matters, as long as such agreements are not incompatible with the AEC legal regime. Per Article II of the Charter, SAARC cooperation does not replace but rather supplements other bilateral and multilateral cooperation; and must be consistent with other international obligations.

Vertical Coherence: Coherence may be vertical or horizontal. *Vertical Coherence* describes nested relations, i.e., relations between organizations at different governance levels – for example, the EAC in relation to the AU and any Regional Integration Organization vis-à-vis the UN. Vertically coherent organizations exist at the universal, continental, interregional, regional, and subregional levels, whether multi- or bilateral; and are mutually reinforcing and generally aligned around basic principles, broad objectives, and wide-ranging shared aspirations.

Upward Vertical Coherence applies in relations between a Regional Integration Organization and other bodies constituted at continental or global levels and to which members of the Regional Organization in question also belong.

At a universal level, Upward Vertical Coherence is reflected in Articles 52(1) and 103 of the UN Charter, per which member states may enter into regional agreements to handle international peace and security matters, as may be appropriate for action at those levels. Yet, action under those agreements

41 Earth Charter, *supra*, p. 7.

must be consistent with Charter principles and purposes and, in case of conflicts, the Charter prevails. We see security matters in the above provisions as being broadly defined to encompass human and environmental security and sustainable development. In this sense, Paragraph 35 of Agenda 2030 recognizes: "Sustainable development cannot be realized without peace and security; and peace and security will be at risk without sustainable development". Following this expansive understanding of security means that there is a wide set of common interests around which a Regional Integration Organization may be formed under the Charter's umbrella.

In Africa, the AU regime has served as a Pan-African institutional umbrella, within which are nested *regional economic communities* (RECs): smaller regional, interregional, and subregional intergovernmental institutions formalized and progressively developed to advance African continental and regional interests. To that end, Article 88 of the AEC Treaty envisions multi-level coordination and harmonization between the activities of Subregional Integration Organizations and the goals of the RECs under which each one sits; as well as between the activities of RECs and the development of the AEC – all to rationalize regional-level integration towards continental unity.

Within the framework of Upward Vertical Coherence, Regional Integration Organizations and their members remain committed to, and participate in, cooperation processes at higher levels. In this sense, Article 3 of the AU Act is about enabling Africa "to play its rightful role in the global economy and in international negotiations"; and Article 92(2) of the AEC Treaty emphasizes cooperative relations with the UN system.

In turn, Article 178 of the Revised COMESA Treaty codifies the Organization's objective to contribute to the implementation of the AEC Treaty and, ultimately, to become an organic entity of that economic Community; and Article 180(3) requires constant engagement with the UN, the AU, and other African organizations, like the UN *Economic Commission for Africa* (UNECA) and the *African Development Bank* (AfDB), as appropriate to support treaty implementation. The Preamble of the Revised CEN-SAD Treaty reaffirms its parties' commitment to UN ideals, principles, and goals; recalls the AU Act and refers back to the development of the AEC as a continental goal; and notes that regional cooperation efforts must neither hinder nor contradict similar endeavors aimed at Pan-African economic integration.

Downward Vertical Coherence applies in relations between a Regional Integration Organization and the sub-regional, basin or sub-basin organizations operating thereunder. As such, Coherence has a role to play in Community-of-Interests.

Horizonal Coherence: This form of Coherence applies generally to relations of Regional Integration Organizations and of their members with other regional organizations or with third countries.

Horizontally coherent organizations target the same, similar, or related common-interest areas, such as trade and/or the environment, and they collaborate with, and exist in parallel to, one another. These organizations may or may not operate under a common continental umbrella yet remain committed, in their mutual relations, to overarching global goals and aspirations.

COMESA pays special attention to cooperation with other RECs. COMESA must work closely and may enter into partnership agreements towards meeting shared objectives with the other organizations in Eastern and Southern Africa that also sit under the AU. Ensuring horizontal Coherence falls upon the COMESA Secretary-General. Article I of the SAARC Charter addresses institutional relations more generally. The provision proclaims that cooperating with regional organizations having "similar aims and purposes" and "with other developing countries" are objectives of the Association.

Coherence also applies to the agreements member states of Regional Integration Organizations may negotiate with third countries. Article 56(2) of the Revised COMESA Treaty requires members to ensure that trade agreements with third countries "do not impede or frustrate [Common Market] objectives".

A concrete example of where horizontal Coherence would apply to treaty negotiations is the future EU-MERCOSUR Partnership Agreement.[42]

4.2 *Cohesion*

Cohesion describes how Regional Integration Organizations organize themselves internally when interfacing with the rest of the world. Cohesion may be *outward* or *inward*.

The term is used in the respective Preambles of two Founding Charters. The EU Treaty references the goal of "reinforced cohesion", whereas the AU Act mentions Cohesion as an ideal underlying the Organization and which guided its founding fathers. The AU Act does not define the term. In the European Union context, Article 174 of the EU Functioning Treaty refers to "economic, social and territorial cohesion", linked to the goal of reducing regional development disparities, as a necessary basis for "overall harmonious development". Herein, we employ Solidarity to express the meaning given to the

42 European Commission, *EU-MERCOSUR Agreement*, at https://policy.trade.ec.europa.eu/eu-trade-relationships-country-and-region/countries-and-regions/mercosur/eu-mercosur-agreement_en.

term *cohesion* in the EU and employ Cohesion in a different sense than that used in the EU Functioning Treaty.

Outwardly, Regional Integration Organizations adopt common positions in the context of international negotiations with external actors. As appropriate for the common interest at stake, outward Cohesion gains different expressions, e.g., the establishment of a common external tariff.

Outward Cohesion is captured in Article 3(d) of the AU Act as an *objective*: to "promote and defend African common positions on issues of interest to the continent and its peoples". That is to say, the African Union positions itself and acts as a cohesive bloc in relation to the rest of the world. Under Article 1 of its Charter, similarly, SAARC intends to strengthen collaboration among members when negotiating with external actors on shared-interest matters.

As a general *commitment*, Outward Cohesion is reflected in CEN-SAD member states' undertaking to harmonize positions on major issues pertaining to priority cooperation areas.

Outward cohesion may also appear as a binding requirement. Under Articles 42 and 94 of the AEC Treaty and Article 3 of the Revised COMESA Treaty, member states must engage as a group and develop and endorse common positions in international forums or in relation to third states, with a view to promoting and safeguarding African interests. To those ends, the AEC prepares studies and reports that may support members in the harmonization of their positions; and the COMESA Secretary-General promotes the adoption of joint positions in multilateral negotiations with third countries or international organizations. Specifically, COMESA members support each other in engaging with the *World Meteorological Organization* (WMO); and they adopt common positions against illegal dumping of toxic waste by third countries.

When reaching agreement on common positions is not mandatory, in general or in certain cooperation areas, Outward Cohesion may entail more basic requirements of interstate coordination. This is the case on science and technology, under Article 51 of the AEC Treaty, requiring that states at least coordinate their positions.

Inwardly, Cohesion is linked to ideals of mutual support in instances where regional and national interests must be safeguarded or when collective action is triggered to protect individual members from external pressures.

Article 46(2)(f) of the AEC Treaty underscores "the protection of regional and continental markets primarily for the benefit of African agricultural products". In the field of navigation, Article 88(q) codifies a general commitment of parties to favor the vessels of member states in the provision of cargo and for berthing and other port services and facilities.

With respect to outside economic threats, Article 54(2) of the Revised COMESA Treaty governs the "dumping or export of subsidized goods by a third country to the territory of a member state that threatens or distorts competition", in which case a request for the imposition of antidumping or countervailing duties can be made.

In the field of collective security, Article 2(c) of the AU *Non-Aggression and Common Defense Pact* considers any aggression against one of the members to be an aggression against them all; and, under Article 4(a)–(b), parties undertake to provide mutual assistance towards common defense and security and to respond in the case of aggression or threat of aggression against any member.[43] In turn, the parties to the EU Treaty aim to implement a common foreign and security policy, including the progressive framing of a common defense policy.

5 Relations among Members States

There are three elements that characterize the *relations among member states* within Regional Integration Organizations:

a) **Unity**, a term employed here based on language found in the AU Treaty.
b) **Solidarity**, a term extracted directly from treaty language, and which appears in different forms in the Founding Charters, implicitly or explicitly, with or without qualifiers; may be thoroughly regulated and/or extensively promoted; may underlie individual commitments and/or obligations, when implicit in specific provisions; and is more developed in Africa than in Asia and in regional integration than under Community-of-Interests.
c) **Nondiscrimination**, a principle well-known in the rules governing trade relations, as well as transboundary basins, albeit with different consequences in each field.

5.1 *Unity*

Unity informs how states strive "to promote joint development in all fields of economic activity".[44] Unity translates into two objectives, which are affirmed

43 AU *Non-Aggression and Common Defense Pact* (AU Assembly, 4th Ordinary Session, Abuja, 31 Jan 2005).

44 Revised COMESA Treaty, *supra*, Article 3(b).

in, and governed by, different kinds of treaty provisions, whether implicitly or explicitly, as follows: *self-reliance* or *self-sufficiency* and *efficient intracommunity movement.*

The AU Act invokes the ideal and objective of Unity among African countries and peoples as an enabler of development, security, and sustainability. Within the AU, Unity is meant to be realized fundamentally through specialization and complementarity – expressions of self-reliance, as well as through improved continental transportation and strengthened communication links, in support of efficient intracommunity movement.

Self-Reliance: The AEC Treaty underscores self-reliance at the regional and national levels, across thematic fields (e.g., industry, agriculture), and for local capacity needs (e.g., human, technological, industrial). Self-reliance within the AEC implies endogenous self-sustained development through integration of African economies; a continent-wide framework to develop, mobilize, utilize, and prioritize African human and material resources and capacities; joint investments in the production and trade of key products and inputs; a strengthened industrial and intracommunity trade base and modernized priority sectors; sale and consumption of regionally manufactured strategic industrial products; and regional industries and industrial specialization for enhanced complementarity among African economies.

For COMESA, *collective self-reliance* is codified as a principle and its normative content is refined within specific cooperation areas. Regional food sufficiency, for example, entails food security; rational production across COMESA; complementarity and specialization of national programs considering individual comparative advantages; a common agricultural policy; and resort to, and coordination between, national research and training institutions. Other aspects of COMESA self-sufficiency involve prioritizing local materials and resources, national consultancy services, and African institutions; pooling resources in cross-border investments; boosting local production in priority sectors; and encouraging conventional low and indigenous technologies. Within CEN-SAD, specific priorities under the umbrella of sustainable development include food security and self-sufficiency.[45] The EAC Treaty captures self-reliance in the context of industrial and agricultural cooperation. The 5th Preambular Paragraph of the SAARC Charter expresses the value of cross-sectoral and multidimensional cooperation to achieve the objective of national and collective self-reliance.

45 Government of Senegal, *supra*, p. 3.

To the extent that achieving self-reliance may require prioritization of internal resources and capacities, a form of Inward Cohesion becomes a precondition for realizing Unity. For example, in Article 51, the AEC Treaty first refers to *individual and collective technological self-reliance* and then requires members to place special emphasis on local technologies. In other words, whereas prioritizing local technologies appears to invoke Cohesion, in this instance, the ultimate goal is self-reliance, which goes beyond the protection of internal products, sectors, markets, and capacities.

Efficient Intracommunity Movement and Communication: This objective includes positive cooperation to gradually remove physical and nonphysical barriers to circulation. This includes facilitating, improving, expanding, harmonizing, complementing, and integrating internal circulation policies, channels, means, and infrastructure, with a view to promoting Unity. Actions in this respect are multidimensional, as they extend to persons, authorities, labor, goods, services, capital, information, and technology.

The AEC Treaty views efficient intracommunity movement as necessary to consolidate and strengthen the African Common Market. Article 61(1) formulates the goal of "harmonious and integrated development of the continental transport and communications network", including through interstate infrastructure integration, regional and continental transport services, and policy coordination and harmonization, as well as cooperation among the competent national authorities. Within CEN-SAD, objectives include removing restrictions that hinder regional integration and free movement.

The Revised COMESA Treaty captures efficient movement through policy coordination and complementarity and calls for specific measures across the areas of transport and communication, monetary affairs and finance, tourism and industry, and economic and social development – e.g., mutual allocation of storage space in one another's facilities; improved and expanded interstate infrastructure; upgraded communications and meteorological facilities; direct telecommunications, radio, and television links; interconnected national electricity grids; free movement for scientists and tourists, and of services and capital; and rights of establishment and rights of residence.

Article 89 of the EAC Treaty calls on partner states to evolve transport and communications policies that are coordinated, harmonized and complementary; and to develop, improve and expand relevant linkages among them – the ultimate goal being to deepen physical integration through, e.g., common design standards; coordination of projects to construct, maintain, rehabilitate, upgrade and rebuild relevant networks; facilitated border-crossing; and electrical grid and other infrastructural interconnections.

Article 1 of the Treaty of Asuncion links the common market to free movement of goods, services and production factors and includes transport and communications among the areas targeted for coordination of macroeconomic and sectoral policies.

5.2 *Solidarity*

Solidarity in Founding Charters may be referenced as an ideal, principle and/or an objective, and in their preambles and/or operative paragraphs. Other than the EAC and SAARC Treaties, all other Charters examined mention Solidarity at least once in their respective texts.

In addition, Solidarity is embedded in provisions on balanced development and special treatment through dedicated programs, projects, and funds. Also employed may be new investments and introduction of tailored technologies for relevant members and indigenous entrepreneurs to improve and diversify economies, capacities, production, and marketing. Other strategies may include development of infrastructure and interstate connectivity and promotion of the water, energy, agricultural, transport, communications, and service sectors.

General Statements: In the AU Act, the Preamble calls for Solidarity among states as a basic guiding ideal; and, in Article 3, as an objective. The Act calls for Solidarity among states, among the peoples of Africa, and on shared environmental challenges. The AEC Treaty mentions Solidarity as a principle, to which parties adhere in pursuing common objectives, and so do the Revised COMESA Treaty in Article 6(b) and the Revised CEN-SAD Treaty in Article 4.

The AEC and EAC Treaties incorporate the objective of attaining a balanced and harmonious development. In this respect, the AEC Treaty emphasizes the *equitable and just distribution of cooperation benefits*, which Article 1, combined with Article 7, define as the "fair and proportionate distribution of benefits" "accruing or to be derived from [Community] operations".

Both the Bangkok Declaration and the ASEAN Charter contain Preambular references to "bonds of regional solidarity" among members as foundations for the Regional Integration Organization and its progressive development. The SAARC Charter alludes to Solidarity when underscoring, in its 2nd Preambular Paragraph, the importance of "mutual understanding" in the context of increasing interdependence and for the achievement of development, peace, and security goals; and when formulating the objectives of mutual trust and "appreciation of one another's problems".

Cooperation Areas: Solidarity may underpin all or specific areas of cooperation. In the case of CEN-SAD, members are to cooperate on the basis of Solidarity across all pertinent domains, while refraining from taking measures that may hinder the achievement of regional objectives.

Under the Revised COMESA Treaty, special assistance for the least developed member states is foreseen in the service, infrastructure, energy and agricultural sectors, as well as in other appropriate areas the Council may identify.

Dedicated Financial Assistance and Differential Treatment: The AU Act establishes the *Solidarity, Development and Compensation Fund* to aid vulnerable members; and, the Revised COMESA Treaty, the *Fund for Cooperation, Compensation and Development*.

Under the AU Act and the EAC and Revised COMESA Treaties, moreover, provisions that invoke Solidarity include those aimed at supporting member states facing difficulties and potential economic imbalances arising from the implementation of integration requirements. The AU Act and the Revised COMESA Treaty also extend compliance exemptions and other special treatment and assistance to those members generally most in need or to other parties affected by extraordinarily challenging circumstances. Also targeted are economically weaker countries and depressed or underdeveloped areas. Competent authorities within COMESA are responsible for making recommendations in this regard and designating countries and regions to receive support.

In the AEC Treaty, Article 4 governs special treatment for least developed states; the adoption of tailored measures in favor of landlocked, semi-landlocked and island countries; and other appropriate assistance for those members to face economic and social difficulties, including through the AEC Fund. In addition, Article 171 exempts from the application of sanctions those members falling behind on budget contributions due to "public or natural calamity or exceptional circumstance that gravely affects [their] economy".

Mutual Assistance: Solidarity underlies mutual-assistance requirements. Article 5 of the CEN-SAD Treaty stipulates a general obligation for states to assist one another, when necessary, in a "spirit of solidarity and fraternity". Article 43 of the AEC Treaty mandates that food security policies be harmonized to enable the mutual provision of aid in scenarios of serious shortage. The SAARC Charter calls for mutual assistance across cooperation fields.

In the EU Functioning Treaty, the so-called *Solidarity Clause* commits the Union and member states to acting jointly if a party suffers a terrorist attack or a natural or man-made disaster. In such instances, the Union mobilizes all the instruments at its disposal to lend assistance, including the military resources made available by members, at the request of the state suffering the event.

5.3 *Nondiscrimination*

Nondiscrimination among member states within Regional Integration Organizations plays its most important role in the field of trade, along with supportive requirements in transport towards free and efficient circulation.

Within the AEC and COMESA, nondiscrimination is expressed in the norms of *most favored nation* and *national treatment* under international trade law, as applied to domestic legislation and administrative measures, and to preferential agreements with third countries. In the Revised COMESA Treaty, measures to protect human life, health, and the environment, or to address economic imbalances and other negative impacts from trade liberalization or treaty implementation, must be applied on a nondiscriminatory basis. In respect of railway, maritime, inland water, and air transport, members agree to charge one another nondiscriminatory tariffs and apply *inter se* uniform rules and regulations. The nondiscrimination principle encompasses persons, mail, and merchandise circulating within the Common Market. Applying the principle of nondiscrimination to a specific stakeholder group, the Treaty requires members to eliminate legislation and customs that discriminate against women with respect to land ownership rights and to access to credit.

6 Relations with Stakeholders: Social Engagement

> *The subjects of law in any legal system are not necessarily identical in their nature or in the extent of their rights, and their nature depends upon the needs of the community. ... [T]he progressive increase in the collective activities of states has already given rise to instances of action upon the international plane by certain entities which are not states.*[46]

The law of co-progressiveness is reflected in Charter provisions that show attention to human flourishing and aim to protect, integrate, and interconnect stakeholders and their interests into the Regional Integration Organization's activities, planning, and priority-setting, and into treaty implementation. We refer here to this characteristic of Close Regional Cooperation as *Social*

46 ICJ, *Reparation for Injuries Suffered in the Service of the United Nations*, Advisory Opinion (1949), p. 174, 178.

Engagement, expressed in the Founding Charters in three complementary ways:

a) **Abstract statements of intent, objectives and/or guiding principles** relating to people-centered cooperation; shared ties and interests among the peoples of the partner states; human rights and fundamental freedoms; stakeholder engagement and partnerships; improved living standards and socioeconomic justice; good governance and democratic principles (accountability, transparency, participation); and sustainable development and the connected concept of present and future generations.
b) **Substantive provisions** enabling Social Engagement, including by targeting specific groups (e.g., women, youth, private sector), and outlining required or encouraged measures in that regard.
c) **Institutional architecture**, through dedicated bodies, including the granting of standing rights for nonstate actors to appear before regional judicial organs.

Statements, Objectives, and Principles: The AU Act emphasizes Solidarity among members and among the peoples of Africa and calls for a partnership between governments and civil society. The Act also codifies and expresses the parties' commitment to good governance and the rule of law, to the promotion and protection of human rights, and to the consolidation of democratic institutions and cultures as objectives of, and principles for, regional integration. Human rights come associated with international and regional law, invoking Africa's own relevant legal instruments and institutions protecting individual rights. Social Engagement appears as an objective in Article 3, alongside cooperation to improve African living standards; and as a principle in Article 4.

In the AEC Treaty, the Preamble recalls how the future of African peoples is endangered by thwarted continental development; and Article 3(h) names, among others, *accountability*, *economic justice*, and *public participation* as principles. In the case of COMESA, the Treaty affirms liberty and fundamental freedoms; human rights' recognition, promotion, and protection; and democratic governance. The Revised CEN-SAD Treaty, *inter alia*, recalls various international and African human rights treaties; and stipulates the wellbeing of the region's populations as the objective to be pursued through the joint development of human and natural resources.

The EAC Treaty highlights transparency, social justice, equal opportunities, and human and peoples' rights protection as guiding principles; consolidation of partnerships with, and a leading role for, the private sector and civil society in development; stakeholder entrepreneurship and engagement across sectors and levels; people-centered development through close cooperation, better understanding, and consolidated political, economic, social, cultural and traditional ties, as well as shared interests, among national populations; gender equality and mainstreaming, and the enhancement of women's participation in cultural, social, political, economic, and technological development; and the granting of observer status to third states and intergovernmental and civil society organizations.

Liberty, democracy, respect for human rights and fundamental freedoms, and the rule of law are also captured in the Preamble of the EU Treaty. The EU Treaty also refers to Solidarity and ever closer union among the parties' peoples. Moreover, the EU Treaty emphasizes economic and social progress and the principle of subsidiarity, under which decisions are taken as closely as possible to citizens. Going beyond other regional integration regimes, the Treaty foresees the establishment of a citizenship common to nationals of their countries.

The Preamble of the SAARC Charter includes three references to the region's peoples: as regards their "common problems, interests and aspirations"; benefits from regional cooperation; and contacts and exchanges to further mutual friendship and understanding. The objectives of SAARC include improving peoples' life quality; promoting sociocultural development; and providing all individuals with opportunities for self-fulfillment. The Charter also centers the community-building process on peoples and their wellbeing, livelihoods, and welfare; and highlights mutual interests and interdependence among member states *and* their peoples.

In the case of ASEAN, Article 1(13) calls upon the Association to be people-oriented, so that "all sectors of society are encouraged to participate in, and benefit from, the [cooperation] process". Article 35 refers to ASEAN's pivotal role in the promotion of "a sense of belonging among its peoples" and to "shared destiny, goals and values". Public empowerment through collaborative human resources development, equitable access to opportunities, and a safe environment for the region's populations are among ASEAN's purposes.

In South America, the Treaty of Asuncion interlinks objectives around scientific and technological development and improved living conditions for the parties' populations.

Social Engagement is also captured in commitments and requirements linked to sustainability and intergenerational equity. The EAC regime endorses and promotes sustainable development and sustainable utilization – expressions respectively defined by Article 1(2) as follows: "development that meets the needs of the present generation without compromising the ability of future generations to meet their own needs"; and "use of resources by present generations, which does not impair the right of future generations to use the same to meet their needs". In the same vein, the SAARC Charter refers to sustainable development for present and future generations.

Intergeneration equity, as a dimension of sustainable development, is also underpinned by Solidarity. The Pact for the Future includes a *Declaration on Future Generations*, which references *intergenerational Solidarity* as a guiding principle.[47]

Substantive Obligations: Founding Charters may also outline substantive provisions, with concrete obligations and commitments, and formulated in response to previously stated general considerations and/or aiming to realize agreed principles and objectives.

In terms of measures to enable Social Engagement, the Preamble of the AEC Treaty refers to a "duty to develop and utilize [Africa's] human and natural resources … for [its peoples'] general wellbeing". The Treaty also envisions bridges among the region's trading organizations through contacts and exchanges of information flows; formulates obligations on scientific and technological capabilities and on the development of African tourism consistent with the protection of the human and natural environment; addresses directly relevant actors in provisions on education, human resources, culture, and social affairs; and requires consideration of gender balance in AEC staff appointment and in its organs' composition.

On social and cultural matters, the Revised COMESA Treaty calls for cooperation on the working environment, e.g., on accident and disease prevention, and labor laws, like on collective bargaining rights; concerted measures to develop human resources and better employ technical knowhow and institutional capabilities, for example, through a regional roster and dedicated plan on knowledge, skills, technological inventiveness, and entrepreneurial abilities, as well as through incentivized technical and student exchange programs; and use of, and support for, national expertise and capabilities in mutual assistance and in all phases of national and regional projects.

The Founding Charters also target specific stakeholder groups. Article 3 of the AU Act governs relations with the African diaspora in decision-making and in the Union's construction. The AEC has dedicated goals and commitments on the protection and engagement of African NGOs towards mobilizing regional resources, enabling Social Engagement, and securing peoples'

47 The Pact for the Future, *supra*, Annex II, ¶4.

support; of socioeconomic organizations and associations, such as of producers, transport operators, workers, employers, youth, women, and artisans; and of children, youth, the elderly, and disabled persons.

For farmers, the COMESA Treaty promotes advances in water supply, rural electrification, and insurance; and participation in agricultural development and intra-sectoral cross-border collaboration.

The AEC has dedicated goals and commitments for protecting and/or engaging women, including through improved socioeconomic and cultural conditions and integration into regional activities. COMESA members undertake to promote women's participation, *inter alia*, through tailored training and technology; education and awareness against gender-based discrimination; and support for the *Federation of National Associations of Women in Business*. The EAC Treaty draws attention to women's essential role in socioeconomic development and business, foreseeing specific obligations to secure their participation and nondiscriminatory treatment.

In the EAC, Chapter 25 of the Treaty is devoted to governing and ensuring that the private sector and civil society benefit from the cooperation process. This includes the formulation of a specific strategy to develop the private sector and the maintenance of ongoing dialogue with nongovernmental actors, both domestically and at the EAC level. The Treaty also calls for active participation of entrepreneurs in EAC policymaking and activities and for direct interaction among domestic private sector bodies. Article 89(d), moreover, requires parties to "maintain, expand and upgrade communication facilities to enhance interaction between persons and businesses" in anticipation of investment opportunities.

The Revised COMESA Treaty provides for the protection of property and contract rights and for the ongoing and active participation of the private sector in the cooperation process, including in policy reform, projects, and the implementation of COMESA decisions, as well as for engagement with chambers of commerce and confederations and for cooperation among those bodies.

Institutional Mandates: Dedicated bodies are another tool through which Regional Integration Organizations engage stakeholders. In the AU Act, Article 22 establishes the *Economic, Social and Cultural Council* as an advisory organ gathering professional and social groups active within member states. The COMESA *Consultative Committee* gathers business representatives and other interest groups, enabling a trilateral dialogue. The *Consultative Committee* advises the *Committee of Experts*; monitors treaty implementation with respect to private sector development and women's engagement in business; and consults with stakeholders and considers their reports. The ASEAN Charter anticipates the establishment of a dedicated human rights body and foresees the ASEAN *Foundation*, tasked with raising awareness of regional values, promoting people-to-people interactions, and facilitating multistakeholder collaboration.

Secretariats may also be given special mandates on Social Engagement. In the EAC, the Secretariat may enter into arrangements with relevant organizations for the delivery of specific services, in addition to performing public relations functions, which include disseminating information among interested actors, the public, and the international community; offering a platform for multistakeholder consultations and exchanges; representing the Organization in press interviews, meetings and seminars; producing press releases and newsletters; and keeping public and private enterprises abreast of current and potential trade and investment opportunities in member states. The COMESA Secretary-General cultivates relations with cooperating partners, including the UN bodies, other international organizations, and donor agencies, on policy development and implementation. The CEN-SAD Executive-Secretary designs and implements the communication strategy directed at the public.

Stakeholders may get a voice in regional integration through dedicated courts. In the AU, persons have standing to appear before the Court established under the Union. The EAC Treaty foresees the adoption of a protocol extending and operationalizing the jurisdiction of the EAC Court of Justice to cover human rights cases; gives standing to legal and natural persons to make referrals about unlawful actions by a partner state or an EAC institution in connection to Treaty application and interpretation; allows residents of a state that is not a party in a given case to apply to the Court to provide evidence; and requires the Court to deliver its judgments, as a rule, in public sessions. In the case of COMESA, legal and natural persons residing in the region may request the Court to determine the legality of an act taken by a member or the Council and intervene in disputes in which such persons have an interest. Where the defendant is a member state, the interested person must first exhaust remedies available through that country's judicial system.

Parliamentary bodies may be yet another venue for the involvement of stakeholders in the Close Regional Cooperation process. The *Pan-African Parliament* under the AU aims to ensure that Africans fully participate in the integration and cooperation process.

The *East African Legislative Assembly* is a vehicle for concrete Social Engagement by means of *indirect* participation in law-making. The Assembly is composed of individuals elected by the national legislatures, representing political parties in power and relevant stakeholders, and with demonstrated experience and interest in the EAC; as well as by *ex-officio* members, who lack voting rights, i.e., the minister with competence over EAC affairs in each partner state, the Secretary-General and the EAC Council. The Assembly passes EAC bills, which then require assent by all heads of state; and handles matters pertaining to EAC competences by providing recommendations to, and requesting proposals from, the Council, and considering the latter's annual report on EAC activities. The Treaty promotes interaction between the *East African Legislative Assembly* and the respective national legislatures. Exchange of records among the latter enables the EAC to consider public opinion as reflected in national legislative debates. The *East African Legislative Assembly* also ensures the transmission of bills introduced and EAC acts adopted from the regional to the national assemblies and cooperation in the pursuit of the common foreign and security policy.

7 Conclusions

Neighboring countries and peoples within a given region are knotted together by physical proximity, which often leads to the emergence of common interests and social, economic, and cultural ties that require Close Regional Cooperation. In other words, regional cooperation founded on common interests has roots in geographic and related bonds, not in the adoption of the Founding Charter or the establishment of the respective Regional Integration Organization. These integration regimes represent an evolution in a history of state interactions as the perceived need for Close Regional Cooperation emerges.

A similar situation exists among states sharing basins. In the case of communities-of-basin-interests, geography plays an even greater role in eliciting cooperation. Physical and related ties may be presumed to be deeper and more in evidence within a drainage basin, where hydrological and derivative connections give rise to a bundle of shared and individual interests among co-basin states. To recall, Community-of-Interests finds its fundamental roots in water's unifying power within the geographic space of the catchment. Other types of ties then emerge from those roots, like economic and social interdependence, until formalizing Community-of-Interests cooperation under the Basin Treaty becomes necessary to safeguard common interests and reconcile individual state concerns. When co-riparians reach that point, they enter into the Basin Treaty, which is tailored to enable and govern stepped-up cooperation under the Theory, much like the Founding Charter of the Regional Integration Organization is designed to assure the realization of regional common interests.

The Founding Charter establishes the principles, rules and guidance through which Close Regional Cooperation unfolds and continues to evolve. This specific type of treaty designs tailored obligations and commitments and a well-developed institutional architecture dedicated to the pursuit of common goals, in addition to setting out an enabling environment for dispute prevention and effective resolution. Under Close Regional Cooperation, joint and active action for common interests prevails over other supplementary forms of state engagement. In addition, rules framed by the law of coexistence remain in the background to address instances of disagreements and noncompliance in swift, fair, and mutually beneficial ways.

Joint or common action gains expression in direct and indirect financing and fundraising; the adoption of regional policies and joint regulations or standards; joint planning and implementation; the joint management of information and knowledge; and even catchall provisions that anticipate the need for joint action in new fields. The adoption of the Charter itself and of supplementary agreements is, itself, a manifestation of joint action. Supplementing joint action, coordination is embedded in requirements for direct and indirect consultations, exchanges on data and other matters, and negotiations on complementary treaties. National action may come under general-undertakings provisions, as well as requirements around enactment of implementing legislation, reporting, and accession to relevant treaties outside the regime.

The pursuit of regional interests also informs how the Regional Integration Organization relates to other international and national actors and how members within such an Organization interact with one another. Vertical and Horizontal Coherence and Inward and Outward Cohesion underpin relations with third countries and with other intergovernmental institutions at various levels. Close Regional Cooperation does not exclude, for the Organization and its members, cooperation at other levels and within other bodies, so long as Coherence with integration goals is respected. In addition, each Regional Integration Organization displays an internal Cohesion of ideals, goals, and priorities, which, outwardly, informs their members' interaction as a unified front in negotiations with the rest of the world; and, inwardly, motivates mutual support among members to protect national and regional interests or to react to outside threats.

Ultimately, in the community of nations, intergovernmental organizations remain linked with one another through overarching values, legal principles, and common interests universally shared. The Regional Integration Organization, in particular, fits within, and remains connected to, the UN and other global organizations, while shaping the cooperation process to the region's characteristics and needs. The Regional Integration Organization may sit under larger regimes serving continental integration interests; and serve as umbrellas for subregional organizations, as well as for communities-of-basin-interests, within which closer cooperation is desired.

Solidarity, Nondiscrimination, and Unity guide relations among members interacting within a Regional Integration Organization. As an enabler of Close Regional Cooperation, Solidarity may gain life in implicit or explicit references, and as an ideal, a principle or an objective. Solidarity is reflected in provisions granting special treatment for disadvantaged members; establishing remedies for negative externalities from trade liberalization; or governing mutual-assistance. Solidarity also influences relations between co-basin states, basin populations, and the shared environment. Solidarity might push states, when appropriate, towards Community-of-Interests. Nondiscrimination has specific applicability in the context of regional trade or may refer to the nondiscriminatory treatment that co-riparian member states afford one another when adopting navigation tariffs and regulations. Unity is realized through self-sufficiency and efficient intracommunity movement.

Social Engagement expresses how Regional Integration Organizations tend to recognize that the rights and roles of actors affected by, or interested in, the cooperation process should be safeguarded and/or proactively promoted. Founding Charters reflect Social Engagement to different degrees and through a variety of formulas. These Treaties may prioritize certain actors, formulate specific obligations and commitments to enable Social Engagement, and/or embed public participation into the functions of specific bodies within the Organization. Taken together, related Charter provisions reveal a concern with human flourishing on the part of Regional Integration Organizations and their member states.

Some of the elements above-presented, with the appropriate adjustments, also tend to characterize cooperation framed by Community-of-Interests. Regional integration regimes and communities-of-basin-interests find commonalities in how they are founded upon Close Cooperation and, consequently, in how:

a) Their **legal-institutional basis** is specifically designed for the pursuit of common interests.
b) **Joint action for shared goals** serves as the primary modality of state engagement, supplemented by coordination and domestic measures, and with coexistence rules playing a necessary and yet subsidiary function.
c) **Coherence** informs relationships with other common-interest regimes within the same region/basin and with other regional, continental or global organizations.

d) **Solidarity** underlies relationships with riparian developing or vulnerable countries, and for the purpose of mutual assistance.
e) **Social engagement** entails stakeholder involvement in the cooperation process – more developed in the case of the Regional Integration Organizations, through general statements and/or specific provisions and through institutional mandates.

In the context of transboundary water cooperation, Unity could translate into obligations around the maintenance of navigation channels or, more broadly, on provisions for cross-border circulation of national authorities competent for water management and of the staff of the Basin Body. In the treaties reflecting the Theory and here examined, however, these characteristics are not sufficiently prominent to elevate Unity as an element of Community-of-Interests.

Nondiscrimination has a context-specific meaning under international water law, as it applies to access to justice and transboundary harm under the UNWC. This meaning of nondiscrimination is captured as a dimension of Social Engagement in the Legal Analytical Framework for Community-of-Interests.

Finally, regarding Cohesion, only one treaty known to reflect the Theory includes specific provisions in that respect.

PART III

The Primary Normative Elements of Community-of-Interests

There are few, if any, absolutes in the law.[1]

Certain treaties and jurisprudence incorporate or apply Community-of-Interests as the theoretical basis for transboundary catchment cooperation centered on shared goals. By examining these precedents, we have identified the legal concepts that make up the Theory's normative content. This analytical approach is supported by Article 2(2) of the 1995 SADC Protocol, which refers to the *principles* of Community-of-Interests, thereby suggesting that the Theory may be unpacked into a set of normative elements.

Here, we present the Theory's four *primary* elements, i.e., those existing across the various precedents examined, and which constitute the first part of the Legal Analytical Framework later used to discuss the functions and status of Community-of-Interests. These elements are:

a) **Basin Scope**, as the biogeographic starting point for the ambit of cooperation framed by the Theory and the application of the other elements.
b) **Basin Treaty** and **Basin Body**, both being context-specific, and designed to consider the entire catchment, as far as possible and as appropriate, and to foster Close Basin Cooperation for common interests as its central purpose.
c) **Close Basin Cooperation**, i.e., co-riparian states cooperating in advanced ways, acting mostly for common interests, through joint action, and with consideration of the basin as a hydrological unity.

Linking the Theory to its primary elements demystifies Community-of-Interests as being contrary to state sovereignty. These normative elements embody well-known and widely applied legal tools – i.e., definition of the scope of transboundary water management, watercourse agreements, joint bodies, and vari-

1 McCaffrey, *supra*, p.185.

ous modalities of riparian state engagement. In other words, the tools in question are not new or controversial in international legal and political discourse, and state practice among co-riparians. In the UNWC, for example, Article 3(3) anticipates the adoption of watercourse agreements; Article 3(4) requires that watercourse agreements "delimit the waters" to which they apply; Article 8(1) codifies the duty to cooperate; and Article 8(2) encourages the establishment of commissions. Going back decades, the Dublin Statement notes that sustainable management of transboundary basins depends on governance arrangements involving international basin organizations under the respective watercourse agreement – both to reconcile and harmonize riparian interests and to design integrated management plans and concerted action programs.

When at play within communities-of-basin-interests, the above legal concepts display particular characteristics, as expressed here in the form of its primary and secondary normative elements. Howden, in this sense, sees in Community-of-Interests "a set of principles and parameters, which, through their interaction, generate new and more progressive interpretations of already existing principles of general international water law".[2] In other words, Community-of-Interests reinterprets consolidated norms and used concepts of international law under Limited Territorial Sovereignty, by further specifying the scope, content, and modes of cooperation among co-basin states for the pursuit of common interests as a principal objective.

The Theory's primary elements inform the effective management of water and related natural resources in a transboundary context, which requires the Basin Treaty enabling Close Basin Cooperation; the Basin Body as the solid institutional home for the community-of-basin-interests in question, including as a mechanism for Social Engagement; and joint action leading to common management tools, like common databases and agreed investment plans.[3]

In the treaties examined, the elements of Community-of-Interests each appear in different formats and to varying degrees, as appropriate to the concrete case. In other words, incorporating the Theory into a treaty does not entail a blind endorsement of its elements, for the Law does not deal in absolutes, just as the Theory is embedded with flexibility and, its application, tied to context. Or, as per the Lake Lanoux Tribunal: "L'unité d'un bassin n'est sanctionnée sur le plan juridique que dans la mesure où elle correspond à des

2 Howden, *supra*, p. 27.

3 *See* UN Water (2018), *supra*, p. 15, describing similar IWRM conditions.

réalités humaines".[4] Cooperation is likely to intensify in tandem with progressive increases in the need or desire to apply Community-of-Interests.

Consider Article 2(2) of the 1995 SADC Protocol, employing the verb *undertake* when codifying the Theory, i.e., the intention to move in that direction;[5] not a strict obligation, but a best-effort commitment to Community-of-Interests. The Theory's elasticity responds to the realities and needs of each basin, recognizing that cooperation is an evolving, long-term process, as co-basin states journey together along the path of formalizing and progressively developing their community-of-basin-interests.

Case Study 2: Evolving Cooperation in the Zambezi

The Zambezi Basin offers a practical example of how Article 2(2) of the 1995 SADC Protocol would play out in practice, with concrete cooperation deepening through time. In the Zambezi, at first, only some of the basin states cooperate, and mostly on technical matters, under a general agreement that does not spell out specific rules of international law. Yet, this general agreement plants the seeds for Close Basin Cooperation within the framework of a jointly agreed action plan.[6] Eventually, all riparians feel ready to adopt a basin-wide treaty, with its corresponding joint body; and, upon entry into force, parties follow that up with the approval of binding and nonbinding instruments further regulating and guiding their relations and interests.[7]

Against this background, each Chapter in this Part delineates the Theory's four primary normative elements on the basis of authoritative treaty and case law. The analysis of the precedents applying Community-of-Interests is mostly organized according to Article 38 of the ICJ Statute: *treaties*, from the global through the regional to the basin levels; *case law*, in chronological order, presenting how jurisprudence has interpreted and applied individual Basin Treaties; and *scholarship*, where necessary to further clarify our conclusions.

4 Lake Lanoux Case, *supra*, p. 304.

5 *See* Plain Language Legal Dictionary, defining *Undertake*: "To guarantee; to set about to do; to engage in; to promise; to perform; to enter upon" (Rocket Lawyer), at https://www.rocketlawyer.com/legal-dictionary.rl.

6 *Agreement on the Action Plan for the Environmentally Sound Management of the Common Zambezi River System*, Botswana-Mozambique-Tanzania-Zambia-Zimbabwe (Harare, 28 May 1987).

7 *See, e.g.*, ZAMCOM, *Procedures for Notification of Planned Measures* (2017).

1 Drainage Basin Scope

The Theory's scope *ratione loci* is expressed herein as *Community-of-Interests Drainage Basin Scope* ('Basin Scope') and is the first and most fundamental of its primary normative elements. The Basin Scope stresses the hydrological and associated interconnections and the physical unity of the transboundary watershed.

As seen above, the biogeographic scope of cooperation under the umbrella of Regional Integration Organizations is determined by the territory made up of neighboring states within a given region, bound together by physical and associated historical, cultural, economic, and other ties, from which common interests emerge.

The scope *ratione loci* of communities-of-basin-interests is also founded upon a geographic element. Hydrological and related interdependencies within a drainage basin, as a biogeographic and legal unit, give rise to common interests – only, in this case, among co-basin states. This same unitary whole, i.e., the shared catchment, informs the primary – albeit not necessarily exclusive – geographic scope of application of Community-of-Interests; and thus, of interstate cooperation on transboundary water planning and management thereunder. The extent to which the Basin Scope is applied depends on the common interests prioritized by the states concerned. For example, the Executive Secretary of the *Lake Chad Basin Commission* has suggested water transfers from the Congo basin to restore Lake levels.[8] In contrast, the High Commissioner of the *Gambia River Basin Development Organization* has stated that the body's "primary concern is to preserve existing ecosystems before considering sharing waters with other basins".[9]

In science, the catchment is defined based on "the water divides formed by the hilltops in the landscape",[10] where "precipitation that does not return to the atmosphere as green water forms blue water";[11] blue water then "feeds the river with rapid flood flow or passes underground as groundwater flow, seeping back to the surface in springs, local hollows, and valley bottoms";[12] then the water "evaporates, feeds riparian forests or recharges the watercourses with a time-stable flow".[13]

8 IISD (2018a), *supra*, p. 4.

9 *Id*, p. 5.

10 Falkenmark, *supra*, p. 358.

11 *Ibid.*

12 *Ibid.*

13 *Ibid.*

As informed by science, therefore, the Basin Scope accounts for three *dimensions of freshwater ecosystem connectivity*: *longitudinal*, along the entire water system; *vertical*, between surface and groundwaters, and with atmospheric waters; and *horizontal*, between water, land, and living resources. For ease of reference, the book calls these linkages *Basin Scope dimensions.*

The Drainage Basin Approach: The Basin Scope is captured in the so-called *drainage basin approach*, going back to the 1996 Helsinki Rules. Adopted by the *International Law Association* (ILA), an expert organization, the Rules attempt to advance the drainage basin approach in transboundary water management. Article II defines an international drainage basin as "a geographical area extending over two or more states determined by the watershed limits of the system of waters, including surface and underground waters, flowing into a common terminus".

Also from the ILA, the more recent Berlin Rules highlight *conjunctive water management*, deemed to be an important trend in the development of the law of transboundary basins.[14] Conjunctive management refers to the need for states to account for the hydraulic connections between underground and surface waters. In this sense, Article 5 calls on states to "use their best efforts to manage surface waters, groundwater, and other pertinent waters in a unified and comprehensive manner". In addition, Article 6 of the Rules calls on states to strive "to integrate appropriately the management of waters with the management of other resources", here reflecting the horizontal dimension of the Basin Scope.

The Basin Scope, as embedded in both the Helsinki and the Berlin Rules, is thus no stranger to the international legal debate on transboundary water cooperation.

The Basin Scope in Policy Discourse: The freshwater community employs different expressions that embed the Basin Scope, but all related paradigms corroborate the centrality of the catchment as the primary management unit for water and related resources. Such is the case with *integrated water resources management* (IWRM) or *integrated river basin management* (IRBM), both falling under the umbrella of the broader *ecosystem approach.* A better understanding of these concepts in policy helps to identify their legal uptake when

14 ILA, *Berlin Rules on Water Resources* (2004) ('Berlin Rules'), *in* ILA, Water Resources Committee, 4th Report ('ILA (2004)'), at https://unece.org/fileadmin/DAM/env/water/meetings/legal_board/2010/annexes_groundwater_paper/Annex_iv_Berlin_Rules_on_Water_Resources_ILA.pdf, p. 13

not explicitly named in relevant legal sources; and thus, the endorsement of the Basin Scope in state practice.

IWRM is first introduced and debated as a policy concept in 1992 at the *International Conference on Water and the Environment* (ICWE). This large expert gathering culminates in the approval of the Dublin Statement. Principle 1 of the Statement calls for a *holistic* approach to resource planning and management, i.e., one that links social, economic, and environmental sustainability, as well as land and water uses, across the entire watershed. The Statement goes on to emphasize the river basin as the "most appropriate geographical entity" for water resources planning and management.[15] The Statement also hints at the geographic scope of cooperation when referring to *transboundary river or lake basins* and to *international watersheds*.[16]

The Global Water Partnership (GWP) describes IWRM as "a process which promotes the coordinated development and management of water, land and related resources, in order to maximize the resultant economic and social welfare in an equitable manner without compromising the sustainability of vital ecosystems".[17] Although this definition does not specify the basin as the basic resource planning unit, GWP itself clarifies that its widely endorsed understanding of IWRM builds on the Dublin Statement[18] and refers to *drainage basins* as "logical planning units for IWRM from a natural system perspective".[19]

For UNEP, IWRM "is an approach that helps to balance competing water demands from across society and the economy, without compromising the sustainability of vital ecosystems … through coordinated policy and regulatory frameworks, management arrangements and financing".[20] In the same report, UNEP emphasizes the need for cross-sectoral coordination and management activities, "particularly at the basin and aquifer levels, … where many of the activities are put into practice, and where the negative impacts of non-action may be most keenly felt".[21]

Tarlock explains that IWRM is a "*catchment area-focused* process [that] builds on the long history of treating *river basin systems as single units* to be

15 ICWE Report, *supra*, p. 6.

16 *Ibid.*

17 A. Agarwal *et al*, *Integrated Water Resources Management*, GWP Technical Advisory Committee (TAC) Background Paper 4 (GWP 2000), p. 22.

18 *Id*, p. 6.

19 *Id*, p. 24.

20 UNEP (2021), *supra*, p. vii.

21 *Id*, p. 20, 52.

developed through comprehensive management regimes".[22] The meaning and content of IWRM is further unpacked in Chapter 18 of Agenda 21.[23]

IRBM is closely related to IWRM. Yet, IRBM more explicitly emphasizes the drainage basin as the basic biogeographic unit for managing water and related resources and better unpacks aspects related to environmental sustainability. To define IRBM, WWF adapts the GWP concept by adding language on resource conservation, and preservation and restoration of freshwater ecosystems; and specifying that such a process takes place within an individual river basin.[24] In other words, under IRBM, the catchment serves as "the spatial context for large-scale environmental planning and management of … aquatic ecosystems linked to rivers, streams and other wetlands."[25] Thus framed by the watershed as the planning unit, IRBM entails long-term basin vision; cross-sectoral integration of policies, decisions, and costs; basin-level strategic decision-making to guide planning and implementation on the subcatchment and local scales; active stakeholder engagement, transparency and public information; capacity-building for basin planning and participation; and a solid knowledge basis of the watershed, its ecosystems, and related socioeconomic conditions.[26]

WWF further explains that watersheds "are dynamic over space and time, and any single management intervention has implications for the system as a whole".[27] For this reason, IRBM is viewed by the conservation community as the "most promising vehicle"[28] for facing the global water challenge, and doing so on a scale appropriate to prevent, control, and mitigate the effects of resource and infrastructure development.[29]

Finally, the ecosystem approach is "a strategy for the integrated management of land, water and living resources that promotes conservation and sustainable use in an equitable way".[30]

22 Tarlock, *supra*, p. 405.

23 Agenda 21, *in* UNCED Report, *supra*, Res.1, Vol.1, Annex II.

24 WWF, *Managing Rivers Wisely: Lessons from WWF's Work for Integrated River Basin Management* (WWF 2003), p. 3.

25 Amazon Waters Initiative, Integrated River Basin Management, at http://amazonwaters.org/the-initiative/integrated-river-basin-management/.

26 WWF, *supra*, p. 3–4.

27 *Id*, p. 3.

28 *Id*, p. 4.

29 Amazon Waters Initiative, *supra*.

30 CBD, 7th Conference of the Parties (COP-7) (Kuala Lumpur, 9–20 & 27 Feb 2004), Decision VII/11: *Ecosystem Approach*, UN Doc UNEP/CBD/COP/DEC/VII/11 (13 Apr 2004), p. 4.

Hence, the integrated management of natural resources and ecosystems within the basin is at the core of IWRM, IRBM and the ecosystem approach. These holistic approaches center governance and management beyond single water bodies to encompass the entire drainage basin, including the "catchment and riparian forests, wetlands, riverine floodplains and associated freshwater and estuarine habitats".[31]

In a transboundary context, accordingly, the Basin Scope accounts for "critical natural connections",[32] interdependencies and mutual vulnerabilities across the freshwater system as a whole, including associated terrestrial and, to some extent, coastal and marine ecosystems. The Basin Scope calls for the drainage basin, as a physical unity, to be holistically managed, developed, and protected. This primary normative element of the Theory emphasizes integrated planning across all dependent sectors and between surface and underground waters, water quantity and quality, terrestrial and aquatic ecosystems, upper and lower riparian interests, and human and environmental needs, including instream flows in adequate quality, quantity, and timing to sustain nature.[33]

Endorsement and Application of the Basin Scope: The Basin Scope, as expressed through ILA's drainage basin approach, may be viewed as a manifestation, in international legal discourse, of IWRM.

Integrated Water Resources Management "has now been accepted internationally"[34] and "progressively adopted as the international water management standard"[35] for sustainable water management and resource allocation. From the adoption of the Dublin Statement to the 1992 Rio Conference, IWRM gains wide support among the world's nations – if not as a legal concept, at least as a best practice policy paradigm to water resources management.

Fast forward to Agenda 2030, SDG-6 "fully commits member states to IWRM and transboundary cooperation over water resources".[36] As recently as 2024, a Resolution of the United Nations Environment Assembly (UNEA) "[c]alls on all member states and members of specialized agencies, and invites relevant international organizations and relevant stakeholders, as appropriate, to implement [IWRM] at all levels, including through transboundary coopera-

---

31 ICWE Report, *supra*, p. 27.

32 *Ibid.*

33 UN Water (2018), *supra*, p. 19; ICWE Report, *supra*, p. 27.

34 Unturbe, *supra*, p. 28. *See also* UN Water (2018), *supra*, p. 11.

35 Tarlock, *supra*, p. 404.

36 UN Water (2018), *supra*, p. 75.

tion".[37] Expert organizations also emphasize the growing importance of collaborative engagement on IWRM policies for good water governance and several targets under the 2030 Agenda.[38]

With regard to a basin approach to water governance and management, specifically, UNEP affirms: "Both indicators 6.5.1 and 6.5.2 [of Agenda 2030] advocate for the management of water resources at the basin or aquifer level, irrespective of whether they cross international borders or other administrative borders".[39] In this sense, participants of the 2023 UN Water Conference emphasized the basin as the "primary solution scale"[40] – for both water quantity and quality issues.

Applying the Basin Scope may be challenging, given the presence of more than one nation state, but it is vital for freshwater sustainability and scientifically sound management. In today's interdependent and changing world, the Basin Scope has become an imperative "to accommodate potential or existing conflicts in instances of multiuse development and to provide the optimum rational development of a common resource for the benefit of each [basin] state".[41] As some pragmatic examples, effective deployment of water reuse, as a component of the water management toolbox, requires the application of a basin-wide approach, since "wastewater from one part of a basin may well be the source of supply for others downstream".[42] Basin-level management is key in the context of climate change adaptation.[43] Countries that start to apply integrated approaches following the appropriate governance reforms benefit socially and economically from improved management practices, including greater advances in infrastructure development.[44] Principles of ecological restoration emphasize the drainage basin as a planning unit required to account for rivers' dynamic nature, enable adaptive management and "create conditions for self-renewal by reestablishing natural biological and physical processes".[45]

To be sure, endorsing Community-of-Interests does not prevent co-riparian states from looking beyond the basin in the pursuit of shared priorities; and,

---

37 UNEA, 6th Session (Nairobi, 26 Feb-1 Mar 2024), Res 6/13, *Effective and inclusive solutions for strengthening water policies to achieve sustainable development in the context of climate change, biodiversity loss and pollution*, UN Doc UNEP/EA.6/Res.13 (5 Mar 2024), p. 2.

38 SIWI (2018a), *supra*, p. 2.

39 UNEP (2021), *supra*, p. 56.

40 UNWC 2023 Summary, *supra*, p. 16.

41 ILA (1966), *supra*, p. 485.

42 UN Water (2018), *supra*, p. 66.

43 *See*, e.g., Tarlock, *supra*, p. 371, FN5.

44 Unturbe, *supra*, p. 3, 29.

45 VWF Report, *supra*, p. 43.

in some cases, doing so may prove necessary for protecting such priorities. As an example, experts have called for more precise forecasting through "intensified observations of climatological and hydrological phenomena within and beyond the river basin boundary".[46] At the same time, catchment-based management may provide the appropriate starting point for dealing with regional or global challenges, since the basin tends to offer "a framework for planning and allocating water … that helps deal with planetary limits".[47]

1.1 *The Concept of Water Systems in International Law*

Embedded in the Basin Scope is the concept of the *water system*. The concept builds on UNWC terminology that defines the Convention's scope of application and recognizes the watercourse as a natural unity. Article 2(a) defines the term *watercourse* as "a *system* of surface waters and groundwaters constituting by virtue of their physical relationship a *unitary whole* and normally flowing into a common terminus".

As thus defined, the water system reflects the longitudinal and vertical connectivity dimensions of the Basin Scope, i.e., all interlinked water bodies that together constitute a unitary whole, such as the river mainstem and its tributaries, along with connected glaciers, reservoirs, canals, wetlands, lakes, and aquifers, even when these components are entirely located within a single state.[48]

The book employs the expression *water system*, instead of *watercourse system*, to spell out the application of the Basin Scope and Community-of-Interests to all river, lake, aquifer, and wetland systems and subsystems, including fossil aquifers and other transboundary systems of waters that may not fall squarely within the UNWC definition.

To compare, the types of *transboundary waters* covered by the ECEWC are determined by the all-encompassing definition of such an expression in Article 1(1): "any surface or ground waters which mark, cross or are located on boundaries between two or more states". In the case of such waters flowing directly into the sea, they "end at a straight line across their respective mouths between points on the low-water line of their banks". Unlike the UNWC, the ECEWC applies to transboundary groundwaters not connected to international watercourses. It is not immediately clear, however, if the ECEWC definition, which does not refer to *systems*, accounts for the longitudinal and verti-

---

46 *Id*, p. 17.

47 Unturbe, *supra*, p. 37.

48 ILC (1994), *supra*, p. 90. On the authority of ILC draft articles, generally, *see* Gabčíkovo Case, *supra*, p. 72.

cal dimensions of the Basin Scope. Compared to the UNWC, the ECEWC contains stronger and more explicit language promoting and stressing an integrated approach to resource use, management, and protection, through the latter's emphasis on the catchment areas of transboundary waters. Within the framework of the ECEWC, "transboundary waters *should* not be limited to a water body (e.g., a river, a lake, an aquifer), but should cover [its] catchment".[49] This suggests that the water-system concept is encouraged by the latter Convention, just as it is in the UNWC.

At the regional level, Article 1(1) of the 1995 SADC Protocol so defines the expression *watercourse system*: "the *interrelated hydrologic components* of a drainage basin ... which constitute a unitary whole by virtue of their physical relationship". Moreover, Article 2(2) elucidates the Theory's scope *ratione loci* by directly connecting Community-of-Interests to shared watercourse *systems*, i.e., to the water-system concept. As codified in the 1995 SADC Protocol, therefore, Community-of-Interests is predicated on the systemic consideration of shared freshwaters, i.e., all the various interlinked water bodies within a system, on the surface and underground.

The Revised SADC Protocol delimits the geographic scope of the regimes created thereunder by practically reiterating UNWC language when defining *watercourse, shared watercourse*, and *watercourse state*. On the basis of those definitions, Article 3 of the Revised Protocol codifies the water-system concept as a substantive principle, per which parties "recognize ... the *unity and coherence* of each shared watercourse" and "undertake to *harmonize* [their] water *uses*" accordingly. In observance of said principle, the same provision requires parties to ensure that development projects "are consistent with the sustainable development of *all watercourse states*". Hence, the new Protocol not only maintains its predecessor's endorsement of the water-system concept but is explicit about the concept implying involvement of all basin countries. In so doing, the Revised Protocol contributes to clarifying the scope *ratione personae* of Community-of-Interests.

At the catchment-level, the Senegal Basin Charter also reflects the water-system concept. Article 3 defines the scope *ratione loci* of the Charter as encompassing the Senegal River *and* associated tributaries, distributaries, and depressions.[50] The consideration of the longitudinal dimension of the Basin Scope here is clear.

---

49 ECEWC *Guide, supra*, p. 14 (emphasis added).

50 *See also* Senegal Basin Charter, *supra*, Art.1(17), defining *bassin hydrographique du Fleuve*: « le Fleuve Sénégal, ses affluent, ses défluents et les dépressions associées ».

On vertical hydrological linkages, Article 3 of the Senegal Basin Charter does not explicitly reference aquifers, but Article 1 defines the term *groundwaters* as the waters contained within porous, permeable, or fractured geological formations, the partial and/or complete recharge of which depends on the hydrological regime of the Senegal River system. In addition, Article 17(4) foresees the cartographic mapping, inventory, and delimitation of recharge zones, with a view to more precisely identifying the interactions between groundwaters and surface waters within the basin. Hence, the Charter does not exclude groundwater from its scope. Aquifers are only absent from Article 3 probably because of insufficient knowledge of vertical interlinkages. Basin states still recognize that, within the framework of the Theory, best efforts must be made, as appropriate, to consider all basin waters in management and allocation decisions.

The Senegal Basin Charter is in line with the commentaries to Article 5 of the Berlin Rules, according to which states ought to endeavor to manage surface and groundwaters conjunctively, but there is no "strict obligation mandating conjunctive management under all circumstances".[51] As long as appropriate measures are being taken, cooperation remains in line with the water-system concept, the Basin Scope and Community-of-Interests.

The Lake Victoria Protocol at the outset approaches the Lake basin – a subcatchment of the Nile basin, as a hydrological unity unto itself. The Lake sub-basin under the Protocol extends across the "geographical areas … within the territories of the partner states determined by the watershed limits of the *system of waters*",[52] both on the surface and underground. In this way, the Protocol incorporates the water-system concept and, therefore, the vertical and longitudinal dimensions of the Basin Scope as a determining factor for the geographic scope of transboundary cooperation. The parties to the Protocol include all five Lake basin states, which, already in the Preamble, recognize that water "must be managed in an integrated and holistic manner". This recognition demands more than unilateral restraint. Treating the Lake Victoria as a water system requires collective consideration of all hydrological connections between the Lake and tributary inflows within the subcatchment.

In contrast, the River Uruguay Statute, per Article 2(b)–(c), is principally concerned with the part of the watercourse that forms the boundary between the two parties.[53] Under Article 35 of the Statute, however, parties undertake

---

51 ILA (2004), *supra*, p. 14.

52 Lake Victoria Protocol, *supra*, Art. 1.

53 This provision defines the term *River* by referring to the *Treaty Concerning the Boundary Constituted by the River Uruguay* (Argentina-Uruguay) (Montevideo, 7 Apr 1961), which demarcates the section of the watercourse forming the border between the two states.

to ensure that the use of tributary and underground waters is compatible with the protection of the river regime and water quality.

In case law, the River Oder Decision establishes the Theory's relation with the longitudinal dimension of the water-system concept. The Decision invokes Community-of-Interests as "the basis of a common legal right [that] extends to the *whole navigable course* of the river",[54] i.e., to the system's mainstem and all shared navigable streams composing it. The Court then finds that this longitudinal dimension of the Basin Scope is among the "essential features"[55] of Community-of-Interests.

The Decision does not fully embrace a water-system concept, which would have extended internationalization to purely domestic tributaries. The Ruling is in line with Article 331 of the Treaty of Versailles, which refers to "all navigable parts of these river systems which naturally provide more than one state with access to the sea". According to the *Reply of the Allied and Associated Powers to the Austrian Delegation*, as transcribed in the PCIJ Decision, the states concerned had pondered whether to extend the international regime to domestic tributaries but conclude that doing so was not in their interest at that point.[56]

Hence, the Decision stops short of delimiting the basic scope of Community-of-Interests absent a treaty directly excluding domestic tributaries. The Court thus leaves the door open for the Theory's continued evolution to include within its ambit even domestic water bodies, as long as these are connected to the large water system.

The above precedents serve as our legal bases for concluding that the Basin Scope, in its vertical and longitudinal dimensions, is a primary element of the Theory.

1.2 *Water Systems and Partial Agreements*

Community-of-Interests does not imply that a Basin Treaty has to cover the entire water system or involve all states within the watercourse. The Theory accommodates *partial agreements*, i.e., those governing state interactions over a subsystem, which means a portion of the water system.

The *Where-Appropriate* Criterium: Article 3(4) of the UNWC foresees two types of context-specific treaties: *water-system agreements*, i.e., those applying to an entire international watercourse; and *partial agreements*, applying to a *part* thereof or to a specific project, program, or use, and/or not involving all

54 River Oder Case, *supra*, p. 27 (emphasis added).

55 *Ibid.*

56 *Id*, p. 30.

co-riparian states. In the ECEWC, Article 9(1) requires states, when designing context-specific agreements, to "specify the catchment area, or *part*(s) thereof, subject to cooperation".

Both Global Conventions employ the term *part* – of a watercourse (UNWC) or of a catchment area (ECEWC), when foreseeing partial agreements. In the River Oder Case, the meaning of the word *part* is one of the points debated, based on language used in the Treaty of Versailles. While one side argues that 'part' applies to a river segment; the other submits that "a part of a river system, in the natural meaning of the terms, is one of the units composing the said system, namely, a tributary or subtributary".[57]

The Court concludes that the Commission's jurisdiction encompasses tributaries suitable for navigation in their entire length. The Ruling goes on to underscore no evidence "of a treaty in which the upstream limit of internationalization of a river is determined by [the last] frontier rather than by certain *conditions of navigability*".[58] The watercourse system is so deemed to include all navigable transboundary tributaries and even their domestic parts located beyond the last international border to the extent that they are suitable for navigation.[59] In short, the Court applies a *where-appropriate* criterium to the question of geographic scope under Community-of-Interests, interpreting the word *part* in the service of navigation, the core common interest behind the dispute.

If we transpose and adjust the River Oder Decision to the context of the non-navigational uses of international watercourses, we can illuminate the interpretation of the term *part*, as employed in the UNWC and the ECEWC, with respect to partial agreements. The ILC clarifies that riparian states "may confine their agreement to the mainstem ..., include within it the waters of an entire drainage basin, or take some intermediate approach."[60] A *part* of a watercourse or catchment can thus refer to an individual body of water, just the groundwaters component, or the river segment that marks the border; or else only "parts of a basin or combining ... parts of several basins".[61] To use our own case studies, a *part* can be a tributary system, like the Lake Victoria, but also a river stretch, as under the River Uruguay Statute, as appropriate to the context in which a Basin Treaty is adopted.

Hence, the same *where-appropriate* criterium applied by the PCIJ – namely, the nature of the common interest at stake (*navigation*), in light of consider-

57 *Id*, p. 26.
58 *Id*, p. 28 (emphasis added).
59 *Id*, p. 29, 31.
60 ILC (1994), *supra*, p. 93
61 Berlin Rules, *supra*, Commentaries, p. 9.

ations of political and factual feasibility (*navigability*) – remains valid with respect to other water uses. Consequently, *appropriateness* informs the interpretation of the term *part* as employed by the Global Conventions and as framed by Community-of-Interests and the Basin Scope.

Both Conventions view transboundary waters as unitary hydrological systems, in line with the Basin Scope, but retain a measure of flexibility when regulating the scope of the treaties that riparian states may adopt to govern individual watercourses. An outright requirement for states only to enter into system-wide management agreements would have meant going a step too far at the level of these umbrella Conventions. The ILC emphasizes, in this sense, "the unquestioned freedom of watercourse states to define the scope of the agreements they conclude";[62] and explains the function of the 1994 Draft Articles – that of facilitating treaty negotiations, whether for system-wide or partial agreements.[63]

There are, however, legal limitations on states' freedom to enter into partial agreements, in order to safeguard the rights of every riparian. The UNWC designs a legal scheme to ensure that partial agreements do not negatively affect the rights of any of the riparian states concerned. This scheme must be considered within the Convention's broader context and in light of its object and purpose.[64]

The UNWC's legal scheme for partial agreements, as designed in Articles 3 and 4, affirms the right of all riparian states to "engage in discussions around a shared watercourse to deal with existing situations where actions or agreements by or between some riparians have repercussions on others".[65] In addition, partial agreements must not significantly[66] interfere with water uses within nonparties, absent their consent; and nothing in partial agreements affects the rights or obligations under the UNWC for states not participating in such agreements. A third riparian state that may significantly suffer as a result of a partial agreement's implementation is entitled "to participate in [relevant] consultations ... and, where appropriate, in the negotiation thereof in good faith with a view to becoming a party thereto, to the extent that its use

62 ILC (1994), *supra*, p. 93.

63 *Ibid.*

64 VCLT, *supra*, Art.31(1).

65 Dellapenna & Gupta (2013), *supra*, p. 14.

66 *See* ILC (1994), *supra*, p. 94, explaining that a significant interference implies an impact "that can be established by objective evidence (provided the evidence can be secured)"; and "a real impairment of use." But such an impact "need not rise to the level of being substantial."

is thereby affected".[67] Finally, all riparian states have the right to participate in relevant consultations and negotiations for, and to become parties to, treaties that apply to the entire watercourse system.

In the same vein, the ECEWC Guide explains that the Convention's "basic provisions and objectives ... can be effectively met only if cooperation extends to all transboundary waters".[68] The language in the ECEWC Guide does not amount to a requirement for partial agreements to cover at least a water *subsystem*, as opposed to a specific body or segment. Still, the Guide does suggest that agreements informed by the water-systems concept are likely to be necessary in most cases – a presumption that, in order for states to address common and unilateral interests, the water system in its entirety is often the most appropriate starting point for treaty negotiations and water governance and management. As the ILC commentary notes, "technical experts consider that the most efficient and beneficial way of dealing with a watercourse is to [treat] it as a whole, including all watercourse states as parties to the agreement."[69] The premise here is that, as a rule, "the establishment of procedures for coordinating activities throughout the system is highly desirable and perhaps necessary".[70]

At the regional level, Articles 1, 3, and 6 of the Revised SADC Protocol govern partial agreements in ways similar to the Global Conventions, by determining that a watercourse agreement must delimit its geographic scope, thus permitting the adoption of partial treaties; enabling and promoting transboundary water cooperation along the entire watercourse system; and outlining interlinked rights and obligations to regulate the adoption of partial agreements.

Under Community-of-Interests, therefore, the principal focus is on agreements based on the water-system concept, without prejudice to the possibility of partial agreements being adopted – where appropriate and using the UNWC provisions as guidance in the case of non-parties to the Convention. Informed by the Theory, the Conventions and the Protocol encourage as much alignment as possible with the Basin Scope, as well involvement of all basin states in the cooperation process, towards the ultimate goal of system-wide Basin Treaties with full state participation.

Examples of Partial Basin Treaties: The approach to partial agreements taken in the above framework legal instruments, reinforced by the ILC Commentaries, is aligned with how Community-of-Interests operates in specific basins, always being tied to context. Contextualized application of a theoretical

67 UNWC, *supra*, Art.4(2).
68 ECEWC Guide, *supra*, p. 64.
69 ILC (1994), *supra*, p. 94.
70 *Id*, p. 86.

framework requires flexibility to be effective. A partial Basin Treaty may be appropriate, within the meaning of Community-of-Interests, when treating the watercourse as a unitary whole is unnecessary or unfeasible. This may be the case where "differences between the subsystems of some international watercourses … are as marked as those between separate drainage basins";[71] or in relation to "problems whose solution is of interest to only some [riparian] states".[72] In such scenarios, a treaty scope other than system-wide may prove better suited to realize the targeted shared goals and thus to serve the community-of-basin-interests in question.

Let us consider as examples of the Theory's contextualized application the River Uruguay Statute and the Lake Victoria Protocol. The River Uruguay Statute sits under the framework of the preexisting Plata Basin Treaty[73] – a system-wide regime that brings together all five co-basin states. Per the Statute, the protection of the part of the River within its scope must be respected by the use of tributary and underground waters outside the border area. Otherwise, the Statute does not explicitly consider the natural relationship of the border segment with the other parts of the River Uruguay water system – neither with other sections of the River Uruguay itself, nor with the other surface or groundwater systems that make up the Plata basin. The Statute, moreover, does not directly clarify the relationship, as to the section of the watercourse within its scope, of its two parties with the other three co-basin states.

On the other hand, Article I of the Statute makes clear that its adoption is "in strict observance of the [parties'] rights and obligations arising from [existing] treaties" – above all, the system-wide Plata Basin Treaty. Article VI of the latter Treaty safeguards its parties' right to enter into "specific or partial bilateral or multilateral agreements designed to achieve the general objectives of [basin] development". Such general objectives are specified in the Sole Paragraph of Article I of the Plata Basin Treaty and include the rational and equitable use of water resources for multiple purposes and the conservation of basin ecosystems. These objectives are subsumed under the overarching goal stipulated in the *caput* of the same provision, namely, joint efforts for "the harmonious development and physical integration of the River Plate Basin and its zones of direct and measurable influence."

Conjunctively reading the above provisions in both legal instruments reveals how the water-system concept is embedded in the River Uruguay Statute.

71 *Ibid.*

72 *Ibid.*

73 *Treaty of the River Plate Basin* (Brasilia, 23 Apr 1969) (in force 14 Aug 1970), Argentina-Bolivia-Brazil-Paraguay-Uruguay, 12550 UNTS 11 (1973) ('Plata Basin Treaty').

The interpretation, application, and implementation of the Statute must be consistent with the general objectives and overarching goal that, when the Statute came into existence, had already been agreed upon among all co-basin states under the Plata Basin Treaty. For Argentina and Uruguay, this consistency requirement implies, *inter alia,* taking account of system-wide hydrological interconnections and the interests of the three other riparians, as appropriate to secure harmonious basin development. In this case, therefore, the River Uruguay Statute embraces the Basin Scope through Coherence, a secondary element of Community-of-Interests analogous to Coherence in the context of Close Regional Cooperation, and which is examined in the next Part.

Lake Victoria is an integral component of the Nile basin. This generates complex interdependencies between the Protocol partner states and other Nile basin countries that are not parties to the Lake Victoria regime. To account for these interdependencies, Article 1 of the Protocol incorporates the water-system concept into its definition of the *Nile River Basin*, seen as encompassing all the Nile connected surface and underground waters that eventually flow into the Mediterranean Sea. On that basis, Article 5(7) refers to the relationship between the Lake Victoria Basin and the Nile River Basin; and requires partner states to "cooperate with other interested parties, regional or international bodies and programs", in light of the hydrological connections and resulting interdependencies that exist and have developed among riparians along the Nile watercourse system in its entire length. Supplementing the foregoing provisions, Article 50 authorizes accession to the Protocol by other countries which join the EAC Treaty. Since all Lake Victoria basin states are parties to that Treaty and to the Protocol, one may presume that, going forward, the parties' aspiration is to extend their Close Basin Cooperation regime progressively across the larger Nile basin.

1.3 *Water Systems, Biodiversity and the Drainage Basin*

The Basin Scope covers all dimensions of freshwater ecosystem connectivity. Whereas the water-system concept focuses on hydrological vertical and longitudinal (and, implicitly, temporal) connections, the horizontal dimension brings into the picture land-water-biodiversity interactions and mutual dependencies.

Framework Approaches to the Horizontal Dimension of the Basin Scope: The UNWC contains no express references to the basin and the definition of a watercourse mentions only the hydrological components of the system.

Yet, several UNWC provisions reveal therein the Basin Scope horizontal dimension and confirm the Convention's implied catchment-wide scope *rat-*

ione loci. The Preamble recalls Agenda 21 principles and recommendations; the valuable contribution of international organizations to international law codification and progressive development; and existing watercourse agreements. Agenda 21 calls for "the integration of land- and water-related aspects ... at the level of the catchment basin or sub-basin."[74] The ILA's Helsinki and Berlin Rules enable and promote not only system-long, but basin-wide management of transboundary waters and related resources.[75] The Rules have no binding power, but "are to be considered as an integral part of the body of the written and unwritten terms of reference"[76] for interpreting the UNWC. As for the Preambular allusion to existing agreements, the Basin Treaties analyzed in this book all account for land-water-biodiversity interactions within the catchment. Based on these references, Tanzi and Arcari remark: "between two possible interpretations of the [UNWC], one leading to retrograde results, the other bringing [the Convention] into line with the most recent international instruments in the field, the latter should prevail."[77]

Moreover, Article 1(1) defines the scope *ratione materiae* of the UNWC as encompassing the use, management, *and protection* of international watercourses and their waters. In its turn, Article 5(1) places the protection of international watercourses at the heart of equitable and reasonable use, remitting the interpreter to Article 20. The latter provision regulates watercourse protection and preservation, referring to the *ecosystem of international watercourses*, i.e., "an ecological unit consisting of living and nonliving components that are interdependent and function as a community".[78] According to Tanzi and Arcari, Article 20 states "a general obligation"[79] that aims to promote "a comprehensive and 'holistic' approach"[80] to watercourse protection. This obligation is well-founded on state practice and the work of international organizations.[81] Finally, Article 21(2) regulates watercourse pollution that may result in significant harm to other co-riparians or *to their environment*, "including harm to human health or safety, to the use of the waters for any beneficial purpose or to the living resources of the watercourse."

To the extent appropriate to comply with the above provisions, parties to the UNWC, when utilizing the watercourse and developing activities within

74 Agenda 21, *supra*, Para. 18.9.
75 *See* Helsinki Rules, *supra*, Arts.I–IV, X; Berlin Rules, *supra*, Arts.1, 3(5), 5–6.
76 Tanzi & Arcari, *supra*, p. 62.
77 *Id*, p. 61.
78 ILC (1994), *supra*, p. 118.
79 Tanzi & Arcari, *supra*, p. 60.
80 *Ibid.*
81 ILC (1994), *supra*, p. 119.

the catchment, must account for potential effects on all basin ecosystems. These ecosystems include the water system itself, aquatic biodiversity and the connected and interdependent wetlands and terrestrial environment within the watershed. Hence, the UNWC delimits the Basin Scope as appropriate to ensure compliance with state obligations thereunder. The horizontal dimension of this element of the Theory may come into play under the UNWC "as the area in which harmful activity is carried forward"[82] (e.g., irrigation runoff); and "as the affected area [where] a certain causal and geographical proximity with the watercourse itself can be demonstrated"[83] (e.g., water infrastructure that impacts migratory fish corridors and lead to watershed degradation through deforestation).

Beyond the use of the watercourse under Article 5(1), Article 20 demands that states diligently protect and preserve ecosystems, without connecting this obligation to potential transboundary impacts. This approach to ecosystem protection and preservation within the territory of riparian states, even where impacts across the border are not yet at play, requires states, at least to some degree, to act and cooperate taking account of horizontal linkages. This is the case, for example, with measures to mitigate land-based water pollution harmful to ecosystems, even if this pollution is not yet affecting other watercourse states but could affect them if left uncontrolled; with coordinated watershed restoration to control erosion and water quality impairment; or with joint action to monitor migratory fish populations throughout the basin.

In the case of the ECEWC, Article 2(6) requires states to cooperate on the development of policies, programs, and strategies "covering the relevant catchment areas, or parts thereof"; and targeting "the protection of the *environment of transboundary waters* or the *environment influenced by such waters*". In other words, resource management and planning tools under the ECEWC must be so designed as appropriate to safeguard all interrelated aquatic and terrestrial ecosystems within the catchment or subcatchment. Per the ECEWC Guide, the general geographic scope of co-riparian cooperation under the Convention is defined around the concept of *catchment area*, thus "encompassing also 'other elements' of the environment, ... *to the extent* that these 'other elements' interact with the relevant transboundary waters".[84] Accordingly, the parties to the Convention are to account for "the complex interrelationship between the

82 Tanzi & Arcari, *supra*, p. 63.
83 *Ibid.*
84 ECEWC Guide, *supra*, p. 14.

hydrological cycle, land, and flora and fauna, based on the understanding that water resources are an integral part of the ecosystem".[85]

Crowning the ECEWC's push for cooperation on horizontal interlinkages, Article 3(1)(i) requires parties to "develop, adopt, implement and, as far as possible, render compatible [governance] measures" aimed at preventing, reducing, and controlling transboundary impact; and, in particular, at promoting "sustainable water resources management, including [through] the application of the *ecosystems approach*".

The ECEWC and UNWC thus offer a template for the implementation of all three dimensions of the Basin Scope in a transboundary context. On the ground, the ECEWC has effectively contributed to integrated and ecosystem-based management of shared freshwaters, with benefits for the riparian states concerned.[86] This indicates that embracing the Basin Scope is not only scientifically preferable, but also politically feasible and likely to lead to positive results.

At the regional level, the two SADC Protocols corroborate the link between the horizontal dimension of the Basin Scope and Community-of-Interests. The Preambles of both the 1995 and the Revised SADC Protocols, like the UNWC, invoke the Helsinki Rules and Agenda 21. In its opening Preambular Paragraph, the new Protocol recalls the adoption of the UNWC, which, as just shown, fully embraces the Basin Scope. Placed in the Preambles of the two Protocols, those two soft-law instruments and the UNWC permeate the interpretation and application of the regional treaties at hand.

Moreover, Article 1(1) of the 1995 SADC Protocol explicitly incorporates and thus defines the expression *drainage basin*: "a geographical area determined by the watershed limits of a system of waters including underground waters flowing into a common terminus" – hence, not just the water system itself. The Protocol then inserts the word *basin* in the definition of a *shared watercourse system*. Article 2(2) employs the expression *watercourse systems and related resources* (i.e., water, land, biota), with Community-of-Interests being explicitly referenced in the same provision. Finally, Article 5(b)(v) of the 1995 Protocol foresees the design of *integrated master plans* for the region's shared watercourse systems. These tools give effect to the Basin Scope.

The Revised SADC Protocol captures the Basin Scope horizontal dimension in ways subtler than its 1995 counterpart, but more explicit in comparison to the UNWC. IWRM is embedded in two provisions: Article 2(c) emphasizes "coordinated and *integrated* environmentally sound development and man-

85 *Ibid.*

86 Unturbe, *supra*, p. 31.

agement" of shared freshwaters; and Article 4(d) mentions *generally accepted international rules and standards* – IWRM being an example of the latter.

Article 4(2) of the Revised SADC Protocol deals with environmental protection: letter 'a' requires states to protect and preserve the *ecosystems of shared watercourses*, basically reiterating Article 20 of the UNWC; and letter 'd' refers to the *aquatic environment, including estuaries*. Letter 'a' appears to be about the wider environment surrounding the watercourse, i.e., the catchment; and, letter 'd', about aquatic ecosystems *per se*, i.e., the water system and its biodiversity.

Articles 1(1) and 3(2) of the Revised Protocol introduce the concept of *environmental use*, i.e., "the use of water for the preservation and maintenance of ecosystems", alongside other forms of resource utilization. The explicit codification of environmental uses represents a clear recognition that the use of water for environmental purposes is no less important than those aimed at meeting social or economic ends. This is in line with Article 10 of the UNWC, according to which, as a rule, priority is not accorded to any particular water use. The Revised Protocol builds on this UNWC provision to cement the rule that the transboundary cooperation process must consider instream environmental uses and needs – and thus, any threats in connection with horizontal linkages within the basin, such as deforestation or overfishing. To note, other uses foreseen in the Protocol also require the maintenance of adequate instream flows, such as recreation, tourism, and fishing.

Horizontal Connectivity in the Basin Treaties: The Preamble of the Senegal Basin Charter views the River as an ecosystem essential for the sustainable development of the riparian states, to be considered as part of the entire hydrological cycle, and in view of all sectoral and intersectoral needs. Placed as such, horizontal connectivity permeates the application, interpretation, and implementation of the entire Charter.

Article 2 includes in the Charter's thematic scope the formulation of rules pertaining to the preservation and protection of the environment, in particular biodiversity, floodplains, and wetlands. Article 3 expressly defines the scope *ratione loci* of the Charter as encompassing the entire hydrographic basin of the River Senegal. Article 5 determines that decision-making on water allocation must consider resource availability by, *inter alia*, mainstreaming the environmental dimension into the management of water and maintaining healthy ecological conditions within the basin.

The horizontal dimension of the Basin Scope also comes to the fore in relation to planned measures within the Senegal basin. Under Articles 10–11 and 24–26 of the Charter, review and approval procedures apply to both proposed direct water uses and to land-based activities capable of modifying significantly the river's hydrological regime or physiographical features; conditions for navigational, agricultural, or industrial water uses; the sanitary status of its waters; or the biological characteristics of aquatic fauna and flora.

Taken together, the above provisions are evidence of the applicability of the Senegal Basin Charter to the entire river system, associated living resources, and its catchment. The Charter accounts for natural linkages within and across environmental realms and the health of all associated aquatic and terrestrial biodiversity. The Charter thus enables the management of the watercourse as a unitary whole, with the drainage basin as a primary planning unit. This includes attention to potential effects from land-based activities on the aquatic ecosystem; as well as from water uses on the wider environment. To recall, even for groundwater, the Charter displays its parties' intent to move towards conjunctive management and thus, to the full application of the Basin Scope.

For the Lake Victoria Community-of-Interests, the Protocol captures the horizontal dimension of the Basin Scope in various provisions. The Preamble starts by identifying the cross-sectoral and multidimensional interests targeted by Lake basin cooperation. These interests include increased investment in key sectors, like transport, communications, livestock, mining, and navigation safety; consideration of the environmental effects of development activities; a clean and healthy environment as a condition for sustainable development; and preservation of the aquatic environment. Building on this set of common interests, Article 3 details the Charter's scope *ratione materiae*, which encompasses sustainable use and management of water, fisheries, forestry and wetland resources; agriculture, irrigation, land use, and tourism; trade and commerce; industry, infrastructure, and energy; health and sanitation; research, capacity-building, and data-sharing; and basin management, environmental protection, and wildlife conservation. All these areas could not be addressed if not within the framework of the Basin Scope in all its dimensions.

Article 1 then confirms the Protocol's geographic scope by referring to the areas delimited by the watershed line, i.e., not just the water system but also connected land. Article 2 defines the expression *water resources* broadly, to include "all forms of water on the surface and in the ground, including the living and nonliving resources therein". Article 4(2)(j) treats basin ecosystems "as units, all of whose components are necessary to their proper functioning".

Crowning the above provisions, Article 4(2)(k) of the Protocol references Community-of-Interests in an international watercourse as a principle governing basin management, whereby all co-riparian states "have an *interest in* [*its*] *unitary whole*". By interconnecting Community-of-Interests and the idea of the catchment as a unitary whole, the Protocol places the Basin Scope at the heart of the Theory, as it is understood among the Lake Victoria riparian states.

In Latin America, the River Uruguay Statute is not only concerned with the water itself – the quality of which is addressed in Chapter x of the Basin Treaty. The Statute accounts for basin-wide interlinkages and promotes the integrated management of all associated natural resources – to an extent appropriate under a bilateral treaty focused primarily on the border section of an individual watercourse. Specifically, Articles 30–34 govern the exploration and exploitation of resources on the riverbed and in its subsoil. Article 35 requires the management of the soil and woodland to be compatible with the protection of the watercourse. Article 36 refers to the maintenance of a healthy ecological status and the control of harmful conditions "in the river *and the areas affected* by it". Articles 37–39 impose cooperation duties with regard to sustainable fishing and aquatic life conservation. Article 41(a) commits parties to the protection and preservation of the riverine environment.

Through the foregoing provisions, the River Uruguay Statute may apply to a variety of activities carried out by each party and which may harm the river segment constituting the main focus of cooperation. Accordingly, the Statute's Basin Scope of application extends to potentially harmful activities that do not involve the water resource itself or which take place outside that border segment, yet along and within the watercourse system and across its wider catchment.

Finally, in the Ecuador-Peru Agreement, the Preamble cites a sequence of treaty and policy instruments agreed upon by the two states over the years, going back to 1971. These documents consistently contain references to transboundary *basins* and include a call for integrated management plans for all such catchments. This indicates that the Basin Scope has been long ingrained in the history of Ecuador-Peru cooperation, and this is reflected throughout the Agreement.

The Basin Treaty at hand directly connects the Theory to the Basin Scope when recognizing, in the Preamble, "la *comunidad de intereses* que unen a ambos Estados en la gestión de las correspondientes *cuencas*".

The same Agreement reflects the Basin Scope in its Article 1-definitions: *Ecosystemic Vision*, which is multidisciplinary, dynamic (adaptive) and integrating, focused on a strategy for the integrated management of natural resources, with an emphasis on the water and its living resources, to contribute to conservation and sustainable use with equity; and *Hydrographic Units or Basins*, as natural spaces delimited by the watershed line, hierarchically organized by levels, with the drainage area extension as the only organizing criterium.

Cementing its embrace of the Basin Scope, the General Objective of the Ecuador-Peru Agreement, as defined in Article 3, builds on an ecosystemic and sustainable vision conducive to the improvement of people's lives and the aquatic ecosystems of the transboundary basins shared between the parties.

1.4 *Directions for Future Legal Development: Source-to-Sea Management*

Some of the treaties herein analyzed account for source-to-sea interactions and shared vulnerabilities, even though transboundary inland waters remain their central concern. Are these indications that the Basin Scope extends, or may be moving in the direction of extending, beyond the freshwater realm to account for natural connections with the coastal and marine environments?

The source-to-sea (S2S) approach pays attention to the continuous flows of water, biota, sediment, materials, pollutants, and ecosystem services, from headwaters on mountains along entire freshwater systems and all the way, through deltas, estuaries, coastlines, and the nearshore, into the sea.[87] With increased use of freshwaters impacting connected ecosystems, experts have emphasized the importance of the approach. Here is a sobering picture of what happens when states fail to account for aquatic connectivity all the way into the ocean. Each year, land-based activities are the source of 8 million tons of plastic reaching the sea. There are six international watercourses among the 10 rivers from which 90% of such marine pollution originates. Eutrophication of coastal and marine waters remains a major challenge linked to inadequate agricultural runoff and wastewater treatment. In some basins, overexploited rivers no longer or rarely reach the sea, with coastal ecosystems becoming deprived of freshwater flows, sediments and nutrients. Around the world, migratory freshwater-marine fish species have been significantly impacted by river fragmentation from poorly planned dam construction.[88]

The source-to-sea approach has been gaining traction in policy discourse. For example, the Dushanbe Declaration calls for integrated and sustainable resource management "from source to sea around the water, food, energy and

87 SIWI, *Policy Brief: Transboundary waters: Cooperation from Source to Sea* (2018), p. 1 ('SIWI (2018b)').

88 *Ibid.*

environment nexus";[89] and for "concentrated and coordinated efforts to build innovative, robust, flexible and fair systems"[90] for the integrated management of the source-to-sea "full continuum".[91]

In Law, the consideration of interlinkages across aquatic ecosystems is incipient. Article 23 of the UNWC, under the umbrella of Article 20 and related provisions, requires riparian states to "take all measures with respect to an international watercourse that are necessary to protect and preserve the marine environment, including estuaries". To that end, watercourse states must act individually and, where appropriate, in cooperation with *other states*, i.e., states outside the basin.

In its turn, the Preamble of ECEWC links the sustainable management of transboundary waters to the challenge of land-based pollution sources affecting the coastal and marine environments. Under this umbrella, Article 1(1) makes clear that the Convention's scope does not extend to the oceans, but Article 2(6) still requires states to cooperate on the development of policies, programs, and strategies to "protect the environment influenced by their transboundary waters, including the marine environment."[92]

In other words, the main scope *ratione loci* of the two Global Conventions is freshwater, but parties must still pay attention to the integrity of the *connected* marine environment. Accounting for source-to-sea connectivity under the Conventions means that transboundary cooperation in shared basins may, at times, have to reach beyond a river's mouth to ensure the protection of the marine environment and promote cooperation between riparian countries and non-riparian coastal states.

How this outreach would take place finds some clarity in relevant provisions of the ECEWC. Article 9(3)–(4) deals with the situation where a coastal state suffers significant detrimental effects transmitted through transboundary freshwaters which such a state does not border. In such cases, the riparian states concerned "can, if they all so agree, invite that coastal state to be involved in an appropriate manner in activities" carried out under the auspices of the respective joint body. In its turn, the joint body in question must invite the intergovernmental institution in place among the coastal states

89 2018 Dushanbe Conference, *supra*, Final Declaration: *Promoting Action and Policy Dialogue* ('Dushanbe Declaration'), at https://dushanbewaterprocess.org/wp-content/uploads/2019/11/2018-06-21-final-declaration-clean.pdf, Preamble, ¶7.

90 *Ibid*, ¶3.

91 SIWI (2018b), *supra*, p. 1.

92 ECEWC Guide, *supra*, p. 14.

directly affected by those transboundary waters "to cooperate in order to *harmonize* their work". These provisions have led an expert organization to point out that the ECEWC plants the seeds for integration of the source-to-sea approach into transboundary water cooperation thereunder, even if not in a comprehensive manner.[93]

Nonetheless, the ECEWC has influenced the drafting of basin agreements in the region that include within their scope the protection of the coastal and marine outlets of transboundary waters. On the Danube, for example, "early recognition of [S2S] priorities ... factors into the success of efforts to reduce nutrient pollution"[94] originating in that River and flowing into the connected Black Sea.

At the regional and basin levels, the endorsement of the source-to-sea approach is less evident. The 1995 SADC Protocol contains no provision in this respect.

Article 4(2)(d) of the Revised SADC Protocol refers to the "aquatic environment, including estuaries", but not to the marine environment more broadly. Still, an argument could be made that the text in that provision was changed in relation to its UNWC counterpart so as to include, under one umbrella, the protection of all aquatic ecosystems – from the freshwater, coastal and marine realms – and their connectivity.

Article 16 of the Senegal Basin Charter provides for its all-encompassing scope *ratione loci*, which extends to the coastal and marine environments. Under that provision, the parties commit to protecting and preserving the riverine ecosystem and managing water resources in a manner that respects ecological balance, with special attention being paid to fragile wetlands and the marine environment.

Case Study 3: Interactions between the Orange–Senqu River Basin and the Benguela Current Large Marine Ecosystem[95]

The discharges of the Orange–Senqu River into the Atlantic Ocean form the freshwater-marine connections that have brought together the *Orange-Senqu River Commission* (ORASECOM) and the *Benguela Current Commission* (BCC) to cooperate and exchange information on the

93 SIWI (2018b), *supra*, p. 1.

94 *Ibid.*

95 S. Matthews, *From Source to Sea: Interactions between the Orange-Senqu River Basin and the Benguela Current Large Marine Ecosystem* (Orange-Senqu River Commission 2013).

shared interests of their members in this globally significant Estuary.[96] Cooperation efforts aim at building a shared understanding "of how these freshwater and marine ecosystems interact and influence each other [and of] the impact of the altered state of the Orange–Senqu River and its catchment with respect to flow, sediment transport, nutrient loads and other water quality issues".[97] Progress has been made around connecting river development with the desiccation of the Estuary's saltmarsh and related restoration actions, as well as, led by ORASECOM, the assessment of environmental flow requirements of coastal ecosystems.[98] Examples of S2S connections in this geography are found in how "nutrients probably enhance the productivity of phytoplankton in the vicinity of the mouth, and hence the zooplankton that feed on them [and] are in turn a source of food for larval, juvenile and adult fish";[99] "the river's plume provides a cue for migration of marine and estuarine-dependent fish into the estuary";[100] and how "overall reduction in river flows probably allows marine sediment to extend slightly further up the estuary than under natural conditions".[101]

1.5 *Conclusions*

The Basin Scope, present across all treaties reflecting the Theory, is the first and more fundamental primary normative element of Community-of-Interests – the element which determines the basic geographic ambit of cooperation thereunder. The Basin Scope informs the design of the Theory's other primary elements, namely: the Basin Treaty, the Basin Body, and Close Basin Cooperation – all of which, as a minimum, must be so structured as to enable catchment-based management, to the extent appropriate in the concrete case.

The Basin Scope is rooted in science, representing connectivity as a key ecological attribute of freshwater ecosystems. This normative element of the Theory finds expression in IWRM and in the drainage basin approach, thus being captured in both policy and legal discourses.

---

96 *Agreement on the Establishment of the Orange-Senqu River Commission* (Windhoek, 3 Nov 2000), Botswana-Lesotho-Namibia-South Africa; *Benguela Current Convention* (Benguela, 18 Mar 2013), Angola-Namibia-South Africa.

97 Matthews, *supra*, p. 2.

98 *Id*, p. 33, 35.

99 *Id*, p. 21.

100 *Ibid.*

101 *Id*, p. 27.

According to the Basin Scope, cooperation framed by the Theory accounts for the interests and rights of all co-riparians and the scope *ratione loci* of each regime is principally (albeit not exclusively) catchment-based, whether basin-wide or at the sub-basin level. Community-of-Interests emerges fundamentally from the physical reality that river, lake, and aquifer systems, and their surrounding environment, form a natural unity unto themselves, in connection with which shared bonds, concerns, goals, priorities, risks, and opportunities may arise and deepen through time. Translating the Basin Scope into practice means accounting for water systems, i.e., the vertical and longitudinal hydrological connections between rivers, their tributaries, lakes, aquifers, wetlands, and so forth; and for ecosystems, i.e., the horizontal linkages between water, land and living resources within the watershed.

All treaties examined account for freshwater ecosystem connectivity in its three dimensions, as embedded in the Basin Scope, taking the hydrographic basin as the basic unit for transboundary water management and interstate cooperation. Those treaties do so to varying degrees and in different ways: context-specific agreements use clear, direct, and detailed terms, whereas framework legal instruments generally take a subtler approach, embracing the basin through a contextualized and coherent interpretation of a combination of related provisions. Regardless of how far each treaty goes in embracing the Basin Scope, they all reflect an acknowledgement on the part of their drafters and parties that hydrological and related interdependencies within a catchment must underpin the formulation of specific treaty norms.

The vertical and longitudinal dimensions of the Basin Scope come together under the water-system concept, which views transboundary river, lake, and aquifer systems as hydrological units, inclusive of all interconnected water bodies. Interlinking the Basin Scope and the Theory through the water-system concept finds corroboration in early navigation agreements, the Global Water Conventions, and the Basin Treaties examined here, as well as in the River Oder Decision.

The Global Conventions consider and promote the water system as a basic management unit, along with the involvement of all co-riparian states in the cooperation process. Yet, the UNWC, the ECEWC and the SADC Protocols do not require that context-specific agreements be always adopted among all states within a basin or that they apply to the entire watercourse. Partial agreements can be consistent with Community-of-Interests, provided that parties pay due consideration to the connectivity of the water system as whole. The UNWC carefully regulates partial agreements to safeguard the interests and promote the inclusion, as much as possible, of all co-riparian states in relevant negotiations and dialogue. The ECEWC emphasizes system-long cooperation as likely the most appropriate scale for the planning, management and protection of transboundary waters. The Revised SADC Protocol follows similar approaches to the treatment of partial agreements. Parties to these partial agreements remain bound by their obligations under international law so that the geographic scope of the treaties into which they enter should take those obligations into consideration.

The horizontal dimension of the Basin Scope has to do with ecological linkages between aquatic, terrestrial and living resources. As framed by Community-of-Interests, the Basin Treaties examined here, even when they do not apply to the entire basin, are structured and designed in ways that promote the management of the basin as a unitary whole, i.e., bearing in mind interconnections and potential transboundary effects on the water system, together with associated lands and biodiversity. As framework treaties, the UNWC, the ECEWC and the SADC Protocols promote consideration of horizontal freshwater ecosystem connectivity – for example, by referring to the *basin/catchment* or to *ecosystems* – concepts that in law, policy, and science are broader than the *watercourse* or the *water system*.

Community-of-interests, therefore, is primarily founded on the Basin Scope but still injects some flexibility into the consideration of hydrological and ecological connections. Flexibility is in line with the Theory's characteristic of not dealing in absolutes and applying fundamentally to where-appropriate situations, so that partial Basin Treaties may be chosen when basin-level planning is unnecessary or unfeasible.

Further, basin-wide management may be supplemented by planning and implementation on other scales, since Community-of-Interests does not foreclose and, indeed, may be advanced through multilevel cooperative efforts, so long as states do not lose sight of basin-wide flows and connections and, where appropriate, act diligently at the catchment level with a view to protecting common interests.

A well-developed community-of-basin-interests is one where all co-basin states come together at least to develop a common understanding of, and vision for, freshwater and related cross-sectoral challenges and opportunities across the entire water system, associated biodiversity, and the surrounding environment. Implementation occurs at the most appropriate level for each activity. In practice, states have embraced the Theory with some degree of flexibility, with the concrete case influencing the appropriate scale of transboundary water cooperation within individual communities-of-basin-interests.

Finally, moving towards source-to-sea approaches would mean extending the longitudinal dimension of the Basin Scope to require riparian countries not only to account for the interests of third coastal states but, as appropriate, to also interact with those states under the Community-of-Interests regime in question. It could be that the UNWC and the ECEWC signal a direction towards which the Theory might evolve, in terms of integrating source-to-sea concerns into freshwater management. However, among the treaties that unequivocally reflect the Theory, there is a lack of consistency. For now, it is not possible to affirm that the source-to-sea approach expresses a fourth dimension of the Basin Scope.

2 Drainage Basin Treaty

> *Transboundary agreements can support a culture of cooperation and trust, allowing for the leveraging and sharing of benefits that are not accessible at national scales.*[102]

The *Community-of-Interests Drainage Basin Treaty* ('Basin Treaty') is the second primary element of Community-of-Interests. As noted previously, there is abundant evidence of the central role of Founding Charters, on their own or in succession, in stepping up cooperation efforts as deemed necessary to advance and safeguard shared interests under the umbrella of Regional Integration Organizations. Here, too, all precedents examined place strong and consistent emphasis on the importance and even necessity of the Basin Treaty to formalize, regulate and institutionalize cooperation framed by the Theory. The Basin Treaty is a special kind of watercourse agreement.

2.1 *Legal Significance of Watercourse Agreements*

Throughout at least the last 800 years, political units have entered into agreements and arrangements for water cooperation at the basin and/or sub-basin levels. UNECE *et al* report a total of 450 of these instruments.[103] Watercourse agreements express the riparian countries' commitment to international cooperation; offer a solid foundation for the channeling of financial and technical assistance; and serve as a platform for engaging stakeholders.

The scope and purposes of transboundary water agreements and arrangements vary – from covering a specific basin, or a part thereof, to encompassing a set of transboundary waters shared between two countries; from enabling cooperation on a variety of water uses to only regulating interstate engage-

102 UNWC 2023 Summary, *supra*, p. 5.

103 UNECE *et al*, *supra*, p. 44.

ment on a specific common-interest project; from being principally concerned with coexistence to centering the regime on common interests, and so forth.

When placed in the context of the broader relations of the basin countries concerned, watercourse agreements enable states to maintain and deepen mutual trust by considering during negotiations a basket of interests and benefits, thus "approaching [points of contention] on a much wider basis".[104] In the case of the Meuse, for example, Netherlands and Belgium tackle their water differences "[b]y including the solution of various other problems ... affecting the relations between the two countries [thus] justifying each party in making concessions which it would not have felt justified in making unless [each party] had received satisfaction in other directions".[105]

Going back to the 1970s, Principle 24 of the Stockholm Declaration already places special emphasis on bilateral or multilateral cooperation arrangements for dealing with potential or actual adverse effects from human activities in ways that account for the interests of all countries. Historically, a key motivation for these instruments has been the primitive status of customary law, with its ambiguities and uncertainties, leaving countries unsure of their rights and obligations and so, less inclined to cooperate and/or more vulnerable to abuse.

The generality of the customary rule of equitable and reasonable use, for instance, may add to tensions rather than aid in the prevention and resolution of disputes when applied in the absence of a water agreement or solely within the framework of Limited Territorial Sovereignty.[106] Dellapenna describes equitable and reasonable use as meaning that "each state recognizes the right of all riparian states to use some water from a common source and the obligation to manage their uses so as not to interfere with like uses in other riparian states."[107] He then questions if the excessively vague notion of correlative rights suffices to guide and govern relations between states amidst growing demands for a stressed shared resource; and concludes: "a more comprehensive and more elaborate system of cooperative management and water sharing"[108] is needed for optimal use and the allocation of mutual benefits.

104 PCIJ, *The Diversion of Water from the Meuse* (Netherlands *v.* Belgium), Judgment of 28 June 1937, Series A/B, Judgments, Orders and Advisory Opinions, Fascicule 70 (1937) ('Meuse Diversion Case'), p. 13.

105 *Ibid.*

106 Dellapenna (1996), *supra*, p. 228, 238.

107 *Id*, p. 229.

108 *Id*, p. 237.

More recently, draft codifications proposed by experts, framework regional and global conventions and the preparatory work preceding them, including those examined in this book, have served as templates for treaty design, helping to clarify the normative content of the principles and rules of international water law. According to the UNWC's preparatory work, the ILC was motivated by the realization that, thus far, states had lacked "firm common ground as a basis for negotiations",[109] and this gap had hampered the adoption of watercourse agreements.

Watercourse agreements apply and adjust customary law, often on the basis of the UNWC and the ECEWC, which, for their part, codify, clarify, and develop international water law. In so doing, the UNWC recalls, in its Preamble, the existing bilateral and multilateral water treaties. In Article 3(3), the UNWC explicitly notes that states *may* adopt context-specific agreements. Hence, the Convention does not impose an obligation on co-riparian states to enter into those agreements.[110]

Yet, the UNWC greatly emphasizes the importance of context-specific treaties for sustainable water management. In effect, as noted by Taylor, the Convention implicitly anticipates the continued need for treaties dealing with individual watercourses.[111] In other words, the Convention acknowledges that optimal and sustainable international watercourse management is "best achieved through an agreement tailored to the characteristics of that watercourse and to the needs of the states concerned".[112]

This is corroborated by Article 3(5), which anticipates the situation where a given riparian country finds that applying and adjusting relevant UNWC provisions "is required because of the characteristics and uses of a particular international watercourse"; and mandates the riparian states concerned to "consult with a view to negotiating *in good faith* for the purpose of concluding" a context-specific treaty. By *mandating* countries to engage in consultations aimed at the adoption of a watercourse agreement upon a request by another riparian, the UNWC goes as far as a framework treaty negotiated at the global level could, in terms of triggering the wider adoption of such agreements. In so doing, the Convention reinforces the place of treaties under Community-of-Interests.

Having started as a regional instrument, the ECEWC goes further than the UNWC. At the outset, the ECEWC Preamble makes clear that transboundary

109 ILC (1994), *supra*, p. 93.

110 *Ibid.*

111 Taylor, *supra*, p. 51.

112 *Ibid.*

water cooperation is to be implemented "*primarily* through the elaboration of agreements between countries bordering the same waters". The word *primarily* here implies *preferably* but does not mean *exclusively*. Building on this flexibility, Article 2(6) of the ECEWC commands co-basin states to cooperate in the design of water management plans and related governance tools, such as policies, programs, and strategies; and to do so, *in particular*, within the framework of bilateral and multilateral agreements. Per Article 9(1), co-riparian countries *shall* enter into agreements, but may choose to adopt other relevant arrangements, as long as they meet the goal of defining their mutual relations and conduct under the Convention.

In Southern Africa, the two SADC Protocols acknowledge the importance of a regional convention to facilitate the adoption of future context-specific treaties. In addition, the SADC Protocols align with the UNWC by not imposing, but encouraging, the adoption of watercourse agreements on the basis of those agreed-upon regional frameworks. In the 1995 SADC Protocol, Article 3(1) lays out a general undertaking among parties to establish joint bodies. The provision implies, as a minimum, an underpinning commitment by parties to negotiate treaties in good faith as part of the process of putting in place the appropriate basin organizations. In turn, Article 2(a) of the Revised Protocol specifies the objective to promote and facilitate the adoption of the agreements and institutions necessary to support the pursuit of the underlying goal of Close Basin Cooperation. Both Protocols, therefore, interconnect the Theory and the Basin Treaty, which governs and guides communities-of-basin-interests.

The UNWC is also designed as a fallback general framework regulating shared watercourses, to be applied when or while the states concerned see no need or lack political appetite for context-specific treaties.[113] The same may be said of the ECEWC and the Revised SADC Protocol. This aspect adds value to the purpose of those instruments to serve as authoritative templates of thoroughly negotiated basic norms.

At two levels, therefore, the two Global Conventions and the SADC Protocol endorse the crucial, where not indispensable, role of legal instruments as enablers of good-faith cooperation, peaceful interstate relations, socioeconomic development, and environmental sustainability.

113 *See* UNWC, *supra*, Preamble, ¶3; ILC (1994), *supra*, p. 92.

2.2 *The Watercourse Agreement* versus *the Basin Treaty*

Despite the use of the UNWC, the ECEWC and other global and regional models by many context-specific treaties, the normative content of watercourse agreements varies considerably. According to the UNWC's preparatory work, an awareness of the different circumstances characterizing the world's international watercourses, and of how such differences posed a challenge to the formulation of globally applicable rules, had been present throughout the ILC's effiorts on the topic.[114] UN Water interprets this variety as indicating the absence of one single formula for the drafting of water treaties.[115]

Any watercourse agreement, including the Basin Treaty, is thus *context-specific*, since each drainage basin – and, in large systems, even individual sub-basins – have their own particular traits, which give rise to state interests tied to local circumstances. Such traits may be linked to environmental features (biodiversity, climate, geography, hydrology, and corresponding degradation drivers and threats), socioeconomic challenges and opportunities (current, future and potential water uses; cultural practices; demography), and governance mechanisms (domestic and international governing frameworks; policies and institutions; management tools; financing).[116]

However, the Basin Treaty is different from agreements based on Limited Territorial Sovereignty. Conversely, not all watercourse agreements can be qualified as a Basin Treaty. Hence, "an agreement on rules that each state implements individually in the national context and with little or no coordination"[117] would not fall within the concept of a Basin Treaty.

Case Study 4: Indus Water Treaty

The Indus Water Treaty[118] is, first and foremost, "a partition agreement";[119] and thus, hardly conducive to the joint pursuit of common interests. The central purpose of this Treaty is to enable peaceful coexistence, specifically by allocating mainstream and tributary waters between India and Pakistan; outlining each parties' related rights and obligations; and supporting the peaceful settlement of interstate disputes when these arise, as they often have.[120] Close Basin Cooperation

114 ILC (1994), *supra*, p. 92.

115 UN Water (2018), *supra*, p. 13.

116 Drawing from Dellapenna & Gupta (2013), *supra*, p. 12.

117 Leb (2013), *supra*, p. 177.

118 *Indus Water Treaty* (Karachi, 19 Sep 1960), India-Pakistan.

119 *Id.*

120 *See*, e.g., A. Swain, Untitled Presentation, Panel IV – Current Transboundary Freshwater Disputes: North Africa, South Asia, and Southeast Asia, International Conference – A

plays a minimal role, with most individual treaty provisions involving principally unilateral restraint, as explained in the following paragraphs.

Under the Indus Water Treaty, Article VII, titled *Future* Cooperation, refers to the parties' "common interest in the optimum development of the rivers"; and, accordingly, declares "their intention to cooperate, by mutual agreement, to the fullest possible extent;" and foresees that either party may request the other to cooperate, by mutual agreement, on river engineering works. While Article VII looks promising, the Treaty does little else in terms of supporting cooperation framed by Community-of-Interests.

After its brief emphasis on common interests, the same Article VII immediately returns to a Limited Territorial Sovereignty mindset by focusing on basic notification and data-sharing requirements in relation to unilaterally planned measures capable of interfering with agreed water allocations. The provision also specifies the scope of future cooperation, proposing the installation and operation of additional monitoring stations within the territory of one party, upon the other's request, for purpose of data-sharing. In contrast, under Community-of-Interests, information would more likely be collected and processed jointly. Similarly, the provision foresees coordination in the development of future drainage works, as opposed to planning and/or execution in common.

To illustrate further, per Articles VI and V of the Indus Water Treaty, India agrees to contribute financially to the construction of irrigation works within Pakistan in conformity with the Agreement's allocation scheme, thus aimed at replacing existing incompatible infrastructure. But Article V then makes clear that said financial contribution is "not to be construed as conferring upon India any right to participate in the decisions as to the system of works". In terms of coordination, Article VI is limited to governing the regular exchange of specified data concerning river flows and water uses; and foreseeing the possibility for additional data to be requested and provided if available.

On the ground, the Indus Water Treaty has not led to concrete cooperative efforts beyond what is required in relation to compliance with agreed water allocations. Swain sums up the Indus Water Treaty as an agreement to *not* cooperate, premised on the lack of mutual trust between the parties, given

---

Bridge over Troubled Waters: Dispute Resolution in the Law of International Watercourses and the Law of the Sea (Luxembourg, 25–26 Sep 2017), Max Planck Institute Luxembourg for Procedural Law ('Swain (2017')), at https://www.youtube.com/watch?v=d3aafljN60Q&list=PLhELkA58aBZt010iJs_HQU3UQF26dqxJm&index=5&t=2772s.

their history. Any vision of less limited cooperation is hampered by the parties' continued reliance on political tactics and provocations. Swain calls for the Treaty to be upgraded into a framework actually committing and better enabling both countries to cooperate.[121] In short, even with its reference to common interests, the Indus Water Treaty is not an agreement based on the Theory. In light of Swain's just noted criticism, the agreement's incompatibility with the Theory reflects upon its implementation, evidencing the importance of adequate treaty design as framed by Community-of-Interests.

If the Basin Treaty is not just any context-specific agreement or arrangement between co-riparian states, how, then, is this normative element of Community-of-Interests different from other watercourse agreements, i.e., those founded principally on Limited Territorial Sovereignty and so not designed to serve communties-of-basin-interests?

Based on the Analytical Framework here constructed, it is possible to draw a clear distinction. The Basin Treaty is negotiated and adopted between the co-riparian states within a particular drainage basin with the *specific intent* to support the pursuit of common interests. The Theory underpins the scope, content, and institutional governance of these agreements. From Argentina's perspective, for example, as described by the ICJ, the River Uruguay Statute "is not merely a bilateral treaty imposing reciprocal obligations on the parties; it establishes an institutional framework for close and ongoing cooperation",[122] i.e., Close Basin Cooperation.

Specifically, the Basin Treaty promotes the Basin Scope; is a binding instrument; serves core purposes linked to the common interests its parties set out to protect; displays special procedural and substantive legal features in support of Close Basin Cooperation; and creates the institutional architecture charged with housing the community-of-basin-interests in question. As a subset of watercourse agreements, Basin Treaties represents the Theory's second normative element – one aimed at formalizing, regulating and institutionalizing a community-of-basin-interests.

Considering the many treaties in existence, Limited Territorial Sovereignty has been the most widely applied theoretical framework for negotiations

121 *Id.* Surfacing the fraught relations between the two countries, and which underlie the character of the Indus Water Treaty as a framework for coexistence based on Limited Territorial Sovereignty, India has recently suspended the Treaty in reaction to a terrorist attack. Foreign Secretary, *Statement on the Decision of the Cabinet Committee on Security* (23 Apr 2025), Ministry of External Affairs, https://www.mea.gov.in/Speeches-Statements.htm?dtl/39442.

122 Pulp Mills Case, *supra* p. 35.

between riparian states,[123] but the agreements and judicial precedents examined in this book, as representative of state practice, contribute to pushing the needle towards Community-of-Interests.

2.3 *Scope* Ratione Loci

The Basin Scope is the most fundamental element of Community-of-Interests and thus informs all others. While this element might seem progressive, UN Water finds that the value of basin-wide agreements has been recognized by numerous countries.[124]

A Basin Treaty designed to further a fully developed community-of-basin-interests would involve all co-riparian states and apply along the whole water system and across the entire drainage basin and its ecosystems.

Where this full endorsement of the Basin Scope is unnecessary or unfeasible, the Basin Treaty incorporates the three dimensions of freshwater ecosystem connectivity as much as possible and, at least, as appropriate to safeguard the common interest at stake and to move towards covering the entire catchment progressively. In essence, the parties to a Basin Treaty accept the prominence of the Basin Scope to inform their cooperation under Community-of-Interests.

The ECEWC, the UNWC, and the two SADC Protocols generally promote the Basin Scope, while allowing for the adoption of partial agreements in compliance with the applicable legal limitations. Where appropriate, the UNWC and the Revised SADC Protocol require full state involvement in relevant treaty negotiations. The ECEWC centers on the catchment, the management of which often entails involvement of all basin states. Hence, the framework instruments tie together the Basin Scope and the Basin Treaty.

At the catchment level, the Basin Treaties that refer explicitly to Community-of-Interests give strong expression and effect to the Basin Scope in delimiting their biogeographic ambit. The Senegal Basin Charter involves all states within the catchment and applies across the entire longitudinal e horizontal dimensions of the Basin Scope, while striving for a gradual integration of groundwaters. The Lake Victoria Protocol incorporates all three dimensions, albeit at the subcatchment level.

In both cases, not all basin states are among the original parties to the Basin Treaty in question. However, both the Senegal Basin Charter and the Lake Victoria Protocol include provisions leaving the doors open for other basin states to join. In the latter case, being a sub-catchment level Basin Treaty,

123 *See*, e.g., Taylor, *supra*, p. 27; McCaffrey (2019), *supra*, p. 135, 218–9; Islam, *supra*, p. 114.
124 UN Water (2018), *supra*, p. 76.

the Protocol also emphasizes the Lake Victoria as part of the broader Nile Basin.

In its turn, the Senegal Basin Charter was initially adopted only among three of the four basin countries, but already during its drafting the eventual inclusion of Guinea into the fold was considered. The Preamble affirms the interest of the original parties in accounting for the Guinean part of the basin when designing relevant policies and programs; and Article 27 leaves the Charter open to accession by all riparians. Accordingly, Article 1 differentiates between *riparian states*, which include all four basin states; and *state parties*, limited to the countries that accede thereto. Framing those definitions, the 17th Preambular Paragraph recognizes a community-of-basin-interests formed of riparian states, as opposed to one involving only the state parties. Through the above provisions, the Charter positions all four basin states as innate members of the Senegal Basin Community-of-Interests, even before each country's accession. In 2006, through the Guinea Membership Treaty, the formalized Senegal Basin Community-of-Interests became complete, enabling its concrete application within all four co-basin states, as had always been intended.

The River Uruguay Statute implicitly incorporates the Theory even though it has a more limited scope. This narrower ambit reflects the priority common interest of Argentina and Uruguay in the watercourse segment that forms the border between them. Even in this latter case, the parties' intent to advance the Basin Scope as much as possible is evident in treaty design, in line with Community-of-Interests.

The Ecuador-Peru Agreement takes a different approach by applying to nine of the countries' shared catchments. When naming those basins, Article 2 views them comprehensively as natural sources of water in its distinct forms, physical states and elements, and which comprise surface and underground continental waters and the resources associated therewith. The same provision draws attention to the specificities and characteristics of each basin, thus viewed as unities in their own right.

2.4 *Formalization of Communities-of-Interests*

The Basin Treaty *formalizes, regulates, and institutionalizes cooperation* centered on common interests, i.e., agreed-upon overarching concerns, which such a Treaty identifies and aims to safeguard and realize. The context-specific agreements that fulfill these three purposes – chiefly, in the service of shared state interests – embody the normative element of Community-of-Interests here examined.

Co-basin states formalize the cooperation process through the adoption of the Basin Treaty because the legal stability and certainty offered by a binding instrument are better suited to enable long-term planning and adaptation to evolving circumstances and changing interests. Only in a treaty, within the meaning of Article 2(1)(a) of the VCLT, states foresee the need for consent to its effects, with resulting rights and obligations under international law.[125] In this sense, a binding agreement serves as a solid legal basis for Close Basin Cooperation under the Theory.

Among the treaties reflecting the Theory, the UNWC and the SADC Protocols refer simply to watercourse *agreements*.

Article 9(1) of the ECEWC mentions agreements *and other arrangements* as adequate bases for co-riparian states to define their mutual relations and conduct. Otherwise, the ECEWC does not explicitly clarify whether, and the extent to which, an agreement *versus* an arrangement may each have a different function in this regard. As a subtle indication in this respect, the Preamble and Article 2(6), on catchment planning, reference only agreements. Under the ECEWC regime, therefore, even if both agreements and arrangements are acceptable as a basis for cooperation, an interpretative Preambular paragraph and the provision on planning suggest that binding instruments are generally presumed to be more adequate to serve the Convention's purposes.

At the basin level, the instruments adopted between the Lake Victoria, Uruguay, and Rhine riparian states, respectively, all consist of binding international agreements, providing formal legal bases for Close Basin Cooperation. The same is true for the Ecuador-Peru Agreement.

In the case of the Senegal basin, the parties view the Charter as a durable and evolutionary *cadre* – i.e., a long-lasting, and yet adaptable, tailored-made binding governing framework – upon which to base their community-of-basin -interests. The adjective *durable* implies a *treaty*, rather than an informal arrangement merely stating political commitments. The adjective *adaptable* is realized through Article 29, the Charter's built-in flexibility mechanism. The provision foresees amendments to the Annexes, which regulate the management of existing installations, in response to changes within the basin.

Indeed, to be effective and long-lasting, the Basin Treaty needs to have some elasticity by including, for example, "specific water and allocation provisions that address variations in water flow and changing needs".[126] As Howden notes, Community-of-Interests "seek[s] a balance between legal predictability and stability and flexibility in order to ensure trust in, and compliance

125 VCLT, *supra*, Art.14(1)(a).

126 Unturbe, *supra*, p. 40.

with, legal rules and regimes, while also respecting and promoting the natural processes and dynamics of the watercourse".[127]

In case law, the Gabčíkovo ICJ Decision emphasizes stability of treaty relations and the rule *pacta sunt servanda* to reject all arguments made to allege that the agreement in dispute had been terminated. The Court remarks on the exceptional character of a claim based on Article 62 of the VCLT as a valid ground for treaty termination; and concludes that even the parties' reciprocal noncompliance with such an agreement cannot affect its continued operation, absent mutual consent to its termination.[128] The Decision goes on to note how parties have implemented the agreement at stake "in considerable measure and at great cost over a period of years",[129] which reinforces the inadmissibility of unilateral termination.

In his Separate Opinion, Judge Bedjaoui points to the importance of providing international commitments with legal certainty and to the role of the ICJ in guaranteeing respect for international law, by affirming "*urbi et orbi* that treaties are not 'scraps of paper' and ... cannot be destroyed by violating them".[130] Unless, therefore, all parties agree, "states cannot and may not rid themselves [easily] of their treaty obligations".[131]

All these precedents suggest that a binding and enforceable agreement, as is the Basin Treaty, is the appropriate framework for Close Basin Cooperation within a *stable* community-of-basin-interests. The Basin Treaty formalizes interdependence and gives parties a strong level of assurance that all basin countries will cooperate in the long-term, thereby safeguarding the stability and effectiveness of the community-of-interests it supports. Within an environment of greater legal certainty, states bound by a treaty are better positioned to pursue common interests and balance individual concerns as these grow in scale and complexity. Conversely, *de facto* interdependent co-basin states "may hesitate to cooperate if through cooperation the game structure could change, and they would no longer be able to reciprocate to the defection of others."[132]

Still, arrangements such as declarations, memoranda of understanding, technical guidelines and model rules may lay the ground for the future adoption of the Basin Treaty. To build on analogies with Regional Integration

127 Howden, *supra*, p. 209.

128 Gabčíkovo Case, *supra*, p. 65, 68.

129 *Id*, p. 68.

130 Gabčíkovo Case, *Separate Opinion*, M. Bedjaoui, p. 138.

131 *Ibid.*

132 Benvenisti, *supra*, p. 392.

Organizations, the ASEAN precedent suggests that a political declaration may be employed as an initial step, appropriate for the early stages of a given regime. In the case of ASEAN, the Declaration was in time succeeded by a Founding Charter, when the states concerned reached agreement on the need for deeper and more systematic cooperation on the basis of binding rules, and under an empowered institutional umbrella with legal personality.

Similarly, soft arrangements may support *de facto* communities-of-basin-interests when common interests are not as pronounced. Such arrangements then serve as steppingstones towards formalization. Within the framework of a nonbinding instrument, for example, states begin to act under the Theory by developing a shared knowledge base, legal and technical capacities, mutual confidence, and political will.

As the states' interests in the watercourse deepen, becoming more evident and entangled, factual interdependence no longer suffices and cooperation framed by the Theory then requires a Basin Treaty to create *legal* interdependence. At that point, the Basin Treaty becomes the appropriate (or necessary), mutually agreed, tailored, and binding legal basis that formalizes the community-of-basin-interests, thereby guaranteeing frequent and long-term exchanges, governing state engagement and joint action, and clarifying the content and applicability of the rules of the game.

In this sense, the Ecuador-Peru Agreement establishes its general aim in Article 3, which is to *consolidate* binational cooperation for *improved* transboundary water management, building on prior political documents and agreements.

In short, informal arrangements may facilitate the early stages of cooperation within communities-of-basin-interests, but the Basin Treaty eventually proves necessary to secure Close Basin Cooperation.

To illustrate, consider the *Pantanal Declaration*, adopted in 2018 by Bolivia, Brazil and Paraguay.[133] The Declaration consists of a nonbinding political statement, outlining commitments and guidelines with regard to the sustainable and collaborative management of the Pantanal – a large wetland within the Plata basin, viewed by the signatories as a major transboundary development hub, endowed with a wealth of biological, cultural, and landscape diversity.

---

133 Bolivia-Brazil-Paraguay, 8th World Water Forum (Brasilia, 18–23 Mar 2018), *Declaração para a Conservação, Desenvolvimento Integral e Sustentável do Pantanal* (Declaration on the Conservation and Integrated and Sustainable Development of the Pantanal) (Brasilia, 22 Mar 2018) ('Pantanal Declaration').

The Pantanal Declaration is a cooperative *arrangement* among co-riparian states, within the meaning of the ECEWC; and, when we take a closer look, the Document appears to reflect Community-of-Interests. The Declaration notes the permanent dialogue among the three signatories, through which they have identified common interests in the region's environment and socioeconomic development; and emphasizes collaboration, integration, and fraternity – all notions linked to Community-of-Interests.

The Basin Scope comes to the fore through references to SDG-6 and the riparians' commitment to attain IWRM through transboundary cooperation; to its signatories' intent to manage water and biodiversity in an integrated fashion; and to the close interconnections and mutual dependence between the region's wetlands, their water sources, and related ecological functions, which require taking the whole of the Paraguay sub-basin as a unity in planning processes. Connecting the Pantanal to the Plata basin, the Declaration refers to regional integration opportunities from linkages between the Pantanal's ecosystems and biodiversity and population and development needs within the wider catchment and to the integration of the trilateral efforts thereunder into a basin-wide ongoing regional initiative.

Linking to the Basin Treaty, the Declaration recalls the three countries' political will and commitment to enter into agreements – as enablers of good governance, enhanced national policies, transboundary coordination and, ultimately, the region's protection, conservation, and sustainable management. Such agreements would contemplate an integrated vision for the protection of the region and its ecological functions as essential bases for sustainable development, within the framework of an integrated territorial vision for the broader Paraguay sub-basin, as well as the creation of institutional mechanisms to ensure the reasonable and equitable use of transboundary waters.

Finally, the Pantanal Declaration touches on Close Basin Cooperation through its emphasis on the cooperation principle, joint action, and coordinated plans, programs, and projects, all aimed, *inter alia*, at maintaining ecological functions; securing sustainable environmental flows; responding to the effects of climate change, including through resilient productive systems; protecting biodiversity, including through protected areas attentive to ecological connectivity and sustainable production practices; preventing, reducing and controlling pollution; exchanging information and technology; and expanding relevant scientific knowledge.

The Pantanal Declaration is thus a governance framework for a community-of-basin-interests under development, possibly moving towards the adoption of a formal legal-institutional regime.

Arrangements may also add value after the Basin Treaty is adopted, as common interests evolve. This has happened in the Lake Victoria, with the adoption of the *Harmonized Guidelines for Establishment and Management of Fish Breeding and Nursery Areas*, endorsed under the *Lake Victoria Fisheries Organization.*[134]

In some cases, informal arrangements may be the only option for the foreseeable future through which states may cooperate and generate positive outcomes. Despite the presence and evidence of common interests, co-riparian states within certain basins lack political appetite to enter into a binding legal instrument or have yet to overcome all their differences. In time, building on informal cooperation, the scenario may change, as is the case in the Nile basin.

Case Study 5: From the NBI to the Nile Cooperative Framework

For over two decades, Nile basin states have engaged in cooperation under the *Nile Basin Initiative* (NBI) – a soft governance mechanism supported by various international actors. The seeds for the NBI were planted during informal exchanges between the states concerned in the 1990s, with facilitation by neutral third parties. The launch took place in Dar-es-Salaam, in 1999, gathering all co-basin states as active participants, with the exception of Eritrea, involved today as an observer.[135] The NBI *Shared Vision Objective* focuses on the pursuit of "sustainable socioeconomic development through equitable utilization of, and benefit from, the *shared* Nile *basin* water resources".[136] The Initiative's basin-wide scope, as implied in this Vision Objective, demonstrates how arrangements may endorse primary elements of Community-of-Interests.[137] The NBI served as a precursor to the *Nile Cooperative Framework*, adopted at last to formalize, deepen, and regulate coopera-

134 Lake Victoria Fisheries Organization, *Harmonized Guidelines for Establishment and Management of Fish Breeding and Nursery Areas in Lake Victoria* (Jinja, 2019), adopted under the *Convention for the establishment of the Lake Victoria Fisheries Organization*, Burundi-Uganda-Kenya-Tanzania (Kisumu, 30 June 1994) (in force 24 May 1996).

135 S.M.A. Salman, *Entry into Force of the UN Watercourses Convention – Where are the Nile Basin Countries?* International Water Law Project Blog (2 June 2014), at https://www.internationalwaterlaw.org/blog/2014/06/02/dr-salman-m-a-salman-entry-into-force-of-the-un-watercourses-convention-where-are-the-nile-basin-countries/.

136 Nile Basin Initiative (NBI), Our Goals, at https://nilebasin.org/our-goals (emphasis added).

137 For examples of cooperation on the ground under the NBI, *see ibid.*, at https://nilebasin.org/projects_all/nelsap-cu & https://nilebasin.org/projects_all/entro.

tion within the basin.[138] The NBI member countries had prioritized from the beginning the adoption of a definitive and formal framework for long-term cooperation. In fact, the NBI was originally conceived with the primary goal to facilitate the adoption of a basin-wide treaty, involving all Nile states; and initial activities in this connection followed immediately the Initiative's formal launch.[139] In line with Community-of-Interests, cooperation is "clearly and unequivocally [the Agreement's] defining theme".[140]

2.5 *Regulation and Institutionalization of Communities-of-Interests*

A watercourse agreement mostly framed by Limited Territorial Sovereignty centers on coexistence. Yet, governing cooperation under the Theory requires more than simply delimiting rights and duties or allocating the resource for continued unilateral use. The Basin Treaty is intentionally designed so as to enable close, long-term, mutually beneficial, and peaceful interstate engagement for the attainment of the parties' agreed-upon goals and objectives. The Basin Treaty is also concerned with coexistence but takes the additional steps of *pinpointing the central common interests* to be pursued and safeguarded thereunder; and, under the umbrella of Close Basin Cooperation, of *promoting joint interstate action as the primary approach to the pursuit of common interests*, with coordination and unilateral measures still being allowed and regulated, but generally as subsidiary forms of state engagement.

The Basin Treaty thus establishes legal obligations and commitments with a view to building a solid and tailored framework for interstate relations within a community-of-basin-interests – one that may evolve, expand, and deepen through time, while withstanding external shocks and potential disagreements among members.

Identifying Common Interests and Enabling Close Basin Cooperation: We consider first the two framework Global Water Conventions as templates for Basin Treaties. When codifying the general duty to cooperate, Article 8(1) of the UNWC spells out what, *in abstracto*, is the core common interest of any group of co-riparian states implementing and negotiating treaties under the Convention, namely: "to attain optimal utilization and adequate protection

138 *Agreement on the Nile River Basin Cooperative Framework*, Burundi-Ethiopia-Rwanda-South Sudan-Tanzania-Uganda (Entebbe, 14 May 2010) (in force 13 Oct 2024) ('Nile Cooperative Framework').

139 Salman (2014), *supra*.

140 *Id.*

of an international watercourse". States may either pursue such an interest within the framework of Limited Territorial Sovereignty through unilateral restraint and some coordination; or states may align their cooperation with Community-of-Interests, through the adoption of the Basin Treaty.

The ECEWC outlines the general purpose of a context-specific agreement or arrangement between riparian parties in Article 9(1), namely: "to define their mutual relations and conduct regarding the prevention, control and reduction of transboundary impact". If we look at this provision in isolation, its focus on transboundary impact would suggest that watercourse agreements under the ECEWC align more closely with Limited Territorial Sovereignty. However, considering the ECEWC as a whole, it is clear that Community-of-Interests is embedded in the Convention's guidance for watercourse agreements. For example, the final sentence of Article 9(1) calls for agreements and arrangements to "embrace relevant [ECEWC] issues" and "other issues on which the riparian parties may deem it necessary to cooperate". Viewed through the Theory's lens, such *other* issues include the diversity of common interests which the states concerned may decide to prioritize in their cooperation process. At the same time, the various topics covered by the Convention serve to guide and inform negotiations between parties on the thematic scope of agreements and arrangements possibly framed by Community-of-Interests.

At the basin level, the 17th Preambular Paragraph of the Senegal Basin Charter expresses the parties' wish to give a framework to the Community-of-Interests that exists among the four riparian states. It is implicit in this language that the Charter, as a governing framework for this particular community-of-basin-interests, has been specifically designed to rule and guide interstate relations as framed by the Theory.

The Lake Victoria Protocol, according to Article 2, aims to "govern" the cooperation process among the partner states towards achieving their overarching common interest: the sustainable development of the drainage basin. The Protocol was drafted and has since been implemented with that central purpose in sight.

The Ecuador-Peru Agreement pinpoints some priority common interests in the Preamble – contamination of rivers and the wider basins; and, in Article 4, the integrated management of water resources in transboundary basins, the conservation of water supplies for human consumption and food security, and climate mitigation and adaptation. These specific areas of common interest come under the umbrella of the general goals formulated in the Preamble, where the parties express the conviction that the Agreement will ensure the sustainable, equitable and reasonable use, development, conservation, planning, and protection of watercourses and their basins. Per Article 1, *equitable and reasonable use* is based on the parties' equality of rights over their transboundary basins, per which utilization must unfold balancing the respective interests and legitimate needs. *Sustainable use* considers the waters of the basin in the context of associated aquatic ecosystems and aims to balance development and environment and conserve resource sustainability.

Under Article 1 of the River Uruguay Statute, the parties' central shared goal is the optimum and rational utilization of the watercourse in its border section. Per the same provision, Argentina and Uruguay "agree on" the Statute to enable and regulate the type of close and systematic cooperation required to pursue that overarching interest.

In the Pulp Mills Case, the ICJ deems the common interest outlined in Article 1 to be at the center of the cooperation regime drawn up by the River Uruguay Statute, and which translates into the harmonization of environmental protection with watercourse uses for enhanced economic prosperity.[141] The Court emphasizes both parties' "reliance ... on the quality of the water ... for their livelihood and economic development";[142] and their common interest in "the continued conservation of the river environment",[143] while retaining their respective "rights of economic development".[144] That common interest and those individual rights are acknowledged, protected, and regulated by the Statute to ultimately realize the joint umbrella goal of sustainable basin development.

The Lake Victoria Protocol, the Ecuador-Peru Agreement, and the River Uruguay Statute show how Basin Treaties regulate the cooperation process with the deliberate intent to identify and promote common interests – the fundamental common interest being linked broadly to sustainable development, management and protection of water and related resources.

In contrast, the Rhine Chlorides Convention demonstrates that the Basin Treaty may regulate a specific issue of common interest to be jointly addressed. Per Article 1(1), the Convention aims to enable its parties to "strengthen their cooperation for the purpose of fighting pollution of the Rhine". The Convention is the product of long negotiations among the states concerned under the auspices of the *International Commission for the Protection of the Rhine*

141 Pulp Mills Case, *supra*, p. 53.

142 Pulp Mills Case, *Request for the Indication of Provisional Measures*, Order of 13 July 2006, ICJ Reports 2006, p. 133 ('Pulp Mills 2006 Provisional Measures').

143 *Ibid.*

144 *Ibid.*

(ICPR),[145] which houses a well-established legal-institutional basin regime, referenced in the Convention's Preamble.

In performing its regulation function, the Basin Treaty may be adopted directly, where no agreement or arrangement existed before; and, once adopted, may exist on its own, as a single agreement informed by the Theory. Often, however, the Basin Treaty is part of an evolutionary process of cooperative relations.[146] For example, the Basin Treaty may come after a nonbinding mechanism, a previous watercourse agreement founded more on Limited Territorial Sovereignty, or even a treaty based on Community-of-Interests but with less advanced characteristics. The original Basin Treaty may be followed by successive amendments, possibly be superseded by an even more developed agreement or complemented by supplementary protocols and soft guidelines that progressively enrich, adapt, and strengthen the formal legal basis for Close Basin Cooperation informed by Community-of-Interests. As interstate relations deepen through a succession of legal acts, cooperation becomes increasingly informed by the Theory, with Limited Territorial Sovereignty playing an ever more residual role.

The Senegal exemplifies the case of regulation through successive Basin Treaties and related instruments, in the context of the long history of cooperation among the riparian states leading up to the Charter's adoption. Starting with the 1972 Status Convention, confirming the river's international status, each agreement in a series builds up the levels of required cooperation and further develops the applicable legal framework to create the existing joint body replacing a preexisting institution;[147] govern joint river development;[148] and record the inclusion of Guinea as a member state.[149] Accordingly, the 11th and 12th Preambular Paragraphs of the Charter affirm the aims of *reinforcing* and *consolidating* the parties' ongoing cooperation and good neighborship bonds under the existing legal-institutional regime.

---

145 *See* Chlorides Case, *supra*, p. 4.

146 *See*, e.g., Leb (2013), *supra*, p. 158, viewing cooperation as an evolving process.

147 *Convention Relative au Statut du Fleuve Sénégal* (Convention on the International Status of the Senegal River) (Nouakchott, 11 Mar 1972), Guinea-Mali-Mauritania-Senegal ('1972 Status Convention').

148 *Convention relative au Statut Juridique des Ouvrages Communs* (Convention on the Legal Status of Common Works and Jointly Owned Infrastructure) (Bamako, 21 Dec 1978), Guinea-Mali-Mauritania-Senegal; *Convention Regarding the Methods of Financing Joint Works* (Bamako, 12 May 1982), Guinea-Mali-Mauritania-Senegal.

149 *Traité relatif à l'Adhésion de la République de Guinée à l'Organisation pour la Mise en Valeur du Fleuve Sénégal* (Treaty on the Membership of Guinea to the OMVS) (17 Mar 2006), Guinea-Mali-Mauritania-Senegal ('Guinea Membership Treaty').

The Rhine Chlorides Convention and its Protocol also represent successive stages in the parties' environmental technical cooperation process; and, therefore, again illustrate the role of the Basin Treaty and related mechanisms in progressively regulating communities-of-interests through the strengthening and/or adaptation of the legal-institutional framework for cooperation, as appropriate.

Institutionalization of Communities-of-Basin-Interests: In addition to regulating communities-of-basin-interests, the Basin Treaty *institutionalizes* them by establishing the Basin Body and outlining its competences to facilitate and/or exercise joint action and promote other forms of state engagement for common interests and, more broadly, to sustain interstate peaceful and mutually beneficial relationships over the long-term.

With the adoption of the Basin Treaty, the community-of-basin-interests becomes housed within a dedicated legal-institutional regime, especially designed to serve Close Basin Cooperation. The Basin Treaty fits ICJ's description of the Founding Charters of international organizations, i.e., "treaties of a particular type",[150] which "create new subjects of law endowed with a certain autonomy".[151] Through a Founding Charter, parties charge the organization with "the task of *realizing common goals*".[152] Founding Charters, therefore, are "conventional and at the same time institutional".[153]

Institutions for transboundary basin cooperation feature prominently in the texts of the framework Conventions and regional Protocols known to reflect the Theory; and the Basin Treaties governing Lake Victoria, the River Uruguay, the Senegal Basin, and the basins shared between Ecuador and Peru, respectively, consistently empower specialized bodies to be at the center of the cooperation process.

As just one example, cooperation under the River Uruguay Statute takes place mainly, and thus has been unfolding, through the *River Uruguay Executive Commission* (*Comisión Administradora del Rio Uruguay* (CARU): "a joint mechanism with regulatory, executive, administrative, technical and conciliatory functions, entrusted with the [Statute's] proper implementation".[154] The Statute establishes CARU to serve the purpose of institutionalization; and, together with the Statute, the Commission forms the *joint machinery* – to

150 Nuclear Weapons Use in Armed Conflict AO, *supra*, p. 75.
151 *Ibid* (emphasis added).
152 *Ibid* (emphasis added).
153 *Ibid.*
154 Pulp Mills 2006 Provisional Measures, *supra*, p. 133.

employ the expression used in Article 1 – required to enable the pursuit of common interests through enhanced levels and means of cooperation. As the ICJ explains, in the course of their long years of stable and productive cooperation, Argentina and Uruguay have "found appropriate solutions to their differences within [CARU's] framework".[155]

2.6 *The Basin Treaty and Incipient Communities-of-Interests*

The Basin Treaty is a tool to upgrade the cooperation process through formalization, regulation, and institutionalization. The Basin Treaty does not create a community-of-basin-interests, which exists because of the interconnections between riparian countries within a shared catchment. These interconnections, not a Basin Treaty, justify the applicability of Community-of-Interests to a particular case. As Vitanyi explains, Community-of-Interests expresses "the existence of a special community of riparians, which has not been created by means of treaties, but derives from nature itself".[156] From this perspective, the Basin Treaty converts a preexisting community-of-basin-interests in its natural state into a formal such community, providing a more solid setting for member interaction.

To compare, motivations for Close Regional Cooperation find their origins in preexisting geographic and related bonds that give rise to interdependencies and, eventually, blossom into shared goals among the states within a region and a desire to cooperate more closely. The Founding Charter builds on but does not give rise to those bonds, interdependencies, and goals.

Both the basin and the region can be seen as a shared neighborhood, from which legal state action emerges: the adoption of the Founding Charter or the Basin Treaty for that regional or basin neighborhood – a special kind of international agreement specifically designed to assist members in their collaborative realization of common interests and commitment to peaceful and mutually beneficial relations in the long-term.

In the case of transboundary basins, up to the point when the Basin Treaty is adopted, there exists an *incipient* community-of-basin-interests. As common interests grow in scale, importance and complexity, that incipient community allows for the progressive development of mutual confidence and political readiness to move towards closer cooperation; as well as to improved awareness of the benefits linked to Close Basin Cooperation and a shared understanding of the resource and the rules of the game.

155 Pulp Mills Case, *supra*, p. 79.

156 Vitanyi, *supra*, p. 33.

From this perspective, the Basin Treaty is a step, albeit one of great significance, in the progressive deepening of a preexisting community-of-basin-interests – the step through which the *de facto* community among basin states is upgraded through formalization, binding regulation, and institutionalization, i.e., the establishment of the Basin Body endowed with legal personality.

The legal effect associated with Community-of-Interests is that even the most basic degree of interstate interaction, if only for coexistence, is required and inevitable once interdependence becomes visible. The materialization of this legal effect does not depend on the existence of an agreement between the states concerned. It so follows that the Theory stands on its own as a theoretical framework for international water law – one that, encompassing Limited Territorial Sovereignty, has framed water agreements, thereby shifting the focus of interstate relations from unilateral to common interests.

The Basin Treaties considered here make this clear. In the Lake Victoria, the 1st Preambular Paragraph of the Protocol notes how the partner states "enjoy *close* historical, commercial, industrial, cultural and other *ties*" under the EAC umbrella. Even before the adoption of the Protocol, as the Preamble also notes, the Lake Victoria riparian states had already designated the basin as an economic growth zone and established a Sectoral Council dedicated thereto. In this sense, the Protocol does not constitute but merely formalizes the existing Lake Victoria Community-of-Interests.

The River Uruguay Statute opens, in its sole Preambular Paragraph, with a reference to the *fraternal spirit inspiring* its parties in the adoption of an earlier agreement for another river section within the same Plata basin. This language serves as evidence of a preexisting Argentina-Uruguay Community-of-Interests based on boundary waters, for which a robust Basin Treaty is eventually adopted to further common state interests.

In case law, the Chlorides Award ascertains that basin states which "decide to create a joint [cooperation] regime ... are *acknowledging* a Community-of-Interests which leads to a *community-of-law*".[157] The Award recognizes the preexistence of a rudimentary community-of-basin-interests and its conversion into a formal community-of-law through the adoption of the joint regime – i.e., the Basin Treaty and the Basin Body established thereunder. The Chlorides Case confirms that the Theory originates from the hydrological and related connections among co-basin states; and that the Basin Treaty, as a primary element of Community-of-Interests, serves to upgrade the cooperation process.

---

157 Chlorides Case, *supra*, p. 40.

The River Oder Decision shows that Community-of-Interests has not been conditioned by the adoption of a treaty going back to its early stages in the law on the navigational uses of international watercourses. The PCIJ refers to a *common legal right* that is "based on the *existence* of a [shared] navigable waterway",[158] i.e., a community-of-navigation-interests founded on the watercourse system and its navigable parts shared among the parties to the dispute. Once multiple forms of water utilization come into play, the fundamental physical basis for Community-of-Interests becomes the entire drainage basin.

2.7 *Conclusions*

The Basin Treaty is a primary element of Community-of-Interests, crucial for its effective implementation. The framework Conventions make clear the significance of watercourse agreements for transboundary basin cooperation. The ECEWC even requires parties to adopt treaties or other arrangements to govern their relations. Under Community-of-Interests, however, not just any kind of context-specific instrument, but one tailored to the pursuit of shared goals, is a Basin Treaty.

The biogeographic scope of the Basin Treaty takes the basin or the sub-basin as its starting point for planning and management. Partial Basin Treaties may remain open to all co-riparians and/or be nested within basin-wide 'mother' regimes. In other words, the Basin Treaty aims to enable the direct or indirect involvement of all co-basin states: *direct*, when all are parties; or *indirect*, when accession or observer status remain open to others or when engagement of nonparty co-basin states takes place through an umbrella regime for the wider basin.

Community-of-Interests does not deal in absolutes, and this applies to the scope *ratione loci* of the Basin Treaty. Co-basin states which do not fully apply the Basin Scope in their agreements may still be cooperating under the Theory to the extent that the Basin Treaty is such designed as to advance the common interests at stake, respect individual state rights and take account of wider ecological connectivity and associated environmental, social and economic interdependencies.

Building on analogies with the Founding Charter, the Basin Treaty performs three specific purposes: formalization, regulation, and institutionalization of the incipient community-of-basin-interests. The formalization function finds evidence in how effective communities-of-basin-treaties have evolved under binding as opposed to nonbinding cooperation frameworks. When compared

158 River Oder Case, *supra*, p. 27.

to arrangements, agreements are generally better suited to sustain communities-of-interests in the long-term. Arrangements that incorporate elements of the Theory may constitute steppingstones towards formalization, supplement agreements as cooperation evolves, or else prove to be the only means by which states are prepared to cooperate informally and still strive to protect common interests to some degree.

The Basin Treaty enables, principally, the pursuit of common interests and, subsidiarily, the balancing of individual state concerns in an equitable and peaceful manner. In regulating and institutionalizing the community-of-basin-interests, the Basin Treaty identifies the common interests to be targeted, defines the institutional architecture for implementation, and foresees all appropriate modes of cooperation, with an emphasis on joint action, and with the ultimate goal of maintaining Close Basin Cooperation into the long-term. At a later stage, the mother treaty may be replaced, amended, or supplemented by other agreements and arrangements that progressively strengthen and adjust the formal legal-institutional setting within which cooperation based on the Theory unfolds and continually evolves.

The Basin Treaty does not create the community-of-basin-interests, just like the Founding Charter does not originate the bonds that have existed historically among neighboring countries, and which underlie a desire to cooperate closely at the regional level. State practice and case law imply the *autonomous existence* of a community-of-basin-interests, which precedes any states' act to formalize it. A community-of-basin-interests among riparian states is formed because of the natural and other linkages within the watershed, which may be politically compartmentalized and yet remains physically unitary. Those connections then create interdependencies and shared interests, including the broad interest in sustainable basin development and in the prevention and the peaceful and swift resolution of disputes. At the point where common interests demand closer cooperation, the Basin Treaty is adopted to step up interstate relations through formalization, regulation, and institutionalization.

3 Drainage Basin Body

> *[T]he realization of community interests depends not only on the creation of norms positing an 'international community' but also on the existence*

of an institutional structure providing for the promotion as well as protection of these interests.[159]

The *Community-of-Interests Drainage Basin Body* ('Basin Body') is the third primary element of Community-of-Interests – an intergovernmental organization, with legal personality, which houses and serves the community-of-basin-interests. The Basin Body is the dedicated and specialized institutional mechanism that supports interstate relations and cooperation under the Theory. The Basin Body is central for Community-of-Interests in the same way that the Regional Integration Organization is key for Close Regional Cooperation.

3.1 *Legal Significance of Joint Bodies*

Multilateral and bilateral intergovernmental institutions have enabled cooperation, treaty implementation, regime-building, and peaceful coexistence across various international law fields, including state engagement for community interests, regional integration interests, and common basin interests.

In our context, treaties use a variety of expressions and definitions to refer to an entity congregating co-basin countries.[160] Under Article 1(5) of the ECEWC, a *joint body* is a "bilateral or multilateral commission or other appropriate institutional arrangement for cooperation between riparian parties". Herein, we may refer interchangeably to basin organizations, joint water commissions, or joint bodies, among other similar expressions, but only the Basin Body, with its inherent traits shown here, is a normative element of Community-of-Interests.

Instituting joint bodies, whether under agreements or arrangements, with or without legal personality, is a common practice among co-riparian states. Leb, for example, having analyzed 200 treaties from Africa, the Americas, Asia, and Europe, adopted between 1902 and 2010, finds that 70% of those instruments establish a basin organization or assign management functions to a

159 Simma, *supra*, p. 285.

160 *See*, e.g., UNWC, *supra*, Arts.8, 24, 33(2), referring, respectively, to *joint mechanisms or commissions*; *joint management mechanism*; and *joint watercourse institutions*; 1995 SADC Protocol, *supra*, Art.3(2)(b), using the expression *river basin commissions*; Revised SADC Protocol, *supra*, Art.4(3)(a) & Art.5(3), referencing, respectively, *joint management mechanism* and *shared watercourse institutions*, which may take the form of *watercourse commissions, water authorities* or *boards*, as appropriate. *See also* 1995 SADC Protocol, *supra*, Art.3(2)(c), calling for the adoption, presumably at the domestic level, of *authorities* or *boards* for each watershed.

preexisting joint body.[161] According to Dellapenna and Gupta, this practice illustrates how "legislative and judicial functions are giving way to administrative rule-making on a day-to-day basis by river basin commissions being set up for the purpose".[162]

Among the framework legal instruments examined by the book, Article 8(2) of the UNWC strongly promotes the establishment of basin organizations as vehicles for cooperation, even if the provision falls short of imposing an obligation on states to create those entities. An emphasis on joint bodies is again strong under the SADC Protocols, with 12 out of 15 shared basins in the region being under the umbrella of a basin organization.[163] Per Article 3(2)(b) of the 1995 Protocol and Article 5(3)(a) of the Revised SADC Protocol, respectively, member states *undertake* to establish such institutions for effective treaty implementation.

In the ECEWC, Article 9(2) determines that context-specific agreements or arrangements *shall* provide for the establishment of basin organizations, thus relying on the institutional mechanism as the beating heart of the cooperation regime. Underlying this approach is an assumption that secondary forms of cooperation would emerge naturally from the adoption of the agreement/arrangement and the joint body created thereunder. Consistent with this assumption is the broad array of potential functions the ECEWC anticipates these bodies to be tasked with by their members.

In international policy, there have been repeated calls for the establishment of joint bodies, "making them appear quite incantatory".[164] The Dushanbe Declaration, for example, recognizes basin organizations as crucial for sustainable water management and declares their establishment a priority for water diplomacy and collaboration.[165]

The centrality of joint bodies in transboundary water cooperation is echoed in scholarship. For Boisson de Chazournes, for example, joint bodies are "necessary corollaries"[166] for the effectiveness of international law in this field.

There is no blueprint for the structure, composition, authority, and mandate of joint bodies, and the significance of results achieved through their

161 Leb (2013), *supra*, p. 177, 258 *et seq.*

162 Dellapenna & Gupta (2013), *supra*, p. 14.

163 SADC, Pillars, Water, at https://www.sadc.int/pillars/water-0.

164 Boisson de Chazournes, *The Role of Diplomatic Means of Solving Water Disputes: A Special Emphasis on Institutional Mechanisms, in* The International Bureau of the Permanent Court of Arbitration ed, Resolution of International Water Disputes (Kluwer Law International 2003), p. 102.

165 Dushanbe Declaration, *supra*, Preamble, ¶11, Body, ¶8.

166 Boisson de Chazournes (2003), *supra*, p. 96.

work varies considerably across watersheds and regions.[167] States have wide room to negotiate and compromise when setting up such bodies to best meet their particular needs and local circumstances. Yet, basin commissions must be designed in a manner responsive to the challenges and characteristics of each catchment. Any governance model, however effective in certain places, must be tailored accordingly, taking account, *inter alia*, of the applicable national legislation and policies, as well as existing agreements across the catchment, present and planned water uses, the basin ecology and hydrology, and socioeconomic and cultural factors.[168] Like water agreements, therefore, watercourse organizations are context-specific, but not just any such organization can be considered a Basin Body.

3.2 *Joint Bodies* versus *Basin Bodies*

The Basin Body is created, structured and empowered to serve common interests, principally. To that end, the Basin Body has legal personality as a permanent, dedicated, and legitimized forum for the governance and management of water and related issues.

The Basin Treaty provides the Basin Body with the mandate and the tools to promote mutual trust, long-term political commitment, legal stability, and progressive confidence- and regime-building, via periodical high-level and technical meetings, Social Engagement, and frequent and intensified interactions and communications among basin countries. As such, the Basin Body "can bridge the inherent gap between sovereigns",[169] allowing for the development of "stable mutual expectations regarding future behavior and reduce[d] ... bargaining costs and uncertainty about the value of proposed transactions".[170]

All this enables Close Basin Cooperation and sustained strategic efforts towards the achievement of shared priorities and maintenance of peaceful relations; reduces transaction costs; and places in relief the potential benefits of cooperation framed by the Theory and risks involved in non-cooperation. By giving riparian states the ability to see beyond their respective immediate needs and potentially conflicting concerns, the Basin Body enables its members to "identify synergies and *common interests*";[171] to see the value in evolving from *ad hoc* efforts centered on coexistence and unilateral development,

---

167 Boisson de Chazournes (2003), *supra*, p. 102.

168 UNW-DPAC, *supra*, p. 21.

169 Benvenisti, *supra*, p. 412.

170 *Ibid.*

171 UNW-DPAC, *supra*, p. 31 (emphasis added).

deemed sufficient under Limited Territorial Sovereignty, to Close Basin Cooperation framed by Community-of-Interests.

Under the UNWC, Article 24(1) requires states to consult with each other, upon request by any of the riparians, concerning international watercourse management, and this "may include the establishment of a joint management mechanism". Article 4(3)(a) of the Revised SADC Protocol mirrors this UNWC provision. In Paragraph 2, Article 24 of the Convention defines *management* to refer to "planning the sustainable development of an international watercourse"; and, in general, "promoting the rational and optimal utilization, protection and control" thereof. Hence, management under the Basin Body, as envisioned by the UNWC, is about more than volumetric water allocation and unilateral restraint; it is about a shared interest in resource sustainability. The provision invokes Community-of-Interests, thereby implicitly emphasizing the Basin Body under the Theory.

In contrast, traditional joint bodies are more focused on individual interests and their equitable balancing. Consider, for example, the permanent joint commissions recommended by the Madrid Resolution, with advisory and/or decision-making powers in relation to planned measures and changes to existing activities liable to generate serious transboundary effects.[172] These would be joint bodies operating mostly under Limited Territorial Sovereignty, with their narrow focus on unilateral projects and associated impacts on neighboring countries.

Recall, also, how the Indus Water Treaty is principally designed, and has thus been applied, to balance interests, as opposed to advancing joint priorities. Mirroring the Treaty, the *Permanent Indus Commission* does not qualify as a Basin Body. The Commission is formed by two high-ranking commissioners, each appointed by its respective government, who ordinarily meet once a year. There is no institutional mechanism under the Commission's umbrella, like an executive secretariat, to sustain joint cooperative efforts in between those meetings. In intersessional periods, communications, in principle, go through the commissioners, but such exchanges do not amount to joint and systematic long-term engagement, as required to identify and pursue common interests. The Commission may consider joint referrals on matters of common concern and respond through studies and reports. Otherwise, the Commission mostly promotes treaty compliance to maintain an equitable balance between parties, *inter alia*, by examining treaty interpretation and

172 Institut de Droit International (Institute of International Law) (IIL), *International Regulation regarding the Use of International Watercourses for Purposes other than Navigation* ('Madrid Resolution'), IIL Session (Madrid, 20 Apr 2011), *in* 24 IIL Yearbook 365 (1911).

application questions, or alleged violations, and endeavoring to settle them promptly; and inspecting river uses and works – on its own initiative, every five years, or upon a party's request. In practice, India and Pakistan seem to go about implementing their own water management programs and only return to the Commission when a unilateral project is planned.[173]

Like the Basin Treaty, the Basin Body is crucial for the Theory's effective implementation because the focus on common interests demands a formal legal-institutional architecture to support and frame systematic state engagement and facilitate Close Basin Cooperation. In its role to nurture the cooperation process, the Basin Body fosters progressive community-building through ever closer and more advanced collaboration, including by facilitating the adoption of successive agreements and arrangements as common interests expand and deepen.

Linking the Basin Body to Community-of-Interests, all Basin Treaties here examined place the organizations they each create at the center of the regime in question. The Senegal basin states first envisioned cooperating through some kind of institutional arrangement back in the 1960s. In the Senegal River Convention, Title I addresses the creation and organization of the *Interstate Committee*; and Art.1 charges such a Committee with promoting and coordinating the studies and works necessary for the development of the River.[174] The 1972 OMVS Convention then creates the *Organization for the Development of the Senegal River* (OMVS).[175] At last, in the Preamble of the Senegal Basin Charter, states highlight their satisfaction with the political and institutional achievements realized under the longstanding OMVS. Adding further institutional muscle to the cooperation process, the Charter establishes and regulates the *Permanent Water Commission* (PWC) within the OMVS. The PWC is composed of member state representatives and has advisory and technical functions.

The *Lake Victoria Basin Commission* (LVBC) is a dedicated institutional machinery for treaty implementation created by the EAC *Council of Ministers* on the basis of Article 33(1) of the Protocol. The LVBC has a broad mandate that includes promoting economic growth and poverty eradication; environ-

173 Swain (2017), *supra*.

174 *Convention Relative à l'Aménagement General du Bassin du Fleuve Sénégal* (Convention on the General Planning of the Senegal River Basin), Guinea-Mali-Mauritania-Senegal (Bamako, 26 July 1963) ('Senegal River Convention').

175 *Convention portant Création de l'Organisation pour la Mise en Valeur du Fleuve Sénégal* (Convention on the Creation of the Organization for the Development of the Senegal River) (Nouakchott, 11 Mar 1972), Guinea-Mali-Mauritania-Senegal ('1972 OMVS Convention').

mental protection and sustainable use and management of natural resources; and navigation safety.

Cooperative efforts and monitoring of progress on river pollution mitigation under the Rhine Chlorides Convention and its Protocol unfold under the auspices of, and through regular reporting to, the ICPR. A duty to notify the Commission, along with other parties potentially affected, applies in relation to relevant accidents or large sudden increases in chloride ions in the Rhine. Consultations on additional control measures, upon a party's request, to address serious environmental risks, must take place under the ICPR's umbrella. The Commission is empowered to request a party to take appropriate measures for halting increases in pollution levels originating from activities in that party's territory. Domestic monitoring operations must follow the applicable ICPR recommendations.[176]

The Ecuador-Peru *Binational Commission for the Integrated Management of the Water Resources of Transboundary Basins* plays a central role in joint planning, a manifestation of joint action, through the bilateral bodies created thereunder specifically to propose and implement transboundary basin plans for the catchments within the Commission's jurisdiction.

The River Uruguay Statute constitutes and regulates the River Uruguay Executive Commission (CARU) in the form of a joint executive commission with international legal personality. As part of CARU's internal architecture, the Secretariat prepares and implements decisions and may decentralize functions through the creation of subsidiary bodies. Dedicated rules and regulations for CARU's procedures and daily functioning have been set out.[177]

The ICJ explores CARU's significance by drawing attention to specific aspects of the Statute. Among other such aspects, the parties are committed to ensuring CARU has the capacity to deliver its functions, along with all resources, information and facilities "essential to its operation".[178] The Basin Body exercises rights and performs duties, and its staff have privileges and immunities. Compliance with substantive obligations is envisioned through procedures linked to CARU. In this sense, the Commission is the heart of the River Uruguay cooperation regime, as evidenced by the scale and diversity of CARU's mandate outlined and detailed by the Statute.[179]

---

176 Rhine Chlorides Convention, *supra*, Arts.2(3), 4(4), 9, 11, 12(2)-(3).

177 *See* River Uruguay Statute, *supra*, Arts.50 & 52; Pulp Mills Case, *supra*, p. 36.

178 River Uruguay Statute, *supra*, Art.50.

179 Pulp Mills Case, *supra*, p. 32, 36, 75; Pulp Mills 2006 Provisional Measures, *supra*, p. 133.

Argentina and Uruguay, the ICJ proclaims, "have a longstanding and effective tradition of cooperation and coordination through CARU".[180] From Argentina's perspective, as described by the Court, CARU is the "core and essence"[181] of the River Uruguay cooperation regime established by the Statute. The ICJ further notes that, through joint collaborative efforts under CARU, the two countries have established a "real Community-of-Interests and rights"[182] in the River Uruguay. This is yet another evidence of the Basin Body being one of the Theory's elements.

To operationalize and sustain communities-of-interests, the mandate of the Basin Body should include tailored provisions for the pursuit of common interests through all modalities of state engagement, principally joint action. These must be supplemented with mechanisms to ensure balanced consideration of unilateral interests, including data-sharing on unilateral projects and robust conflict resolution alternatives. As remarked by the ICJ in the Pulp Mills Case, the two CARU members aim to provide their Close Basin Cooperation with "the best possible guarantees of stability, continuity and effectiveness".[183] The parties intend to make the Commission "a central component in the fulfilment of their obligations to cooperate".[184] So, "far from being merely a transmission mechanism between the parties, CARU has a permanent existence of its own".[185] The states must ensure continuity in CARU's work and proceed with the cooperation process through the Commission, so that it may propose and design the tools necessary to foster sustainable river development and protection.[186]

3.3 *Jurisdiction*

The geographic ambit of watercourse agreements not framed by Community-of-Interests differs from Basin Treaties. It is the same with Basin Bodies, which are unlike ordinary basin organizations as regards jurisdiction.

The Basin Body, as much as the Basin Treaty, embraces the Basin Scope in ways as expansive as possible and, minimally, as appropriate to meet the common needs and interests of the states concerned. In structuring the Basin Body, the Basin Treaty goes as far as feasible or as appropriate within the

180 Pulp Mills Case, *supra*, p. 70.
181 Pulp Mills Case, *supra*, p. 35.
182 *Ibid* (emphasis added).
183 *Id*, p. 36.
184 *Ibid.*
185 *Id*, p. 35.
186 *Ibid.*

particular circumstances of each community-of-basin-interests to promote the Basin Scope. The Basin Treaties reviewed here do so by foreseeing the progressive uptake of the full water system and its biodiversity and by accounting for, or at least acknowledging, interconnections and related common interests across the entire basin.

In this sense, the Basin Treaty envisions the ultimate scope *ratione loci* and *ratione personae* of Close Basin Cooperation as being catchment-wide, including in how such a Treaty designs the institutional architecture thereunder. This overall endorsement of the Basin Scope, tempered by the relative nature of Community-of-Interests, which states apply where and as appropriate, is thus reflected on the geographic mandate of Basin Body.

Under Article 9(5) of the ECEWC, for example, the Basin Bodies operating within the same catchment would "endeavor to coordinate their activities", as needed to strengthen actions aimed at preventing, controlling, and reducing transboundary impacts in the areas within their respective jurisdictions. The Convention's call for basin-wide institutional coordination advances the Basin Scope.

Article 2 of the Ecuador-Peru Agreement centers the purpose of the Binational Commission on the integrated management of transboundary water resources as framed by an ecosystemic vision; and Article 18 calls on the Commission to progressively incorporate IWRM for specified shared catchments. In fact, the very name of the Basin Body, with its explicit reference to integrated management of transboundary basins, reflects the Basin Scope.

In the case of the Senegal basin, when consideration of the need for a Basin Body first started, in the 1960s, it was then recognized that only an organization common to the four riparian countries could enable coordination of activities among the competent domestic organs and facilitate concerted international action.[187]

Case law is also illustrative. In the River Oder Decision, the PCIJ interlinks the scope of the Basin Treaty being interpreted, the jurisdiction of the respective Basin body, and the interests of states in navigation along the whole course of the river. For the Court, "when a Commission is set up, it is natural to suppose that the territorial limits of the 'régime' and of the 'administration' by the Commission, whose function is to make practical application of the principles of the régime, are coincident".[188] The Decision finds nothing in the treaty in question justifying a possible differentiation in territorial limits.

---

187 Senegal River Convention, *supra*, Preamble, ¶5.

188 River Oder Case, *supra*, p. 23.

To the contrary, "a precise indication that the régime and administration coincide [is found in] the matters confided to the Commission's powers ... exactly corresponding to the régime".[189] The Court concludes that "the competence of a river [navigation] commission ... extends to all the internationalized portions of the river and river system."[190]

In other words, when designing the basis for cooperation, it makes sense to overlap the scope of the legal and institutional components of the regime. Informed by the Basin Scope, both the geographic ambit of the Basin Treaty and the jurisdiction of the Basin Body are then delimited so as to serve the chief purpose and common interests that motivate the regime's existence. This is true whether the regime is focused on navigation or has a broader scope dealing with multiple water uses.

3.4 *Mandates*

The powers and functions of the Basin Body differentiate it from other joint organizations. As its core mandate, the Basin Body is established to enable Close Basin Cooperation for common interests. As a supplementary competence, the Basin Body ensures coexistence. In these respects, the Basin Body is similar to the Regional Integration Organization.

To illustrate, Article 2 of the Ecuador-Peru Agreement determines the overarching purpose of the Binational Commission as that of tapping on the potentialities and complementarities between the parties and establishing joint mechanisms to solve matters of common interest.

The Basin Body supports Close Basin Cooperation through *indirect* and *direct* interstate joint action: *indirect*, i.e., when the organization performs its mandate by acting through its organs (e.g., a technical group monitoring water quality and quantity); or *direct*, i.e., coordination and monitoring of activities carried out jointly by the members themselves (e.g., support for national parliaments working on policy harmonization). Actions on both fronts, as submodalities of the category of joint action, make up the principal approach of the Basin Body to pursue common interests.

In furthering joint action for common interests, the Basin Body may be given competences, for example, to create and maintain joint databanks; facilitate or exercise joint fundraising; design joint standards or regulations; coordinate or directly conduct joint basin investigations; plan, execute and/or

189 *Id*, p. 24.
190 *Id*, p. 23.

operate joint projects; and supervise, monitor, facilitate, and report on treaty implementation.[191]

A number of such and other examples of possible powers and functions of the Basin Body are found in the ECEWC, centered on the protection of the environment as an overarching common interest. Per the Convention, the Basin Body may have the mandate to draft common regulations in the form of water-quality objectives and criteria, taking as starting points the guidelines contained in Annex III to the ECEWC. In such a case, the Basin Body would be directly responsible for taking action on a specific matter; and so, their members pursue common interests by cooperating through those bodies. In other areas, both sub-modalities of joint action are combined – under and through the Basin Body: in relation to planning, the Basin Body may be asked to design and propose programs and measures for pollution control and the maintenance or enhancement of water quality. In their turn, member states would review such programs and measures and, upon jointly approving those documents, implement them in a coordinated manner within their respective territories. Closing the circle, the process for dealing with pollution would go back to the Basin Body to evaluate implementation effectiveness.

Yet, regimes framed by the Theory are not exclusively focused on common interests, since disagreements may also emerge among states cooperating closely. The Basin Body manages individual interests under Limited Territorial Sovereignty to supplement its core mandate of advancing shared priorities. Exercising this supplementary mandate, the Basin Body may be called upon, when disagreements or disputes emerge, or in instances of noncompliance, to ensure continued peaceful coexistence. For example, the Basin Body may intermediate the regular exchange of basic data and other communications; facilitate interstate consultations, negotiations, and coordination on major unilateral projects; provide technical or legal advice on eventual disagreements; mediate negotiations; and deal with compliance issues, whether through the use of 'carrots' or 'sticks'. These functions of the Basin Body based on Limited Territorial Sovereignty are essential to preserve the integrity of a community-of-basin-interests.

When the Basin Body exercise this supplementary mandate, it does so in ways different from traditional basin organizations, still under the mindset of Close Basin Cooperation and building on the historical prevalence of joint action. In contrast, traditional organizations stay within their realm of coordinating *ad hoc* exchanges, considering disputed matters upon referrals, and

---

191 *See* Caponera, *supra*, p. 329 *et seq*, for a detailed assessment of the functions and other characteristics of joint bodies, including examples from around the world.

offering advice when so requested, without playing a more proactive and preventative long-term planning role.

To illustrate, Article 28 of the River Uruguay Statute requires parties to provide CARU with biannual detailed reports of unilateral projects authorized or implemented during the period. Such reports are meant to enable CARU to assess the likelihood of cumulative impacts amounting to significant harm. This reporting obligation is not foreseen in the UNWC framework provisions on planned measures. Within specific communities-of-interests, therefore, when compared to regional and global water treaties, the governance regime for unilateral projects is likely to be more sophisticated, including by involving the Basin Body.

As another example, Article 8(e) of the Ecuador-Peru Agreement tasks the Binational Commission with proposing dialogue and dispute resolution mechanisms for employment within its Basin Committees.

3.5 *Specific Powers and Functions*

Under its general core and supplementary mandates, the specific functions and powers of each Basin Body are underpinned by the *Principle of Speciality*. Under the Principle, international organizations "are invested by the states which create them with powers, the limits of which are a function of the common interests whose promotion those states entrust to them".[192] *Speciality* applies to international organizations in general, whether they have multiple or only two members;[193] and whichever shared goals they advance.

Applying the Principle of Speciality to our context means that the specific functions and powers of Basin Bodies are defined on a case-by-case basis and by agreement among the states concerned, *in light of the common interests at stake*. In other words, institutional objectives, and the common interests thus prioritized, determine institutional functions and powers for each Basin Body. As noted by the ICJ, CARU's powers are those "necessary to achieve [its] object and purpose".[194]

In this sense, for the pursuit of optimal utilization and adequate protection of an international watercourse, the core common interests under the UNWC, Article 8(2) encourages states to create bodies "as deemed necessary ... to facilitate cooperation on relevant measures and procedures".

Article 5(3)(b) of the Revised SADC Protocol states that the responsibilities of shared watercourse institutions are "determined by the nature of their

192 Nuclear Weapons Use in Armed Conflict AO, *supra*, p. 78.

193 Pulp Mills Case, *supra*, p. 36.

194 *Ibid.*

objectives". Per the same provision, the objectives and mandates thus outlined must respect the principles of the Revised SADC Protocol, wherein Community-of-Interests is embedded. Speciality, in the Theory's context, requires co-riparians to consider the core and supplementary mandates of the Basin Body and correlated common interests when working out the institutional basis for Close Basin Cooperation. Some flexibility, which is inherent to Community-of-Interests, remains but the targeted common interests, and the functions and powers required to advance those interests, are the guiding light for the design of treaty provisions structuring the Basin Body.

An advanced Basin Body would develop and implement a joint management plan to identify, prioritize, and safeguard shared goals. Where, however, political appetite for the joint design of those plans has yet to materialize, the Basin Body can lay down the seeds for progress, by coordinating, across the basin, decision-making and implementation within each riparian state. As countries develop a greater understanding of, and appreciation for, the benefits to be gained through joint planning, they may expand the Body's powers, give it more joint action functions, and strengthen the Secretariat's planning capacities in tandem with deepening common basin interests.

Where joint planning takes place, this needs to be harmonized with actions at the domestic level. Combining both joint and national action in basin planning, Article 8(b) of the Ecuador-Peru Agreement mandates the Binational Commission to establish formulas for the application of national IWRM strategies in transboundary basins and the protection and conservation of natural water sources. In this sense, joint action through the Commission serves sustainable management measures within each member's territory.

Specific Functions to Advance Common Interests: The ECEWC envisions different possibilities of joint action with regard to *data management*. The Basin Body may itself be responsible for collecting, compiling, and evaluating information on pollution sources expected to produce effects across the border and for preparing related inventories. Alternatively, co-riparian parties may prefer to limit the data-management powers of their Basin Body to designing a catchment-wide monitoring program. Each member would then implement such a program within its respective territory, albeit still under the Basin Body's oversight.

At the regional level, the 1995 SADC Protocol envisions Basin Bodies preparing catchment development strategies; following national implementation of management plans; tracking compliance with national laws and regulations by resource users within the catchment; monitoring the environmental effects of navigation on shared watercourses; and promoting measures to protect the environment, e.g., by proposing a list of banned or controlled substances, to be adopted jointly among the states themselves. Under the same Protocol, the Basin Body could be tasked with conducting data collection, analysis, storage, retrieval, dissemination, exchange and use; and designing and carrying out studies, research, and surveys. In addition, the Basin Body could recommend appropriate domestic governance reforms, propose the enactment of new statutes; and promote interstate harmonization of relevant laws and regulations. For their part, basin states would collect and review national legislation; jointly assess the Body's advice; and coordinate with one another when carrying out the appropriate domestic reforms.

As for specific Basin Treaties, under Article 33(3) of the Lake Victoria Protocol, the LVBC, *inter alia*, supports harmonization of domestic laws, regulations, policies, and standards; promotes capacity and institutional development; carries research and pilot projects; guides program and project implementation; monitors and assesses compliance with applicable policies and agreed measures; ensures safety and security on the Lake; develops, for Council approval, a management plan accounting for the respective national strategies, plans, and programs, which states must design anew or harmonize with the Protocol; and reviews national implementation reports.

Within the LVBC, the *Sectoral Council* offers overall common policy directions and guidance to program and project implementation; formulates joint regulations, directives, decisions, opinions, and recommendations; reviews and adopts the budget and work programs of the Basin Body; and considers and approves measures for parties to undertake towards treaty implementation. The *Coordination Committee* presents reports and recommendations to the Sectoral Council and gives effect to the latter's decisions; and oversees sectoral committees and promotes linkages among sectoral bodies, such as the Lake Victoria Fisheries Organization. *Sectoral committees* deal with specific topics within the Protocol's scope, including by preparing and reviewing relevant programs. The *Secretariat* manages data, including promoting information exchange, creating a regional database and developing information systems. The Secretariat also mobilizes resources in support of project and program implementation, which encompasses designing a permanent funding mechanism, on the basis of financial rules and regulations laid out by the Sectoral Council. *National Focal Points* are to be established in each partner state to coordinate national initiatives.

In the River Uruguay, CARU's responsibilities cut across most matters of treaty implementation.[195] On navigation, CARU leads on joint planning and

195 *Id*, p. 53.

management by periodically allocating to the parties tasks for the conservation, dredging, and buoying of channels. CARU has comprehensive competence to trigger joint rulemaking processes on themes of common interest, such as pollution and biodiversity. Further, the Commission coordinates scientific studies to be carried out jointly by the states, particularly to assess the river in a comprehensive manner. CARU itself publishes and updates the official map of the River.

Under Article 8 of the Ecuador-Peru Agreement, the Binational Commission proposes for implementation by the IWRM Basin Committees, under the Basin Body's umbrella, climate adaptation and mitigation measures, as well as early warning systems for extreme events establishing information exchange mechanisms. In their turn, the Committees elaborate technical proposals and apply binational policies and strategies in the management of water resources, as determined by the Commission regarding the development, implementation, monitoring and evaluation of IWRM plans.

The Technical Secretariat of the Binational Commission articulates political and technical coordination between the Basin Committees and the highest organ within the Basin Body. In so doing, the Secretariat supports the flow of binational policies, strategies and instruments, as well as the demands of management systems that transcend the jurisdiction and mandates of individual Committees. Furthermore, the Secretariat coordinates with the Committees the formulation, establishment and implementation of protocols and mechanisms for technical information exchange to support the design and execution of IWRM plans; and formulates recommendations for monitoring and evaluation, which are conducted by the Committees.

Doctrine of Implied Powers: Not all functions required to meet common interests need to be explicitly established by the Basin Treaty. Per the *Doctrine of Implied Powers*, implied competences may be conferred upon an international organization, even though the rule is for institutional mandates to be outlined explicitly in the founding treaty.

Yet, at times, "the necessities of international life may point to the need for organizations, in order to achieve their objectives, to possess subsidiary powers which are not expressly provided for in the basic instruments which govern their activities".[196] Subsidiary powers would be at play, for example, where a Basin Body begins informally to put together a joint database with a

196 Nuclear Weapons Use in Armed Conflict AO, *supra*, p. 79.

view to facilitating day-to-day activities, even if the Basin Treaty itself does not mandate the institution to do so.

Functions and Powers Framed by Limited Territorial Sovereignty: Article 33(2) of the UNWC illustrates the possible function of the Basin Body as a dispute settlement mechanism, in the event the parties to a dispute fail to reach an agreement through negotiations; and, per Article 5 of the 1995 SADC Protocol, the Basin Body could become involved in planned measures by encouraging the completion of the respective environmental impact assessment.

The ECEWC also envisions various functions that a Basin Body could perform under Limited Territorial Sovereignty, such as serving as a platform for information exchange on existing and planned measures capable of causing transboundary impact, including by participating in the corresponding environmental assessments. Article 13 requires co-basin states to exchange, within the framework of their agreements or arrangements and thus, under the institutional umbrella, reasonably available information on, e.g., water permits, relevant legislation and technical guidelines, and planned ecosystem protection measures. Article 10 governs interstate consultations, through the Basin Body, on all issues covered by the Convention, including on the basis of the rules of equitable and reasonable use and harm prevention. Consultations may be triggered by a request from a basin state and are guided by reciprocity, good neighborliness, and good faith – the first two principles being hallmarks of Limited Territorial Sovereignty.

At the basin level, the Senegal riparian states interpret, apply, and implement equitable and reasonable use through the OMVS. Article 17 of the Charter tasks the Organization with an annual prospective evaluation of water quantity and quality within the basin. The *Permanent Water Commission* exercises joint regulatory and planning functions on water allocation across sectors, in accordance with the applicable Charter provisions and annexes. This includes prioritizing among competing water needs and identifying the required water volumes to be consumed, while taking account of demand. The Commission also proposes, for Council approval, the annual infrastructure management program for the whole basin. In addition, the Commission issues advisory opinions addressed to the *Council of Ministers* regarding all proposed water management projects and programs.

CARU plays its own part in dispute prevention and settlement, including in the case of unilateral projects. On planned measures, Articles 7 *et seq.* of the Statute lay out detailed consultation and cooperation rules and procedures. In this respect, the ICJ has affirmed that the parties are required to act in good faith, through CARU, in implementing related provisions, as envisioned by the

Statute.[197] In other words, Argentina and Uruguay must follow the consultation framework established by the Statute and centered on CARU; and "neither … may depart from that framework unilaterally [by putting] other channels of communication in its place."[198] Per Article 58 of the Statute, the parties may unilaterally refer disputes to CARU to trigger a conciliation procedure. Before the parties get to the point of requiring conciliation, CARU plays a key role in mediating between the parties so that, as much as possible, eventual disagreements regarding the River do not evolve into more serious disputes.

3.6 *The Basin Body and Incipient Communities-of-Interests*

The *formal nature* of the Basin Body mirrors that of the Basin Treaty, the same as between a Regional Integration Organization and its Founding Charter. The Basin Body, being created by the Basin Treaty, requires legal personality to advance effectively common interests. The points above on the stability of treaties *versus* arrangements apply equally to this discussion on treaty-based *versus* soft institutions. As Leb explains, treaty-based joint bodies "represent the preferred choice of management structure [and an] appropriate method to steer utilization of shared waters."[199] Among the Basin Bodies here examined, all have legal personality.

For regional integration regimes, the step of *formal* institutionalization – consisting of a Regional Integration Organization being created through the Founding Charter – represents the moment when the states concerned decide to deepen the cooperation process in response to evolving common interests. As with the case of ASEAN, which had started as a soft body, it may suffice for a community-of-basin-interests, in its early stages, to convene in periodic ministerial summits where information is exchanged and political statements may be adopted. When common interests deepen, the Basin Body is created to enable Close Basin Cooperation.

Case Study 6: Guarani Aquifer System

All four aquifer states participated in a Global Environmental Facility Project.[200] For the purpose of project implementation, *ad hoc* institu-

---

197 Pulp Mills 2006 Provisional Measures, *supra*, p. 134.

198 Pulp Mills Case, *supra*, p. 36.

199 Leb, *supra*, p. 177.

200 GEF, *Environmental Protection and Sustainable Development of the Guarani Aquifer System Project*, Argentina-Brazil-Paraguay-Uruguay (2003–2009), Project Details, at https://www.thegef.org/project/environmental-protection-and-sustainable-integrated-management-guarani-aquifer.

tional arrangements were created, with positive results on the ground and in diplomacy, in particular the adoption of the Guarani Aquifer Agreement. These results include reduced risks connected to overextraction, pollution and transboundary impacts; delivery of an improved knowledge base; well-drilling and protection manuals; groundwater models; local land use and solid waste management standards; and limits for sustainable geothermal water use.[201] Upon the conclusion of the Project, the ratification process to secure entry into force of that Agreement proved longer than expected; and, in the absence of the institutional arrangements active during the Project and pending the creation of the body foreseen by the Agreement, cooperation levels started to decline. In this respect, Sindico *et al* compare the degree and modalities of state engagement during and after the conclusion of the GEF Project and pending the full ratification of the Agreement: from 2002 to 2010, the four countries proactively worked together, including on knowledge-building and treaty negotiations, under the Project's institutional architecture; between 2010 and 2017, state cooperative engagement appreciably declined, by the end largely consisting of *ad hoc* bilateral projects and informal bilateral cooperation between border cities of different Guarani countries.[202]

Hence, project-based, time-bound, soft institutions, however well-designed, are likely to be less well-suited to serve long-lasting communities-of-basin-interests than their treaty-based counterparts.

Importantly, the establishment of the Basin Body does not constitute the community-of-basin-interests; it only provides an existing community-of-basin-interests with a formal institutional home. It is thus a misunderstanding to claim that "joint bodies create a [community-of-basin-interests] among the participating states".[203]

3.7 *Conclusions*

The creation of international organizations is a common and long-standing practice in international relations and an important tool to enhance cooperation among states. For our purposes, the Basin Body has a central place in cooperation founded on the Theory, as recognized in both treaty and case law. Created and designed by the Basin Treaty, the Basin Body has mandates

201 World Bank, *supra*, p. 4, 6–7.
202 Sindico *et al*, *supra*.
203 Howden, *supra*, p. 87.

that are characteristic of Community-of-Interests. In this sense, Basin Bodies are similar to Regional Integration Organizations.

The core mandate of the Basin Body is to enable the attainment of common interests, with powers and functions directed at fostering and sustaining Close Basin Cooperation, mostly through joint action. Member states interact with each other under or through the Basin Body. The Basin Body takes action itself when acting through its organs, within which states work together; and/or facilitates direct state action and interaction under its institutional umbrella; or, as in the case of the recent US-Mexico Memorandum of Understanding on the sanitation and environmental crisis in the Tijuana–San Diego Region (24 July 2025), acts on instructions formulated within the framework of such direct communications.

This core mandate of advancing common interests is supplemented by a competence to service Limited Territorial Sovereignty, i.e., to aid states in the balancing of individual interests, with a view to ensuring that the parties remain engaged when conflicting goals, actual disagreements or more serious issues arise. After all, it is not realistic to conceive of a community-of-basin-interests that has overcome entirely Limited Territorial Sovereignty and focuses only on common interests. Within the framework of Close Basin Cooperation, the Basin Body is placed at the center of requirements and procedures pertaining to equitable and reasonable use, harm prevention and dispute settlement, as is the case with CARU, the LVBC, and OMVS. In contrast, water commissions other than the Basin Body prioritize direct *ad hoc* negotiations or dispute settlement interactions on a case-by-case basis, as with the Indus example.

The jurisdiction of the Basin Body matches the geographic scope of the Basin Treaty that creates and regulates it. Both the Basin Treaty and the Basin Body are informed by the common interests at stake, embracing the Basin Scope as appropriate to safeguard those interests. The Basin Scope is the thread interlinking the Basin Treaty's ambit, the Basin Body's mandate and the common interests pursued by the co-riparians. This conclusion reinforces the characterization of the Basin Scope as the element of Community-of-Interests that underpins the Basin Treaty and the Basin Body.

When fully applying the Basin Scope is not necessary or feasible, the countries concerned have adapted this normative element to embrace its dimensions to the extent appropriate for safeguarding common interests, while creating entry points for the progressive realization of catchment-based management. This is reflected in institutional mandates, as much as it is on the scope *ratione loci* of the respective Basin Treaty. States, therefore, retain flexibility to adjust the elements of Community-of-Interests to their particular circumstances and needs. A legal-institutional regime that only partially adopts the Basin Scope is so designed to allow for cooperation to evolve, so that the full realization of this element remains the ultimate goal and underlying guidance for treaty interpretation, application, implementation, and progressive development under the auspices of the Basin Body.

Established by the Basin Treaty, the Basin Body has legal personality. Formal institutions secure a high degree of interdependence through continued interactions, thereby maintaining mutual trust, legal certainty, and political stability. This state of affairs, in turn, produces an environment conducive for a community-of-basin-interests to endure and prosper.

4 Close Drainage Basin Cooperation

> *When we try to pick out anything by itself, we find it hitched to everything else in the universe.*
>
> JOHN MUIR, naturalist, explorer, and writer.

Community-of-Interests Close Drainage Basin Cooperation ('Close Basin Cooperation') is the fourth primary element of Community-of-Interests. Like the neighbors that collaborate under the auspices of the Regional Integration Organization, the basin states that come together to formalize, regulate and institutionalize a community-of-basin-interests do so because they are committed to Close Cooperation. These states realize that advanced forms of interstate engagement are necessary to enable them to meet their shared aspirations, while sustaining peaceful relations in the long-term.

In Founding Charters, as in the precedents unequivocally reflecting Community-of-Interests, the centrality of Close Cooperation finds expression in treaty references, for example, to *mutual benefit*; *close, meaningful, greater, enhanced* or *increased* collaboration; or *active* or *positive* cooperation. Article 4(3) of the EU Treaty, for example, codifies the "principle of sincere cooperation".

In the context of transboundary waters, the 1st Preambular Paragraph of the ECEWC notes that the sound protection and use of transboundary waters are "important and urgent tasks", which can only be effectively accomplished through "enhanced cooperation". The Preamble of the 1995 SADC Protocol draws attention to the environmental impacts of the region's plans for social and economic development; and, on that basis, emphasizes the need for "close cooperation" between watercourse states. The Revised SADC Protocol reiterates the Preambular reference to "close cooperation"; and, in Article 2, underscores "closer cooperation" as an overarching goal.

These expressions may appear in preambles, as guiding ideals, goals, or principles; codified in the body of treaties as general or specific obligations or rules (binding) or commitments or standards (non-binding); or embedded in the mandates of the Basin Body. In case law, the ICJ affirms that "close and continuous"[204] cooperation between the two co-riparian countries is the only avenue for securing the protection of the River Uruguay.

Close Basin Cooperation is more than engaging in casual exchanges and negotiations on a case-by-case basis but actually accomplishing things in common directed at shared goals. Cooperation framed by the Theory is a specific application of the general duty to cooperate, central to how states interact within shared watersheds, and strongly reflected in the framework and Basin Treaties examined here. The UNWC and the ECEWC both codify, clarify, and develop cooperation as a general requirement. The SADC Protocols lack provisions expressly codifying the general obligation to cooperate. However, Article 3(3) of the Revised Protocol contains a catchall provision on respect for international law, which injects the *general* duty to cooperate into the SADC legal regime. Customary rules bind all states, regardless of treaty language stating as much. Viewed through the lens of Community-of-Interests, under which collaboration is the general rule, rather than the exception, Article 3(3) embeds the duty to cooperate.

In policy discourse, the proclamations of the *International Decade for Action, 'Water for Life', 2005–2015,*[205] the *International Year of Water Cooperation, 2013,*[206] and the *International Decade for Action, 'Water for Sustainable Development', 2018–2028,*[207] have aimed to advance cooperation at all levels, which includes transboundary, as a means to achieve internationally agreed goals. The current Decade explicitly emphasizes integrated management of water resources among its objectives. UN Decades and Years intend to draw political attention to priority topics which, to be effectively addressed, demand sustained and long-term focus on the part of the global community and at the regional and/or national levels.[208]

---

204 Pulp Mills Case, *supra*, p. 34.

205 UNGA, 58th Session, Res 58/217, *International Decade for Action, 'Water for Life', 2005–2015* (23 Dec 2003), UN Doc A/RES/58/217 (9 Feb 2004).

206 IYWC Res, *supra*.

207 UNGA, 71st Session, Res 71/222, *International Decade for Action, 'Water for Sustainable Development', 2018–2028* (21 Dec 2016), UN Doc A/RES/71/222 (7 Feb 2017).

208 Unturbe, *supra*, p. 6.

Under the umbrella of Close Basin Cooperation, *joint action* is the prevailing modality of state engagement in the pursuit of common basin interests, being supplemented by coordination, harmonization, and unilateral measures. Joint action may be exemplified by the design of long-term basin management plans worked out collaboratively among co-basin states.

4.1 *The Duty to Cooperate under Community-of-Interests*

Close Basin Cooperation, i.e., the cooperation duty as framed by Community-of-Interests, displays four specific and characteristic features. These are hallmarks not found in regimes framed by Limited Territorial Sovereignty, based on which we propose a typology for the obligation to cooperate under Community-of-Interests.

Prevalence of Joint Action: The emphasis on joint action permeates regional integration regimes and is also present under Community-of-Interests. Article 8 of the UNWC captures both the general duty, i.e., cooperate in good faith; and a specific modality of joint action, which is to cooperate through a joint body. Paragraph 1 requires states to "cooperate on the basis of sovereign equality, territorial integrity, mutual benefit and good faith in order to attain optimal utilization and adequate protection of an international watercourse." Since the reference is to cooperation, without qualifiers or specifications, states realize common interests by resorting to various modalities of engagement and interface with one another, as appropriate; but the explicit reference to cooperation via *joint mechanisms or commissions* in Paragraph 2 suggests a special place for this particular manifestation of Close Basin Cooperation under Community-of-Interests.

The Senegal Basin Charter requires joint action in connection with ecosystem protection and preservation, environmental management, and the sustainable development of the basin. In particular, the role of the OMVS in preparing, for joint adoption by its members, an environmental action plan reveals the practice of joint and affirmative cooperation as part of overall basin planning, rather than just for specific matters.

Supplementary Forms of State Engagement: Under Close Basin Cooperation, joint action prevails but is supplemented by coordination and domestic measures also employed for the achievement of shared goals.

As anticipated by Article 8(1) of the UNWC, advancing basin interests does not presuppose joint action for all issues at all times. The same is implicit in Basin Treaty provisions referring generally to *cooperation* or implicitly invoking various possible stage engagement modalities that may be appropriate in the concrete case. It may be that some activities are better delivered if each country takes them up individually, at its own pace; in other cases, mere coordination or exchange may suffice. For certain purposes, otherwise, a mix of different modalities of state engagement may be required, including joint action.

For example, in complying with a Basin Treaty, it is likely that states would have to adopt measures domestically outside the institutional umbrella. To be clear, national measures coordinated or facilitated by the Basin Body express joint action. What we mean here instead can be illustrated by Article 2 of the Berlin Rules, envisioning national-level implementation measures without explicitly involving the Basin Body in their execution. These measures may entail enacting laws and regulations for treaty implementation; adopting administrative measures, such as management plans; and improving technical capacity for water management in the context of educational and research programs.

Joint Action for Coexistence: Close Basin Cooperation places joint action at the service of Limited Territorial Sovereignty, as is the case when the Basin Body plays a central role in the equitable and reasonable allocation of uses or in conflict resolution.

Consider the approach of Article 46 of the Lake Victoria Protocol to peaceful dispute settlement. Parties must first resort to negotiations. If those fail, either partner state may unilaterally refer the dispute to the EAC Court for a final decision. The EAC Secretary-General is then competent to refer pending disputes to the Court when parties do not. This provision puts the institutional machinery at the center of efforts to solve the dispute, in the interest of ensuring that unresolved disagreements do not fester, and the normal status of cooperation based on Community-of-Interests is restored as soon as possible. In so doing, the Protocol maintains its overall emphasis on Community-of-Interests, under which Limited Territorial Sovereignty plays a residual part.

Direct Interstate Engagement: Close Basin Cooperation may entail direct interstate engagement, i.e., members working together without the involvement of the Basin Body on a given task towards a specific goal.

In the case of incipient communities-of-interests, absent the Basin Body, states can engage directly with each other in the name of emerging common interests. Sometimes, provisions in Basin Treaties simply require interstate cooperation but do not specify if countries must interact under the Basin Body or if they may do so directly, i.e., outside the institutional umbrella. Direct cooperation duties may also apply for periods when the corresponding institution is not fully operational, for whatever reason. Finally, direct interstate engagement includes instances of collaboration and joint decision-making between national authorities, as with the adoption of the above-mentioned US-Mexico MoU. Close Basin Cooperation, therefore, may take place through or under the institutional umbrella or imply direct state interaction outside the Basin Body.

In practice, where a Basin Body is in place, most interactions tend to involve the institution in one capacity or another, thereby amounting to joint action. Seen in this light, the significance of the Basin Body, as the preferred forum for state engagement, as opposed to outside interactions, consolidates the importance of the institution as an expression of joint action under Close Basin Cooperation.

Under the River Uruguay Statute, for example, Article 46 governs enforcement in relation to domestic actors, which entails national action, direct communications between the parties, and rule-making by CARU. Each party has primary responsibility for exercising related powers within its respective territory. An exception applies where one party's authority detects a violation occurring along the river, but across the border. In such cases, the acting authority "may seize the offender and must place him at the disposal of [the] party" where the offence had taken place. Competent authorities may also cross the border in the pursuit of vessels that commit an offence within their own jurisdiction and then enter the territory of the other party. The requirement in both cases of border-crossing for the purpose of enforcement is of immediate notification of the event to the party concerned. The distance from the coast up to which this prerogative may be exercised is determined for each section by CARU.

4.2 *Joint Action for Shared Goals under Community-of-Interests*

Similarly to the Founding Charters, treaties framed by the Theory favor joint action in the pursuit of common interests under the umbrella of Close Basin Cooperation. Other state engagement modalities may be employed for activities or in situations where joint action is not politically, technically or financially feasible; or when coordination and harmonization are sufficient or even the more appropriate courses of action for achieving shared goals.

The UNWC follows a pattern of requiring parties to act *individually and, where appropriate, jointly*, in protecting basin ecosystems and managing international watercourses, ultimately to safeguard a higher common interest in a healthy environment. Parts 4 and 5 of the Convention explicitly or implicitly require states, in various instances, to move beyond mere coordination by acting jointly, if necessary, to achieve certain outcomes pertaining to the use, management and protection of the watercourse.

The SADC instruments also rely heavily on joint-action requirements, with preambular references to the *common* utilization and management of shared watercourses. In the 1995 SADC Protocol, emphasis on joint action is made concrete mostly through the detailed description of the possible functions of the Basin Body, thus placed at the center of cooperation efforts. To illustrate the intent behind the approach followed by the 1995 SADC Protocol, consider Articles 11(h) and 14(l) of the Ecuador-Peru Regulation, which mandate the Binational Commission to foster the joint design of technical instruments that advance common objectives and, through its IWRM Committees, to promote and execute approved binational projects.

Joint Action for Environmental Protection: Joint-action requirements, as framed by Community-of-Interests, may apply towards environmental protection regardless of the potential for transboundary impact. This indicates that such requirements are not framed by the harm-prevention rule. In other words, protection obligations are triggered with the aim to safeguard and manage the basin itself, untangled from the applicability of related Limited Territorial Sovereignty provisions. Yet, protection obligations of joint action enable compliance with the harm-prevention rule.

As an umbrella provision, Article 20 of the UNWC requires states, individually and, where appropriate, jointly, to protect and preserve the ecosystems of an international watercourse.

On water quality, the UNWC definition of *pollution* in Article 21(1) does not include a reference to cross-border injury, thus serving as a template for countries to define common goals on the topic, including for the purpose of transboundary impact avoidance. Paragraph 3 of the same provision determines that a request by a basin state on water quality issues originates for all other riparians a duty to "consult with a view to arriving at mutually agreeable measures and methods" aimed at pollution prevention, reduction, and control. This may include joint regulations or guidelines on water quality objectives and criteria; joint techniques and practices; and joint lists of controlled or banned substances. Joint action permeates these measures and methods as examples of commonly agreed steps states might employ to address pollution together. Here, the common interest in sustaining ecosystem health is the principal concern, bringing states together to act jointly, where appropriate, as interdependent members of a community-of-basin-interests.

Following the approach of Articles 20 and 21 of the UNWC, letters (a) and (d) of Article 4(2) of the Revised SADC Protocol command parties to protect and preserve watercourse ecosystems – individually and, where appropriate, jointly; and the aquatic environment – individually and, where appropriate, in cooperation with other states. This reference to *cooperation* in general regarding the aquatic environment implies any modality of collaborative state engagement deemed *necessary*, including joint action.

Article 2(11)–(12) of the 1995 SADC Protocol takes the same approach. The provision mandates parties, regardless of the potential for transboundary harm, to act diligently in preventing that alien aquatic species, potentially harmful to ecosystems, are introduced into shared freshwaters; and to prevent pollution and environmental degradation by providing for the protection and conservation of shared basins and the infrastructure located therein. Acting diligently to conserve the environment under the 1995 SADC Protocol includes, per Article 2(8), domestic measures putting in place minimum environmental licensing requirements. Similarly, Article 4(4)(b) of the new Protocol requires each party to set up, in its respective territory, a permitting system for water abstractions and discharges. These domestic measures supplement joint action.

Among the Basin Treaties, the 19th Preambular Paragraph of the Senegal Basin Charter affirms the parties' determination to combat, *jointly*, potentially harmful water management practices. The language employed, once again, does not apply only to instances of transboundary water risks but reflects the parties' common interest in improving water management across the entire basin.

Informed by this general commitment, Article 16 of the Charter unpacks the obligation of ecosystem protection and sustainable water management into two components, with the duty of acting jointly arguably applying to both, as appropriate: the control of every measure capable of significantly modifying the river or its waters, its biodiversity and surrounding environment; and the adoption of all appropriate measures to prevent, reduce and control events or conditions, whether resulting from natural causes or human activities, and which may lead to harm to the riverine environment or to human security and health. Specifically, states are to take "concerted action" to prevent the introduction into the river of new or alien animal or plant species capable to altering the basin ecosystem; jointly establish list of substances whose presence in the water is to be prohibited, limited, studied, or controlled; jointly define water quality objectives and criteria, in accordance with the relevant uses; engage in concerted work on measures to tackle point and nonpoint pollution sources; and work together on the development of techniques and best practices to ensure efficient water use.

To supplement these joint-action obligations, Senegal basin states pursue the above objectives separately, through national legislation that governs environmental issues in relation to drainage basins; and agree to harmonize such legislation.

The Lake Victoria Protocol incorporates joint-action obligations in connection with a common interest in nature protection, alongside progressive environmental law provisions.[209] Article 6(1) requires partner states to protect, conserve, and rehabilitate the basin and its ecosystems through all appropriate individual or joint measures. The same provision unpacks this ecosystem conservation duty into the following aspects: water quantity and quality protection; prevention of the introduction of potentially detrimental alien or new species; conservation of migratory and endangered species, forests, wetlands, and fisheries; restoration and rehabilitation of degraded natural resources; mapping of biodiversity components within the basin; and biodiversity conservation strategies. This listing of priority environmental management activities illustrates intervention areas likely to require joint efforts across the entire Lake basin to be effective.

Partner states also undertake to harmonize national laws and policies through the LVBC – and thus, jointly. Article 32(1) applies a general harmonization duty specifically to pollution from vessels.

Joint Planning and Management: A joint management plan, as may be mandated by the Basin Treaty, and which results from states efforts under or through the Basin Body, concretely expresses the meaning of joint action; breathes life into the Basin Scope; and illustrates the different elements of Community-of-Interests being applied simultaneously to reinforce one another. A joint basin plan could, for example, determine environmental flows on a basin-wide scale, thereby integrating infrastructure and biodiversity planning; and define no-go zones and free-flowing tributaries or stretches, as necessary to protect environmental hotspots and the basin's overall hydrological connectivity.

Joint basin plans result from a long process of data gathering and analysis, and definition of key objectives and a monitoring framework, with the involvement of all co-riparian states and in consultation with stakeholders. This means that the very process for developing such plans reflects the Theory, by enabling states to come together around technical rather than political issues; to identify common concerns; and to develop jointly agreed baselines

209 *See*, e.g., Lake Victoria Protocol, Art.4(2), referring to the environmental law principles of precaution and polluter-pays.

from which to assess progress towards collective water security and healthy ecosystems in the long-term. In the context of climate change, with all the uncertainties it imposes on managers regarding future water availability and variability, such plans are of great importance. Management plans are built to allow for ongoing monitoring and periodical adjustments as more information becomes available and as water allocation and management approaches and strategies are tested and, their effectiveness, assessed.[210]

Article 24(2) of the UNWC gives the word *management* a broad connotation, encompassing "planning the sustainable development of an international watercourse and providing for the implementation of any plans adopted; and otherwise promoting the rational and optimal utilization, protection and control of the watercourse". The first sentence refers to the overall, long-term process of resource planning, leading up to a joint plan or to coordinated planning tools. The second sentence encompasses other activities aimed at enabling the basin's sustainable use, protection, and control.

Under the ECEWC, Article 2(6) mandates co-basin states to cooperatively design, adopt, and implement *harmonized* policies, programs, and strategies for preventing, controlling, and mitigating transboundary impact and ensuring environmental protection. According to the ECEWC Guide, the term *harmonized* here means "common, or *at least*, coordinated"[211] planning tools, encompassing different degrees of cooperation – "from coordination of relevant national actions to the development of a single river basin management plan".[212] But the insertion of the expression *at least* in the Guide's explanation of the provision implies that, while there is some flexibility in this regard, joint planning and management tools are prioritized.

Per Article 17 of the Senegal Basin Charter, parties are to jointly adopt a general environmental action plan. The plan serves, *inter alia*, to better delimit OMVS' regulatory and enforcement powers, which is exercised taking account of existing permits. These powers encompass taking provisional measures to limit or suspend certain water uses, in response to conditions of scarcity or to the threat or effects of a natural disaster; outlining procedures to map out and categorize pollution sources and to monitor effluents; establishing conditions under which the exercise of water rights may be controlled, suspended, limited, or prohibited; and issuing special regulations for installations, activities and practices. Measures to ensure domestic compliance with

210 ILA (1966), *supra*, p. 456, 522–23.

211 ECEWC Guide, *supra*, p. 33 (emphasis added).

212 *Ibid.*

international obligations generally remain within the exclusive domain of each state's competent agencies.

In South America, the Ecuador-Peru Agreement envisions 5-year basin-level IWRM plans. Article 4(2) views these plans – their development, implementation, monitoring and evaluation – as the tools for achieving the objectives of water availability, use and sustainability. These plans are designed and proposed by each Basin Committee, along with technical-financial implementation proposals; and approved by consensus by the Basin Body, thereupon becoming binding on parties, per Article 8(c) of the Agreement. The *Binational Technical Secretariat* is responsible for the overall monitoring of the activities of the Basin Committees and of the plans' implementation. The Secretariat also establishes mechanisms and recommendations for the Committees to apply in the monitoring, joint follow-up, and evaluation of the IWRM plans. These plans are linked to, and aligned with, national water resources and basin management plans adopted by each country. Article 18 of the Basin Body's Regulation so defines the basic contents of the IWRM plans adopted under the Agreement: situation analysis; common objectives; binational actions (plans and projects); evaluation indicators; and financial mechanisms for implementation.[213]

Around the world, several transboundary basin management plans illustrate the promotion of joint action as a modality of cooperation.[214]

Pollution: The Preamble of the ECEWC fosters complementarities across different levels of intervention by calling for strengthened *national and international measures* targeting the prevention, control, and reduction of hazardous substances releases into freshwaters, as well as the abatement of eutrophication and acidification. The Convention offers guidance for the drafting and implementation of relevant national laws and policies. For example, pollution

213 *Regulation of the Binational Commission for the Integrated Management of the Water Resources of the Transboundary Basins between Ecuador and Peru*, Ecuador-Peru ('Ecuador-Peru Regulation').

214 *See, e.g.*, *Regional Strategic Action Program for the Nubian Aquifer System* (Vienna, 18 Sep 2013), Egypt-Libya-Sudan-Chad, *at* https://iwlearn.net/resolveuid/eba4ee45685b4654b5d8a5e278823c49; *Strategic Action Program: Regional Strategy for Integrated Water Resources Management in the Amazon Basin* (2018), *at* http://otca.org/en/ctp_otca_projetos/acto-unep-gef-project-integrated-and-sustainable-management-of-transboundary-water-resources-of-the-amazon-river-basin-considering-variability-and-climate-change/; *Strategic Framework for Adaptation to Climate Change in the Dniester River Basin* (2015) & *Implementation Plan* (2017), *at* https://dniester-commission.org/en/publications/climate-change/.

must be tackled preferably at source; and control measures must not lead to cross-media pollution transfer, whether directly or indirectly.

Monitoring: Joint action may serve monitoring objectives. Under Article 11 of the ECEWC, co-basin states must design joint monitoring programs targeting the conditions of transboundary waters and potential transboundary impacts; and implement them under the umbrella of the Basin Body *or* within the framework of a separate, dedicated arrangement. As part of monitoring efforts, the states concerned must adopt a common set of target pollution parameters and pollutants and then regularly monitor their discharges and concentrations; as well harmonize rules on "measurement systems, devices, analytical techniques, data processing and evaluation procedures, and methods for the registration of pollutants discharged".

Article 11 of the ECEWC also requires basin states to regularly assess, jointly or in a coordinated manner, the present and evolving conditions of transboundary waters, in light of measures adopted to prevent, control and reduce transboundary impact. Article 4 then mandates parties to put in place water resources monitoring programs. Presumably, national action in this respect is meant to supplement or carry out the joint monitoring program required by Article 11; or, in the absence of that program or pending its approval, to ensure that monitoring is taking place at least domestically, thus building the seeds for the establishment of a joint program in the future.

On monitoring, therefore, while the ECEWC combines requirements of joint action with domestic, harmonization and coordination measures, the latter three are to be implemented to further, and in accordance with, the overarching joint program adopted in common by the parties concerned. The ECEWC does not go as far as to mandate or explicitly foresee the establishment of joint databases.

At the basin level, Article 16(1) of the Lake Victoria Protocol deals with the identification within each country's territory of potential human-made and natural risks to basin people and ecosystems. Article 25(2) calls for the establishment of monitoring and surveillance stations and control laboratories for both water quality and quantity. Article 16(2) foresees the adoption of standardized monitoring equipment and methods in relation to natural phenomena. Article 25(1) covers the harmonization of national water quality standards. Article 25(3) governs the exchange of water quality and quantity data in accordance with jointly adopted guidelines.

Case Study 7: Joint Monitoring in Practice in the Danube

Article 9 of the *Danube River Protection Convention* governs cooperation on monitoring and assessment, which builds on domestic activities, coordination, and joint action.[215] The Article envisions, *inter alia*, harmonization of methods; joint monitoring systems and programs; inventories on point pollution sources and estimates of water pollution from non-point sources; agreements on monitoring points, river quality characteristics, and pollution parameters; and publication of the results. Article 9 is supplemented by Article 12, dealing with information exchange. Within this governing framework, "the major monitoring activities in the Danube River are performed through basin-wide joint programs".[216] Examples of how these provisions are operationalized through joint action include the *Joint Danube Survey*, "an extensive and intense sampling trip along the whole course of the river and its major tributaries";[217] the *Transnational Monitoring Network* (TNMN) for the collection of water quality data and publication in the ICPDR online yearbooks;[218] and the *Danube River Basin Geographic Information System*, the ICPDR data-sharing public platform, which "seeks to integrate and store the watercourse states' relevant data in a coordinated format".[219]

Research and Development: Article 12 of the ECEWC requires co-basin states – through joint bodies or arrangements, to "undertake specific research and development activities in support of achieving and maintaining [agreed] water-quality objectives and criteria". Joint action is also embedded in Article 13(4), on technology exchange, including through joint ventures enabling "direct industrial contacts and cooperation", as well as "joint training programs".

Article 45 of the River Uruguay Statute refers to "joint scientific studies of common interest" for parties to carry out. To that effect, Article 44 requires parties to authorize each other's representatives to conduct relevant research across the border, subject to prior notice via CARU describing the intended work, its locations, and timetables. Only exceptionally and for a limited time

215 *Convention on Cooperation for the Protection and Sustainable use of the Danube River* (Sofia, 29 June 1994) ('Danube River Protection Convention').

216 Howden, *supra*, p. 347.

217 *Id*, p. 348.

218 *Ibid*

219 *Id*, p. 349.

may such requests be rejected. At the same time, it is the authorizing party's right to join the work, receive information of its completion, and have access to its findings.

Joint Regulations: Under Article 17 of the Senegal Basin Charter, parties are to *jointly* adopt environmental regulations, *inter alia*, to determine the conditions under which domestic enforcement measures are applicable to shared waters.

Joint regulation for Senegal basin states also applies with regard to jointly owned, built and operated dams and reservoirs. Incidentally, shared ownership of infrastructure on international watercourses is rare in state practice.[220] With respect to such infrastructures, Articles 14 and 15 refer to the *Management Manual for the Manantali and Diama Dams*, as jointly established in Annexes 2 and 3 to the Charter. The *Joint Operation Scheme* sets out rules for the operation of the dams in question, which must be considered in the prioritization of uses and in the planning and operation of future infrastructure on the river and its tributaries.

In relation to the regulation of audits of existing facilities likely to generate significant environmental impact, Article 14(1) of the Lake Victoria Protocol requires states to adopt domestic laws, regulations, and policies as guidance for the operators of such facilities; and explicitly determines that such governance instruments be in line with the applicable EAC guidelines. These, in turn, are formulated jointly in a participatory process led by the EAC Secretariat.

Case Study 8: US-Mexico IBWC Minutes as Joint Regulations

The US and Mexico are parties to the *Treaty Respecting the Utilization of the Waters of the Colorado and Tijuana Rivers and of the Rio Grande*.[221] The Treaty institutes the *International Boundary and Water Commission* (IBWC), which is empowered to propose regulations, called *Minutes*, on specific topics for joint approval by the two countries. Minute 331, "*Measures to Improve the Reliability and Predictability of Rio Grande Water Deliveries to Benefit the United States and Mexico*", aims to ensure more regular water deliveries from Mexico to the US and to reduce or prevent shortfalls in such deliveries, subject to prior U.S. agreement. The

220 UNW-DPAC, *supra*, p. 33.

221 *Treaty Respecting the Utilization of the Waters of the Colorado and Tijuana Rivers and of the Rio Grande*, US-Mexico (3 Feb 1944) (in force 8 Nov 1945).

broader goal is to deal with growing water scarcity and shared environmental challenges, including regarding water quality and salinity.[222]

Sectoral Cooperation: The River Uruguay Statute prioritizes joint action with regard to various *specific common interests* across sectors, including through CARU, in the following provisions: Article 4, on jointly agreed navigation safety provisions; Article 36, on coordination, through CARU, of actions appropriate to prevent changes to the basin's ecological balance, as well as to control harmful conditions, including pests, on the watercourse and across connected surrounding areas; Article 39, on information exchange on fishing activities, including catches – again, through CARU; Articles 37 and 56(a), on joint regulations to ensure that living resources are protected and preserved, e.g., via the establishment and periodical adjustment of equally shared maximum catches per species; and Article 56(d), on CARU's role of coordinating with the competent national authorities activities aimed at preventing and prosecuting environmental offences and crimes.

Article 10 of the Lake Victoria Protocol deals with tourism, calling on parties to design "a collective and coordinated approach" for the sector's development and marketing. This provision for tourism should be read under the framework of Article 27(1)(b), requiring each partner state, within its respective territory, to "integrate, as far as possible and as appropriate, the conservation and sustainable use of [basin] resources … into relevant sectoral or cross-sectoral plans, programs and policies." This requirement of national-level mainstreaming of environmental sustainability supplements, enriches and enables collective and coordinated planning for tourism.

A broader call for dealing with sustainability as a transversal issue is present in Article 2 of the ECEWC, per which parties must act with due diligence in their territories towards the achievement of environmental sustainability, in particular by mainstreaming the goals of ecologically sound and rational management, conservation and protection into resource use and promoting ecosystem conservation and restoration.

Economic Instruments and Financing: Article 18 of the Lake Victoria Protocol codifies and details the user-pays principle, according to which states must, *jointly or individually*, "put in place measures for recovery of costs for the large-scale [water] uses". The provision does not clarify how that might be done jointly, merely stating that funds collected domestically are to be spent

222 IBWC, *IBWC Signs Minute 331 Focused on Improving Reliability, Predictability of Rio Grande Water Deliveries* (9 Nov 2024) (on file).

by each partner in meeting basin management costs within its respective territory. Given the lack of state practice in joint application of the user-pays principle within transboundary basins, it would be interesting to see if the riparians have put such measures in place.

With regard to joint financing, Article 8(g) of the Ecuador-Peru Agreement empowers the Commission to establish financial mechanisms through international cooperation; and Article 27 of the Regulation deals more broadly with the mandate of the Commission to design cooperation and coordination mechanisms with international, regional and national organizations, in support of the effective management of the transboundary basins under the Agreement.

Hence, under regional integration and Community-of-Interests regimes, there is a pattern of states prioritizing joint action, but also undertaking to coordinate, exchange, harmonize, consult, negotiate, regulate, notify, etc., in a mutually reinforcing manner. In other words, modalities of state engagement other than joint action supplement the latter in the pursuit of common interests. In particular, *implementation* of treaty obligations still largely occurs at the domestic level, inextricably linking national and international water governance systems.[223]

The approach of mixing intervention modalities and preserving some flexibility in terms of how states are to engage acknowledges that, in some basins and for certain matters, riparian parties may not *yet* be prepared to cooperate principally through joint action. When this is the case, other forms of state engagement are necessary in the meantime to generate basic data, build mutual confidence and develop the parties' experience and comfort levels with transboundary water cooperation, thus viewed as an evolving process.

4.3 *General Obligation to Participate*

Equitable and reasonable use is a cornerstone of the UNWC and of international water law, but it is the manifestation of the principle as Equitable and Reasonable *Participation* which holds greater significance under Community-of-Interests. Framed by equity and reasonableness and underpinned by the duty to cooperate, as codified in the UNWC, Participation is a key expression of Close Basin Cooperation for mutual benefit.

Invoking de concept of Participation, *Mutually beneficial cooperation* is often highlighted within the Founding Charters of Regional Integration Organizations. As an example, Article 6(e)-(f) of the EAC Treaty includes among its

223 F. Bernardini, *in* Unturbe, *supra*, p. 30.

principles *cooperation for mutual benefit* and *equitable distribution of benefits*. Specifically, Article 5(2) calls for the fair and proportionate allocation of the benefits arising from "harmonious and balanced development and sustained expansion of economic activities".

Equitable and Reasonable Participation under the UNWC: Article 5(2) determines that watercourse states "*shall* participate in the use, development and protection of an international watercourse in an equitable and reasonable manner". Participation is thus formulated as an obligation, which entails state engagement in watercourse management, use and protection, whether in measures, works, activities, planning tools or governance instruments, as would enable sustainable development and shared enjoyment of associated benefits.[224] Per the second sentence of Paragraph 2, Participation "includes both the *right to utilize* the watercourse and the *duty to cooperate* in the protection and development thereof". The UNWC's formulation of equitable and reasonable Participation is fully incorporated into Article 3(7)(b) of the Revised SADC Protocol.

The legal effect of the above provisions is that, conversely, basin countries "have a *right to the cooperation* of other watercourse states [on various matters], as appropriate under the circumstances".[225] Such a right is implicit in the respective rights of riparian countries to use the resource within their territories in line with equitable and reasonable use and respecting the harm-prevention rule. The relationships between riparian states here resemble that of fraction owners within buildings who accept they must meet a fair share of maintenance and improvement costs; and are aware that, without the administration of common parts, "the use and the value of a private part will be deeply affected".[226]

Under the UNWC and the Revised SADC Protocol, equitable and reasonable Participation is a hybrid application of equitable and reasonable use and the general duty to cooperate. Combining into one duty the substantive and procedural aspects of the rules just mentioned, equitable and reasonable Participation informs the application and interpretation of all other articles under the Convention and the Revised SADC Protocol.

To grasp the centrality of Participation for Community-of-Interests, consider that equitable and reasonable use is predominantly concerned with the allocation of water rights; the rule refers to the right of riparian countries to

224 *See* ILC (1994), *supra*, p. 97.
225 *Ibid* (emphasis added).
226 Magalhães, *supra*, p. 83.

make use of transboundary waters within their respective territories as "an attribute of sovereignty";[227] and this right is "qualitatively equal to, and correlative with, those of other watercourse states".[228] Equitable and reasonable use is the framework rule that applies as states independently exercise their rights within the basin, even if sometimes owing neighbors specific cooperation duties. As such, equitable and reasonable use had not been designed and neither has evolved or much applied to address common interests, such as the protection of ecosystems in their own right, i.e., when "environmental harms ... do not conflict with other riparian party's use of the river."[229]

In contrast, the fundamental vocation of Participation is to advance common interests, even if the rule may be employed to balance rights. As explained by the ILC, equitable and reasonable Participation carries "an implicit right to the cooperation of other watercourse States in maintaining an equitable allocation of the uses and benefits of the watercourse".[230] But Participation requirements also apply to broader sustainable management objectives dependent on *active* state engagement in the design of plans, programs and measures to tackle issues such as floods, droughts, erosion, pollution, disease vectors, security of infrastructure, and environmental protection.[231]

Participation as a Positive Obligation: Participation is more than the sum of its parts, being characterized by its *affirmative nature.* Going beyond the procedural and abstract content of the duty to cooperate and beyond the focus of equitable and reasonable use on unilateral restraint, Participation calls for *proactiveness*, i.e., *positive* cooperation.[232] *To participate*, within the meaning of the UNWC and the Revised SADC Protocol, is to *act*, in the sense of *taking initiative*, as opposed to simply *reacting* to specific circumstances or *passively waiting* for explicit requests for cooperation. Viewed through the lens of Community-of-Interests, the Duty to Participate entails the proactive engagement of co-riparian states, on an equitable and reasonable basis, in the pursuit of common interests connected to the sustainable development, protection and management of the watercourse and associated ecosystems.

The general obligation to participate does not exclude but supplements obligations to *react*, where required or appropriate. Consider the duties for

227 ILC (1994), *supra*, p. 98.
228 *Ibid.*
229 Hunter *et al* (2015), *supra*, p. 888.
230 ILC (1994), *supra*, p. 97.
231 *Ibid.*
232 *Ibid.*

states to enter into consultations under Articles 6(2) and 24(1) of the UNWC, respectively: *when the need arises*, on the application of equitable-and-reasonable-use factors; and *at the request of any of them*, with respect to basin management. Consider, also, Article 26(2), on the obligation to respond to requests for consultations on "the safe operation and maintenance" of infrastructure, as well as on the protection of infrastructure "from willful or negligent acts or the forces of nature". The obligation is triggered when a co-basin state "has reasonable grounds to believe that it may suffer significant adverse effects" in this regard. Under these three Articles, states wait for a need to arise or to receive a request – and only then must engage in some modality of dialogue or exchange.

In contrast, Article 25 of the UNWC may entail both passive and active cooperation. The provision deals with the regulation of an international watercourse, i.e., the "use of hydraulic works or any other continuing measure to alter, vary or otherwise control the flow of the waters of an international watercourse." Paragraph 1 requires states to "cooperate, where appropriate, to respond to needs or opportunities" pertaining to flow regulation. Per the ILC Commentary, the expression *where appropriate* in the provision means that "the obligation is not to seek to identify needs and opportunities, but to respond to those that exist."[233]

Yet, an interpretation underpinned by Community-of-Interests starts from the use of the term *cooperate* used in Article 25(1), which encompasses all possible modalities of state engagement. In turn, Paragraph 2 of the same provision is a specific application of equitable and reasonable Participation that requires states to "participate on an equitable basis in the construction and maintenance or defrayal of the costs of such [agreed-upon] regulation works". If there is a requirement to participate in the execution of appropriate regulation measures, Participation may also apply, where appropriate, at the planning stage of those measures. So, *as appropriate*, Article 25(1) may entail a proactive obligation to seek out and plan for relevant regulation needs and opportunities.

Passive cooperation may be appropriate under certain circumstances, but one could hardly conceive of a thriving community-of-basin-interests that does not prioritize proactiveness. Tanzi and Arcari point out that equitable and reasonable Participation "enhances the vision of an international watercourse as a 'river community', entailing … the obligation for the co-riparians to act affirmatively for the purposes of its protection and control".[234]

233 *Id*, p. 127.

234 Tanzi & Arcari, *supra*, p. 118, 120.

Benefit-Sharing: Participation means that states must share the benefits, and the costs, associated with the management, protection, and use of a transboundary basin. Article 26 of the Regulation of the Ecuador-Peru Agreement, for example, commits the parties to channeling the funds necessary so as to ensure the Binational Commission's effective functioning. In its turn, the Commission establishes public financing mechanisms for the performance of its own activities and for the implementation of IWRM plans.

Joint financing as an expression of Participation for environmental protection could also be exemplified by the joint design and construction of migratory fish ladders on a proposed dam within one of the riparian countries, with the costs and benefits from such measures being shared among the states concerned.

In the context of the UNWC and the Revised SADC Protocol, benefit-sharing connected to Participation is guided by the criteria of equity and reasonableness. In determining the manner and extent of their Participation, countries must consider all relevant factors, as exemplified in Article 6 of the UNWC, including the extent to which the states concerned would benefit from its solution.[235] According to the ILC, equitable Participation means that states' "contributions ... to joint protection and preservation efforts be at least proportional to the measure in which they have contributed to the threat or harm to the ecosystems in question".[236]

Equitable and reasonable Participation does not require that the watercourse always be put to its most efficient use, i.e., efficiency may be a factor to weigh in allocation decisions, but it is not an overriding consideration. In addition, per Article 10(1) of the UNWC, not one use enjoys inherent priority over another.

The basis for sharing under Participation, however, need not always be equity. In Tarlock's view, benefit-sharing goes beyond volumetric resource allocation to center on *resource use efficiency* – it "substitutes money for the use and control of wet water."[237] Development then becomes more efficient and equitable when "the focus is less on the gallons used by each country and more on the potential or real economic benefits [to] be derived from joint management".[238] For example, countries could agree on a scheme under which the project proponent pays another not to dam the watercourse. The

235 ILC (1994), *supra*, p. 119.

236 *Ibid.*

237 Tarlock, *supra*, p. 397.

238 D. Hunter, J. Salzman, D. Zaelke, *International Environmental Law and Policy*, 2nd ed (Foundation Press 2002), p. 802.

recipient may then employ the funds thus received to serve related domestic needs in another cost-effective way.[239]

This distribution of benefits may also gain concreteness through specific joint projects, which are better enabled in the context of Community-of-Interests than of Limited Territorial Sovereignty; and Participation is likely better realized as part of a long-term process of interstate engagement. As such, Participation framed by the Theory is embedded in Tarlock's conception of *joint management*, put in place to "correct the defects of a static equitable apportionment"[240] through continued and affirmative engagement.

Forms of Proactive State Engagement: A state may proactively contribute to, or participate in, the sound management of an international watercourse by strengthening management measures within its own territory and/or coordinating those same measures with its co-basin states. Individual initiative can be illustrated by a state that maintains its portion of a watercourse free of barriers to navigation, imposes on domestic users pollution control requirements recommended by the Basin Body even before those recommendations are formally endorsed, or initiates engagement with neighbors to assess the best locations for the siting of monitoring stations.

Under Article 26(1) of the UNWC, each state, within its own territory, undertakes to maintain and protect relevant installations, facilities, and other works, which exemplifies its Participation in proper infrastructure management.

Proactive coordination may include regular updates in the case of an emergency or when various states coordinate the operation of individual dams along the watercourse to ensure sustainable flows for multiple uses.

Often, however, Participation is likely to entail some degree of joint action, the prevalent modality of state engagement under Community-of-Interests. Hypothetically, riparian countries participating in the protection of migratory species depend on joint action to cover their entire range when assessing status and occurrence, identifying threats, defining and monitoring appropriate conservation measures, and ensuring that relevant benefits and costs are equitably shared.

Hence, effective Participation in basin protection, management, and development tends to demand joint assessment and planning, even if implementation then takes place domestically. The very notion of Participation in the pursuit of common interests is embedded in joint action. Joint-action obligations provide further specificity to Participation, when full compliance there-

239 Tarlock, *supra*, p. 397.

240 *Id*, p. 402.

with entails the states proactively coming together to act on an issue, i.e., where specific circumstances demand *common and positive action* in transboundary basin management. An example of proactive joint action is the development of a baseline assessment of the states' respective equitable contributions and corresponding benefits linked to the protection and sustainable use of the watercourse and related ecosystems.

Under Community-of-Interests, therefore, joint action and Participation develop a symbiotic, albeit not exclusive, relationship with each other. Absent explicit agreement between the parties, however, Participation, joint action or Community-of-Interests do not entail common property of the resource or a consent requirement for unilateral watercourse development.

4.4 *Common Property, Mutual Consent and Joint Action*

Condominium and mutual consent are not inherent to Community-of-Interests, nor are they part of international customary law. Yet, there have been claims wrongly associating with Community-of-Interests these controversial notions of *common, joint or shared property or ownership* of transboundary waters, held as such by the respective co-basin states;[241] and the *derivative requirement of mutual consent* or a *veto power* for the implementation of unilateral projects capable of affecting other countries within the basin.

We use the word *derivative* interlinking the two concepts because, when one qualifies an international watercourse as common property, one would have to concede to the existence of a veto power that could be yielded by a potentially affected country over another's unilateral project. As Hartig explains, if riparian states are deemed to be co-owners of the unity formed by the watercourse, they "can act only by mutual consent in respect of this inseparable *res*".[242] Similarly, for Caflisch, mutual consent necessarily flows from common property, i.e., if one accepts that a condominium exists between co-basin states, they must be prepared to assume that each such state holds a veto right over the implementation of a new measure planned by another.[243]

241 In the context of navigation, an early reference to joint ownership is found in a French Decree declaring that "the course of rivers is common ... property of all riparian land". French Government, Interim Executive Council, Decree of 16 Nov 1792, *quoted in* Caponera, *supra*, p. 270.

242 Hartig, *quoted in* McCaffrey (2019), *supra*, p. 229.

243 L. Caflisch, *Règles Générales du Droit des Cours d'Eau Internationaux*, 219 RCADI 9 (1989), p. 61.

Case Study 9: Lake Lanoux Dispute and the Misunderstanding over Community-of-Interests, Joint Ownership and Veto Power
Spanish claims in the Lake Lanoux Case illustrate the misunderstanding around the Theory and the two concepts at hand. Relevant passages of the Spanish assertions, invoking the applicable boundary treaty, consist of the following references: "eaux du bassin versant qui sont communes par nature";[244] "une conception unilatérale, contraire au régime de communauté";[245] and "l'aménagement des eaux suivant leur bassin versant naturel".[246] On those bases, Spain invokes "l'idée de l'accord mutuel nécessaire qui informent tout le régime du *communauté de pâturages*".[247] Spain confusingly mixes together Community-of-Interests, the idea of common resources, the Basin Scope, and the mutual consent requirement. In response, the Award states: "Le Tribunal ne saurait méconnaître la réalité, au point de vue de la géographie physique, de chaque bassin fluvial, qui constitue ... 'une unité'. Mais cette constatation n'autorise pas les conséquences absolues que voudrait en tirer la thèse espagnole".[248]

Common Property in International Water Law: Common property over transboundary river systems has roots in the domestic law concept of the *condominium*. Hartig embraces common property for the same reasons "a farmer could [not] acquire an exclusive property right in just one leg of a live cow."[249] Co-basin countries are thus "in the same position as any co-owners of a *res* which consists of one unit and cannot be split into parts."[250]

Hartig's imagery unveils the full meaning of joint ownership and yet are not representative of the opinion of most scholars.[251] The widespread understanding seems to be that the ownership of transboundary basins is not shared, so that countries must use the resource in a rational and fair way without being bound by a mutual-consent requirement. McCaffrey, for example, views the

244 Arbitral Tribunal, *Affaire du Lac Lanoux* (Spain *v.* France), Award of 16 Nov 1957 ('Lake Lanoux Case'), p. 296.
245 *Ibid.*
246 *Id*, p. 298.
247 *Id*, p. 297.
248 *Id*, p. 304.
249 Quoted in McCaffrey (2019), *supra*, p. 229.
250 *Ibid.*
251 *See*, e.g., Benvenisti, *supra*, p. 399, noting the lack of consensus in scholarship in this respect; Howden, *supra*, p. 220, remarking on the absence of support for linking Community-of-Interests and joint ownership.

watercourse as a unitary whole that ties together the riparian states as, not joint, but *neighboring* property owners within an extended neighborhood across the entire catchment.[252]

In state practice, joint ownership receives little endorsement nowadays. McCaffrey finds references in older treaties and relevant unilateral statements to watercourses as shared property, but the same is less often the case within legal instruments adopted from the 1900s onwards.[253] For Caflisch, co-basin states may agree to incorporating the notion of joint ownership into a water treaty, but said notion does not reflect customary law.[254]

When co-basin states *together opt* to enter into a treaty endorsing common property and veto power, this may be seen as a commitment to an *extreme expression of joint action*. In this sense, Benvenisti considers that reviving common property in transboundary waters "could elucidate and thus enhance the riparians' duty to cooperate".[255]

Otherwise, common ownership might apply to infrastructure built jointly on international watercourses by co-riparian states. Article 56(i) of the River Uruguay Statute mentions *binational works and installations* – a practice also found under the Senegal community-of-basin-interests. In the case of the Uruguay River, it falls upon CARU to establish the legal and administrative regime governing such joint projects, as well as to manage them.

Jointly-Owned *versus* Shared Resources: Doubts, sensitivities, and resistance to applying the concept of common property to transboundary waters are clear in the work of the ILC on transboundary aquifers. In his 2nd Report, following a round of discussions with states, the Rapporteur clarifies his choice to use the term *transboundary*, so as to avoid the ideas of world heritage or common ownership that the word *shared* could entail.[256]

While the Rapporteur's concerns are legitimate, there is a difference between the concepts of common property and of *shared resources, basins, or watercourses*. In the case of transboundary aquifers, the ILC seems to give in to political pressure and government statements that *incorrectly* assume that a basin said to be shared is jointly owned. The Rapporteur's clarification creates confusion as to the meaning of the word shared under Community-of-

252 Benvenisti, *supra*, p. 237.

253 McCaffrey (2019), *supra*, p. 223.

254 Caflisch, *supra*, p. 60–1.

255 Benvenisti, *supra*, p. 399.

256 C. Yamada (Special Rapporteur), *2nd Report on Shared Natural Resources: Transboundary Groundwaters*, UN Doc A/CN.4/539 (2004), p. 260.

Interests, possibly instigating resistance to the Theory itself. Viewing transboundary waters as *shared* resources is a common feature of the treaties that reflect Community-of-Interests. The Revised SADC Protocol employs the expression *shared* watercourses throughout its text; and, per the definitions in Article 1 of the Senegal Basin Charter, the River is a resource *shared* among the riparian states, and the waters of the river are *shared waters*. In fact, going back to the early stages of cooperation, the Senegal has been understood as an *international river*, so expressly declared by the basin states in 1963 and reaffirmed in 1972.[257] In case law, the ICJ finds that the River Uruguay is a *shared resource*[258] and characterizes the Danube as a *shared* river system.[259] In none of those cases, there is an implicit or explicit indication of joint ownership.

Hence, qualifying a basin as being shared between the states concerned possibly signals an endorsement of Community-of-Interests. Referring to a basin as shared is not the same as deeming it to be common property. This distinction is relevant for detecting the presence of Community-of-Interests in specific treaties through acknowledgements that the waters at stake are shared among the states concerned. The mere use of the term shared, however, does not imply endorsement of the common-property concept.

Veto Power in International Water Law: Like with common property, international water law does not support a mutual-consent requirement, and most watercourse agreements do not create a veto power with regard to planned measures.

In Latin America, Article V of the River Plate Basin Treaty makes clear that states remain free to implement unilateral actions within their own territories, as long as they comply with their duties under international law. The same is true in Africa, where the general state practice has been "to formulate an obligation or duty to consult the competent commission",[260] rather than to condition new developments to prior agreement among basin states.

Case law has also repeatedly rejected the mutual-consent requirement, within the field of international water law and beyond. The Pulp Mills Decision, for example, rejects Argentina's claim that, pending their judicial dispute, Uruguay would be required to hold off implementation; and rules that

257 *See*, respectively, Senegal River Convention, *supra*, Art.13; 1972 Status Convention, *supra*, Art.1.

258 Pulp Mills Case, *supra*, p. 38.

259 Gabčíkovo Case, *supra*, p. 54.

260 M.M. Mbengue, *A Model for African Shared Water Resources: The Senegal River Legal System*, 23:1 RECIEL 59–66 (2014), p. 61.

the River Uruguay Statute does not codify a no-construction obligation, neither explicitly nor implicitly.

Case Study 10: Lake Lanoux Dispute and the Veto Power
In the same dispute over Lake Lanoux, the Arbitral Tribunal makes clear that the mutual-consent requirement cannot be regarded as a customary rule and even less as a general principle of law. Although examples of this veto power exist in state practice, such cases are exceptions.[261] The Tribunal draws attention to a hypothetical situation where the planning state is unable to obtain its neighbor's consent, with the two parties failing to come to an agreement on the unilateral measure in question. In such a case: "il faut admettre que l'État normalement compétent a perdu le droit d'agir seul, par suite de l'opposition inconditionnée et discrétionnaire d'une autre État"[262] – a '*droit d'assentiment*' "qui paralyse, à la discrétion d'une État, l'exercice de la compétence territoriale d'un autre État".[263]

In scholarship, Caflisch underscores that a right of a riparian state to veto planned measures on international watercourses does not exist.[264] Conversely, for the veto power to exist, the countries concerned must have agreed on its applicability to their mutual relations.

An exception appears to apply to projects that would visibly extrapolate a country's equitable share of the watercourse. In such cases, consent seems to be required. In the Gabčíkovo case, Slovakia carries out a major diversion of the Danube – one deemed by the Court to deprive Hungary of its own equitable and reasonable rights. In respect to such extreme cases, the ICJ indicates that a riparian country cannot "proceed with a unilateral diversion of this magnitude without [the other's] consent."[265]

For planned measures other than those amounting to a patent violation of equitable and reasonable use, accepted substantive and procedural norms of international law condition their implementation. Shared ownership goes beyond those norms by imposing consensus among all basin states as a precondition for the development of the basin – in fact, for any decision pertaining to its overall management.

261 Lake Lanoux Case, *supra*, p. 306, 308.
262 *Id*, p. 306.
263 *Id*, p. 308.
264 Caflisch, *supra*, p. 61.
265 Gabčíkovo Case, *supra*, p. 56.

Norms Governing Planned Measures: Part 3 of the UNWC does not require consent. Instead, the Convention lays out a robust body of rules and procedures governing notification, information exchange, consultations, and negotiations for the review of planned measures. The Revised SADC Protocol imports various UNWC provisions on the topic and applies and adjusts them to the region's context.

Neither the UNWC nor the Revised SADC Protocol subject the implementation of water development projects to the consent requirement. Under both instruments, a state is free to proceed, albeit at its own risk, with the execution of the planned measure in question upon full compliance with the applicable rules and procedures. The approach codified in the Convention and the Revised SADC Protocol finds support in the Lake Lanoux Case, where the Tribunal considers that it is up for each state to reasonably and in good faith assess the circumstances of, and rules applicable to, the case.[266] In moving forward with the project, per the Award, the implementing state "prend le risque de voir sa responsabilité internationale mise en cause s'il est établi qu'elle n'a pas agi dans la limite de ses droits".[267]

In this same sense, the Pulp Mills Decision concludes that, "in proceeding with the authorization and construction of the mills, Uruguay necessarily bears all risks relating to any finding on the merits that the Court might later make".[268]

Case Study 11: ICJ, Passage through the Great Belt

The ICJ considers whether to determine the suspension of works for the construction of a bridge pending its final decision, in order to protect free passage rights for certain ships. The Court decides to allow the project to proceed under the premise that, once informed of the concerns expressed by the potentially affected state, it is for the implementing country to weigh the risks of a potential ruling against it and related effects on project implementation; and then decide on the merits of possible modifications or delays.[269]

266 Lake Lanoux, *supra*, p. 310.

267 *Ibid.*

268 Pulp Mills Case Provisional Measures, *supra*, p. 133.

269 ICJ, *Passage through the Great Belt* (Finland *v.* Denmark), Provisional Measures, Order of 29 July 1991, I.C.J. Reports 1991, p. 12, 19 ('Great Belt Case').

In line with the Great Belt Case, the ILC notes that, in proceeding with implementation, the state concerned remains under the obligation to consider the interests of other potentially affected countries.[270]

Like the UNWC and the Revised SADC Protocol, the River Uruguay Statute designs a detailed safeguard mechanism for interstate engagement that conditions the implementation of unilaterally planned measures capable of affecting navigation, water quality or the river regime, including the construction and modification of channels. The difference here is that the River Uruguay Statute places CARU at the center of states' exchanges, thereby reflecting joint action. The safeguard mechanism, as governed by Articles 7–12, well-illustrates how Community-of-Interests deals with unilaterally planned measures. While the rules and procedures under the Mechanism are strict and detailed, they do not include obtaining prior approval from the other party.

Per the safeguard mechanism, the implementing party informs CARU of its plans, which triggers a collaborative review process. It falls upon CARU to make a preliminary determination of the project's potential to result in significant transboundary impact. If there is such a risk, or where the Commission's analysis is inconclusive, the implementing party notifies its counterpart, through CARU, enclosing the technical and other information required for assessing the project's likely transboundary effects. An EIA is required for informed decision-making on projects likely to cause significant transboundary impact, as evidence of diligent and vigilant preventive behavior. The notified party has 30 days to inform the other state, through CARU, in case the information provided is incomplete, or else 180 days to reply with its feedback. CARU may extend this response period in light of a project's complexity. In the absence of objections or a reply, project implementation may proceed.

Where the notified party detects a risk of significant transboundary impact, it must notify the other riparian state through CARU, detailing relevant aspects of the project and related technical considerations; and proposing appropriate changes to the original plan. A 6-month negotiation process is triggered, failing which any one party may submit the dispute to the ICJ. After the end of the consultation procedure, the implementing party remains bound to its obligations under the Statute and international law. Article 10 secures for the notified party "the right to inspect the works being carried out in order to determine whether they conform to the plan submitted."

---

270 ILC, *Draft articles on Prevention of Transboundary Harm from Hazardous Activities*, with Commentaries, 53rd Session, *in* ILC Yearbook (2001), Vol.II, Part Two, UN Doc A/56/10, Art.9(3).

The ICJ deems this safeguard mechanism to be "comprehensive and progressive",[271] with CARU as its center; and thus, "an appropriate means, accepted by the parties, of achieving the objective"[272] in Article 1: the parties' overarching common interest in the sustainable use of the watercourse.

Rules governing planned measures short of requiring mutual consent are also present in the Lake Victoria Protocol. Article 4(2)(d)-(e) codifies prior notification and environmental impact assessment as guiding principles for basin management. Under Article 13, the planning party must issue the corresponding notification to the other partner states *and* the EAC secretariat, providing all information needed to assess potential impacts. This step is followed by interstate consultations, with the implementing party required to account for the interests of the other partner states in project development. Article 12 requires an implementing state, which finds that its project might cause significant transboundary impacts, to share the respective EIA for comments, both with the other partner states and the EAC Secretariat; and to take account of feedback thereafter received, when deciding on whether or not to approve the assessment. If the implementing party fails to do so, the interested partner state may trigger the Protocol's dispute settlement mechanisms.

The UNWC and the Revised SADC Protocol embody the current state of international water law. The River Uruguay Statute and the Lake Victoria Protocol go further by giving the Basin Body a central role in the context of planned measures. Notification, consultation, and negotiation procedures enable states to be aware of their neighbors' intentions and have an early and effective opportunity to present their opinion, voice concerns, assess opportunities for benefit-sharing, and consider the need for compensation. Those procedures build an environment conducive to cooperation between the parties, "enabling them to assess the plan's impact on the river on the basis of the fullest possible information and, if necessary, to negotiate the adjustments needed to avoid the potential damage".[273]

In the Pulp Mills Case, the ICJ also affirms the applicability, throughout the entire course of the consultation and negotiation proceedings, of another safeguard not explicitly captured by the Statute: pending completion of all steps required by the Mechanism, Uruguay is to refrain from initiating or authorizing construction works related to the unilateral project in dispute. The ICJ sees this so-called suspension duty as being implicit in the Statute's object and purpose, in the absence of which the mechanism would lose its very *raison*

---

271 Pulp Mills 2006 Provisional Measures, *supra*, p. 133.

272 Pulp Mills Case, *supra*, p. 34.

273 *Id*, p. 40.

d'être; and considers it to be an established requirement of international law founded on the principle of good faith that governs interstate cooperation.[274]

Under both the UNWC and the Revised SADC Protocol, in the case of a request by the potentially affected state, a mandatory suspension of implementation activities applies during the course of consultations and negotiations, for up to six months.

This approach, as a means to create an enabling environment for successful negotiations, is recognized in the Lake Lanoux Case as representing international practice.[275]

Agreement on the Application of the Veto Power: According to Dellapenna, the mutual-consent requirement illustrates "a high degree of joint development of a basin's water resources"[276] – a modality of Close Basin Cooperation whereby mutual consent, on the basis of an agreement between the states concerned, replaces equitable and reasonable use as the governing rule for river development and states forego their right to explore independently their respective portions of the watercourse.

This is the case in the Senegal Basin Community-of-Interests. The applicable legal-institutional regime is an exception to the rule of certain constraints being imposed on the unilateral development of the watercourse without amounting to veto rights. None of the treaties adopted for the basin over the years mentions explicitly joint ownership. Yet, the mutual-consent requirement has been embedded in this advanced and continuously evolving community-of-basin-interests since the signing of a 1963 treaty and retained in the Senegal Basin Charter.[277] The latter treaty, in fact, strengthens and further details veto rights.

The Senegal Community-of-Interests subjects unilateral or joint projects to prior approval by the OMVS. In Mbengue's words, "the idea of a *community-of-law* [has been] inseparable from the need to establish a *community-of-management*",[278] in which states perceive unilateralism "as distorting the very objective of solidarity [as] the ultimate end that justifies full adherence to the legal regime."[279] In other words, the basin states endorse the mutual-

274 *Id*, p. 47.

275 Lake Lanoux Case, *supra*, p. 311.

276 Dellapenna (1996), *supra*, p. 240.

277 *See* Senegal River Convention, *supra*, Art.8. The Convention was later replaced by the 1972 Status Convention, *supra*, where Art.4 codifies mutual consent.

278 Mbengue, *supra*, p. 62 (emphasis added).

279 *Id*, p. 63.

consent requirement as the legal safeguard for securing the effectiveness and predictability of their collectively chosen cooperation path: to manage the entire basin together, viewed, per the Charter's Preamble, as an ecosystem essential for sustainable development.

Under the Charter, Article 10 subjects all water uses, except for those serving domestic purposes, to a regime of prior review. Decision-making in this regard must consider third-party and existing rights, as well as management scenarios and agreed thresholds in relation to both water quantity and quality. Obtaining prior OMVS *authorization*, through the Council of Ministers, is required for water projects that involve the construction and operation of installations and works; or which may endanger public health and security, interfere with the free flow of waters, reduce resource availability, degrade the riverbed, or undermine the quality or biodiversity of the aquatic environment. For such activities, the Charter requires the interested state to transmit an authorization application to the OMVS High Commissioner, who then adds any relevant information thereto and submits it to the Commission for an opinion. The power to approve applications lies with the Council of Ministers. The Council may also withdraw a granted authorization for lack of use or in the public interest.

Other potentially harmful activities pertaining to water uses may require a *declaration* as a precondition for implementation. The Charter maintains the mandate to enforce this requirement with the competent national authorities in each party; and requires such authorities to transmit the declarations they issue to the OMVS High Commissioner.

Article 24 of the Charter outlines additional notification and consultation requirements for all projects within the basin likely to have *significant* impacts on the characteristics of the river regime, the water body, conditions for various water uses, water quality or aquatic biodiversity. These projects are governed by detailed norms pertaining to information exchange and mutual consultations on potential effects through the Council of Ministers. Prior to implementation, early notification must be sent, through the High Commissioner, to the other parties, accompanied by the relevant documentation, including the respective EIA. Potentially affected states have three months to reply, with the absence of response amounting to consent. An application for authorization must be addressed to the Council, via the High Commissioner. The Commission must be consulted to emit a technical opinion on the subject. With all those procedural requirements met, preapproval by the parties, deliberating through the Council of Ministers, is mandatory before implementation may begin.

For emergency projects, the implementing state must issue a formal declaration to the High Commissioner, who must then submit it for ministerial negotiations.

Case Study 12: Boundary Waters Treaty
Outside the Basin Treaties here examined, another precedent to mention is the *Boundary Waters Treaty*, between the US and Canada.[280] Articles 3–4 of that Treaty incorporate the mutual-consent requirement, through the International Joint Commission, for certain planned measures.

The Senegal basin precedent, on its own, is insufficient to justify including the concept of common property, along with its mutual-consent requirement, among the primary elements of Community-of-Interests. At the same time, the prominent presence of veto rights in the Senegal basin must not be ignored. This leads to the conclusion that common consent expresses an advanced degree of integration reached by a given community-of-basin-interests and a joint state intent to deepen the Theory's application as a governing framework for cooperation. Only in a tightly knit community-of-basin-interests could the concerns expressed by the Arbitral Tribunal in the Lake Lanoux Case be fully addressed. One may assume that the states within such communities would not abuse their veto rights, especially when applied in conjunction with a long history of cooperation, deep and multisectoral interdependence, and an implied commitment to intra-basin Solidarity. Accordingly, the mutual-consent requirement is a *possible* but not a primary element of Close Basin Cooperation under Community-of-Interests.

Otherwise, a regime founded on veto rights could sometimes be detrimental for people and nature. Where mutual consent is a requirement among multiple basin states, it could push them into rushed negotiations and decisions on tradeoffs behind closed doors. In such cases, projects may be accepted among states on the basis of reciprocity, sometimes with no or little regard for the value of ecosystem services or the needs of riparian communities that depend on those services for their lives and livelihoods. In any event, imposing agreement among all basin states as a requirement for development would prove unfeasible in most places.

280 *Boundary Waters Treaty*, US-CAN (Washington, 11 Jan 1909) (in force 5 May 1910).

4.5 *Limited Territorial Sovereignty under Community-of-Interests*

Communities-of-basin-interests are predicated on Close Basin Cooperation for sustainable basin management as an overarching shared goal. The normal state of affairs among states within a formalized community-of-interests is Basin-Scope cooperation, as governed by the Basin Treaty and the Basin Body, on the basis principally of joint action and Participation – all aimed at safeguarding common interests.

Yet, no matter how well-developed a cooperation regime or how friendly the relations between the countries concerned, water or related disputes are bound to occur. Consider the long history and tradition of Close Basin Cooperation between Argentina and Uruguay. As noted by the ICJ, through CARU, the two countries have been coordinating their activities and resolving the problems that periodically arise, having invoked the Statute's provisions on judicial dispute settlement for the first time in relation to the Pulp Mills Case. The Court so notes immediately after recognizing the existence of a real community-of-basin-interests-and-rights between the two countries.[281]

Case Study 13: Meuse Diversion (Netherlands *v.* Belgium)

The PCIJ considers whether certain works by each of the states concerned are consistent with the legal regime for the use of the Meuse system in connection with navigation and irrigation interests. The Court deems the river in question to be a "waterway of common interest"[282] for the parties; and notes the treaty provision regarding "works for the improvement of the navigability of the Meuse … and for the financial participation of Belgium in the carrying out of these works".[283] Hence, the Treaty in question, at least with regard to navigation, appears to embed Community-of-Interests. Demonstrating how Limited Territorial Sovereignty may support the Theory's implementation, the Court's Decision is based on self-restraint, i.e., the legal limitations imposed on each party as to how they act within their respective territories. Finding no evidence of harm to the interests safeguarded by the Regime, the Court affirms the parties' freedom to modify, enlarge and transform the canals covered by the Treaty, as well as to fill them in and increase the volume of water in them from new sources. Yet these actions must respect the requirements "to maintain the normal level and flow in the

281 Pulp Mills Case, *supra*, p. 70, 79.

282 Meuse Diversion Case, *supra*, p. 12.

283 *Id*, p. 30.

Zuid-Willemsvaart"[284] and not interfere with navigation interests on the Meuse.[285]

Like with Regional Integration Organizations, therefore, fully developed communities-of-basin-interests are unlikely. A cooperation regime based on Community-of-Interests may be less or more developed but still reflect the Theory. The degree of development of a community-of-basin-interests may be determined by the extent to which it reflects the Theory, with not all its normative elements being necessarily represented to their fullest extent in a given regime.

In the same way that rules for coexistence subsist within the Founding Charters, therefore, rules framed by Limited Territorial Sovereignty are present under Community-of-Interests. This is the case even with the Senegal and Lake Victoria Basin Treaties and the multi-basin regime between Ecuador and Peru, all three of which expressly refer to Community-of-Interests.

Rules framed by Limited Territorial Sovereignty are those principally focused on the protection and balancing of individual state interests. These rules consist of *equitable and reasonable use* and *harm prevention,* along with obligations on domestic action and coordination that support compliance with the former two, linked to *information exchange*, *planned measures*, and *dispute settlement*. On equitable and reasonable use, for example, McIntyre considers it to be the principle that usually articulates Limited Territorial Sovereignty in the context of international watercourses.[286] In the framework Conventions underpinned by Community-of-Interests, as well as in the Basin Treaties examined, these rules perform a necessary, if subsidiary, function.

Equitable and Reasonable Use and Harm Prevention: In the UNWC, Article 5 codifies *equitable and reasonable use* and Article 7 embodies the duty of riparian states *to exercise due diligence in avoiding significant transboundary harm*, when utilizing an international watercourse. The UNWC sheds light on the relationship between these two rules, bringing precision to issues that had long been debated by both governments and scholars. The Convention governs the scenario in which, despite the adoption by the state of origin of all appropriate prevention measures, significant harm nevertheless occurs, and agreement to the harmful use is absent. In such a case, the state of origin must take all appropriate measures, with due regard for equity and reasonableness,

284 *Id*, p. 26.

285 *Id*, p. 23.

286 McIntyre, *supra*, p. 23.

and in consultation with the affected country, "to eliminate or mitigate such harm"; and, "where appropriate, to discuss the question of compensation". The UNWC designs "a process aimed at avoiding significant harm as far as possible while reaching an equitable result in each concrete case"[287] – with the intent to balance and reconcile conflicting state interests.

The ECEWC also codifies rules framed by Limited Territorial Sovereignty, and the Convention's very structure is compelling in this respect. The ECEWC's main provisions are organized in two core sections: Part 1, mostly outlining norms for all *parties*; and Part 2, with articles applicable between *riparian parties*, i.e., co-basin states.[288] Part 1 largely invokes Limited Territorial Sovereignty, whereby countries act mostly independently, but remain bound by their duties under harm prevention and equitable and reasonable use. In Part 2, Community-of-Interests comes to the fore through its primary normative elements.

Compared to the UNWC, the ECEWC pays greater attention to the rule of harm prevention and provides useful guidance for its interpretation, application, and implementation. The expression *transboundary impact* is broadly defined in Article 1(2) to include all possible cross-border environmental and related detrimental effects. Building on this definition, Articles 2 and 3 clarify the normative content of the harm-prevention rule, in the form of the following duties: "take all appropriate measures to prevent, control and reduce any transboundary impact"; "ensure that transboundary waters are used in a reasonable and equitable way" as regards activities with actual or potential cross-border effects and that actions adopted under the Convention do not result in an increase in transboundary impact; and mainstream the principles of precaution and polluter-pays into relevant national governance frameworks.

Possible national measures to be adopted in compliance with the harm-prevention rule under the ECEWC include water quality objectives and criteria; environmental assessments and prior licensing; wastewater discharges monitoring and control; release standards for hazardous substances and municipal wastewater; low- and non-waste technology at source; stricter requirements, including bans, where appropriate; reduction of nutrient inputs from point (best available technology) and nonpoint sources (best environmental practices, to be developed in light of the guidelines in Annex 2); contingency planning, including for accidental pollution; and groundwater protection measures. In addition, Article 7 requires parties to "support appro-

287 ILC Draft Articles (1994), *supra*, p. 103.

288 ECEWC, *supra*, Art.1(4).

priate international efforts to elaborate rules, criteria and procedures in the field of responsibility and liability."

The Revised SADC Protocol codifies equitable and reasonable use in Article 3(7) as a specific objective: to "advance the sustainable, equitable and reasonable utilization of the shared watercourses". In Article 3(10), the Revised Protocol incorporates the duty of harm prevention, drawing from Article 7 of the UNWC; and, in Article 1(1), takes the additional step of facilitating implementation of harm prevention by so defining the expression *significant harm*: "nontrivial harm capable of being established by objective evidence without necessarily rising to the level of being substantial". In contrast, the 1995 SADC Protocol codifies equitable and reasonable use among its general principles, in Article 2, but the instrument is not explicit about harm prevention.

In the Senegal Basin Charter, Article 4 refers to equitable and reasonable use and outlines the principles meant to guide water allocation. The Lake Victoria Protocol codifies equitable and reasonable use and harm prevention as basic management principles, alongside Community-of-Interests. On equitable and reasonable use, the Protocol emphasizes optimal and sustainable use and benefits; requires that states consider the interests of their co-riparians; enumerates factors that may inform the norm's application; and indicates how such factors are to be assessed and weighed against one another – all in line with the UNWC. On harm prevention, Article 15 of the Lake Victoria Protocol requires states, when exploiting basin resources within their territories, to act with due diligence with the aim of avoiding significant environmental harm of a transboundary character, while accounting for other states' vital interests, whether economic, social, or cultural.

Obligations Ancillary to Equitable and Reasonable Use and Harm Prevention: Article 9 of the UNWC governs the *regular exchange of information*, including "that of a hydrological, meteorological, hydrogeological and ecological nature and related to the water quality as well as related forecasts." The provision outlines steps and certain requirements for information collection and processing by each riparian country. This is supplemented by obligations to exchange information regularly, respond to data requests and facilitate the use of produced data by other states.

Article 9 of the UNWC is underpinned by Limited Territorial Sovereignty, since obligations are to be carried out mostly unilaterally, supported by a minimum degree of coordination, and no joint-action measures are envisioned. At the same time, data of an *ecological* nature relates "to the living resources of the watercourse itself",[289] and the forecasts envisaged include "the condition or movement of living resources".[290] To the extent that such information assists states in complying with Article 20, in addition to Articles 5–7, Article 9 may support common interests as well, albeit in a narrower sense than joint data management as would occur under Community-of-Interests.

On planned measures, as noted above, the UNWC, the Revised SADC Protocol and the River Uruguay Statute design a solid and clear safeguard system based on notification, impact assessment, information exchange, consultations, and negotiations. In all three legal instruments, the governance systems for national projects aim, first and foremost, to protect and balance unilateral state interests – i.e., one state's right to develop the resource equitably and reasonably *versus* the other state's right not to suffer significant, inequitable, and fault-based transboundary impact.

Protecting ecosystems, as elements of a wider common interest in sustainable development, is part of the equation in norms governing planned measures, but not the primary motivation. The ICJ considers that the relevant provisions in the River Uruguay Statute approach equitable and reasonable use as an instrument to balance economic and environmental considerations and, by doing so, to realize sustainable development. The Court ponders that developing the river without consideration for the interests of co-riparians in the same resource, including in its protection, fails to meet equity and reasonableness requirements. The Decision then demands the implementing state to perform ongoing monitoring of possible environmental effects from the activity – once it becomes operational and, where appropriate, for the project's entire lifecycle.[291]

Joint Action in the Service of Limited Territorial Sovereignty: Another characteristic of cooperation framed by the Theory is the employment of joint and positive action in support of Limited Territorial Sovereignty. To build on Magalhães' lessons, whether for buildings or in his Earth Condominium, institutions play a central role within communities-of-owners – both in safeguarding common interests and in resolving eventual disagreements.

It is not surprising, therefore, that the framework and Basin Treaties reviewed here do not simply codify norms like equitable and reasonable use and harm prevention and supporting duties on information exchange and peaceful dispute settlement. Those same agreements design such rules as part of a

289 ILC Draft Articles (1994), *supra*, p. 108.
290 *Id*, p. 109.
291 Pulp Mills Case, *supra*, p. 54, 61.

sophisticated normative package that places Limited Territorial Sovereignty as an intrinsic dimension of Community-of-Interests. Compliance with equitable and reasonable use and harm prevention then happens not only through *ad hoc* national action and coordination, but also under the auspices of the Basin Body or through other joint-action duties.

This is the case, for example, with explicit or implicit joint-action requirements under Articles 21(2) (pollution), 22 (invasive species) and 27 (harmful conditions) of the UNWC, which contribute to compliance with the harm-prevention duty. The Convention requires the states concerned, individually and, where appropriate, jointly, to take measures aimed at preventing, reducing, and controlling pollution; as well as to "take steps to harmonize their policies in this connection", harmonization being bound to require a measure of joint effort. The same language referring to domestic measures and joint action, as appropriate, is employed regarding the prevention and mitigation of "conditions related to an international watercourse that may be harmful to other watercourse states" – natural or manmade. On invasives, a requirement for joint action is implicit in the call for basin states to "take all measures *necessary* to prevent [their] introduction" into the shared watercourse.[292]

Under the ECEWC, Article 3(1) requires that relevant legal, administrative, economic, financial, and technical measures be developed, adopted, implemented and, "as far as possible, render[ed] compatible", in order to ensure compliance with harm prevention. This duty is further supported by Article 13(2), mandating riparian parties to share information on their relevant national regulations, as a basis for enabling the harmonization of emission limits.

Article 2 of the 1995 SADC Protocol refers to *close cooperation* on the assessment and implementation of planned measures. Such Close Cooperation may entail taking account of relevant joint standards that may have been adopted between the states concerned among the factors to be considered in the application of equitable and reasonable use. The same approach of requiring Close Cooperation on projects is present in Article 3(5) of the Revised SADC Protocol; and here, said requirement might entail conducting joint impact assessments.

The Senegal Basin Charter generally requires states to adopt all appropriate measures to avoid transboundary impact. The placing of the harm-prevention rule under the heading of Article 16, which explicitly foresees joint action, suggests that, where appropriate, such measures must be taken jointly.

292 *See also* Revised SADC Protocol, *supra*, Arts.2 & 4.

Under the River Uruguay Statute, CARU plays a central role in the cooperative consideration of planned measures. The format of negotiations must be conducive to a solution under which, with CARU's support, both parties remain compliant with the Statute.[293] The ICJ concludes that, through the review process established by the Statute, the co-riparian states "can *jointly* manage the risks of damage to the environment"[294] that may arise in connection with unilateral projects.

In the case of Lake Victoria, Article 12(2) of the Lake Victoria Protocol mandates the LVBC Secretariat to refine the notion of *significance* involved in determining which projects ought to require an EIA under domestic legislation.

On information exchange, a general requirement under Article 13(3) of the ECEWC is supplemented by several provisions on joint data management. The same approach is followed in other treaties, which elevate Basin Bodies in this respect. The obligation to exchange available data is formulated in general terms in Article 2(5) of the 1995 SADC Protocol, which then further elaborates on the topic when outlining the functions foreseen for Basin Bodies. Per Article 5(b), these functions include data collection, analysis, storage, retrieval, dissemination, exchange and utilization and assistance for member states to collect and analyze data within their own territories. In the Lake Victoria Protocol, Article 24 unpacks the information exchange obligation in ways similar to the UNWC; and then Article 42(1)(c) tasks the Secretariat with establishing a regional – thus joint – database. These examples also reinforce the point made before about the general prevalence of joint action under Close Basin Cooperation, whether for common interests or coexistence.

In addition, Community-of-Interests supports state action on *emergencies*, even though Limited Territorial Sovereignty is the main governing framework on the topic. The relevant UNWC, Lake Victoria Protocol and ECEWC provisions do not govern disaster risk reduction and management in general, i.e., *all* accidents or incidents that may impact an international watercourse. The focus is on emergency situations that "may have transboundary effects" and so from which "other potentially affected partner states" or "other potentially affected states" need protection.[295] The 1995 and 2000 SADC Protocols deal with emergencies along the same lines as the UNWC. In other words, the Law here is concerned with transboundary effects and aims primarily at the protection of territorial integrity.

293 Pulp Mills Case, *supra*, p. 38, 41, 46.

294 *Id*, p. 32 (emphasis added).

295 ECEWC, *supra*, Art.14; Lake Victoria Protocol, *supra*, Art.26(1); UNWC, *supra*, Art.28(2).

Still, the influence of Community-of-Interests remains strong in all five instruments, since measures required are to be implemented cooperatively and do involve joint action, including in collaboration with or through a joint body, where one exists. The UNWC elevates the role of relevant international organizations, such as, presumably, joint commissions. Those organizations are among the actors to be promptly notified if an emergency occurs, together with the states that may be affected. Where appropriate, response measures must be taken in cooperation with those organizations, in addition to the potentially impacted countries. *Cooperation* here implies all possible modalities of collaboration as may be appropriate in the case, including joint action. The UNWC, moreover, orders the joint development of contingency plans, as necessary to prepare for, and respond to, emergencies; and to do so, again, where appropriate, in cooperation with relevant international bodies.

Article 14 of the ECEWC governs the topic through a mix of requirements for unilateral, coordinated and joint action on the part of co-basin states, namely: to promptly notify others of critical situations likely to cause transboundary impact; where appropriate, establish coordinated or joint communication, warning, and alarm systems as tools to obtain and transmit information; operate such systems based on jointly agreed and mutually compatible procedures and facilities for data management; and exchange information on designated authorities and focal points competent to act in emergency situations. At the same time, the ECEWC foresees joint bodies being tasked with the establishment of warning and alarm systems.

Article 26 of the Lake Victoria Protocol governs emergencies in a manner similar to the UNWC, with its requirements of timely notification; cooperation towards the adoption of all measures necessary to address harmful effects – hence, with an implicit call for joint action, where appropriate; and joint development of disaster preparedness plans. Throughout this process, the state of origin must cooperate and engage with the LVBC, among other competent international organizations.

On dispute resolution, the UNWC outlines a robust and comprehensive process in Article 33, through which countries move from one stage to another, as the chosen pathway fails to lead to a solution. The provision is supplemented by an Annex setting out arbitration clauses. With its focus mostly on dispute settlement, Article 33 reflects *principally* Limited Territorial Sovereignty. Still, an instance of joint action enabling coexistence is found in Paragraph 2, which, among alternative methods, lists the possibility of resort to watercourse institutions. As interpreted by the ILC, Article 33(2) mentions joint bodies as more than just another option but as the alternative being encouraged.[296] In subsequent provisions, Article 33 lays out non-binding and non-confrontational fact-finding procedures, which, within a community-of-basin-interests, would be conducted through a Basin Body.

The ECEWC provides for dispute settlement in less detail than the UNWC. Article 22 of the former refers to negotiation and other means, as agreed by the parties concerned; and envisions the possibility of states declaring acceptance as compulsory of submission of unresolved disputes to the ICJ or to arbitration. The ECEWC takes a step further by relying on a dedicated body that supports interested parties through informal and nonconfrontational implementation and compliance review.[297] Through this 'carrot' approach, the ECEWC infuses the principle of peaceful dispute settlement with Community-of-Interests content.

The Revised SADC Protocol governs conflict resolution, albeit in a superficial manner. Article 7 requires the parties concerned to seek the amicable settlement of disagreements connected to Protocol implementation, interpretation, or application; and, where that is not possible, to bring the dispute in question before the SADC Tribunal. However, for many years now, the Tribunal has not been operational.[298] The absence of a clear dispute settlement mechanism could challenge continued cooperation under the Protocol. The SADC example illustrates how Limited Territorial Sovereignty rules in framework instruments may not suffice and why the Basin Treaty should provide for appropriate and tailored mechanisms to ensure disputes are resolved peacefully.

Article 30 of the UNWC governs situations in which "serious obstacles to direct contacts between watercourse states" exist. This may be the case due to ongoing armed conflict, lack of diplomatic relations, or nonrecognition of an entity's statehood status. In such cases, the states concerned remain bound by the customary rules of international water law and must comply therewith through the *indirect procedures* of their choosing. Said procedures may entail resorting to the good offices of the leaders of third states or to organizations, as

296 *See* ILC (1994), *supra*, p. 134.

297 ECEWC, *Implementation Committee*, at https://unece.org/environment-policy/water/about-the-convention/convention-bodies/implementation-committee.

298 For more information on the status of the Tribunal and why it has been suspended, *see* Media Defense, *Advanced Modules on Digital Rights and Freedom of Expression Online, Module 6: Litigating Digital Rights Cases in Africa* (Mar 2024), p. 38–39, at https://www.mediadefence.org/ereader/wp-content/uploads/sites/2/2022/12/Module-6-Litigating-digital-rights-in-Africa-2024.pdf.

the parties involved may deem appropriate.[299] Limited Territorial Sovereignty underlies Article 30, as a fallback provision aimed at sustaining or promoting water cooperation between unfriendly nations until normal diplomatic relations become feasible. Because of the *de facto* community-of-interests that exists between co-riparians even in these situations, the countries concerned cannot ignore their customary law duties connected to reasonable and equitable use, harm prevention, and cooperation, along with requirements ancillary to those duties.

4.6 *Conclusions*

Regional integration regimes, as much as communities-of-basin-interests, focus on Close Cooperation for common interests. As a primary element of the Theory, Close Basin Cooperation for shared aspirations is realized principally through joint action – under or through the Basin Body, i.e., states acting through the Body's organs or interacting directly under its umbrella. In this sense, the Basin Treaties examined generally prioritize obligations and commitments founded on joint action, both to achieve common interests and to balance individual state concerns.

The Theory does not require nations to act jointly under all circumstances and in all situations. In fact, Community-of-Interests builds on supplementary and subsidiary modalities of state engagement for common interests, i.e., national action, coordination, and harmonization, as well as direct interstate interactions outside the Basin Body. Each of those modalities may be sufficient or better suited to serve a given common interest.

The treaties examined establish duties linked to Limited Territorial Sovereignty, such as basic rules on information exchange. Limited Territorial Sovereignty is inherent to Close Basin Cooperation because states will always hold interests of their own that may conflict with other interests considered as common. Still, under the Theory, the central focus is on common interests, pursued principally through joint action. Coexistence norms remain largely in the background, coming to the fore under especial circumstances. Such would be the situations where the cooperative spirit or friendly relations falter, and rules based on Limited Territorial Sovereignty are invoked to prevent dialogue breakdown and to enable a speedy return to interstate cooperation framed by Community-of-Interests. Under the Theory, duties linked to Limited Territorial Sovereignty are complemented by joint-action requirements, including

299 M.M. Farrajota, *International Cooperation on Water Resources*, *in* J.W. Dellapenna & J. Gupta eds, *The Evolution of the Law and Politics of Water* (Springer 2009), p. 347.

measures under or through the Basin Body. In such instances, Community-of-Interests is put at the service of Limited Territorial Sovereignty.

All four manifestations of Close Basin Cooperation – joint action for common interests, direct cooperation, other engagement modalities also for common interests, and joint action in the service of Limited Territorial Sovereignty, when viewed as a package, characterize Community-of-Interests.

Each manifestation can be informed by a duty of Participation, the core trait of which is that it invokes proactiveness, as opposed to passive behavior. Under the UNWC and the Revised SADC Protocol, Participation brings together equity and cooperation as a hybrid substantive and procedural obligation characteristic of the Theory and to be applied taking account of all the relevant factors and circumstances, in an equitable and reasonable manner. The relevant articles in each instrument contain an overarching and catchall provision on the duty to cooperate into which a *general obligation for active joint action*, where appropriate, is embedded. Participation informs the interpretation, application, and implementation of the UNWC and the Revised SADC Protocol as a whole, in particular Parts IV and V, on protection, preservation, management, harmful conditions and emergencies. By incorporating equitable and reasonable Participation among their core rules, the UNWC and the Revised SADC Protocol reinforce Close Basin Cooperation, with joint action and Participation at its center, as a primary element of Community-of-Interests.

The general obligation to participate is supplemented by obligations to *react*, where required or appropriate. Moreover, Participation means that states must share the benefits, and the costs, associated with the management, protection, and use of a transboundary basin, thereby advancing mutually beneficial cooperation. Participation does not necessarily or always entail joint action, though, on the ground, resorting to joint action would be almost inevitable in the context of positive cooperation for realizing common interests.

Common property and mutual consent are not elements of Community-of-Interests. Embracing Community-of-Interests does not exclude the right of states to proceed unilaterally but it means conditioning the exercise of those rights to compliance with the obligations deemed appropriate by the states concerned to safeguard common and individual interests in a balanced manner. Except for the Senegal regime, the Treaties examined do not incorporate joint property and veto rights, and jurisprudence and scholarship reject those two concepts in the absence of explicit agreement endorsing them. Instead, the UNWC, the Revised SADC Protocol, the River Uruguay Statute, and the Lake Victoria Protocol design systems of substantive and procedural safeguards. Under Community-of-Interests, the Basin Body is placed at the center of the implementation of those safeguards; and joint planning, a manifestation of joint action, is prominent in guiding domestic and transboundary basin management and coordinated implementation, as informed by the Basin Scope.

5 Conclusions

Community-of-Interests brings states closely together to cooperate jointly and proactively, as the normal state of affairs in their relations, on the basis of a system-wide, long-term outlook. This environment is conducive to states sharing the benefits and together tackling the risks that emerge from the interdependencies bound to exist and deepen within a transboundary catchment.

The primary normative content of Community-of-Interests can be unpacked into four elements: *Basin Scope, Basin Treaty, Basin Body,* and *Close Basin Cooperation.*

The *Basin Scope* considers the drainage basin as the fundamental biogeographic unit for the planning, use, management, and protection of water and related resources and ecosystems. The Theory envisions cooperation across the entire unity of the catchment or subcatchment. The Basin Scope encompasses, but transcends the concept of water systems, so that all spatial dimensions of connectivity are captured thereunder: *vertical* (surface waters and connected groundwaters), *longitudinal* (the mainstream and all connected water bodies along the watercourse system), and *horizontal* (water and related resources and aquatic and terrestrial ecosystems within the larger catchment). Going forward, the Basin Scope could expand further to embrace the entire source-to-sea continuum.

The Basin Scope does not exclude the possibility of cooperation at other levels and the adoption of partial Basin Treaties, as appropriate for the common interests at stake in a particular basin. This would be the case if working closely together at the level of an entire drainage basin or a sub-basin is deemed unnecessary, or not feasible – politically, financially or technically; or else when the riparian states within a part of the basin wish to provide further specificity or greater stringency to their cooperation goals and modalities and strengthen enabling normative conditions for joint action and Participation.

The *Basin Treaty* is an agreement adopted among co-basin countries with particular features that make it tailored to enable Close Basin Cooperation on common interests, while maintaining stable interstate relations in the long-term and ensuring that the process is not disrupted by eventual disputes. The

Basin Treaty is placed at the center of cooperation framed by the Theory, as the constitution of a community-of-basin-interests. This element formalizes, regulates, and institutionalizes transboundary basin cooperation that is informed principally by the acknowledged need to address shared concerns, risks and opportunities through Close Basin Cooperation. The watershed is the overarching determinant of the scope (*ratione loci* and *ratione personae*) of the Basin Treaty, being informed as it is by the Basin Scope.

Although, as a rule, communities-of-basin-interests are governed by Basin Treaties, informal arrangements may be employed to serve common interests at an early stage of the cooperation process, thereby building the path towards formalization and institutionalization.

The *Basin Body* is an international organization established among co-riparian countries by the Basin Treaty, endowed with legal personality. Unlike other transboundary water commissions, the Basin Body is designed and structured by the Basin Treaty specifically to enable Close Basin Cooperation for common interests. This element of the Theory enables joint action and Participation, on the basis of agreed-upon common interests, while maintaining stable interstate relations in the long-term. The Basin Body is placed at the center of the cooperation process to form, together with the Basin Treaty, the legal-institutional home for the community-of-basin-interests in question.

Like with the geographic scope of the Basin Treaty, the Basin Scope underpins the jurisdiction of the Basin Body. Institutional mandates go as far as appropriate within each particular case to promote the Basin Scope and the progressive embrace of its spatial dimensions; and to account for, or at least acknowledge, interconnections and related common interests across the entire basin. The specific competences of the Basin Body vary but fall under two subcategories of joint action: those realized when the Basin Body takes action itself, through the organs that make up its institutional architecture, or those involving direct interstate interactions facilitated by the Basin Body.

Close Basin Cooperation is cooperation between basin states centered on common interests, and which gains concrete expression mostly through joint action and Participation as modalities of state engagement. State practice on Community-of-Interests brings a variety of examples of joint-action measures, like the joint administration of data, knowledge and information, or the joint adoption of basin management standards, regulations, and plans. Joint action is connected to the obligation to participate, as explicitly codified in the UNWC and the Revised SADC Protocol and practiced by basin states through Basin Treaties. Exceptionally, joint action *may* go as far as embracing the notion of common property and the mutual-consent requirement, but those are not inherent traits of Community-of-Interests.

Requirements or expectations for state engagement within communities-of -basin-interests are not limited to joint action for common interests. Unilateral or coordinated modalities of involvement in the management of transboundary waters, including in combination with joint action, may be appropriate, i.e., sufficient or necessary – whether to safeguard specific shared goals (Community-of-Interests) and/or to facilitate the process of balancing individual state concerns, in line with equitable and reasonable use and harm prevention (Limited Territorial Sovereignty). This makes Limited Territorial Sovereignty an inherent but subsidiary manifestation of Close Basin Cooperation.

PART IV

The Secondary Normative Elements of Community-of-Interests

The secondary elements of the Theory govern the interactions of the Basin Body and its members with one another, with other cooperation regimes and with stakeholders, as expressed in specific obligations or commitments.

The general contours of these secondary elements have been pulled out of the analysis of Founding Charters as the lens through which to analyze treaties reflecting Community-of-Interests. Elements of institutional relations appear more explicitly and consistently, better developed, and in more modalities under Close Regional Cooperation than under the Theory. Transposed to the latter's context, the secondary elements of Community-of-Interests consist of the following:

a) **Coherence**, which may be vertical (with broader or narrower cooperation regimes) and horizontal (with parallel cooperation regimes).
b) **Solidarity** in internal relations, i.e., among co-basin states.
c) **Social Basin Engagement**, i.e., the involvement of stakeholders in the cooperation process.

When contrasted with the primary elements examined in Part 3, secondary elements are not as strongly and as consistently present across all the agreements examined. For these reasons, the book considers Coherence, Solidarity, and Social Basin Engagement as *secondary* elements of Community-of-Interests. The two sets of elements are interconnected: the Basin Scope, the Basin Treaty, the Basin Body, and Close Basin Cooperation incorporate and give effectiveness to the Theory's secondary elements. At the same time, Coherence, Solidarity, and Social Basin Engagement supplement the primary elements in the realization of common interests.

1 Coherence in Relations with Other Cooperation Regimes

Coherence characterizes the external relations of communities-of-basin-interests. Among the traits found in Founding Charters, Coherence is the one most apparent under the Theory. In the context of shared basins, Coherence translates into a multilevel and multiscale integration structure interlinking cooperative action on shared interests in water resources and related

 | HTTPS://DOI.ORG/10.1163/9789004507036-006

goods. Coherence is crucial because "resources management issues must be addressed at the local, national and at appropriate regional and international levels".[1]

Through *Horizontal Coherence*, sub-catchment communities-of-interests are physically connected to each other in the basin and, through *Vertical Coherence*, may sit under the umbrella of basin-wide regimes.

Vertical Coherence is also expressed in McCaffrey's view that the state groupings sharing freshwaters are "bound together"[2] by the basin, consequently forming a community-of-interests in that same basin – "a unity unto itself",[3] while, at the same time, "a part of the hydrological cycle".[4] Although, therefore, cooperation regimes founded on the Theory are geographically bound by the basin, those regimes remain connected to global and regional regimes through the role that freshwater plays in sustainable development.

The two SADC Protocols, for example, are placed explicitly in the context of broader regional priorities. In its 3rd Preambular Paragraph, the 1995 SADC Protocol recalls the region's "socioeconomic development programs ... and their impact on the environment" – a text later reproduced in the Preamble of the Revised Protocol. Article 2 of the latter instrument defines its objective as being to "advance the SADC agenda of regional integration and poverty alleviation"; and, in Article 3(1), commits states to ensuring that watercourse interventions "observe the objectives of regional integration and harmonization of their socioeconomic policies and plans". The successive Protocols serve as mechanisms for the pursuit of regional water interests, with each set of co-riparian states expected to contribute to the wider regional agenda through their respective basin cooperation processes. The SADC Protocols *promote* regional water cooperation but *govern* transboundary waters as assets shared exclusively at the basin level. The two Protocols do not qualify shared watercourses as regional public goods but do affirm the central role of these resources in the realization of the region's development and integration goals.

Coherence, therefore, has to do with how cooperation regimes founded on Community-of-Interests view and interact with the outside world, i.e., the states or groups of states outside a given community-of-basin-interests. Community-of-Interests regimes do not exist in isolation and the achievement of the objectives shared by co-riparians is linked to other cooperation efforts –

1 Unturbe, *supra*, p. 39.
2 McCaffrey (2019), *supra*, p. 232.
3 *Ibid.*
4 *Ibid.*

on transboundary waters or correlated topics, and on different scales, like the catchment or subcatchment; the subregion or region; the continent or the globe. Accordingly, the basin states that enter into a Basin Treaty to formalize a community-of-basin-interests acknowledge that their cooperation regime is part of a larger, more complex structure entailing institutionalized cooperation at various levels.

1.1 *Communities-of-Interests within the Same Drainage Basin*

The Basin Scope is the primary element of Community-of-Interests that informs all others. Hence, a Community-of-Interests regime formalized via a partial Basin Treaty, i.e., where not all basin states are involved, may be subject to a basin-wide cooperation regime. Sub-basin communities-of-interests then interact through the catchment-wide Basin Body and may be required to abide by the umbrella Basin Treaty applying across the watershed. Even absent the umbrella regime, sub-catchment regimes depend on and influence other communities-of-interests within the same watershed. Horizontal Coherence thus interconnects separate communities-of-interests within the larger basin and partial regimes may or may not be nested within a basin-wide framework.

In this sense, the Lake Victoria Protocol and the River Uruguay Statute are partial Basin Treaties, and illustrate Coherence *vertically*, when a sub-basin community-of-interests sits under a basin-wide regime; and *horizontally*, i.e., across parallel subsets of co-basin countries. These relations supplement and reinforce one another.

In the Plata, several watercourse agreements are in place across the basin, each instituting regimes that exist in parallel to another, but which may affect portions of the basin under another body's jurisdiction. Cooperation between Argentina and Uruguay on the border section of the watercourse sits under the Plata basin regime in force among all five riparian states. Coherence is reflected in the River Uruguay Statute in relation to the Plata Basin Treaty: Argentina and Uruguay both remain bound by the Plata Basin Treaty for issues outside the Statute's geographic or thematic scope.

Case Study 14: The Guarani Aquifer System and the Plata Basin

The Guarani Aquifer, shared among Argentina, Brazil, Paraguay, and Uruguay, discharges into the Plata basin via specific tributaries, including the Uruguay River. In view of this vertical connectivity, the *Guarani Aquifer System Strategic Action Program*, endorsed by the four aquifer countries, considers institutional governance options and selects the Plata basin-wide regime as the appropriate umbrella within which to nest Guarani Aquifer cooperation. This choice results from intergovernmental negotiations conducted over several years under a GEF Project;[5] and positions the countries to promote, within the frameworks of Coherence and the Basin Scope, the integrated governance of underground and surface waters within the Plata basin.[6]

In the case of Lake Victoria, the sub-basin states form a community-of-*subcatchment*-interests vertically coherent with and nested within the Nile Basin Initiative, as the Protocol itself recognizes, and now under the Nile Cooperative Framework. Horizontal Coherence here expresses the subsisting connection, through the drainage basin as a unitary whole, between the subset of Lake basin countries that cooperate more closely and the other co-basin states outside that formalized community-of-basin-interests.

Still on the issue of external relationships, states within regional integration regimes tend to operate as units in their interactions with the outside world. This Outward Cohesion refers to the consolidation of common positions that are internally negotiated, adopted, and held among the states concerned in international negotiations with third states and/or institutional actors; and have special relevance in the face of stronger counterparts. For an illustration, Article 41(4) of the ASEAN Charter requires that members, in their foreign relations, "coordinate and endeavor to develop common positions". The Charter refers to such common positions as the *ASEAN views*, which the Secretary-General presents at meetings with external parties.

For communities-of-basin-interests, the Lake Victoria Protocol is the only Basin Treaty foreseeing its parties employing Outward Cohesion as a strategy to protect common interests in relation to the other Nile basin states. Under Article 33(2)(h), the *Lake Victoria Basin Commission* has the mandate to "prepare and harmonize" members' negotiating positions vis-à-vis those of all other riparian states on basin matters. In other words, Protocol parties act as a united front, as a bloc, in international negotiations and cooperation with the other Nile co-basin states; and, thereby, affirm their legal status as a community-of-basin-interests unto itself.

Because, however, Outward Cohesion is reflected only in the Lake Victoria Protocol, among the sources known to reflect Community-of-Interests, it is not considered among the Theory's secondary elements.

5 *See* Sindico *et al*, *supra*, p. 53.
6 *See* World Bank, *supra*, p. 28.

1.2 *Communities-of-Basin-Interests under Umbrella Regimes*

Coherence also informs how communities-of-basin-interests interact with countries and international organizations outside the catchment. These interactions happen vertically when cooperation regimes framed by the Theory are formalized under a given overarching umbrella regime. When this is the case, different individual communities-of-interests in separate drainage basins may hold horizontal relationships with each other under that same overarching regime. Individual communities-of-basin-interests may be linked, formally or informally, through a regional or continental cooperation regime; and/or through a regional or global regime under which international water law is codified and implemented.

Both the Lake Victoria and Senegal Communities-of-Interests are linked to regional integration regimes. The Lake Victoria Protocol has gained shape within the framework of the EAC, as an additional component of the integration process. Accordingly, the text of the Protocol consolidates strong region-basin linkages. Article 4(1) requires parties to manage basin resources in line with the EAC Treaty and, in particular, with Articles 5–8 thereof, which outline EAC objectives, fundamental and operational principles, and general undertakings, and mention equitable benefit-sharing and mutually beneficial cooperation. Article 34 creates the *Lake Victoria Basin Commission* as an EAC institution. Article 47 clarifies that the Protocol forms an integral part of the EAC Treaty, with the latter prevailing in the case of inconsistencies. In its turn, the Senegal basin regime builds on continental values and principles, with the Preamble of the Charter invoking the African Union Act.

In so doing, the Senegal and Lake Victoria Communities-of-Interests show the role of water in sustaining and/or generating interdependencies beyond the drainage basin, further strengthening common interests among co-basin states and with other nations.

On the basis of Coherence as well, a community-of-basin-interests may be linked vertically to a treaty that transcends a specific watershed. This is the case when the co-basin states enter into an agreement for the multiple catchments they share, like the Ecuador-Peru Agreement. A regime framed by the Theory may also be nested within a framework treaty applying to all transboundary waters within the region, as exemplified by the two SADC protocols. Finally, a Community-of-Interests regime may be adopted within the framework of a global convention – specifically, the ECEWC and the UNWC. Coherence guides the above vertical relationships of communities-of-basin-interests with their overarching umbrella regimes; as well as the horizontal relationships between those various communities-of-interests under said regime –

e.g., through exchanges in lessons, experience, and relevant information, as well as collective meetings.

In the case of the ECEWC, Vertical Coherence gains shape in the form of overarching obligations that all parties must respect in their mutual relations within a given catchment. This is why the Convention's goals and related provisions go beyond the primary aim of governing interstate relations among co-basin states. Guiding the Convention's interpretation and application, the Preamble stresses a shared concern with the environmental, social, and economic harmful effects that may result for all parties from changes in the conditions of transboundary waters. In other words, the ECEWC parties view themselves as together forming a community interested in the long-term sustainability of all transboundary waters within the Convention's geographic ambit.

According to the ECEWC Guide, the Convention seeks "to protect the *common interest* of the community of its parties in the preservation of the environment."[7] With the environment being the core common interest to be safeguarded in this context, the Guide excludes the possibility of a party responding to another's breach by way of reciprocal noncompliance; and of the ECEWC regime condoning actions leading to "serious and irreversible"[8] transboundary environmental harm or involving environmentally unsustainable water uses.[9] Accordingly, obligations *erga omnes partes* under the Convention "create a set of indivisible corresponding rights for the community of the parties",[10] from which states may not derogate, even by common agreement.

In this sense, Article 5 of the ECEWC requires *all* parties, whether within the same catchment or not, to engage in cooperative research and development on technics aimed at addressing transboundary impact; and to share the respective results with the wider community of ECEWC parties. The same provision indicates priority challenges in this respect that exist across basins, such as toxicity or noxiousness assessment methods; pollutants' occurrence, distribution and environmental effects; environmentally sound technologies and sustainable production and consumption patterns; appropriate disposal methods for hazardous substances; restoration of transboundary waters; and sustainable infrastructure. Exploring these themes is in the interest of the entire community-of-parties and not necessarily just of the riparians of a specific international watercourse.

---

7 ECEWC Guide, *supra*, p. 16 (emphasis added).
8 *Ibid.*
9 *Ibid.*
10 *Ibid.*

In Articles 6 and 8, respectively, the ECEWC binds all parties *inter se*, not just as between co-basin states, to exchange relevant data as widely and as early as possible, while safeguarding rights connected to protected information, defined as such by the applicable national or supranational laws. Article 9(1), moreover, requires that context-specific agreements be compatible with the ECEWC's basic principles.

Consistent with this community *inter partes* under the ECEWC, its parties have entered into various basin-specific cooperation regimes framed by the common interest in environmental sustainability, in addition to other specific interests that may arise at the basin level in each concrete case. These basin cooperation regimes are vertically coherent with the ECEWC community-of-parties and thus mutually reinforcing and horizontally compatible with, and supportive of, each other.

1.3 *The Role of the ECEWC regime and the SADC in Promoting Coherence*

The well-developed institutional governance architecture of both the ECEWC and the SADC have historically built on Coherence to advance treaty interpretation, progressive development, and implementation by framing, supporting and interlinking basin cooperation regimes.

To those ends, the ECEWC organs prepare guidelines, model provisions, and protocols; design, adopt, fund, test, implement, monitor and/or support programs, activities, and projects; and promote knowledge development, capacity-building, and the exchange of information, experiences and best practices.

The wealth of work enabled by organs of the ECEWC enriches the activities of the various joint bodies created thereunder.[11] Looking at the Convention through the work of its organs, acting on behalf of all parties' interests, allows us to see the ECEWC regime through the lens of multiple communities-of-basin-interests collectively housed under the ECEWC regime, with a "much more advanced [institutionalization] than in the context of a simple diplomatic conference".[12]

Part 3 of the ECEWC establishes its two core institutions, from which other subsidiary bodies, such as working groups and taskforces, have periodically derived. Supported by Secretariat, the Meeting of the Parties (MoP) gathers every three years as the supreme decision-making body to track implementation. The MoP's functions under this broad mandate include, *inter alia*, to review relevant implementation policies and methods employed by parties;

---

11 UNW-DPAC, *supra*, p. 14.

12 Runavot, *supra*, p. 36.

and consider and adopt amendments and protocols. The MoP advances and tracks Community-of-Interests at the basin level by facilitating the negotiation and implementation of context-specific agreements and arrangements; and reaching out to competent international institutions, including joint bodies. The MoP benefits from a catchall mandate in Article 17(2)(f), namely, to "consider and undertake any additional action" as may be necessary to achieve the Convention's goals.

Through this institutional structure, the ECEWC has contributed to the effective application and progressive development of international law in the field and has shaped and enhanced state practice on transboundary water cooperation, mostly in the Pan-European region, but increasingly also beyond, and often with tangible results on the ground.[13]

In the case of the SADC, basin cooperation regimes in the region are developed, formalized, and governed within the framework of the Regional Integration Organization and, specifically, of the Revised SADC Protocol. The central mandate to facilitate and guide the Protocol's interpretation, application, implementation, and progressive development falls upon the dedicated set of SADC institutions outlined in Article 5.

At the highest level, the *Committee of Water Ministers* directs and monitors treaty effectiveness, in addition to guiding and coordinating cooperation and, at the same time, assisting parties in the resolution of eventual disputes. In maintaining and furthering Vertical and Horizontal Coherence, this Ministerial Committee promotes the harmonization of laws, policies, strategies, programs, and projects, both within and across basins; and serves as the water-sector link to the SADC Council, by providing thereto policy advice and keeping it abreast of progress – with regard to the Protocol as a whole and within individual basins.

The *Committee of Water Senior Officials* (CWSO) reviews reports and other documents it receives from lower organs; initiates and advises the Ministerial Committee on proposed policies, strategies, programs and projects for consideration and approval by the SADC Council; and regularly updates the Ministerial Committee on the status of Protocol implementation. The CWSO operates with the advice and support of the *Water Resources Technical Committee* (WRTC).

13 G. Reichert, *Entry into Force of the UN Watercourses Convention – Should Europe Care?*, International Water Law Project Blog (21 July 2014), at https://www.internationalwaterlaw.org/blog/2014/07/21/dr-gotz-reichert-entry-into-force-of-the-un-watercourses-convention-should-europe-care/.

The *Water Sector Coordinating Unit* (WSCU) has executive functions linked to guiding Protocol interpretation and implementation monitoring, with findings reported annually to the Ministerial Committee. The Unit acts as the institutional link to other SADC sectors and coordinates SADC external relations with other competent organizations. The WSCU plays a direct role in tracking and supporting basin cooperation regimes by, *inter alia*, advising member states on Protocol-related matters; organizing and managing technical and policy meetings; facilitating fundraising or directly mobilizing financial and technical resources for implementation; and maintaining an inventory of the watercourse agreements and bodies within the region.

In this way, framework global and regional instruments on international water law further Coherence.

1.4 *Conclusions*

External relations of communities-of-basin-interests are framed by Coherence, placed among the Theory's secondary elements. Communities-of-basin-interests, like the cooperation regimes founded on regional common goals, coexist and interact, horizontally and/or vertically in a coherent manner, with one another and with external actors, within or beyond the drainage basin.

Coherence signals the possibility of partial Basin Treaties formalizing communities-of-basin-interests at the subcatchment, water body and/or boundary levels, within a basin. Sub-catchment communities-of-interests are then connected through Horizontal Coherence with other riparian states or parallel partial regimes. These partial regimes may also be nested within a community-of-interests in place for the entire basin, with such relations then characterized by Vertical Coherence. In this way, partial cooperation regimes remain in line with the Theory's Basin Scope.

Beyond the basin, communities-of-basin-interests may have been formalized within the framework of regional cooperation regimes. In this case, the co-basin states concerned form part of a coherent vertical structure, on the basis of common interests that transcend the drainage basin and yet remain, to some extent, interrelated. Moreover, communities-of-basin-interests may be linked to transboundary waters framework regimes, whether covering different basins shared among the countries concerned or operating at the regional or global levels. As examples, the communities-of-interests under the EAC and the ECEWC, respectively, are closely connected to those regimes, as well as with each other, in ways that are mutually reinforcing and ensure Vertical and Horizontal Coherence across basins and among wider global and regional cooperation efforts. These external institutional relations examined may be nurtured by the organs that make up the internal architecture of the international regime under which the respective Basin Bodies are created.

2 Solidarity: Relations within Communities-of-Basin-Interests

> *[W]e need a water ethic – a guide to right conduct in the face of complex decisions about natural systems we do not and cannot fully understand.*
>
> SANDRA POSTEL, Last Oasis: Facing Water Scarcity

Solidarity is the element of Community-of-Interests that guides interactions among co-basin states and in relation to the shared environment. In the cases studied here, Solidarity comes to the fore in the context of the special needs of vulnerable countries, mutual assistance in disaster situations, equitable and reasonable use or due-diligence obligations, and Participation in environmental protection through derogation of equity and polluter-pays.

The presence of Solidarity is less evident and more inconsistent in the treaties known to reflect Community-of-Interests. Those agreements hint at but neither expressly refer to Solidarity, nor uniformly indicate what Solidarity entails. Nevertheless, the Chlorides Case establishes a clear link between Solidarity and Community-of-Interests.

Because, however, the precedents examined do not go far in developing the normative content of Solidarity in the context of the Theory, here we expand our baseline for analysis by considering the concept in international law and in the water policy discourse. These findings are later transposed to the transboundary water context and cooperation under Community-of-Interests.

2.1 *Solidarity in International Law*

International law authors have approached Solidarity in different ways. From a historical perspective, von Bogdandy unveils the roots of Solidarity in social sciences in the 19th Century's teachings of Durkheim, and remarks that Solidarity is still in its youth.[14] Von Bogdandy recalls Duguit's theory of public law, which draws from Durkheim to propose Solidarity as a democratic pillar; a counterbalance to power, to the centrality of the state, its will and authority – until then, the prevailing pillar of the public legal edifice.

---

14 A. von Bogdandy, *Opening Address, in* R. Wolfrum & C. Kojima eds, Solidarity: A Structural Principle of International Law (Springer 2010), p. 1.

In the early decades of the 1900s, Scelle introduces conceptions of Solidarity into international law.[15] Since then, and particularly in the context of progressive legal development, Solidarity has had a place in the international legal discourse.[16] For Wellens, Solidarity appears in international law "first as a *notion*, then as a *political* and finally as a *legal* principle".[17] Wellens interlinks Solidarity and justice: he views the former to be "one of the multifunctional, constituent elements of the [latter] in public international law."[18] Further, Wellens offers an *ethical* perspective on Solidarity as a legal principle strongly imbued with value, and which injects considerations of morality and ethics into modern international law.[19] Along the same lines, Wolfrum places Solidarity in the context of "the transformation of international law into a *value-based* international legal order requiring *close cooperation* among the actors".[20]

Viewed through an ethical light, Solidarity's influence on general international law invokes Yee's law of co-progressiveness and its strong attention to moral concerns. It is thus pertinent to recall the parallel traced before between the ongoing evolution of general international law into a law of co-progressiveness and the development of the law of transboundary basins towards Community-of-Interests. We build on the thinking of Wellens to see Solidarity as a value-driven principle that permeates both co-progressiveness and Community-of-Interests, and which could gain in persuasiveness were those two Theories to be embraced in widespread state practice.

At the regional level, Solidarity receives significant attention, both as a general guiding principle cutting across entire Founding Charters and as embedded into specific obligations and commitments within provisions dealing with the special treatment of disadvantaged states and with mutual assistance. Solidarity often appears and is developed, explicitly and/or implicitly, alongside other approaches guiding those communities' intra-institutional relations. As an example, the Preamble of the ASEAN Charter envisions its members as part of a "caring and sharing community"; and calls for stronger "existing bonds of regional solidarity" in the name of the regional cooperation regime, thus positioned "to effectively respond to current and future challenges and opportu-

15 *Id*, p. 1–2.

16 *Id*, p. 2.

17 K. Wellens, *Revisiting Solidarity as a (Re-)Emerging Constitutional Principle: Some Further Reflections, in* Wolfrum & Kojima, *supra*, p. 4.

18 *Id*, p. 7.

19 *Id*, p. 5.

20 R. Wolfrum, *Solidarity amongst States: An Emerging Structural Principle of International Law*, 49 Indian Journal of International Law 8–20 (2009), p. 8 (emphasis added).

nities".[21] Within ASEAN, Solidarity is an overarching value-based element that invokes ideals of empathy and compassion and contributes to holding the cooperation regime together by guiding relations among member states.

Specific international legal fields have responded to, and have been feeding from, the development of Solidarity in general international law and in state practice on Close Regional Cooperation. In peace and security, Solidarity has for long played a significant role.[22] In other areas, such as development, human rights, humanitarian assistance, disasters, and the environment, Solidarity has reached varying degrees of evolution, plays specific functions, and is embedded into both primary and secondary rules. Wellens concludes that Solidarity has reached constitutional status as a principle that safeguards "fundamental values of the international community".[23]

Solidarity displays different dimensions from field to field, some of which are present within treaties known to reflect Community-of-Interests. Under international disaster law, the Preamble of the ILC Draft Articles adopted on the topic proposes a normative framework structured around four interlinked pillars: *sovereignty* and, as its direct consequence, the *primary role of affected states*; *Close Cooperation* along the entire disaster cycle; and *Solidarity's fundamental value* in international relations.[24]

The four pillars are to be viewed harmoniously, so that Solidarity and cooperation not only preserve but, indeed, depend upon the ability of the affected state to exercise effective territorial sovereignty and control by requesting or consenting to assistance and managing the overall process of relief provision. As explained by the accompanying ILC commentary, Solidarity and cooperation "cannot be interpreted as diminishing the sovereignty of affected states and their prerogatives within the limits of international law".[25] As such, Solidarity and cooperation form "the background against which the entire set of Draft Articles is to be understood."[26] In this field of international law, therefore, Solidarity guides relations between states within the framework of territorial sovereignty and Close Cooperation, as it does, under Community-of-Interests, in relation to harmful conditions and emergency situations.

---

21 *See also* ASEAN Charter, *supra*, Annexes 3 and 4, respectively, referring to Solidarity when describing components of the ASEAN Flag and the ASEAN Emblem.

22 At the global level, *see*, e.g., UN Charter, *supra*, Arts.49–50.

23 Wellens, *supra*, p. 5.

24 ILC, *Draft Articles on the Protection of Persons in the Event of Disasters, with commentaries* (2016) ('ILC Draft Articles (2016)'), *in* ILC Report, 68th Session (2 May–10 June & 4 July–12 Aug 2016), UN Doc A/71/10.

25 *Id*, p. 2.

26 *Id*, p. 3.

The Pact for the Future places Solidarity at the heart of the concept of *complex global shocks*, i.e., events with "severely disruptive and adverse consequences for a significant proportion of countries and the global population"; "impacts across multiple sectors"; "disproportionate impact on the poorest and most vulnerable"; and "usually ... disastrous consequences for sustainable development and prosperity". In the Pact, governments "recognize the need for a more coherent, cooperative, coordinated and multidimensional international response"[27] to such events, to be guided by the principles of national ownership and consent, equity, *Solidarity* and cooperation, with full respect for international law.[28]

In the area of international environmental law, Solidarity underpins the fundamental and widely studied and endorsed principle of *common but differentiated responsibilities* (CBDR),[29] which considers the varying needs and circumstances of different countries. CBDR entails attributing differentiated duties to countries at different levels of development and capabilities as a means to meet shared goals. The Pact for the Future illustratively refers to the *concept of climate justice*.[30]

In the context of international development law, almost all Founding Charters codify and regulate differentiated obligations and advantages for the benefit of certain states, such as the least developed, small island and enclosed countries.

2.2 *Water Policy Discourse and Hydrosolidarity*

Solidarity displays tailored contours when applied to the fluid nature of water and in response to the characteristic manifestations of the global water challenge and transboundary cooperation. Discourse and scholarship on water policy have paid great attention to Solidarity for its potential to strengthen resource governance, guide interstate relations, and balance users' interests, particularly in shared basins.

The over 40-year-old *Mar del Plata Action Plan* emphasizes the need for national policies that consider the mutual right of co-basin states to equitable and reasonable use "as the means to promote *bonds of solidarity* and cooperation."[31] The 2009 Istanbul Declaration recognizes interstate Solidarity as a

27 The Pact for the Future, *supra*, ¶82.
28 *Ibid.*
29 Wellens, *supra*, p. 4.
30 The Pact for the Future, *supra*, Annex II, ¶18.
31 *Mar del Plata Action Plan, in* Report, UN Water Conference (Mar del Plata, 14–25 Mar 1977), UN Doc E/CONF.70/29 (UN 1973), Recommendation 91 (emphasis added).

central ingredient for realizing a sustainable water world within transboundary basins and calls on governments "to implement tools that will help us accomplish Solidarity".[32]

First crafted in scientific and social sciences, the term *hydrosolidarity* has its roots in, and owes its progressive refinement to, the writings of Falkenmark, starting in the late 1990s and continually developed through successive publications. As conceived by Falkenmark, hydrosolidarity is an ethics-based tool that draws from religious and philosophical teachings and the science on the functioning of lifegiving ecological systems to oppose *hydroegoism*, an extreme or exclusive logic of self-interest and competition.

Gerlak *et al* also place hydrosolidarity in opposition to hydroegoism, at any level and in any sector, as well as to *hydrosovereignty*, i.e., reliance on the theories of absolute territorial sovereignty or integrity; to *hydrohegemony*, meaning resort to hegemony in transboundary water relations to promote self-interests; and to *hydrocide*, referring to the destruction of water systems, loss of vital water-related ecological services, or significantly reduced water availability downstream.[33]

Hydrosolidarity is applicable at all levels, from the global through the regional and national to the catchment, as well as on the scale of transboundary basins. At each level, the concept manifests itself in different ways – for example, global, through intra- or inter-regional exports and imports of virtual water; catchment-level integrated land, water and ecosystem management with ethical foundations; or resource-sharing in a transboundary context.[34]

Between various water users and co-riparian states, hydrosolidarity aims to reconcile conflicting claims over natural resources of land and water users operating upriver *versus* those located downriver and beneficiaries of sustained water availability and related ecosystem services. A need for reconciliation emerges as a long-term global interest because of the interdependencies water creates along the watercourse system. An effective reconciliation process that protects the peace and the resource base requires legitimate negotiating platforms, capable of fostering the open and deliberate assessment, discussion and valuation of negative and positive externalities connected to resource development in the context of upstream-downstream linkages.[35]

32 Istanbul Declaration, *supra*.

33 Gerlak *et al* (2009), supra, p. 312; A.K. Gerlak *et al*, *Hydrosolidarity and Beyond: Can Ethics and Equity Find a Place in Today's Water Resource Management?* 36:3 Water International 251–65 (2011), p. 257, 261.

34 Gerlak *et al* (2009), *supra*, p. 314; Gerlak *et al* (2011), p. 256–7.

35 Falkenmark, *supra*, p. 360–1.

Hydrosolidarity remains, like water itself, a fluid concept. The through-line across disciplines and writers is that hydrosolidarity is tailored to tackle the water challenge, but consensus beyond that has proven difficult within a world water community that cuts across and bridges multiple levels, sectors, professions, disciplines, themes, and stakeholder groups. Complexity and diversity among water actors are necessary due to the very nature of the target resource but have led to a proliferation of proposed hydrosolidarity definitions and possible functions – yet none singled out for general endorsement by researchers or policymakers and most still vague or undergoing refinements. Gerlak *et al* sum up the history and status of hydrosolidarity as follows: "the term initially acquired greater specificity, only to be enlarged and rendered vaguer later [with] several distinct, but often simultaneous, definitions in practice".[36]

Among legal scholars, Magsig views hydrosolidarity as a value-driven principle embedded with strong ethical underpinnings; based on collective action and interdependence; gaining expression across different international law fields; and whose main purpose is to transition water governance from competing national interests to common benefits.[37] Magsig makes the point that hydrosolidarity, as a guiding policy concept for progressive legal development, "can only be of any benefit if it is being supported by an effective legal framework";[38] and yet, to his mind, a "guiding principle in international water law which provides a framework for the concept to thrive"[39] does not exist. This may explain why Solidarity remains underdeveloped in international water law and in state practice on Community-of-Interests.

In water law and policy, hydrosolidarity may be viewed as a water-related "*nirvana-concept*",[40] not readily implementable like a concrete recipe. Rather, hydrosolidarity inspires and serves as an umbrella benchmark for sustainability in the form of "idealized normative aims"[41] for public policy. Hydrosolidarity is proposed as an ethics-based "grand manifesto [with] potential for alleviating conflict over shared water resources".[42]

Like the principle of Solidarity in international law, therefore, hydrosolidarity has an *ethical basis*. Ethical considerations, still largely missing from solu-

36 Gerlak *et al* (2011), *supra*, p. 256.

37 Magsig, *supra*, p. 67–8, 102.

38 *Id*, p. 84.

39 *Id*, p. 85.

40 F. Molle, *Nirvana Concepts, Narratives and Policy Models: Insights from the Water Sector*, 1:1 Water Alternatives 131–56 (2008).

41 Gerlak *et al* (2011), *supra*, p. 252.

42 Gerlak *et al* (2009), *supra*, p. 324.

tions put forward for the water challenge, shape hydrosolidarity into an overarching framework for peaceful water-sharing and cooperation for the benefit of humans and nature, now and into the future. Through the application of Solidarity, ethical ideals would underpin water negotiations and management, making discussions between water users more balanced and, ultimately, influencing decision-making in a positive way.

Gerlak *et al* view hydrosolidarity as a "socio-ethical annex"[43] to IWRM. As we know, the Basin Scope expresses integrated water resources management in a transboundary context. Gerlak *et al* also consider that the functional value of hydrosolidarity refers to the concept's vocation to draw on ethical considerations for persuading states of the need to enhance water governance. This enhancement would take place in particular through the creation of joint bodies, the adoption of common management tools, the engagement of stakeholders, the development and exchange of knowledge and data, and the promotion of integration and coordination on the scale of the drainage basin, across sectors and between interconnected biomes.[44] In unpacking the ethical content of hydrosolidarity along those lines, Gerlak *et al* emphasize fairness; ideals of common good and social justice; human rights and human welfare; dialogue and mutual understanding; and conflict reduction.[45]

Hydrosolidarity, an ethical and policy concept, and Community-of-Interests, a legal theory, are aligned with each other. The uptake of hydrosolidarity by the Theory would translate into ethical considerations percolating into individual communities-of-basin-interests. At the same time, Community-of-Interest might fulfill the role of an international water law Theory framing hydrosolidarity as a basis for the progressive development of norms in this field.

2.3 *Solidarity as an Element of Community-of-Interests*

The treaties known to reflect the Theory, examined through the lens of international law and policy, as delineated in the two previous subchapters, offer the bases to further refine Solidarity within communities-of-basin-interests. Consideration is given to how Solidarity is captured by the law of co-progressiveness; regional integration cooperation; specific international legal fields closely related to international water law; and international policy, as expressed through the concept of hydrosolidarity. Treaty provisions that embed the dimensions of Solidarity studied above signal an implicit endorse-

43 Gerlak *et al* (2011), *supra*, p. 257.

44 Gerlak *et al* (2009), *supra*, p. 317–20.

45 Gerlak *et al* (2009), *supra*, p. 312–16, 323; Gerlak *et al* (2011), *supra*, p. 252, 259–60.

ment of this element in the law of transboundary basins and indicate the normative content of this secondary element of Community-of-Interests.

The three dimensions of Solidarity thus identified are the *special status of developing countries*, reflecting common but differentiated responsibilities (CBDR); *mutual assistance* in the case of disasters; and *Participation* in environmental protection.

Special Status of Developing Countries: In the UNWC, the 7th Preambular Paragraph expresses an "aware[ness] of the special situation and needs of developing countries", meaning that the special status of these states informs the application and interpretation of the Convention as a whole. Developing countries that join the UNWC comply with its provisions in accordance with their own capabilities and poverty alleviation priorities, and by means of the needed assistance to be provided by the international community or by co-basin states able to do so.

Equity is at the heart of equitable and reasonable use and harm prevention and guides states in transboundary water negotiations. Under Article 5 of the UNWC, equity mandates countries to take account of one another's interests and of those of water users within the others' territories, consistent with the protection of transboundary basins and related ecosystems. As between co-riparian states in different stages of development, this unbalance would be among the factors to be weighed in the application of equitable and reasonable utilization. To be sure, Article 6 of the UNWC, under which such balancing process takes place, is merely illustrative in its list of factors and circumstances.

Solidarity with developing countries is implicit in the expression *all appropriate measures*, contained in Article 7 of the UNWC. Such are the measures that must be taken with a view to preventing significant transboundary harm in connection with the use of an international watercourse; and, where such harm nevertheless occurs, to ensuring its elimination or mitigation. *All appropriate* reflects the standard of due diligence, which encompasses, among other considerations, the financial, technical, and other capabilities of the basin state utilizing the watercourse. The same expression appears in Article 27 – a specific application of the harm prevention rule, and governing harmful conditions related to an international watercourse. The measures required thereunder are those that, in addition to fitting the facts on the ground, would have been "reasonable in view of [states'] circumstances [and] capabilities ..., in so far as their means of knowing of the conditions and their ability to take the necessary measures".[46]

46 ILC (1994), *supra*, p. 129.

Elsewhere in the UNWC, Articles 20, 21(2), 22, 23, 26(1), and 28(3) either omit the expression *all appropriate measures*, employ terms such as *necessary* or *practicable*, or refer to *best efforts*. Notwithstanding the variety in formulations and expressions used, all those provisions are due diligence-based, and thus, embed some measure of Solidarity by accounting for the special conditions of developing countries.

Finally, the special needs of developing countries are embedded in the obligation of equitable and reasonable Participation. This obligation may involve the provision of technical assistance and joint financing,[47] *inter alia*, to aid the parties that so require in making required progress on pollution control, preservation of estuaries, or watercourse regulation.

The ECEWC considers the special status of developing countries in Article 13(4), when requiring that states facilitate the exchange of best available technology through technical assistance. In this sense, under Community-of-Interests, Solidarity entails more than just acting in an equitable and reasonable manner on the basis of unilateral restraint and *ad hoc* coordination.

Mutual Assistance: Article 28(1) of the UNWC defines *emergency* – or, as under the ECEWC, a *critical situation*, as "a situation that causes, or poses an imminent threat of causing, serious harm to watercourse states or other states and that results suddenly from natural causes ... or from human conduct".

For such instances, Article 15 of the ECECW governs mutual assistance. The provision requires basin states to respond to requests for assistance by engaging in the process of designing and agreeing on relevant procedures and providing the necessary aid accordingly. Among other issues, such procedures should address assistance "direction, control, coordination and supervision"; "local facilities and services to be rendered by the [requesting] party"; "arrangements for holding harmless, indemnifying and/or compensating the assisting party and/or its personnel"; "transit through territories of third parties"; and reimbursement methods for services provided.

At the basin level, Coherence means that the Solidarity embedded in the AU and EAC treaties, respectively, permeates the Senegal Basin Charter and the Lake Victoria Protocol. In its Preamble, the Senegal Basin Charter invokes the AU Act, which refers explicitly to Solidarity. In the case of Lake Victoria, parties are required to abide by EAC principles and objectives in basin-level cooperation. Such principles and objectives include a call on coastal states to provide landlocked parties with facilitated access to port and maritime serv-

47 *Id*, p. 122, FN363.

ices. Among the Lake Victoria basin states, Burundi, Rwanda, and Uganda stand to benefit from this particular aspect of Solidarity captured in the EAC Treaty. Solidarity-based ideals and objectives thus inform the interpretation, application, implementation, and development of the Senegal and Lake Victoria Communities-of-Basin-Interests.

Solidarity as a Basis for Participation: The Chlorides Award explores Solidarity as a basis for Participation and allocation of responsibilities in environmental protection. The Award makes explicit the connection between Solidarity, as an overarching ideal, and Community-of-Interests, as a theoretical framework for transboundary water relations.

The Award starts by noting that the parties to the dispute endorse Solidarity as being applicable to their relations under the Protocol, in view of that instrument's object and purpose, as elucidated by the circumstances of its adoption. According to France, the promotion of Solidarity is at the core of the Protocol, with each Rhine riparian state having an "equal interest"[48] in water quality and the activities taking place in their respective territories contributing differently to pollution.[49] Solidarity gains expression in "the form of actions taken by each of the states ... on its own behalf, and also of collective financing of necessary measures".[50] In its turn, The Netherlands acknowledges the importance of Solidarity for resolving the dispute. This is evidenced by the documentation taken as the agreed-upon starting point for subsequent negotiations, and which proposes solutions "respecting the *principle of solidarity*".[51]

Pondering upon the above views, the Tribunal finds that the parties "decided to opt for a system that established a solidarity between them".[52] The Award highlights Solidarity as the guiding factor for expense allocation in connection with measures to mitigate Rhine pollution, i.e., for the approach chosen among the avenues that the states concerned had jointly considered. Solidarity allows for an optimal, cost-effective solution to safeguard a common interest in water quality, by requiring France to take jointly planned and jointly funded measures that benefit all riparian countries.[53]

48 Chlorides Case, *supra*, p. 17.

49 *Id*, p. 18.

50 *Ibid.*

51 *Id*, p. 40 (emphasis added).

52 *Ibid.*

53 *Ibid.*

As explained by Boisson de Chazournes, the Rhine Chlorides Regime does not apply the polluter-pays principle,[54] to which France and Holland, absent the Protocol at hand, would have been subject per Article 2(5)(b) of the ECEWC. When considering the applicability of the polluter-pays principle to the case, the Award highlights the contrast between the presence of that principle in relevant legal instruments and its absence from the Rhine Chlorides Regime; and concludes that the principle in question should play no part in the Regime's interpretation and application. The Protocol adopts a different solution derogating from the polluter-pays principle.[55] In other words, the parties could have decided to follow equity (i.e., equitable and reasonable Participation) or polluter-pays, as normative guidance for determining their respective contributions to dealing with their common problem of chlorides pollution. Yet those states opt for framing their obligations on the basis of Solidarity,

Upon placing Solidarity at the center of the Rhine Chlorides Regime, the Tribunal invokes the River Oder Decision and interprets the establishment of a joint regime as an acknowledgement by its parties of a community-of-interests, with the latter then evolving into a community-of-law.[56] Within the framework of Community-of-Interests, therefore, states may choose Solidarity to guide the framing of Participation in the protection, management and sustainable development of the transboundary basin.

The Award concludes: "Solidarity between the bordering states is undoubtedly a factor in their community-of-interests."[57] Here, the Tribunal hints at the role of Solidarity in informing the internal relations of the Rhine Community-of-Interests, thus placed as an element of the Theory. Of note, the analysis does not seem to apply exclusively to the Rhine and its riparians, as the Award refers to the countries along *an*, and not *the*, international watercourse; as well as to *a*, and not *the*, joint resource use regime by which *a*, and again not the, community-of-law is created.[58]

2.4 *Conclusions*

Solidarity applies as between the members of the community-of-basin-interests as a secondary element of the Theory, even if it is the least visible among them. None of the water treaties above examined mention the term

54 Boisson de Chazournes (2008), *supra*, p. 3.

55 Chlorides Case, *supra*, p. 40.

56 *Ibid.*

57 *Ibid.*

58 *Ibid.*

Solidarity; and they are all subtle and limited in their endorsement of the concept. Yet, all treaties known to reflect Community-of-Interests include provisions embedded with one or more of the three dimensions of Solidarity, namely: special status of developing countries, especially the disadvantaged, less powerful or under-developed, with treaty provisions possibly foreseeing aid and equitable treatment; mutual assistance in the case of emergencies or harmful conditions; or a basis for how states apply Participation with regard to their shared duty to contribute to the advancement of the community-of-basin-interests.

Solidarity under Community-of-Interests is founded on the multidimensional connections and interdependencies within a drainage basin and calls for states in shared watercourses to move away from absolute control claims, even in international negotiations, and to inject ethical values into their mutual relations.

As a young concept, Solidarity remains characterized by open-endedness. This is true with regard to the concept's multidisciplinary origins and to its legal delineation as it progressively penetrates various international law fields and the policy and legal discourse on transboundary water management. Solidarity has an ethical footing, including in the context of transboundary basin management, which aligns it with the law of co-progressiveness.

Being an element of justice, Solidarity permeates Community-of-Interests, as conceptualized in the River Oder Case. As a legal concept specific to certain international legal fields, Solidarity gains expression through obligations and commitments linked to mutual assistance in disaster law; and common but differentiated responsibilities in environmental and development law. Solidarity is endowed with normative force when reflected in specific treaty provisions, in the form of guiding principles or shaped as specific obligations.

In international policy discourse, hydrosolidarity is aligned with the Theory and supplements Community-of-Interests with ethical underpinnings. On the one hand, hydrosolidarity remains without an accepted definition, and this may pose a challenge to its greater penetration into international water law. On the other, hydrosolidarity's *nirvana* nature would allow the members of a community-of-basin-interests to adjust the concept to their particular needs and circumstances, as in the Rhine joint clean-up efforts.

3 Social Basin Engagement: Relations with Stakeholders

> *[T]he term 'community' is associated with inclusiveness and unity, as well as a sense of common spirit and identity [and] this understanding of the term favors, rather than excludes, the inclusion of non-state actors.*[59]

Simson, when writing about the accelerated process of globalization, explains: "while free markets have expanded rapidly to cover most of the globe, democratic governance has not advanced in tandem".[60] Simson's observation leads to a reflection on how neglecting interested actors in the international legal order has been to the detriment of a more cooperative and integrated search for solutions to global and transboundary challenges.

Across basins, there are precedents of stakeholders participating in transboundary management.[61] In the context of Community-of-Interests, the various treaties that reflect the Theory attempt, in different ways, to consider the interests of stakeholders as part of the Close Basin Cooperation process. We refer to this characteristic of cooperation founded on Community-of-Interests as *Social Basin Engagement* – another secondary element of the Theory and which informs the relationships of co-riparians with other actors within a given catchment. Why only a secondary element? Because, while so present, Social Basin Engagement as part of state practice on Community-of-Interests, at least as disciplined in the agreements examined here, is less developed and mainstreamed than the Theory's primary elements.

To identify the various dimensions of Social Basin Engagement, we build on the earlier analysis of relevant trends in general international law, in particular the law of co-progressiveness, and the Founding Charters of Regional Integration Organizations, in terms of how they govern relations with their members' peoples.

59 Howden, *supra*, p. 263.

60 Simpson, *supra*.

61 *See*, e.g., A. Earle & D. Malzbender eds, *Stakeholder Participation in Transboundary Water Management: Selected Case Studies* (African Centre for Water Research 2006); C. Bruch et al eds, Public Participation in the Governance of International Freshwater Resources (United Nations University Press 2005); R.T.P. Denoon *et al, Engaging non-state actors in the negotiation and implementation of international watercourse agreements: Experiences and Lessons Learned from Canada*, 45:4 Water International, 311–328 (2020); M. Tignino & K. Sangbana eds, *Public Participation and Water Resources Management: Where Do We Stand in International Law?* (UNESCO 2013); UNECE et al, supra, p. 3–4.

3.1 *Democratic Governance and Common Interests in International Law*

In the traditional definition of Article 2(1)(i) of the VCLT, an *international organization* is an "*intergovernmental* organization", i.e., only states can be represented there, with their will manifested through government-nominated delegates.[62] Nowadays, international institutions have emerged which include nonstate actors or display public engagement values in their Charters.

Following these developments, stakeholder involvement within both regional integration regimes and communities-of-basin-interests falls under the umbrella of *international democratic governance*, i.e., the opportunity that ought to be granted to a given the nonstate actor, in line with the overarching goals of human flourishing and intergenerational equity, to have a say in intergovernmental agenda-setting or decision-making processes that might affect the rights or interests of said actor.[63] Democratic governance transcends the national level in the face of challenges that do not respect political borders and inevitably require interstate cooperation.

Social Engagement has been long, often, and widely emphasized by experts, practitioners and even some governments as a requisite for sustainable development. This emphasis finds expression in the development of human rights law and of the rights to public participation, access to information and justice at all appropriate levels and fields. To illustrate, the Earth Charter calls on states to safeguard, with the appropriate national and international resources, the human rights to potable water and safe sanitation, as well as to clean air, food security, uncontaminated soil, and shelter; and promotes stronger multilevel institutional democratic governance, with transparency and accountability, as well as participatory decision-making, and access to justice.[64]

With the continued prevalence of the intergovernmental model, there remains a deficit in democratic governance that permeates all fields of international law, including the protection of the environment and the management of shared natural resources. The inadequacy or insufficiency of democratic governance in most international organizations is probably a key factor behind a backlash against globalization.

Calls for democratic governance in the water context go all the way back to 1992, when participants at the ICWE encouraged integrated approaches to

62 Runavot, *supra*, p. 21.

63 A. Bummel, Guest Article: *Let's imagine global citizen participation at the UN*, CIVICUS (undated), at https://www.civicus.org/index.php/re-imagining-democracy/overviews/3335-let-s-imagine-global-citizen-participation-at-the-un.

64 Earth Charter, *supra*, Principles 9(a) & 13.

water management consisting of "political commitment and involvement from the highest levels of government to the smallest communities".[65]

Along these lines, Principle 2 of the Dublin Statement incorporates Social Engagement into the IWRM paradigm. Stakeholder participation is inherent to the way IWRM intends to consider and reconcile all relevant sectors; to harmonize all three dimensions of sustainable development; and to integrate all aspects of the management of water resources, water services and related ecosystems. IWRM relies "on the input and involvement of a range of stakeholders operating at different levels";[66] and identifies "the different users and their different roles and responsibilities in ensuring water security and in managing the resource sustainably"[67] – all in order to account for "how water resources link different parts of society and how decisions in one sector may affect water users in other sectors"[68] within the larger drainage basin.

Scholarship on IWRM can guide communities-of-basin-interests looking for models and good practices to integrate nonstate actors into their cooperation process. For example, in addition to the general pointers already noted, IWRM entails "full public consultation and involvement of users in the planning and implementation of water projects";[69] decentralization, i.e., "decisions at the lowest appropriate level, … as close as possible to those affected",[70] to "ensure [appropriate] representation … and integration of sectoral demands";[71] and awareness-raising "of the importance of water among policy-makers and the general public".[72] Public access to relevant information, in particular, is an indispensable enabler of effective decision-making, public participation and accountability. The data to be so available needs to consist of "timely, updated, accurate, and understandable water information developed by multisectoral and multistakeholder processes".[73]

Underpinned by IWRM, communities-of-interest tend to enable Social Basin Engagement, in addition to what individual governments may provide for in terms of local and national stakeholder involvement. The materialization of international democratic governance for human flourishing in transboundary basins presupposes that Community-of-Interests recognizes stakeholders as

65 ICWE Report, *supra*, p. 12.
66 Unturbe, *supra*, p. 28.
67 *Id*, p. 29.
68 UN Water (2018), *supra*, p. 11.
69 Dublin Statement, *supra*, Principle 2.
70 ICWE Report, *supra*, p. 13–4.
71 *Id*, p. 16.
72 *Id*, p. 13–4.
73 VWF Report, *supra*, p. 75.

having rights and interests that are relevant and merit protection thereunder; and provide for mechanisms by means of which stakeholders are able to exercise such rights and demand the tutelage of such interests. Among such mechanisms, for example, is the granting of observer status to representative organizations with regard to certain meetings, bodies, or activities of the organs of the Basin Body.

3.2 *Community-of-Interests State Practice on Social Basin Engagement*

> *Being ... built on shared interests in a common resource, the community-of -interest*[s] *that arises around such a resource should be representative of all interests at stake – not only at the state level.*[74]

Treaties reflecting Community-of-Interests tend to consider the interests of nonstate actors, demonstrating a concern with human flourishing. Those treaties do so in ways similar to the Founding Charters, albeit with less frequency and legal detail. Social Basin Engagement is expressed in the promotion of water and related rights and environmental access rights, as well as in the definition of the mandates of Basin Bodies. This normative element entails that a basin state gives due consideration to its own nationals and does the same in relation to populations across the border.

For clarity as to the actors that benefit from this element of the Theory, Article 1 of the Lake Victoria Protocol defines the term *stakeholder* broadly, to include "all persons, legal or natural and all other entities being governmental or nongovernmental, residing, having interest or conducting business in the basin".

The Founding Charters examined may declare that, as part of the cooperation process, parties intend to account for nonstate interests and/or enable stakeholder involvement. General statements may underscore human rights, including by invoking democracy and good governance principles. Substantive and procedural obligations and commitments may target individual stakeholder groups and/or establish guarantees and mechanisms for effective representation. In the latter case, a combination of provisions outlines the procedures and organs through which different public involvement rights may be exercised and coordinated.

In our context, Social Basin Engagement may be represented in acknowledgements, guarantees, and provisions referencing intergenerational equity

74 Howden, *supra*, p. 37.

or the rights and interests of stakeholders in a transboundary context. The Preamble of the Ecuador-Peru Agreement states the goal of improving life standards for the populations of the parties through the sustainable use of water resources on the basis of cooperation and the search for mutually satisfactory solutions. Other treaties have preambular references to intergenerational equity in the context of sustainable development.

Additionally, Social Basin Engagement may appear as part of the scope *ratione materiae* of the Basin Treaty. Article 3 the Lake Victoria Protocol includes in its thematic ambit the strengthening of human health and sanitation services and the incorporation of the gender dimension into all activities carried out within the basin. Article 3 of the Ecuador-Peru Agreement refers to the generation of positive impacts on the quality of life of populations in the General Objective of the Basin Treaty.

Among substantive provisions, Social Basin Engagement may be expressed through equitable and reasonable utilization and associated provisions acknowledging requirements for future uses and for dependent populations or calling for special attention to be paid to vital human needs in water allocation and management. This is the case with the UNWC. The more advanced Senegal Basin Charter internalizes Social Basin Engagement by directly recognizing the human right to water[75] and related rights, such as the right to a healthy environment and to food security.

Agreements reflecting the Theory may enable the exercise of procedural access rights, i.e., the rights to public participation, information and justice.

Finally, Social Basin Engagement may be reflected in the mandate of specific organs of the Basin Body, with those organs acting as interfaces between member states and their peoples. Related powers and functions in this respect may include proposing guidance and procedures for the exercise of access rights; ensuring data dissemination; channeling public input into basin planning; and building local capacities.

Case Study 15: Kasikili/Sedudu Island

How does Social Basin Engagement play out as part of transboundary basin cooperation? In a case between Namibia and Botswana, the ICJ is asked to determine the international boundary around the Kasikili/Sedudu Island on the Chobe River, on the basis of the applicable treaties

75 For a thorough discussion on the human right to water in the international law of transboundary basins, *see*, e.g., C. Leb, *The Right to Water in a Transboundary Context: Emergence of Seminal Trends*, 37:6 Water International 640–653 (2012), DOI: 10.1080/02508060.2012.710950.

and relevant international law. Upon finding the Island to be within Botswana, the Court reminds parties of their commitment, under the *Kasane Communiqué*, not to impede the continuation of economic activities, such as fishing; ongoing social interactions among local peoples; the free movement of tourists; and navigation on both channels under the standard of equal treatment for nationals and vessels of both nations, including with regard to connected environmental protection requirements.[76] The Court observes how it is "not uncommon for the inhabitants of border regions in Africa to traverse such borders for purposes of agriculture and grazing, without raising concern on the part of the authorities on either side of the border".[77] In its Declaration, Judge Ranjeva highlights "a right of free access to the surrounding waters and to the territory of the Kasikili/Sedudu Island".[78]

Sustainable Development and Rights of Present and Future Generations: Care for present and future generations is present in the UNWC, in the ECEWC and in Basin Treaties as a facet of sustainable development. The Preamble of the UNWC adopts sustainability as an overarching goal and priority common interest to be pursued and protected. The ECEWC expressly references sustainable development, which must inform the adoption of measures to prevent, control and reduce transboundary impact; and refines the concept as entailing the management of transboundary waters that meets the needs of the present without compromising the needs of the future.

Among Basin Treaties, the Senegal Basin Charter calls for optimal, sustainable, and efficient resource use and integrated and equitable water management for the benefit of present and future generations. The Ecuador-Peru Agreement expresses the parties' conviction that their Basin Treaty will ensure optimal and sustainable basin management and watercourse use now and into the future.

Substantive Rules: Equitable and Reasonable Use and Participation and Harm Prevention: Social Basin Engagement is embedded in the normative content and application of equitable and reasonable use and of equitable and reasonable Participation under the UNWC.

Under the banner of sustainable development, equitable and reasonable use and Participation imply the sustainable utilization of the shared water-

76 Kasikili Case, *supra*, p. 59–60, 65–67.

77 *Id*, p. 53.

78 *Id*, *Declaration*, Judge Ranjeva, p. 69.

course and related contributions by the different states, taking account of their interests, and consistent with the protection of related ecosystems in the long-term. State *interests* here include individual and common and, as emphasized in Article 6(1)(e) of the UNWC, interests in "existing and potential uses" and Participation in their realization – as may be required to satisfy the needs of future generations. Similarly, Article 3(4) of the Revised SADC Protocol translates sustainable development into a state obligation to balance resource use so as to improve human wellbeing and promote environmental conservation. This provision reiterates the normative content of Article 2(3) of the 1995 SADC Protocol.

An emphasis on long-term thinking, inherent to equitable and reasonable Participation, sustainable development and intergenerational equity, is clear in Article 24(2)(a) of the UNWC. This provision encourages the joint management of an international watercourse, which entails designing and implementing long-term plans for its sustainable development. Doing so is crucial to ensure the sustainability of the basin for the generations of today and tomorrow.

For the application of equitable and reasonable use and Participation, Article 6(1)(c) of the UNWC includes, among the relevant factors and circumstances to be considered, the dependence of the populations of the riparian states on the watercourse. In other words, the needs of nonstate actors connected to the basin must be weighed in the balancing process required for the operationalization of equitable and reasonable use and for compliance with the Duty to Participate. The same approach is taken by Article 3(8)(a)(iii) of the Revised SADC Protocol, but it is not explicitly captured by its predecessor – the latter having preceded the UNWC.

For its part, the ECEWC interlinks *harm prevention* and Social Basin Engagement. Article 1(2) designs a broad definition of transboundary harm that includes environmental dimensions alongside human health and safety, historical monuments or other physical structures, cultural heritage, and socio-economic conditions.

Human Right to Water and Sanitation: Article 10 of the UNWC states that, absent agreement to the contrary, all water uses enjoy the same level of consideration. In case of conflict, however, special regard should be given to "vital human needs", i.e., "sufficient water to sustain human life, including both drinking water and water required for the production of food in order to prevent starvation".[79] In instances of conflicting uses, therefore, the populations'

79 ILC (1994), *supra*, p. 110.

reliance on the watercourse receives a higher weight relative to other relevant circumstances and other categories of uses, but only to the extent appropriate to supply basic needs of dependent nonstate actors. Under special circumstances, the UNWC so safeguards vital human needs by authorizing departure from its general rule of no priority between uses – for example, for drinking water during an emergency or for domestic livestock through an extended drought.

According to the ILC, Article 10 of the UNWC is about conflicting uses and not about disputes between states.[80] This means that the exception foreseen by the provision applies to protect vital human needs even where states' interests are aligned but are contrary to those vital needs. Imagine three co-basin states that operate a joint system of dams primarily for energy generation. During a prolonged drought, experts recommend that states agree on retaining more water in the system as the optimal solution for meeting vital human needs, but which would reduce the amount of energy generated. In weighing their own common interest in energy generation against the basic needs of dependent populations, all states would be required to give special consideration to the latter, even if to the detriment of energy production.

The ILC Commentary also emphasizes that the requirement to give special regard to vital human needs applies only where customary or treaty law do not establish otherwise.[81] Hence, could co-riparian states, among themselves, agree to prioritize their common development interests, as defined by an agreement or custom, to the detriment of local populations? Since the adoption of the 1994 ILC Draft Articles and the Commentaries thereto, a rights-based approach to access to water and sanitation has gained strength, to the point of becoming recognized as a fundamental human right with autonomous standing,[82] as opposed to existing solely in connection to a right to life, to health, etc.[83] Such developments reveal the arrival of the law of co-progressiveness and its focus on human flourishing, and must be considered for a *current* interpretation of article 10 of the UNWC.

Inspiration for the development of human rights under international water law can be found in the Senegal Basin Charter. The same 17th Preambular Paragraph containing the explicit reference to the Theory proclaims the parties' wish to guarantee, for each state and each river user, the benefit of an

80 *Ibid.*

81 *Ibid.*

82 UNGA, Res 64/292 (2010): *The Human Right to Water and Sanitation*, UN Doc A/RES/64/292 (3 Aug 2010).

83 *See* Leb (2012), *supra*, p. 642–3, explaining the trajectory of the human right to water: "from nowhere to be seen into the spotlight of attention".

equitable and reasonable water use, in accordance with international law. Building on these considerations, Article 4 of the Charter codifies explicitly the human right to water. The provision determines that water allocation principles aim to secure, for the populations of the riparian states, the full enjoyment of the resource, consistent with human security and infrastructure safety, as well as of the fundamental human right to clean water, all under the umbrella of sustainable development. These provisions are aligned with the position of the UN Special Rapporteur on the Human Rights to Safe Drinking Water and Sanitation, for whom "states are accountable to the population in their territory … and to those that are affected by the cross-border activities of the state".[84]

The Human Right of Access to Participation in Decision-Making: Both the Ecuador-Peru Agreement and the Senegal Basin Charter refer to IWRM. The former Basin Treaty includes IWRM among its Specific Objectives, underscoring the engagement of institutions and organizations of water users and civil society. The Preamble of the Senegal Basin Charter notes that water allocation, management and utilization must involve the different actors concerned, such as resource users, managers, decision-makers, developers, and experts.

Article 2 of the Senegal Basin Charter foresees the formulation of a framework and modalities to enable stakeholder involvement in relevant decision-making within the basin. Together with OMVS, the parties must provide for the education of riparian populations – a fundamental requirement for meaningful Social Basin Engagement – through awareness-raising centered on the ecologically rational utilization of water resources.

Similarly, Article 22 of the Lake Victoria Protocol mandates partner states to "create an environment conducive for stakeholders' views to influence governmental decisions on project formulation and implementation". As concrete tools to create such an enabling environment and thus ensure effective Social Basin Engagement, Article 21(1) requires parties to "promote and encourage awareness of the importance of, and the measures required for", sustainable basin management; and to design relevant educational and public awareness programs, in cooperation, as appropriate, with other states and international organizations.

84 L. Heller, *Report of the Special Rapporteur on the Human Rights to Safe Drinking Water and Sanitation*, *in* UNGA, 73rd Session, Note by the Secretariat, UN Doc A/73/162 (16 July 2018), p. 5.

Under Article 3(l) of the Lake Victoria Protocol, promoting Social Basin Engagement in planning and decision-making is a topic specifically contemplated under the Regime's scope. Article 4(2)(h) codifies public involvement as a principle, "whereby decisions about a project or policy take into account the views of the stakeholders". Article 6 requires partner states to act diligently towards ensuring the protection, conservation, and rehabilitation of the basin and its ecosystems; and, where appropriate, to do so involving all stakeholders. Targeting a specific group of nonstate actors, Article 44(1) requires riparian states, in implementing the Protocol, to enter into partnership agreements with development partners, thereby aiming to integrate such entities into the concrete activities of the Community-of-Basin-Interests.

While the River Uruguay Statute contains no relevant provisions, the Pulp Mills Decision notes that "both parties agree that consultation of the affected populations should form part of an [EIA]".[85] The Court then finds that such consultations by Uruguay did take place, including with stakeholders located in Argentina.[86]

Article 24(3) of the Lake Victoria Protocol requires states to take appropriate measures to facilitate cross-border stakeholder collaboration on research and data-sharing, under the auspices of the LVBC.

Right of Access to Information: Article 16(1) of the ECEWC requires states to make certain key information publicly available, namely, "the conditions of transboundary waters, measures taken or planned to be taken to prevent, control and reduce transboundary impact, and the effectiveness of those measures". As a specific application of the above obligation, Article 11(3) commands parties to ensure public access to the results of individual assessments conducted to generate or update such key information.

Among the Basin Treaties, Article 13 of the Senegal Basin Charter requires parties to make all relevant information accessible to the public, such as the status and quality of water resources and measures planned or taken to regulate river flows. In practice, however, "the sharing of information with actors other than the member states is weak. Only a very limited number of documents are published on the OMVS website or are in other ways made accessible to the public."[87]

85 Pulp Mills Case, *supra*, p. 63.

86 *Id*, p. 64.

87 Howden, *supra*, p. 343. *But see* UNW-DPAC, *supra*, p. 33, noting that Social Basin Engagement into the Senegal community-of-basin-interests has been happening in practice,

Right of Access to Justice: Article 32 of the UNWC incorporates access to justice through the principle of *nondiscrimination* as between one riparian state in relation to nationals of another co-basin country.

The provision aims to protect the interests of the persons residing in, and/or dependent upon, the basin, in the event of transboundary impacts taking place in connection with a shared watercourse. For such persons, the Convention safeguards nondiscriminatory access to judicial or other procedures for claiming compensation or other relief in the state of origin of the actual or potential injury, as laid out in the latter's domestic legislation.

This guarantee reflects Social Basin Engagement in the form of a concern with the interests of nonstate actors as they may be impacted by decision-making over a shared basin and its uses. The same approach is reproduced in Article 3(10)(c) of the Revised SADC Protocol. In contrast, the 1995 Protocol does not capture nondiscrimination.

The reference to *threat* in Article 32 indicates that the nondiscrimination principle applies both to actual and potential harm; and, because administrative procedures are often better suited to deal with the risk of detrimental impact before it actually materializes, the UNWC guarantees nondiscriminatory access to judicial *and other* avenues.

Between Article 32 of the UNWC and the corresponding provision in the ILC Draft Articles, the only edit is the deletion of the expression *under its jurisdiction* and its replacement with the words *in its territory*. As such, the ILC commentaries in this respect remain valid in relation to both the UNWC and the Revised SADC Protocol.

In interpreting the principle, the ILC explains that discrimination is not allowed in relation to the exercise of the right of access to justice – whether based on nationality, residence, or the place of occurrence of the harm contested. A state that causes significant transboundary injury through an international watercourse may not foreclose access to its justice system to persons thus injured by arguing that such harm was suffered outside its territory. Further, a requirement for nonresidents or aliens to post a bond before they may utilize the court system, as a means to cover related costs, is not contrary to the principle, since access to justice is to be granted in conformity with national law.[88]

The Commission also draws attention to the opening phrase of Article 32, in the sense that the provision applies unless states have agreed otherwise. Arti-

---

with the involvement of various stakeholders, including competent national agencies, water users, NGOs, and scientists.

88 ILC Draft Articles (1994), *supra*, p. 132.

cle 32 is thus a residual rule, as with other UNWC provisions and in line with the Convention's framework character. The states concerned remain free to agree on alternative means – diplomatic or otherwise, for complying with the nondiscrimination principle, but such alternative means may not result in a form of discrimination.[89]

During the drafting of Article 32, an ILC member rejected the provision, since the future convention was meant to "deal with relations between states and should not extend into the field of actions by natural or legal persons under domestic law."[90] That the ILC finds it important to point out that some resistance had to be overcome for this provision to be retained signalizes that the UNWC represents progress in this regard.

Institutional Mandates: Article 5(b)(iv) of the 1995 SADC Protocol charges joint bodies with "stimulating public awareness and participation in the sound management and development of the environment, including human resources development". The Revised Protocol does not reproduce that provision, having excluded the exemplification of the potential functions of watercourse commissions. Given, however, that the Revised Protocol continues to be framed by the Theory, the institutional dimension of Social Basin Engagement, as highlighted in the 1995 Protocol, may still guide the design of Basin Treaties.

The Senegal Basin Charter and the Lake Victoria Protocol offer concrete examples of the use of the Basin Body to further Social Basin Engagement. Article 23 of the former Basin Treaty governs the granting of observer status before the Permanent Water Commission (PWS) to entities within the members representing water users, as well as to subnational political units, NGOs, and decentralized management committees. Once holding such status, these entities are meant to participate meaningfully in the Commmission's activities.

Article 33(3)(b) of the Lake Victoria Protocol explicitly tasks the Basin Body with promoting Social Basin Engagement. Per Article 42(2), part of this promotional role consists, where appropriate, of involving relevant intergovernmental organizations and NGOs in coordination processes for "the preparation, negotiation and implementation of national and regional programs". Among the Body's organs, Sectoral Committees ensure broad-based stakeholder representativity therein, alongside the partner states themselves. The Committees bring together senior government officials, public and regional

89 *Ibid.*

90 *Id*, p. 133.

institutions, business and industry, civil society, and other relevant sectors. On access to information, Article 37(4) requires each party to establish a national focal point, and task it with sharing data with the Basin Body and other stakeholders.

In the case of the Ecuador-Peru Agreement, the Basin Committees, created within the structure of the Binational Commission, are charged with coordinating with the competent authorities for the dissemination of the IWRM basin plans foreseen by Article 13. The composition of the Committees includes irrigation associations (Ecuador) and water users organizations (Peru), as well as local communities. Representatives from other sectors, such as agriculture, mining, energy, public health, and transport, may also participate in the Committees if the parties so agree. Surprisingly, given the Agreement's strong focus on sustainability, the environmental sector or organizations are not mentioned in the formation of the Committees.

Rights of Nature: Movilla ponders on how to further transcend a "strict interstate outlook"[91] in the management of shared freshwaters based on the Theory. Movilla proposes an expanded Theory of Community-of-Interests that could ultimately lead to improved basin cooperation and resource sustainability, on the basis of a wider ecocentric viewpoint – one that "allows a broader and holistic interpretation of that community, including the interests of the local riparian populations, the interest of the water body itself and the interest of its related ecosystems."[92]

Along these lines, Howden suggests that an international watercourse could have rights such as "respect for its natural processes; the right to voice its interests and opinions in matters relating to its utilization or in matters where its health and functioning could be affected, such as the construction of projects, diversion of its waters, industrial or agricultural discharge into the basin; and the interest of being governed from a basin-wide perspective".[93] This, of course, would presuppose all of the basin states agreeing to grant the watercourse legal personality,[94] thereby formally introducing the natural entity underlying their community-of-basin-interests "as a stakeholder in its own management".[95]

91 Movilla, *supra*.

92 *Ibid.*

93 Howden, *supra*, p. 126.

94 *Id*, p. 131.

95 *Id*, p. 132.

3.3 *Conclusions*

Social Basin Engagement is a secondary element of Community-of-Interests given that all treaties examined provide for the engagement of interested actors but do so in limited ways. This normative element of the Theory must be considered in the light of the calls and concrete recommendations for improved international democratic governance, which include the role of the Basin Body.

Within the Founding Charters, Social Engagement tends to be, at a minimum, an ideal that states commit to pursue; and, under the more progressive regimes, a general commitment realized through dedicated obligations and procedural and institutional mechanisms.

In our context, there is considerable attention paid to nonstate actors in the Basin Treaties that refer explicitly to Community-of-Interests. Both the Lake Victoria Protocol and the Senegal Basin Charter advance in significant ways the notion of communities-of-interests among co-basin states and their peoples, including by embedding access rights into institutional mandates. The Lake Victoria Protocol entails active stakeholder involvement and specific cooperation areas to advance their interests. The Senegal Basin Charter goes further by explicitly codifying the human right of access to water. The Ecuador-Peru Agreement places Social Basin Engagement in the context of joint planning and, like in the Senegal and Lake Victoria Regimes, into the functions of the Basin Body.

Attention to stakeholders is missing from the text of the River Uruguay Statute, although Social Basin Engagement has been practiced as part of its implementation process, in accordance with the findings under the Pulp Mills Case.

The other agreements reflecting the Theory do not go as far but still recognize the interests of non-state actors by incorporating one or another dimension of Social Basin Engagement, namely: intergenerational equity; consideration of social factors and local dependencies as part of equitable and reasonable use and Participation; the right to water and sanitation; and procedural access rights.

The UNWC reflects Social Basin Engagement in three articles, with two of those instances pertaining to the factors and circumstances that inform the application of equitable and reasonable use and Participation to a concrete case. A more developed consideration of Social Basin Engagement in transboundary water cooperation would have been desirable; and the UNWC's timid approach on this topic is a weakness often emphasized.[96] This weakness reflects a deficiency across international water law as a whole, which "has traditionally been skewed towards state-state relations".[97]

In general, the agreements in question endeavor to promote Social Basin Engagement – even if they do so by following less consistent approaches and to a more limited degree than the Founding Charters. To the extent that the Global Conventions, the SADC Protocols and the Basin Treaties envision engaging interested actors within communities-of-interests, the corresponding provisions in each instrument are evidence that Social Basin Engagement is at least a secondary element of the Theory. While communities-of-basin-interests are concerned with the shared aspirations of states, they strive to integrate stakeholders, more so than states might do under Limited Territorial Sovereignty. Were riparian states to heed the calls for enhanced stakeholder involvement in transboundary cooperation, Social Basin Engagement would develop further and, in time, perhaps become a primary element of Community-of-Interests.

The different approaches to Social Basin Engagement taken by the treaties examined form together an analytical framework to examine other watercourse agreements, so that we could better grasp what this normative element of Community-of-Interests entails and look for its presence beyond the instruments known to reflect the Theory.

The same diversity means that states have negotiating space in this respect; that Community-of-Interests gives riparian states a degree of flexibility and discretion to decide together, as appropriate, on the extent to which to integrate stakeholders and on the choice of methods for doing so. This is consistent with the point being made about Community-of-Interests throughout the book: the Theory does not deal in absolutes. The primary and secondary elements of Community-of-Interests most often apply and come into play as appropriate to realize jointly defined interests and, as needed, to reconcile individual state concerns. At the same time, freedom to negotiate does not amount to a blank check to completely ignore or exclude stakeholders. This general limitation becomes clear from the ILC interpretation of the principle of nondiscrimination.

Social Basin Engagement gains special relevance in the balancing of the interests of the members of a community-of-basin-interests. By expanding the interests to be considered beyond those of the riparian states themselves

---

96 *See*, e.g., Islam, *supra*, p. 369–70.

97 Z. Yihdego & A. Rieu-Clarke, *An Exploration of Fairness in International Law through the Blue Nile and GERD*, 41:4 Water International 528–549 (2016), p. 532.

in ways that include the needs and voices of the stakeholders within the basin, the Theory adds a layer of protection for ecological and human interests. Social Basin Engagement contributes to empowering civil society and other groups to monitor compliance by their own governments with international law in the fields of transboundary waters, the environment and human rights. For that to happen, safeguards applicable to planned measures are imperative, whether developments are planned unilaterally or jointly by two or more states. Such safeguards provide the legal basis and appropriate platform for a state's constituencies, as citizens of the basin taken as a whole, and preferably in collaboration with their potentially affected counterparts across the border, to participate meaningfully in decision-making; to review plans and project documents; and, ultimately, to influence the management of transboundary waters in the common interest of not only the states themselves but of the environment and people as well.

4 Conclusions

The Theory's secondary elements have to do with the institutional relationships of Community-of-Interests Regimes.

Coherence refers to a general consistency between the fundamental shared objectives of communities-of-basin-interests and the overarching goals pursued by other actors, such as regional organizations, like the EAC and the AU; basin-wide regimes in relation to communities-of-interests at the subcatchment level and between these latter communities; and framework water conventions, like the UNWC, the ECEWC and the SADC Protocols, and water agreements dealing with multiple basins.

Solidarity serves as a guiding ethical standard that may inform relations among co-riparian states within a community-of-basin-interests – with regard to the special needs and conditions of developing countries; mutual assistance in the case of disasters; and the application of the rule of Participation.

Social Basin Engagement entails a legal acknowledgement and implementation of the rights and interests of stakeholders within the basin and/or their engagement in the cooperation process through rules and institutions designed to ensure access to information, participation, and justice.

PART V

Functions of Community-of-Interests

The Legal Analytical Framework formed of the primary and secondary elements of Community-of-Interests is here applied as the lens through which to demonstrate the functions of the Theory linked to the codification and clarification, application and interpretation, and progressive development of three basic norms in the field, a "triangle of cornerstone principles … which interact, overlap and mutually support one another as general principles of international water law",[1] namely: equitable and reasonable use, harm prevention, and the duty to cooperate.

1 International Water Law Codification and Clarification

As traditionally regarded, equitable and reasonable use and harm prevention, "the most fundamental"[2] rules under international water law, do not principally aim to protect shared aspirations, but to enable coexistence through basic forms of cooperation. In watercourse agreements not informed by Community-of-Interests, those two rules operate chiefly through unilateral efforts and some coordination, tempered with minimum cooperation commitments. When framed by the Theory, equitable and reasonable use and harm prevention transcend those roles.

For its part, the general duty to cooperate is codified and developed as an obligation and legal pillar of interstate transboundary water relations in the UNWC and the ECEWC. Taylor relates the duty to cooperate under the law of transboundary basins to the law of cooperation in general international law and draws attention to the wide endorsement of such a cooperation duty in international water law scholarship.[3] Leb concludes that the general duty to cooperate "is a general obligation with a legal nature of its own: it has all of the attributes of a legal principle and yet is an obligation of general nature".[4] For

1 Leb (2013), *supra*, p. 105 (emphasis added).

2 S. McCaffrey, *The Entry into Force of the 1997 Watercourses Convention*, International Water Law Project Blog (25 May 2014), at https://www.internationalwaterlaw.org/blog/2014/05/25/dr-stephen-mccaffrey-the-entry-into-force-of-the-1997-watercourses-convention/.

3 Taylor, *supra*, p. 50.

4 Leb (2013), *supra*, p. 81.

 | HTTPS://DOI.ORG/10.1163/9789004507036-007

McCaffrey, cooperation over international watercourses "is probably now required by general international law.[5] Furthermore, Tanzi and Arcari remark on how Article 8 of the UNWC "enhances the development of cooperation as an autonomous legal obligation".[6] Like with equitable and reasonable use and harm prevention, the Theory influences how the duty to cooperate is codified and clarified.

1.1 *Equitable and Reasonable Use and Harm Prevention*

The way the ILC describes equitable and reasonable use captures the purpose this rule serves under Limited Territorial Sovereignty: "where the quantity or quality of the water is such that all the reasonable and beneficial uses of all watercourse states cannot be fully realized, a 'conflict of uses' results".[7] In that scenario, "some adjustments or accommodations are required in order to preserve each watercourse state's equality of right [and] are to be arrived at on the basis of equity".[8]

In a similar sense, Article IV of the Helsinki Rules proposes the following formulation for equitable and reasonable use: "Each basin state is entitled, within its territory, to a reasonable and equitable share in the beneficial uses of the waters of an international drainage basin". Article I of the IIL *Resolution on the Use of International Non-Maritime Waters* proclaims: "Every state has the right to make use of the waters flowing across or bordering its territory … That right is limited by the right of use by the other states concerned".[9] In both texts, and in the ILC explanation, the basic focus of equitable and reasonable use is on reconciling domestic uses of the watercourse, without an obvious wider concern with sustainable management or human needs.

In contrast, Article 5 of the UNWC goes beyond those earlier attempts at the rule's codification. Evidence that the UNWC, having been framed by Community-of-Interests, takes equitable and reasonable use further is in the ILC Commentary to the effect that the rule in question is "laid down *and elaborated upon*"[10] in Draft Article 5(1).

As in the Draft Articles, Article 5(1) of the UNWC embeds a traditional notion of equitable and reasonable use in its opening sentence, which applies

---

5 McCaffrey (2019), *supra*, p. 758. *See also Ibid.*, FN29, for evidence corroborating the customary status of the duty to cooperate in relation to transboundary waters.

6 Tanzi and Arcari, *supra*, p. 183.

7 ILC (1994), *supra*, p. 97.

8 *Ibid.*

9 IIL, *Resolution on the Use of International Non-Maritime Waters*, IIL Session (Salzburg, 11 Sep 1961), *in* 49 IIL Yearbook 381–4 (1961).

10 ILC (1994), *supra*, p. 97 (emphasis added).

the rule at hand to govern how a state uses a watercourse within its respective territory. The provision, however, goes on to identify the three overarching criteria for determining the legality of a particular water use, namely: the goal of *optimal and sustainable utilization and associated benefits*; the consideration of not just needs, but the *interests, common or unilateral,* of all states; and *watercourse protection.*

The UNWC integrates the three criteria into the very definition of equitable and reasonable use, meaning those requirements frame other factors that may be appropriate to consider in a specific case, such as those enumerated in Article 6. The same requirements are the entry point through which the drafters of the Convention inject into equitable and reasonable use a Community-of-Interests flavor. To be sure, the ILC refers to Article 5(1) as stating the basic rule of equitable and reasonable use[11] – hence, its complete text for the purpose of codification.

The requirement that countries pursue equitable and reasonable utilization and associated benefits in conformity with the umbrella goal of sustainability, considering the interests of the countries concerned, invokes the common interest that all co-basin states share in the long-term conservation of the resource. Hence, the interests of all states within the catchment align under a shared umbrella goal of optimal and sustainable use and protection, to be safeguarded, pursued and promoted in an equitable and reasonable manner. When equitable and reasonable use is thus framed, it is more likely that the desired scenario envisioned by the ILA and the ILC would materialize, i.e., of all states enjoying maximum benefits from using the watercourse and, in that connection, suffering minimum losses and unmet needs.[12]

The ILC further clarifies that watercourse protection, "while primarily referring to measures undertaken by individual states, ... does not exclude cooperative measures, works or activities undertaken by states jointly".[13] In prioritizing domestic measures, the ILC's interpretation reflects Community-of-Interests, but still assumes a world where unilateral restraint and domestic action almost always suffice to implement equitable and reasonable utilization; where the application of equity to the law of international watercourses may be subsumed under the idea that a basin country "has both the right to utilize an international watercourse in an equitable and reasonable manner

11 *Ibid.*

12 ILA (1966), supra, p. 487; ILC (1994), *supra*, p. 97.

13 ILC (1994), *supra*, p. 97.

and the obligation not to … deprive [co-riparians] of their right to equitable utilization."[14]

However, realities have changed since the approval of the 1994 ILC Draft Articles. Considered as a whole, the UNWC, with its various provisions that reflect Close Basin Cooperation, allows for a more progressive reading of equitable and reasonable use. Meeting the core equitable-and-reasonable-use criteria stated in Article 5(1) will often demand basin-wide cooperation, which transcends the notion of states exercising rights domestically in a manner that does not interfere with one another's interests.

Article 5(1), therefore, encompasses the implied function that equitable and reasonable use may perform in safeguarding common interests. Such a role for equitable and reasonable use cannot be considered an afterthought on the part of the UNWC drafters, as if it had been included in a separate paragraph or article; and even less so a simple best practice recommendation, since the term employed in said sentence is not *should* but *shall*. The explicit references to sustainability and state interests are additions to the 1994 ILC formula, inserted during the negotiations on the final draft of the UNWC.[15] Under the Convention's formula, equitable and reasonable use is more than a tool for balancing conflicting interests and may also serve communities-of-basin-interests. As framed by the Theory, equitable and reasonable use enables the pursuit of the interest that *all* states within a basin share in the goal of long-term optimal and sustainable use and adequate protection of the watercourse.

Whereas the Theory's flavor is implicit in the way the UNWC codifies the rule at hand, Article 2(2) of the 1995 SADC Protocol makes that connection explicit when calling on parties to "respect and abide by the principles of Community-of-Interests in the equitable utilization" of shared watercourses. Similarly, Article 5 of the Lake Victoria Protocol codifies equitable and reasonable use while referring back to Community-of-Interests and the other governing principles enumerated in Article 4.

By situating equitable and reasonable within the context of Community-of-Interests, the UNWC and the 1995 SADC and Lake Victoria Protocols show how the Theory underpins the codification and clarification of that basic rule of international water law.

On harm prevention, compare the language used in the Indus Water Treaty, from which Community-of-Interests elements are largely lacking, and in the Lake Victoria Protocol. Under Articles IV(2)–(3)(a), (6), and (9)–

14 *Ibid.*

15 *Ibid.*

(10) of the former, each party undertakes to take all appropriate measures to avoid causing transboundary damage in relation to certain unilateral schemes, such as those for flood control or sandmining; non-consumptive uses; maintenance of natural channels; operation of dams and irrigation canals; and control of pollution. In contrast, Article 4(2)(c) of the Lake Victoria Protocol imposes on partner states a duty to prevent transboundary harm "whereby [they] shall individually and jointly take all appropriate measures" to that effect.

In this sense, the Lake Victoria Protocol requires joint action to secure coexistence, consistent with the typology of the obligation to cooperate under the Theory, as examined earlier. Here, joint action is codified as an ancillary obligation to the harm-prevention rule. As proposed by McCaffrey, the concept of *supportive or ancillary obligations* allows us to explore *where-appropriate* scenarios in the application and interpretation of the duty to cooperate specifically through joint action – the modality of state engagement prevailing under the Theory. Where-appropriate scenarios unfold when apparent that joint action is required to ensure full compliance with harm prevention.

Community-of-Interests may thus influence how states codify and clarify the normative content of equitable and reasonable utilization and harm prevention, as accepted norms of international law, using language that places these two cornerstone rules under the umbrella Community-of-Interests.

1.2 *General Duty to Cooperate*

Under general international law, as in the law on transboundary waters, the duty to cooperate is broadly delineated, with an open-ended and flexible normative content, which poses a challenge to effective compliance therewith. Yet, when codified and clarified through the lens of the Basin Treaty, the Basin Body and Close Basin Cooperation, the duty to cooperate gains more specificity.

Article 8 of the UNWC links the cooperation duty to the concept of mutual benefit. In so doing, the Convention provides a clue as to how states are to cooperate under Community-of-Interests, i.e., by seeking mutually beneficial collaboration paths, which are themselves intrinsic to the pursuit of shared goals. The ECEWC codifies and further clarifies the normative content of the duty to cooperate in Article 6(2) when requiring parties to interact within the framework of specific agreements or arrangements and under the umbrella of dedicated formal or informal organizations.

In the UNWC, moreover, Article 8 refers to cooperation on the basis of *good faith*, which, as McCaffrey explains, is needed for the implementation of substantive and procedural obligations under the Convention.[16] This good-faith 'hook' suggests that, in a concrete case, a where-appropriate obligation may arise for state parties to consider cooperating under the umbrella of a Basin Treaty and a Basin Body. In the situation where this where-appropriate obligation arises, it would do so for being a requirement ancillary to the general duty states have to cooperate *in good faith* – ultimately, to fulfill other international law obligations.

In the same vein, Article 64(1) of the Berlin Rules states: "When necessary to ensure the equitable and sustainable use of waters and the prevention of harm, basin states shall establish a basin-wide or joint agency or commission". The Rapporteur's Commentary clarifies that, for the achievement of equity and sustainability, "basin-wide management mechanisms will be [often] the best or even a necessary means".[17] The adoption of these mechanisms may not be an independent requirement under customary law but may become an ancillary duty to other recognized obligations.

This understanding is reflected in Article 1 of the River Uruguay Statute, adopted "to establish the joint machinery *necessary*" for the watercourse to be used optimally and rationally. In the Pulp Mills Case, the ICJ finds this joint machinery to consist of CARU, together with the set of substantive and procedural duties set out in the Statute. According to the Court, "whereas the substantive obligations are frequently worded in broad terms, the procedural obligations are narrower and more specific, so as to facilitate … a process of continuous consultation between the parties".[18] Under CARU's umbrella, procedural and substantive obligations "complement one another perfectly, enabling the parties to achieve the object of the Statute",[19] i.e., their overarching common interest in the equitable and reasonable use of the watercourse, consistent with its protection. In the Uruguay River, therefore, putting in place a joint machinery for an individual watercourse, in the form of the Basin Treaty and the Basin Body, within the framework of Community-of-Interests, has enabled compliance by both basin states with good-faith cooperation and, ultimately, with equitable and reasonable use and harm prevention.

16 McCaffrey (2019), *supra*, p. 757.

17 ILA (2004), *supra*, p. 50.

18 Pulp Mills Case, *supra*, p. 31.

19 *Id*, p. 32.

Case Study 15: Argentina-Bolivia Treaty on Environment[20]

This framework Agreement establishes a legal and institutional umbrella for environmental cooperation. According to the Preamble, the parties consider that environmental, development and integration issues demand joint action to identify and apply joint solutions; and that the effects of environmental problems cross national borders, and require the progressive construction of a regime that sustains joint responsibilities.[21] This language suggests that the *appropriateness* of instituting a regime arises out of the particular circumstances of the environmental challenges and resources the two countries share in common, including with respect to water resources.

Beyond the UNWC and the River Uruguay Statute, good faith "dominates the interpretation and application of the entire body of international law".[22] Accordingly, requirements ancillary to the duty to cooperate and linked to elements of Community-of-Interests may apply more widely. Taking Article 3(3) of the UNWC as interpretative guidance, the scenario in which Close Basin Cooperation becomes indispensable to address the specificities of the basin triggers the general requirement for states at least to come to the table to discuss the appropriateness of a Basin Treaty and a Basin Body. For non-UNWC parties, an ancillary obligation to engage in good-faith consultations and eventual negotiations on a Basin Treaty with the requesting co-basin state could still flow from the general duty to cooperate in good faith. Here, Community-of-Interests contributes to clarifying the meaning of good-faith cooperation between co-riparians.

In this respect, the Lake Lanoux Case Award notes how it might not be appropriate to speak of "l'obligation de négocier un accord".[23] In reality, what we have before us is a state obligation "à rechercher, par des tractations préalables, les termes d'un accord".[24] Pending negotiations, and even if these fail, states are free to continue the exercise of their sovereign rights, as long as they do so in accordance with international water law. This duty to seek the terms of an agreement may involve diverse forms and scope of commitments

20 *Tratado sobre Medio Ambiente*, Argentina-Bolivia (Buenos Aires, 17 Mar 1994).
21 *Id*, Preamble, ¶¶ 5 & 7.
22 Chlorides Case, *supra*, p. 27.
23 Lake Lanoux, *supra*, p. 306.
24 *Ibid.*

and related implementation procedures. Yet a state may not contest these commitments and noncompliance may be sanctioned.[25]

Therefore, an obligation linked to the Basin Treaty, as ancillary to the duty to *cooperate in good faith*, is not an obligation to reach an agreement, but to enter into good-faith negotiations with the aim of concluding said agreement, i.e., "les États doivent tendre à conclure de tels accords".[26] The general obligation to respect the rules of good faith is thus supported by a *treaty-negotiations duty*, which, for its part, encompasses obligations to refrain from disruptive behaviors likely to hinder positive outcomes, such as unjustifiably terminating discussions; causing abnormal delays; disregarding the foreseen procedures; and systematically refusing to consider the other parties' proposals or interests.[27] The treaty-negotiations duty also entails good-faith mutual acceptance of communications and contacts so as to enable goodwill on both sides and a conducive environment for an agreement to be reached. These requirements apply to both procedure and substance, i.e., to how states negotiate and to what they propose, to the effect of demonstrating appropriate understanding and meaningful consideration of the interests of the opposing state – during negotiations and in the design of the final solution.[28]

Complementarily, the ICJ unpacks the duty to enter into negotiations towards the goal of reaching an agreement as a special application of the principle of peaceful dispute settlement codified in Article 33 of the UN Charter. According to the Court's Ruling in the North Sea Continental Shelf Cases, the parties to the dispute must keep in mind their ultimate goal – the agreement, "and not merely ... go through a formal process of negotiation".[29] Engaging in meaningful interactions is the opposite of "when either of them insists upon its own position without contemplating any modification of it".[30]

Case Study 16: Fisheries Jurisdiction Case

The Fisheries Jurisdiction Case deals with the common interest of the UK and Iceland in sustainable development and conservation of marine biodiversity. The case involves the risk of overexploitation of fishery resources on which both countries depend – a risk calling for the intro-

25 *Id*, p. 306–7.

26 *Id*, p. 308.

27 *Id*, p. 307.

28 *Id*, p. 308, 317.

29 ICJ, *Cases Concerning the North Sea Continental Shelf* (Germany *v.* Denmark & Germany *v.* Netherlands), Judgment of 20 Feb 1969, ICJ Reports 3 (1969) ('North Sea Continental Shelf Cases'), p. 47.

30 *Ibid.*

duction of jointly agreed environmental protection measures, such as catch or spatial limitations, "for the benefit of all"[31] – i.e., measures to safeguard shared concerns. Per the Court, an obligation to negotiate in good faith entails, *inter alia*, giving "due regard to the interests of other states in [resource] conservation and equitable exploitation";[32] exercising exploitation rights "to the extent compatible with"[33] protecting the common interest at stake; and monitoring the state of fishery resources. The Court also calls on states to "examine together, in the light of scientific and other available information, such measures as may be required for [resource] conservation and development, and equitable exploitation"[34] – within the framework of existing or future treaties that may result from continued negotiations.

The above precedents illuminate the possible meaning, under the Theory, of the duty to enter into negotiations on a Basin Treaty, where appropriate to ensure compliance with the duty of good-faith cooperation as framed by the Theory. In short, we are dealing here with a *due-diligence* obligation, i.e., to enter into good-faith treaty negotiations; and not with an obligation of result, which would mean actually adopting the sought-out treaty. Further, this obligation is not autonomous, but rather ancillary to accepted customary duties under the law of transboundary basins.

1.3 *Conclusions*

Community-of-Interests informs the codification and clarification of the rules of equitable and reasonable use, harm prevention and general cooperation.

Underpinned by Community-of-Interests, the UNWC and the Revised SADC Protocol expand on previous attempts at codification of equitable and reasonable use, such as through the introduction of the criterium of protection of the watercourse. The same evolution in how equitable and reasonable use is codified happens under the 1995 SADC and Lake Victoria Protocols. In these treaty precedents, the rule at hand gains a greater role in advancing common interests and explicitly recognizes the need for joint action alongside domestic measures.

The same happens with harm prevention, as is clear when we compare the language used in a traditional watercourse agreement *versus* a Basin Treaty.

31 ICJ, *Fisheries Jurisdiction* (UK *v.* Iceland), Merits, Judgment of 25 July 1974, ICJ Reports 3 (1974), p. 31 ('Fisheries Jurisdiction Case').

32 *Id*, p. 35.

33 *Ibid.*

34 *Id*, p. 34–5.

Here, joint action is emphasized along domestic efforts and, as a manifestation of Close Basin Cooperation, may become binding when playing a supportive role to the general obligation of states to diligently prevent transboundary harm through the use of the watercourse.

On cooperation, agreements framed by Community-of-Interests specify the content of the general duty to cooperate with references to mutual benefit and good faith. The good-faith qualifier, which permeates international law, may give rise to obligations ancillary to the duty co-basing states have to cooperate with each other and, where appropriate, this cooperation comprises, along with other dimensions, the obligation to enter into negotiations with a genuine intent to arrive at a Basin Treaty.

2 International Water Law Application and Interpretation

To the extent that embracing one or more of the Theory's elements appears necessary for a basin state to comply diligently and in good faith with its duties, Community-of-Interests enhances the normative ambit of the relevant rules by underlying their application and interpretation in concrete cases. In such instances, through the binding force of accepted rules, Community-of-Interests informs collaboration requirements accessory or ancillary to equitable and reasonable use, harm prevention and cooperation, both when the Theory appears implicitly in a treaty and when it is expressly stated therein. The Theory does so, *where appropriate*, through its normative elements.

2.1 *Equitable and Reasonable Use and Harm Prevention*

The way Community-of-Interests frames international water law interpretation and application in relation to equitable and reasonable use is illustrated by the River Oder and Gabčíkovo Decisions. Interpreting the two Rulings together, we find the Theory being placed as a bridge between relevant values (justice and utility) and a rule of international water law (equitable and reasonable use).

In the River Oder Case, the PCIJ relates Community-of-Interests with "fulfilling the requirements of *justice* and the considerations of *utility*".[35] We see justice and utility here as values embedded in the Theory and inherent to the management of transboundary basins. In the Gabčíkovo Decision, Commu-

35 River Oder Case, *supra*, p. 27 (emphasis added).

nity-of-Interests is invoked in direct connection to the rule of equitable and reasonable use, underpinning that rule's application to a concrete case.

Comparably, the North Sea Continental Shelf Cases deal with the application of equitable principles to delimitation negotiations on adjacent continental shelfs. There, the ICJ considers that, from a conceptual perspective, or "as a matter of abstract justice",[36] its "decisions must by definition be just, and therefore in that sense equitable";[37] and that, concretely, a decision based on the rule of equity "finds its objective justification in considerations lying not outside but within the rules [calling] for the application of equitable principles."[38] In the case in question, therefore: "On a foundation of very general precepts of justice and good faith, actual rules of law are here involved"[39] – actual rules which require "the application of equitable principles".[40]

The three Decisions above are founded on the rule of equity and, indirectly, on equitable principles and on the value of justice – all of which fall within the legal realm. Applying specifically to international water law, the River Oder and Gabčíkovo Decisions invoke Community-of-Interests to interlink justice and equity and equitable and reasonable use; and this interlinkage characterizes how Community-of-Interests may underpin the interpretation and application of a rule of international water law.

The Theory may do the same through the Basin Scope, Close Basin Cooperation requirements and Social Basin Engagement. When commenting on the harm-prevention rule, the ILC explains how the systemic nature of an international watercourse means that "human intervention at one point ... may have effects elsewhere [and so] equitable utilization could be affected, or significant harm caused",[41] because of the river's unity along its entire length. The Commentary hints at the possibility of the longitudinal dimension of the Basin Scope gaining binding power under specific circumstances, i.e., acting and cooperating within the framework of an integrated approach to a watercourse system would become mandatory when doing so were necessary to comply with harm prevention and equitable and reasonable use.

This may be the case, for example, when activities on a tributary entirely within 'State A' may significantly impair the mainstem flowing only through 'State B'. Here, applying certain elements of Community-of-Interests may no

36 North Sea Continental Shelf Cases, *supra*, p. 47.
37 *Id*, p. 48.
38 *Ibid.*
39 *Id*, p. 46.
40 *Id*, p. 47.
41 ILC Draft Articles (1994), *supra*, p. 90–1.

longer be an option or a strongly recommended good practice, but an ancillary obligation for State A to abide by the law of transboundary basins, regardless of the existence of a watercourse agreement determining as much. In a scenario of deep interdependence, considering the basin as a whole, engaging in joint action, and involving stakeholders across the border may be *sine qua non* for meeting the due diligence requirements under the harm-prevention rule. There is nothing in Article 7(1) of the UNWC and in Article 2(1) of the ECEWC to imply that the envisioned appropriate measures are limited to those that may be adopted unilaterally within the state of origin; and, if cooperative measures are subsumed under that expression, it may be that cooperation in a given case must be close and system-wide in relation to the tributary and the mainstem, in order to be effective in meeting the obligations at stake.

Consider the UNWC provisions governing the adoption of context-specific treaties. Thereunder, the Basin Scope, under certain circumstances and via accepted rules of Limited Territorial Sovereignty, may frame concrete rights and obligations – in this case, constrain states' freedom to enter into partial agreements. The right of a third riparian state to participate in related negotiations emerges from the unity of an international watercourse and thus from Community-of-Interests. Yet, such a right is not absolute; it is only triggered when the unity of the system generates circumstances relevant under international law, namely, the possibility of the partial agreement significantly affecting that third state's interests and rights in the watercourse. In other words, if the state concerned "would not be [so] affected ..., the physical unity of the watercourse does not of itself require that the state have these rights".[42]

Conversely, where the interest of another riparian state is at risk, Community-of-Interests informs the interpretation and application of the harm-prevention rule and correlated international law obligations. The consequence is that a specific obligation would then arise for the state implementing the project, an obligation to apply the Basin Scope to the planning, consultation and implementation process with the potentially affected co-riparian. Framed by the Basin Scope, joint-action obligations (Close Basin Cooperation) and requirements for cross-border consultations (Social Basin Engagement) could also arise.

Case Study 17: Amazon Basin and Dam Planning

Best practices around dams stress basin-wide impact assessments as part of broader transboundary infrastructure planning.[43] Yet, in the

42 *Id*, p. 96.

43 World Commission on Dams (WCD), *Dams and Development: A New Framework for Decision-Making* (Earthscan 2000) ('WCD Report'), p. 306–7.

Amazon, multipurpose dam planning and construction have been "a chaotic, project-focused endeavor with little regard for the larger regional picture."[44] This still prevailing practice is not conducive to optimal and sustainable dam-siting and to the consideration of connectivity impacts on a basin scale. For millions of years, profound physical connections have existed between the River Amazon and its headwaters in the Andes: most sediments, nutrients and organic matter feeding the Amazon mainstem and sustaining its rich floodplains and biodiversity come from Andean tributaries – which also serve as spawning grounds for fisheries of significant economic and ecological value, including long-distance migratory species. Continued system fragmentation through dam construction on still largely free-flowing Andean tributaries, by failing to consider the entire basin, could lead to large-scale, serious and unpredictable impacts.[45] From a scientific perspective, "the placement of dams within a river network and relative to one another is just as important to consider as the total number and size of the dams."[46] As with dam-building, the "large-scale development of agriculture, mining, oil and gas, … timber and fisheries in the Amazon in the last three decades have set the environmental stage for the *necessity* of IRBM"[47] – thus, in a transboundary context, of the Basin Scope.

In the Amazon,[48] as elsewhere, transboundary basin-wide assessments are often constrained by the lack of reliable, consistent and/or comprehensive data across riparian countries, e.g., on the nature and location of infrastructure projects, the river routes used by aquatic migratory species, the state of fisheries that support local livelihoods, and the location of key biodiversity aquatic areas. These challenges further strengthen the case for basin-scale interstate efforts that generate the regional data required "to complement localized planning [and] identify more effectively the most sustainable, and the most destructive, dam locations."[49]

On this basis, in order to prevent significant transboundary harm, while pursuing equitable and reasonable use, basin states in situations similar to the Amazon riparians might already be under a requirement to apply the The-

44 Finer & Jenkins, *supra*, p. 6.
45 *Id*, p. 1–2.
46 *Id*, p. 2.
47 Amazon Waters Initiative, *supra*.
48 Finer & Jenkins, *supra*, p. 1, 6.
49 *Id*, p. 6.

ory by treating and cooperating on their shared resource as a unitary whole. This may include, in line with the Basin Scope and Close Basin Cooperation, as appropriate, comprehensive catchment-wide planning; data generation along the entire watercourse system and across the basin; and evaluation of impacts of existing and future dams – ultimately allowing infrastructure planning in optimal ways that mitigate environmental harm and the risk of transboundary impacts, while enabling socioeconomic benefits.

As they advance their Community-of-Interests regimes, co-riparians may consider broadening collaboration beyond dams *per se*. By placing dams within the context of cross-sectoral planning, riparian states may come to realize that certain projects become unnecessary when related needs can be met through existing infrastructure within the basin; or else that collaborative interventions framed by the water-food-energy nexus can lead to a wider basket of common interests being achieved. Biswas, for example, refers to a partnership between Bhutan and India involving a scheme of cost- and benefit-sharing in the Brahmaputra basin in connection with projects on hydropower, agriculture, industry, intermodal transportation, and environmental protection.[50] Biswas' example about integrated water planning carries lessons for multisectoral projects and programs conceptualized at the basin level.

The Pulp Mills Decision further contributes to elucidating the where-appropriate legal trigger for the mandatory consideration of the Basin Scope as ancillary to harm prevention and equitable and reasonable use. When ruling on the disputed breadth of its jurisdiction, the Court considers Argentina's claims regarding various transboundary environmental impacts and determines which among them involve the Statute's interpretation and application, within the meaning of its compromissory clause. Argentina alleges treaty violations on the part of Uruguay through various types of environmental harm that would be reaching across the border – from direct water quality impacts to broader effects occurring within the space of the basin but not affecting the watercourse or its ecosystems. Purported broader effects include air pollution, noise, visual nuisance, and impacts on tourism from bad odors. According to Uruguay, the Statute applies to "any pollution or type of harm caused to the River Uruguay, or to organisms living there",[51] including "air pollution which

50 A.K. Biswas, *Water and Regional Development*, *in* A.K. Biswas, O. Ünver, C. Tortajada eds, Water as a Focus for Regional Development (OUP 2004), p. 4, 10–12.

51 Pulp Mills case, *supra*, p. 25.

has harmful effects on the quality of the waters of the river or on the aquatic environment";[52] but otherwise not to "every type of environmental damage."[53]

In deciding on the matter, the ICJ states that its jurisdiction only encompasses claims founded on the River Uruguay Statute and thus falling within its scope. According to the Court, within the meaning of Article 36,[54] this is not the case with regard to noise pollution, visual nuisance, and bad odors, absent a demonstrated relationship between those impacts and the aquatic environment.[55] The Court thus clarifies the Statute's scope, founded on the watercourse, its ecosystems, and the surrounding environment. Conversely, where appropriate, i.e., if a clear connection exists between harmful effects from unilateral activities taking place in the surrounding environment and the health of the watercourse itself, the parties' obligation to take all measures to prevent transboundary impact entails application of the Basin Scope and possibly of other normative element of Community-of-Interests, as further explored next.

2.2 *General Duty to Cooperate*

Community-of-Interests guides states in pinpointing how collaborative engagement ought to unfold in different situations, thereby underpinning the interpretation and application of the duty to cooperate. Specifically, the Theory may inform the interpretation of the duty to cooperate as giving rise to joint-action requirements.

Implicit joint-action obligations may arise, for example, in relation to the collaborative design of a basin plan that brings different elements of freshwater management into one comprehensive, coherent, and systematic package, setting out targets and strategic actions, enabling harmonization of national development agendas, identifying benefit-sharing opportunities, and fostering cooperation among national authorities and stakeholders.[56] Experts emphasize the "*need for* [an Amazon basin] strategic plan to maintain free-flowing connectivity ... from headwaters to estuary"[57] – a joint management plan identifying and setting aside for protection priority tributary systems.

---

52 *Ibid.*

53 *Ibid.*

54 Refers to the maintenance of a healthy ecological status and the control of harmful conditions "in the river *and the areas affected* by it." (emphasis added).

55 Pulp Mills Case, *supra*, p. 26.

56 *See* ICWE Report, *supra*, p. 23; Dushanbe Declaration, *supra*, Preamble, ¶11, Body, ¶8.

57 Finer & Jenkins, *supra*, p. 6 (emphasis added).

In the treaties founded on Community-of-Interests, the Theory plays this function of influencing the interpretation and application of the cooperation duty across different provisions.

Being framed by Community-of-Interests, all UNWC Articles governing the common interests of states in water use, protection and management may demand joint action – whether or not the provision in question includes the formula '*individually and, where appropriate, jointly*' – if needed to ensure compliance with the duty to protect and preserve the ecosystems of shared basins. For example, Article 23 requires basin countries, where necessary to protect and preserve the marine environment as it may be affected through an international watercourse, to act *in cooperation with other states*. Although the provision refers to interstate cooperation in general, a requirement for joint action under Article 23 emerges where necessary to safeguard coastal and oceanic ecosystems, e.g., as appropriate "to protect the marine environment from pollution carried there by an international watercourse."[58]

Article 6(2) ECEWC requires collaborative water planning and management through the design, adoption and implementation of policies, programs, and strategies, with the goals of transboundary impact prevention, control and reduction, and environmental protection. Although there is no reference to joint action in the Article, this modality of state engagement might be required to perform a double function: facilitating compliance by states with the harm-prevention rule, while enabling co-riparian parties to pursue their overarching common interest in environmental sustainability. In such cases, Community-of-Interests underpins the duty to cooperate in good faith.

Articles 17, 19 and 20 of the Lake Victoria Protocol govern pollution by outlining state obligations in connection with economic incentives and discharge fees; regulation, enforcement and liability; mining, agriculture and forestry; municipal waste discharge into the Lake; land use planning and soil conservation; and sanitation and hygiene. The Protocol does not specify that states may also be required to act jointly in the pursuit of common water-quality goals. Yet, because Community-of-Interests informs the application and interpretation of the entire Protocol, a requirement of joint pollution prevention and minimization could be triggered, where appropriate to demonstrate compliance with good-faith cooperation. Such action, for example, could take the form of jointly crafted regulations or guidelines, based on which national measures would then be designed and implemented.

58 ILC (1994), *supra*, p. 125.

Moreover, Article 16(3)–(4) of the Lake Victoria Protocol determines that, when faced with an environmental threat, parties "shall undertake … precautionary and preemptive measures … even where there is no scientific certainty, according to their capabilities". When viewed within the Theory's framework, the requirement to act with caution in the face of risk may entail common efforts, as appropriate, even if the above provisions do not mention joint action or even cooperation explicitly.

2.3 *Conclusions*

In order to secure full compliance with equitable and reasonable use and harm prevention, states may be compelled to follow the Basin Scope in all its dimensions. Put differently, Community-of-Interests may reinterpret those two rules to turn them into a requirement for closer, deeper, long-term, and dynamic transboundary interstate relations; and so, to adapt equitable and reasonable use and harm prevention to an increasingly interconnected and rapidly changing world, in which where-appropriate situations are becoming ever more obvious and frequent.

Under Community-of-Interests, moreover, a joint-action requirement is triggered when necessary, *or appropriate*, to safeguard common interests or enable coexistence, as underpinned by the basic rules of international water law. In specific cases, other elements of the Theory may also be relevant, such as the principle of nondiscrimination as part of Social Basin Engagement. This is arguably the case even in the absence of specific provisions within the Basin Treaty spelling out a joint-action requirement to address the problem in question.

3 Progressive Development in International Water Law

> *[I]n international law as in every other system of law, the existing law should be questioned from time to time – this is the surest way of furthering its progressive development.*[59]

In addition to informing the codification, clarification, application, and interpretation of existing rules of international water law, Community-of-Interests may be contributing to progressive legal development through its primary elements.

---

59 Fisheries Jurisdiction Case, *supra*, p. 38, *Declaration*, Judge Ignacio-Pinto.

This contribution relates to equitable and reasonable Participation and, otherwise, could eventually lead to the emergence of norms associated with the Basin Scope, the Basin Treaty and the Basin Body.

3.1 *Participation*

Community-of-Interests has possibly informed the progressive development of international law through the design of equitable and reasonable Participation, a normative standard laid out in the UNWC and reiterated in the Revised SADC Protocol and applied more widely within the communities-of-basin-interests examined here.

The book has already examined the concept of Participation in detail, as a component of Close Basin Cooperation often operating together with joint action. Here, the focus is on connecting equitable and reasonable Participation and progressive legal development as framed by Community-of-Interests.

The norm formulated in Paragraph 2 of Article 5 of the UNWC "complements",[60] "flows from, and is bound up with",[61] equitable and reasonable use. Equitable and reasonable Participation is also linked to, while specifying the normative content of, the general obligation to cooperate in Article 8, by calling, specifically, for active cooperation.[62] Hence, Participation under the UNWC regime remains subject to equity considerations and falls under the umbrella of general cooperation.

These linkages notwithstanding, under the UNWC, equitable and reasonable Participation stands itself as a rule, supportive of, but still independent from, the duty to cooperate and the rule of equitable and reasonable use. Confirming this rule's autonomy, with the potential to gain customary status in its own right, the ILC recommends the adoption of water treaties to regulate collaboration based on equitable and reasonable Participation but makes clear that "the obligation and correlative right … are not dependent on a specific agreement for their implementation".[63]

Beyond the UNWC and the Revised SADC Protocol, Participation is present in other sources unequivocally reflecting Community-of-Interests. Participation is captured in the definition of the term *cooperation* in Article 1(6) of the

60 ILC (1994), *supra*, p. 97.
61 *Ibid.*
62 *Ibid.*
63 *Ibid.*

Ecuador-Peru Agreement, namely: "the general obligation of the countries to *participate jointly* and in good-faith in the management of water resources in transboundary basins". Building on this definition, Article 8(a) tasks the Binational Commission with the design of strategies to promote transboundary IWRM towards the establishment of coordination, joint action and Participation mechanisms. Finally, under Article 11(i) of the Regulation, the Basin Body promotes Participation of the two states in the integrated management of shared water resources.

The Rhine Chlorides Regime also embraces Participation, with the difference that the basis for sharing there is Solidarity, and not equity, as under the UNWC. The Solidarity-based cost-sharing mechanism finances pollution control activities carried out primarily within France. The mechanism is jointly designed, agreed-upon, and financed among the states concerned, on the basis of a predefined cost-sharing formula. Parties thus participate by financing cleanup efforts within a single country that benefit them all. This is the optimal solution found by parties during negotiations, considering that, only in the case of France, it had been possible to single out the main pollution source, namely, the Alsace Potassium Mines.[64] Participation in cost-sharing under the Regime entails both joint and domestic measures. The Protocol governs water quality protection by providing for the joint financing of agreed measures by France and the Netherlands.[65] At the same time, Article 5 of the Rhine Chlorides Protocol requires each party, within its respective portion of the basin, to prevent an increase in chlorides discharges into the river; as well as to monitor chloride-ion discharges above 1 kg/s. Per Article 12(1), each party is "responsible at the agreed measuring stations for the installation and operation of the measuring equipment and system used to monitor the concentration of chloride ions in the waters".

Precedents of states proactively participating in the management, use, and protection of international watercourses exist beyond the treaties examined here.

Case Study 18: US-Mexico

Adopted under the auspices of the *International Boundary and Water Commission*, Resolution 12 of Minute 331, a regulation for the use and management of the Rio Grande, foresees mutually beneficial efforts by

64 Boisson de Chazournes (2008), *supra*, p. 1.

65 Chlorides Case, *supra*, p. 40.

both countries to "explore joint cooperative actions that could include US investment in water conservation projects in Mexico".[66]

Case Study 19: Canada-US
The *Summary of the Agreement in Principle to Modernize the Columbia River Treaty Regime* foresees flood risk management within Canada to protect the US downstream. The US would be entitled to pre-planned storage space behind Canadian dams, so as to enable the management of high flows originating in Canada and maintain predictable flows in the Columbia Basin. The US would then compensate Canada with monetary payments for those services. Shared benefits from this scheme would advance common interests around shipping operations, irrigation and agriculture, recreation, and protection of regional salmon populations.[67]

Participation guides states in pursuing mutually beneficial cooperation within the framework of Community-of-Interests. Guided by positive cooperation, states within a community-of-basin-interests share the waters *and* the benefits associated therewith. Yet, with the brief analysis conducted above, it is not possible to affirm with certainty that Participation has crystalized as a customary law norm.

The consolidation and more widespread uptake of Participation would serve two key purposes towards strengthening international water law, as it moves from Limited Territorial Sovereignty towards Community-of-Interests: to infuse affirmative normative content into the vague duty of co-basin countries to cooperate in good faith when addressing common interests; and to overcome the limited focus of equitable and reasonable use on coexistence and unilateral restraint.

Going forward, Participation may become a necessity for countries to meet water security and sustainability concerns, as expressions of common goals, but also potential triggers for aggravating conflicting interests. To illustrate, consider how Colombia approaches the need for basin plans. Per Article 314

66 IBWC, *supra*.

67 Office of the Spokesperson, *Factsheet: Summary of the Agreement in Principle to Modernize the Columbia River Treaty Regime*, (11 July 2024); Government of British Colombia, Negotiations to Modernize the Columbia River Treaty, *Agreement-in-Principle Content* (on file).

(d) of the *National Environment Code*,[68] the State must coordinate and promote the sustainable development of managed basins. According to Article 316, the *management* of a basin means planning for the coordinated use of its land, water, flora, and fauna. Per Article 318, the State must determine that a given basin be so managed – and thus, that a management plan be developed – when ecological, economic, and social conditions exist that require as much. In Colombia, therefore, designing a management plan for an individual basin is not an absolute legal requirement, but doing so may become mandatory for the administration where specific circumstances so demand, which are bound to grow in importance as countries become increasingly vulnerable to climate and other impacts.

As at the domestic level, international law is likely to move in the same direction, with the progressive legal consolidation of Participation – *inter alia*, in the design of basin-wide management plans – as informed by Community-of-Interests.

3.2 *Normative Status of the Primary Elements of Community-of-Interests*

Another way to evaluate the influence of Community-of-Interests in legal progressive development is to examine the normative status of its primary elements themselves, in particular, the Basin Scope, the Basin Treaty, and the Basin Body. Said analysis, to be authoritative, ought to be developed on the basis of the classic sources of international law and in light of state practice and opinion, including at the domestic level.

Given the complexity of the matter, the book does not purport to exhaust the discussion, much less to provide definitive answers as to the status of those three normative elements in international law. Ours is a *preliminary* investigation aimed at directing how a more thorough review of sources could determine which among those elements, if any, might be undergoing a process of legal crystallization in its own right – or else the prospects for this crystallization eventually happening.

Were it possible to identify an emerging rule among the Theory's elements, then a strong argument could be made that Community-of-Interests is indeed informing progressive development by potentially giving rise to new duties in the field. Such a finding would strengthen the persuasive legal force of the Theory itself.

---

68 Decreto-Ley 2811 (1974), *Código Nacional de Recursos Naturales Renovables y de Protección al Medio Ambiente* ('National Environment Code').

Basin Scope: The Basin Scope encourages the involvement of all states within a basin or sub-basin; and, as appropriate, cooperation among all such states across the entire biogeographic unit to safeguard and advance common interests. The ILC notes how countries generally "recognize in their practice the importance of dealing with international watercourse systems in their entirety."[69]

Globally, there are examples of cooperation involving all basin states and applying across the entire natural unit, and a trend exists in that same direction. When commenting on levels of transboundary IWRM implementation, the UN so addresses the question of geographic scope: "negotiations have moved more from being bilateral to multilateral, *basin-wide*".[70] In the Ganges-Brahmaputra, Swain reports that India, Bangladesh, Nepal, and Bhutan are attempting to cooperate with one another at the sub-basin level for resource management and development, *inter alia*, through hydropower and navigation, as they begin to transition from strict bilateralism to catchment-based multilateralism.[71] On vertical connectivity, UNECE *et al* observe "a greater willingness of countries … to interpret river and lake basin arrangements in a way that recognizes connected aquifers".[72]

Yet, persistent bilateralism remains predominant in certain places and most internationally shared water systems still lack cooperative frameworks adequately designed to enable integrated river basin management in a transboundary context. Aquifers, in particular, are typically excluded from the geographic scope of watercourse agreements.

Case Study 20: Tigris-Euphrates Basin

In the Tigris-Euphrates, although there are more than two basin states, bilateral water allocation agreements are limited in both geographic and thematic scope, covering only the Euphrates portion of the watercourse system – between Turkey and Syria (1987) and between Syria and Iraq (1990), respectively. In addition, Turkey, Syria, and Iraq are members of the *Joint Technical Committee* (JTC), created in the early 1980s. However, unilateralism and lack of coordination prevail, since the three co-basin

69 ILC (1994), *supra*, p. 91.

70 Unturbe, *supra*, p. 29 (emphasis added).

71 A. Swain, *Water Cooperation on the Ganges–Brahmaputra River,* Course on Governance for Transboundary Freshwater Security: 1b. Case study, *at* https://learning.edx.org/course/course-v1:SDGAcademyX+TBW001+2T2020/block-v1:SDGAcademyX+TBW001+2T2020+type@sequential+block@ca04fe41d0e146b3a75695f0a712ac66/block-v1:SDGAcademyX+TBW001+2T2020+type@vertical+block@3ced3eea0f1a4d98af18fa99f7b79d6b.

72 UNECE *et al*, *supra*, p. 11.

states have yet to agree on a set of clear JTC competences and to use Committee meetings as a space for identifying shared interests and common challenges and for exchanging on relevant domestic policies and practices.[73]

Hence, it is not possible to claim now that the Basin Scope amounts to a general requirement under international customary law. If not for certain an existing or emerging customary norm, could the Basin Scope qualify as a *principle of international water law* or a *general principle of law*?

In the operative part of the River Oder Decision, the PCIJ concludes that the governing norm capable of settling the question of jurisdiction "is the *principle* laid down"[74] in Article 331 of the Treaty of Versailles. The provision in question captures the longitudinal dimension of the Basin Scope, as applied to navigation. Here, therefore, the PCIJ conceives of the longitudinal dimension of the Basin Scope as a principle of navigation law. Yet, the Decision offers little to clarify the normative status of the Theory's scope beyond navigation.

The third path for investigating the status of the Basin Scope in international law is based on the element's significant penetration in domestic legislation (albeit under varying rubrics), across various regions and legal systems. Indeed, most states are actively engaged in IWRM implementation efforts; have developed IWRM plans; and have adopted laws and policies informed by integrated basin approaches.[75]

Brazil, a major basin country in the Amazon and Plata basins, among other transboundary waters, is a case in point. Federal Law 9433/97 considers the river basin as the fundamental territorial unit for purposes of planning and implementation, taking account of the interactions across water, land and living resources, and the connections between surface and underground waters.[76] In Articles 6 to 8, Law 9433/97 mandates and regulates the elaboration of plans at the basin, state, and national levels to guide integrated water management nationwide. In regulating this Law, Article 2 of Resolution CNRH

73 A. Kibaroğlu, *Water Security and Peace on the Euphrates-Tigris River*, Course on Governance for Transboundary Freshwater Security: 1d. Case Study, *at* https://learning.edx.org/course/course-v1:SDGAcademyX+TBW001+2T2020/block-v1:SDGAcademyX+TBW001+2T2020+type@sequential+block@832541b7e8c14205a836e2f2c45e7234/block-v1:SDGAcademyX+TBW001+2T2020+type@vertical+block@d2fbea28c1fd48bf815667354ea20ed1.

74 River Oder Case, *supra*, p. 32 (emphasis added).

75 UN Water (2018), *supra*, p. 84; Unturbe, *supra*, p. 29.

76 Federal Law 9433/97 (8 Jan 1997) (*Política Nacional de Recursos Hídricos*) ('National Water Resources Policy Act').

22/2002 requires those management plans to describe the interrelations between aquifers and other surface and underground systems of water, as well as with the surrounding environment, in order to enable integrated management,[77] i.e., the Basin Scope.

In Colombia, Article 312 of the *National Environment Code* describes the drainage basin in line with the Helsinki Rules definition, including therein both surface and groundwaters and, otherwise, both permanent and intermittent streams. In further promoting conjunctive management, Article 313 deals with the possibility of an aquifer system connected to a given basin not coinciding entirely with the latter's watershed. In such an event, for planning purposes, the basin area will be extended to include the entire aquifer system.

Article 314 of the same Code outlines broad and cross-cutting government functions and powers so as to enable the integrated management of surface waters, groundwaters, and atmospheric waters; the water, land and living resources within the basin; water resources *per se*, the channels through which they flow, and the aquatic ecosystems that depend thereon; water quantity and quality; basin planning, development, and conservation; and the environment, social and economic factors influencing decision-making and priority-setting. Article 315 governs inter-basin transfers by imposing a requirement of prior authorization for the transfer of the water itself to another basin; and for the use of services that water provides, such as electricity, outside the basin of origin. The Code does not forbid but controls inter-basin transfers, indicating that each individual basin remains the primary – albeit not exclusive – biogeographic unit for planning.

In line with the above, there may be an argument to make that Community-of-Interests has influenced progressive legal development by fostering the emergence of the Basin Scope as a general principle of law. More thorough research, however, is necessary to investigate the element's uptake in national legal systems and the theory of formation of such sources of international law.

Basin Treaty and Basin Body: These two primary elements of Community-of-Interests are intimately related and, when combined, form the cooperation regimes within which communities-of-basin-interests flourish.

The legal status of *watercourse agreements*, generally considered, has been approached by courts and scholars in the context of the rejection of the concept of mutual consent. According to the ILC, building on state practice and

77 National Water Resources Council (Conselho Nacional de Recursos Hídricos), Res 22/2002 (24 May 2002).

international decisions, basin states are under no "obligation to conclude an agreement *before using* the waters of the international watercourse".[78]

Affirming, however, that an obligation to enter into watercourse does not exist in relation to unilateral projects does not provide a satisfactory answer to the question of whether co-basin states have an obligation to enter into a basin agreement or arrangement, not as a precondition for the unilateral use of the resource, but to enable sustainable long-term management, in line with Community-of-Interests. The Basin Treaty is concerned with but transcends specific development projects, in order to govern a broader joint planning outlook across the basin. Hence, when we ask if the applicable law requires states to enter into watercourse agreements, such an obligation could exist even if it is not a prerequisite for the unilateral use of shared basins.

As a key precedent here, the ECEWC codifies an obligation for co-riparian parties to conclude agreements or arrangements and places such instruments, together with joint bodies, at the heart of its cooperation requirements, without forbidding unilateral use pending negotiations. The ECEWC does not link the obligation to adopt agreements or arrangements to a veto power in relation to planned measures; nowhere does it state that, until such instruments are in place, states may not unilaterally develop transboundary waters.

In scholarship, Rieu-Clarke *et al* take this wider perspective when addressing the status of watercourse agreements. The authors consider that entering into specific agreements is not required but recommended so that shared catchments may be effectively managed and developed.[79] Those authors, however, do not provide an exhaustive analysis of current state practice and opinion.

Doubts also remain with regard to *joint bodies*. After all, the establishment of a joint commission requires the states concerned to adopt some kind of instrument clarifying the body's legal status and determining its mandate. If it is uncertain that adopting such instruments can be seen as a duty under customary law, it would be logical to extend this same lack of clarity to the creation of joint bodies.

This conclusion is reinforced by the dissent in scholarship on the matter. Benvenisti finds that current international water law does not include a rule requiring institutional cooperation. Neither could Tanzi and Arcari locate extensive *opinio juris* indicating the existence of an obligation on states to

78 ILC Draft Articles (1994), *supra*, p. 94 (emphasis added).

79 A. Rieu-Clarke, R. Moynihan, B.O. Magsig, *UN Watercourses Convention User's Guide* (UNESCO 2012), p. 94.

establish basin organizations.[80] Yet, relevant widespread state practice "can be ascertained to be based at least on a consistent *opinio necessitatis*".[81]

For Boisson de Chazournes, in contrast, the establishment of joint bodies should not be "expected to flow ... from the good will"[82] of co-basin states; and thus, water law actually requires such countries to create the appropriate institutions to support the sustainable management of transboundary waters: "What still needs to be clarified ... is the range of functions to be accomplished by those mechanisms".[83]

Looking into the future, the International Law Association states, with regard to Article 64 of the Berlin Rules and other provisions not reflecting existing custom, that "such progressively developed rules will [soon] become settled customary international law". But no further evidence is provided.

That this debate appears to be ongoing should not, as it has been argued, "cloud the urgent necessity of the creation of such a legal rule and to its existence already as a rule of international morality as well as of the community of Nations".[84]

Legal Effects of Successful Codifications: Where there is debate on the status or content of customary norms, successful codification efforts may contribute to clarifying open questions and thus to accelerating progressive legal development.[85] Given the uncertainty regarding the status of three of the elements of Community-of-Interests, what have the impacts been in connection with the entry into force of the UNWC and the global opening of the ECEWC? What would widespread endorsement of either or both Conventions mean for the progressive development of international law, as it pertains to the elements of the Theory?

Both the UNWC and the ECEWC strongly encourage but do not impose the Basin Scope. The Global Water Conventions then take different approaches when regulating watercourse agreements and bodies: whereas the UNWC strongly encourages, the ECEWC explicitly mandates the establishment of joint bodies through the agreements or arrangements riparian parties are required to adopt. Despite their different approaches, could both Conven-

80 Benvenisti, *supra*, p. 412.

81 Tanzi & Arcari, *supra*, p. 191. *See also* ILA (2004), *supra*, p. 404.

82 Boisson de Chazournes (2003), *supra*, p. 103.

83 *Id*, p. 105.

84 E.J. Manner & V.M. Metsälampi, *The Work of the International Law Association on the Law of International Water Resources* (Finnish Branch of International Law Association 1988), p. 172–3.

85 Dellapenna & Gupta (2013), *supra*, p. 6–7.

tions play a role in the development of customary rules linked to the Basin Treaty and the Basin Body?

Scholarship and jurisprudence have captured the role of treaties in the evolution of customary law. Such a role encompasses being "an important (and quite often the main) component of the practice accepted as law";[86] codification, such as with equitable and reasonable use in the UNWC; and progressive development, when treaties are seen as "crystalizing received or at least emergent"[87] custom. For Pellet, a fourth scenario arises when a treaty becomes "the point of departure"[88] for new custom to form. This is premised on the treaty provision in question being "supported by *consistent and representative* state practice".[89] Consistent and representative state practice exists for both water agreements and joint bodies.

In the North Sea Continental Shelf Cases, the ICJ considers the status in international customary law of the so-called equidistance principle as a delimitation method, in view of its codification in Article 6 of the Geneva Convention[90] and ensuing state practice. The ICJ assesses "the status of the principle as it stood when the Convention was drawn up, as it resulted from the effect of the Convention, and in the light of state practice subsequent to the Convention".[91] The Court concludes that the equidistance concept remains no more than a conventional rule, pointing to the insufficiency of state practice to demonstrate the alleged formation of customary law around that concept since the adoption of the Geneva Convention.

Before thus concluding, the ICJ develops a thorough analysis of what would be required for a conventional rule to give birth to a customary norm. The scenario proposed is that in which a given article, upon the treaty's adoption, expresses a purely conventional norm; later, if certain conditions are fulfilled, that same article progressively evolves into a rule-creating provision and, the rule therein embedded, into a custom. According to the ICJ, not only may this process unfold, but it has taken place throughout history; and, in fact, even if its development and conditions must be always carefully assessed, this pro-

86 A. Pellet, *Art.38, in* A. Zimmermann *et al* eds, The Statute of the International Court of Justice: A Commentary, 2nd ed (Oxford 2012), p. 849.

87 North Sea Continental Shelf Cases, *supra*, p. 43.

88 Pellet, *supra*, p. 849.

89 *Ibid* (emphasis added).

90 *Convention on the Continental Shelf* (Geneva, 29 April 1958) (in force 10 Jun 1964), 499 UNTS 311 (1965) ('Geneva Convention').

91 North Sea Continental Shelf Cases, *supra*, p. 37.

cess is a recognized method for new customary rules to emerge and crystallize within the body of international law.[92]

Based on the North Sea Continental Shelf Cases, the four conditions for customary law crystallization, which must be met concurrently, may be summarized per the paragraphs that follow.[93]

First, a *rule-creating essence* expresses the normative content of the provision in question. In the case of Article 6 of the Geneva Convention, the Court considers that, on the surface, it appears to possess such a character, but certain aspects thereof raise doubts, such as the placing of the equidistance principle *after* the obligation of delimitation by agreement – the latter thus becoming an express derogation of the former, which would be "an unusual preface to what is claimed to be a potential general rule of law";[94] the reference to *special circumstances* as another possible exception to the equidistance concept; and the significant lack of agreement on the precise normative content of the concept in question.

To compare, Article 9 of the ECEWC establishes the obligations about agreements/arrangements and bodies in the first sentences of each of its first two paragraphs, respectively; introduces Part II, where the provisions relating to riparian parties are outlined; and uses the term *shall* without any qualifiers or foreseen exceptions. Article 9 is drafted in a straightforward manner, with the obligations in question clearly formulated and prioritized – in the provision itself, in the context of the Convention as a whole and as a well-defined and understood (at least among parties) normative requirement deemed necessary to structure transboundary water cooperation. As such, the relevant parts of Article 9 arguably possess a norm-creating essence and, accordingly, have the potential to originate a new rule of international water law.

Second, *participation* refers to the conditions that must be met regarding the countries that join the convention. Specifically, those countries must represent a very widespread number, come from very representative locations, and encompass specially-affected nations.

The participation criterium for the ECEWC has yet to be met, but prospects for that to happen look increasingly positive. Current parties (57) stand at over ¼ of the number of UN member states (193) and come mainly from the Pan-European region. Yet, new ratifications, including from outside Europe and Central Asia, keep materializing and that has been the case for years. With regard to specially-affected states, in the present context, these would be the

92 *Id*, p. 41.

93 *Id*, p. 41–4.

94 *Id*, p. 42.

153 countries that share transboundary waters, just over 1/3 of which are represented among the current parties to ECEWC. Overall, bringing more countries into the fold has been a standing priority for the ECEWC parties and bodies.

Third, the criteria of *time and state practice* must be fulfilled. The ICJ ponders that the Geneva Convention had been in existence for a decade and, in force, for less than five years. The ECEWC, on the other hand, completed 33 years in 2025, having been in effect for almost three decades.

Failure to meet the requirement of time does "not necessarily, or of itself",[95] impede the progressive legal development process of a conventional rule. Yet, the correlated requisite of state practice is indispensable. The Court refers to state practice, including that of especially-affected countries, which is "*extensive and virtually uniform* in the sense of the provision invoked";[96] and carried out "in such a way as to show a general recognition that a rule of law or legal obligation is involved".[97]

To assess extensiveness and uniformity, the ICJ considers the number of cases of continental-shelf delimitation presented in relation to those yet to be delimited.[98] In our case, the number of delimitation cases translates into the proportion of transboundary basin area already covered by operational cooperation mechanisms vis-à-vis the total surface area of the globe drained by shared waters. This data is precisely what has been measured for the last few years by UN agencies and governments under the monitoring and reporting process for SDG Indicator 6.5.2. An *operational cooperation arrangement*, which can be based on a treaty or other arrangement,[99] entails a joint *body* being in place; interstate meetings and information exchange happening at least annually; and agreement on joint objectives, strategies or plans.[100] The emphasis on arrangements, joint bodies and joint action means that these elements are crucial tools for countries striving for progress towards water-related sustainable development goals.

As of 2024, among the 153 countries sharing freshwaters, 84% have provided data and the SDG 6.5.2 indicator value has been calculated for 117 states. Among those, 43 have 90% or more of their transboundary basins under oper-

95 *Id*, p. 43.
96 *Ibid* (emphasis added).
97 *Ibid.*
98 *Ibid.*
99 *Step-by-Step Monitoring Methodology for SDG Indicator 6.5.2* (2020), *at* https://unece.org/DAM/env/water/activities/Reporting_convention/SDG_652_Step-by-step_methodology_2020_ENG.pdf.
100 UNECE *et al*, *supra*, p. xx.

ational arrangements, but these instruments are absent in over 20 countries. Coverage of transboundary basin areas by operational arrangements, per country, averages 59%.[101]

These numbers indicate that, although agreements/arrangements and bodies for transboundary basins abound, much the world's transboundary surface and underground waters remain without effective legal and institutional cooperation frameworks among the basin states concerned. Ongoing monitoring efforts will enable the determination of whether state practice framed by Article 9(1)–(2) of the ECEWC eventually becomes representative and uniform, in addition to already being extensive and long-standing.

Fourth, the *opinio juris sive necessitatis* is probably the greatest obstacle to prove, eventually, that the ECEWC obligations in question have entered into the realm of international law as independent and binding norms. As the ICJ explains, there is no evidence or reason to presume that the states employing equidistance, whether or not parties to the Geneva Convention, had been doing so because "they believed themselves to be applying a mandatory rule of customary international law"[102] – or for other many possible reasons, such as courtesy, convenience or tradition. In other words, "acting, or agreeing to act, in a certain way, does not of itself demonstrate anything of a juridical nature".[103] Widespread and uniform state practice, even when collectively considered, does not amount to *opinio juris*. The existence of a customary rule cannot be proven without a demonstrated "sense of legal duty".[104]

It will not be a simple task, therefore, to assess whether, going forward, states not parties to the ECEWC, and which enter into future watercourse agreements and establish joint bodies do so out of a sense of obligation under international water law; or if other, more pragmatic factors, such as the desire to cooperate on infrastructure development or pollution control, are what motivates them in most cases.

Among parties, these, "presumably, so far as they [are] concerned, [act] actually or potentially in the application of the convention".[105] For other states, finding evidence of the element of *opinio juris* would be also a challenge unless future agreements explicitly state, or at least imply, that their adoption is motivated, among other factors, by a rule under international water law

101 *Id*, p. iii, xx, xxv.
102 North Sea Continental Shelf Cases, *supra*, p. 44.
103 *Ibid.*
104 *Ibid.*
105 *Id*, p. 43.

enjoining them to adopt water agreements/arrangements and create basin organizations.

In any case, as more countries join and implement the Global Water Conventions, the status of these framework instruments as codifications of international water law beyond those rules today recognized as custom would strength. The legal push for integrated river basin management would become more persuasive, given that both the UNWC and the ECEWC stress, promote and enable the Basin Scope.

The same is true for the Basin Treaty and the Basin Body. The international community has long recognized and increasingly emphasizes the legal and practical significance of cooperation regimes for sustained and effective interstate cooperation and the sustainability of transboundary waters. To briefly recap with some examples, experts, from the early 1990s, have recommended that states develop legal norms and institutions to govern, organize, coordinate, and implement transboundary basin management.[106] The 2009 *Istanbul Ministerial Statement* explicitly references *agreements/arrangements* and *institutions*.[107] A 2013 high-level declaration directly refers to *legal frameworks* and *river basin organizations*.[108] UNEP highlights the importance of having in place "a legal body that can attract and manage finances, supported by a clear and transparent legal framework and mandate".[109]

In literature, Kramer *et al* draw attention to the role of cooperation regimes as negotiation platforms conducive to confidence- and trust-building; and thus, capable of handling existing and potential conflicting interests, as well as shared concerns and mutually beneficial solutions. Regimes ensure that each country's interests are considered in decision-making, and common solutions are identified through the consolidation of basin-wide perspectives and jointly managed information.[110]

Going forward, where-appropriate *situations* are becoming increasingly visible, frequent, and widespread and that, along with growing interest in the ECEWC, might push state practice and opinion to accelerate the formation of rules involving treaties and bodies, with emphasis on those framed by the Theory for being better suited to tackle deepening interdependencies.

---

106 ICWE Report, *supra*, p. 40.

107 WWC (2009), *supra*, Ministerial Process, *Istanbul Ministerial Statement* (22 Mar 2009), ¶¶2, 9, 16.

108 Government of Tajikistan, High-Level International Conference on Water Cooperation (Dushanbe, Tajikistan, 20–21 Aug 2013), *Declaration* (20–21 Aug 2013).

109 UNEP (2021), *supra*, p. 60.

110 Kramer *et al*, *supra*, p. 10.

3.3 *Conclusions*

States widely recognize and are striving to implement IWRM, including in a transboundary context. In so doing, states are practicing Community-of-Interests. Proliferating state practice linked to widespread accessions to the global Conventions and faster endorsement of IWRM in connection with Agenda 2030 could trigger the revision or adoption of water agreements to reflect fully the physical reality that watercourses are *systems* of surface and underground waters and associated biodiversity, dependent upon and capable of affecting their wider drainage basin; and, as a rule, should be developed, managed, and protected as such. These combined processes could accelerate the emergence of the Basin Scope as a customary norm.

With regard to the Basin Treaty and the Basin Body, the ECEWC's attainment of global status strengthens the prospects that the endorsement of those elements will accelerate across regions. This is conditioned on the Convention progressively succeeding in boosting cooperation framed by the Theory, both among parties and non-parties; and that this happens ever more often because states feel legally compelled to so cooperate.

If we consider the evolving water challenge and the combined legal-political force of the UNWC, the ECEWC and Agenda 2030 in progressively building up state practice and *opinio juris* with respect to the Basin Scope and to legal-institutional regimes framed by Community-of-Interests, new customary rules or at least legal principles of international water law in this regard could progressively emerge, including on Participation. Already, SDG Indicator 6.5.2 "has inspired countries, such as those sharing the *Senegalo-Mauritanian Aquifer System*, to work together to accelerate progress on the adoption of arrangements and joint bodies for transboundary water cooperation or make existing arrangements operational".[111]

4 Conclusions

Global, regional and Basin Treaties demonstrate how Community-of-Interests frames the codification and clarification of equitable and reasonable use, harm prevention, and the obligation to cooperate, going further than previous attempts at codification. The basic norms of international water law are injected with a Community-of-Interests flavor to better safeguard common goals. Where appropriate, the elements of the Theory may become mandatory

111 UNECE *et al*, *supra*, p. xxv.

as ancillary to the above existing rules to ensure compliance with good-faith cooperation, the normative content of which the Theory helps to clarify.

When informing international water law interpretation and application, Community-of-Interests may also give rise to ancillary obligations linked to its normative elements, even if international law does not *a priori* impose the Basin Scope or joint action and even in the absence of watercourse agreements or explicit rules in an existing treaty.

For example, where not explicitly required, joint action may still be mandated in order to demonstrate good-faith compliance with the general cooperation rule – itself a means to fulfill the substantive requirements of equitable and reasonable use and harm prevention. In such cases, Community-of-Interests shifts the emphasis under the duty to cooperate from unilateral or coordinated efforts to joint action. The Theory operates as a catchall principle mandating the application of its elements to the extent that, in a concrete case, they prove necessary to ensure compliance with existing international water law rules.

It is not possible to assert that Community-of-Interests is already giving rise to customary rules of international water law. Participation could be an instance of an emerging new rule. However, this book lacked the space to develop evidence as to how widespread Participation is in state practice or as to whether the motivation for its application is factual or legal.

On the elements of Community-of-Interests, the need for the wider uptake of the Basin Scope, the Basin Treaty, and the Basin Body is growing. In this moment in history, it is at least clear that countries are increasingly interested in, and committed to, strengthening transboundary water cooperation; and that watercourse agreements continue to be negotiated, adopted, or revised.[112] In the future, the Theory could eventually give rise to new obligations under international water law in connection with its normative elements, obligations such as those currently formulated in the UNWC and the ECEWC.

112 UN Water (2018), *supra*, p. 84.

PART VI

Status and Uptake of Community-of-Interests

Community-of-Interests, as shown in the previous Part operates as a legal principle underpinning the codification and clarification, interpretation and application and possibly the progressive development of international water law. However, the evidence examined here is not enough to demonstrate that Community-of-Interests has indeed attained the normative status of a legal principle. We have arrived at this conclusion after revisiting how treaties, jurisprudence and scholarship address the status of the Theory, which reveals inconsistency in the use of terminology; exploring definitions for the various categories of standards under international law and policy; and going back to the elements and functions of Community-of-Interests presented in this book.

As an encouragement for further research in this regard, this Part also applies our Legal Analytical Framework to test two additional watercourse agreements on their possible endorsement of Community-of-Interests, supplementing those instruments already examined and known to be framed by the Theory. Ultimately, the idea is to expand the use of the Legal Analytical Framework to more water treaties in effect around the world, with a view to reassessing the normative status and accurate degree of uptake of the Theory.

1 Treatment of the Status of Community-of-Interests in Treaties, Jurisprudence and Scholarship

According to Verschuuren, standards that have appeared repeatedly *as principles* in authoritative legal documents, such as treaties and statements, "can be considered to be legal principles".[1]

Of the four treaties referring explicitly to the Theory, two codify Community-of-Interests as a principle: Article 4(2)(k) of the Lake Victoria Protocol references the Theory as a principle governing transboundary basin management; and the 1995 SADC Protocol codifies the Theory among its general principles. The Senegal Basin Charter and the Ecuador-Peru Agreement simply mention the Theory, without any qualifiers that could illuminate the question

1 J. Verschuuren, *Sustainable Development and the Nature of Environmental Legal Principles*, 9:1 PER/PELJ 209–61 (2006), p. 235.

 | HTTPS://DOI.ORG/10.1163/9789004507036-008

of normative status. The Charter invokes the Community-of-Interests among the riparian states; and, the latter, the Community-of-Interests that unites the states in the management of transboundary basins. These precedents arguably confer upon the Theory normative value, beyond a mere policy or ideal. Yet, such treaty references, on their own, are insufficient to qualify the Theory unequivocally as a legal principle or as another legal or policy standard.

We must then consider how Community-of-Interests is invoked in case law. The premise is that a standard that the courts apply as a principle *might* be deserving of that title. Yet, a single such reference does not suffice: "There has to be a continuing reference by the courts to a norm before it can be called a principle."[2] The Theory has been applied in a string of decisions, each calling back on the relevant legal precedent, albeit not consistently as a legal principle.

In the River Oder Case, the PCIJ reformulates the question posed by the parties to the dispute: "[W]hat is the *law* which should *govern* the determination of the upstream limits of this jurisdiction?"[3] The Court is unable to rely on a literal interpretation of the treaty provision in question, thus reading it in light of Community-of-Interests, viewed as one of the "*principles* governing international fluvial law in general". But the Decision then affirms: "It is on this *conception* that international river law ... is undoubtedly based".[4] Having referenced Community-of-Interests first as a principle and then as a conception, the River Oder Decision is inconclusive as to the Theory's status. In the Gabčíkovo Case, the ICJ invokes the River Oder Case to proclaim: "Modern development of international law has strengthened this [Community-of-Interests] *principle* for non-navigational uses of international watercourses as well".[5] In the more recent Chlorides Case, the Award refers to the Theory as "a *notion* used by the PCIJ".[6]

Together, the above judicial precedents confirm that the Theory has normative weight – either as a principle of international water law or as another *legal* standard, but certainly not simply as an ethical or policy concept. Beyond this conclusion, the cases examined, like the treaties reviewed before them, do not give us a definitive answer as to the legal status of Community-of-Interests.

---

2 *Ibid.*

3 River Oder Case, *supra*, p. 16.

4 *Id*, p. 27 (emphasis added).

5 Gabčíkovo case, *supra*, p. 56.

6 Chlorides Case, *supra*, p. 40 (emphasis added).

In scholarship, renowned authors use a variety of terms when examining Community-of-Interests, without always justifying why or getting into a discussion around the Theory's normative status. Among those who do take a position on the matter, no consensus exists.

To illustrate, McIntyre concludes that Community-of-Interests is an *approach* to basin management in a transboundary context.[7] The words *notion* and *concept* have been used by Leb when exploring the status of Community-of-Interests.[8] Hildering refers to the Theory as an *emerging concept*;[9] and Lammers as a *normative concept*.[10] Sievers uses the expression *foundational policy* in reference to all four theories of international water law.[11] Tanzi and Arcari employ the term *theory*.[12] McCaffrey examines the Theory alongside the other three proposed theoretical bases of international water law, but refers to Community-of-Interests interchangeably as a *theory*,[13] *doctrine*,[14] *concept*,[15] *notion*,[16] *approach*,[17] and *principle*.[18]

Digging a little deeper into the issue, Howden chooses the term *approach*, though also sometimes using *legal approach*,[19] as the one best suited to describe Community-of-Interests, thus seen as "a manner of doing or thinking about something; a specific way to approach a topic".[20] In justifying this opinion, that author builds on various definitions, namely: *principles* have a "general or overarching character ... aimed at protecting shared values, often of common benefit", in addition to being "more exact [than a theory] as [a principle] covers one specific idea or value";[21] a *theory* "implies a collection of ideas and principles that are intended to explain a phenomenon",[22] and may

7 McIntyre, *supra*, p. 28–9, 32.
8 Leb (2013), *supra*, p. 51 *et seq.*
9 A. Hildering, *International Law, Sustainable Development and Water Management* (Eburon 2004), p. 100.
10 Lammers, *supra*, p. 507.
11 Sievers, *supra*, p. 15.
12 Tanzi & Arcari, *supra*, p. 21, 23.
13 McCaffrey (2019), *supra*, p. 226, 231, 235, 236, 237, 238, 329.
14 *Id*, p. 133 (FN 119), 236, 283.
15 *Id*, p. 221, 223, 231, 236, 318, 346, 740.
16 *Id*, p. 220-21, 224–25, 228, 230–31, 233, 236, 240.
17 *Id*, p. 223-24.
18 *Id*, p. 229, 330, 422.
19 Howden, *supra*, p. 13, 15, 17, 38, 166, 213, 402.
20 *Id*, p. 27.
21 *Id*, p. 26.
22 *Id*, p. 25.

contain several principles and ideas";[23] a *concept*, *doctrine* and *approach* "are all slightly vaguer and at the same time more encompassing"[24] than a principle or a theory; a *concept* is an "idea or [a] principle that seeks to protect a specific value";[25] a *doctrine* can be "one single principle or a collection of ideas and principles with the same aim as a concept".[26] She concludes that Community-of-Interests "might not be sufficiently complex to merit the label 'theory';"[27] that the term principle is "too narrow to cover the [Theory's] full content";[28] and, finally, that the Theory, as a collection of principles serving a specific goal, "could be labelled a doctrine, and probably also a concept as the definitions of these terms are not rigid and the terms are commonly used".[29]

In her turn, Boisson de Chazournes has used the terms *concept* and *notion*,[30] but, in more recent writings, refers to Community-of-Interests as a *principle*, to be considered alongside other international water law principles, such as freedom of navigation and freedom of commerce.[31] When reviewing the Chlorides Case, Boisson de Chazournes opines that the Tribunal implicitly sees Community-of-Interests as a principle, "thus further confirming the status accorded to it in the case law".[32] Elsewhere, the same author reaffirms that Community-of-Interests "has become a core principle of contemporary international water law".[33] Boisson de Chazournes' position in this respect does not represent a cemented opinion among her peers and yet, she is a highly respected scholar in this field, so that her views are not to be taken lightly.

A contributing factor to the lack of agreement and the multitude of terms used in reference to the Theory might be that, in the various sources where Community-of-Interests comes up, neither scholars nor the courts pause to reflect on the definitions that may exist for the various terms employed themselves.

---

23 *Id*, p. 26.
24 *Id*, p. 27.
25 *Ibid.*
26 *Ibid.*
27 *Id*, p. 26.
28 *Ibid.*
29 *Id*, p. 27.
30 L. Boisson de Chazournes, *Fresh Water in International Law* (Oxford 2013), p. 22, 211, 244.
31 L. Boisson de Chazournes, *The Permanent Court of International Justice, The International Court of Justice and International Water Law: Versatility in Consistency*, in S.C. McCaffrey, C. Leb, R.T. Denoon eds, Research Handbook on International Water Law (Edward Elgar 2019), p. 286, 290.
32 Boisson de Chazournes (2008), *supra*, p. 15.
33 Boisson de Chazournes (2019), *supra*, p. 286.

2 Hard and Soft International Law Standards

Primary and secondary sources do not offer precise, definitive, and universally agreed definitions around categories of standards under international law and policy. Verschuuren draws attention to the misunderstandings and superficiality that dominate discussions around legal standards, with especially the word *principle* being often misused in reference to a rule or a policy. For Vershuuren, policies, principles, and rules, for example, are important for advancing ideals and they can influence one another. Yet, these are different categories of standards, with each performing characteristic functions in the international legal order.[34]

Illustratively, such standards may be classified as *approaches*; *policies*; *legal concepts*; *ideals or values*; *theories* and *doctrines*; principles, whether *general principles of law* or *legal principles*; and *rules*.

Approach, Policy, and Concept: An *approach* is "a way of dealing with someone or something; a way of doing or thinking about something such as a problem or a task".[35] An approach is devoid of normativity.[36]

Policies are not legal norms either and thus are not capable, directly and on their own, of substantiating legal decisions and, more generally, of legally compelling specific human behavior. To gain international normative content, policies must be codified in a legal instrument, become embedded in a principle or rule of customary law, or bind a decision-maker under administrative law. Policies lack the stability of legal norms, which are not as easily altered or superseded. Policies may influence ideals and vice-versa. Principles and rules may drive policies, but these latter standards depend on rules to be enforceable.[37]

A *concept* is seen as "an abstract or generic idea generalized from particular instances".[38] From a legal perspective: "All legal rules and standards … are

34 Verschuuren, *supra*, p. 209, 211, 242, building on R. Dworkin, *Model of Rules I*, *in* Taking Rights Seriously (Duckworth London 1996), to differentiate among rules, principles, and policies and to unpack the meaning of ideals.

35 Oxford Learner's Dictionary: *Approach* (noun), *at* https://www.oxfordlearnersdictionaries.com/us/definition/american_english/approach_2.

36 *See*, e.g., McIntyre, *supra*, p. 29, describing *common management* of international watercourses as "an *approach* to managing water problems *rather than* a *normative* principle of international law" (emphasis added).

37 Verschuuren, *supra*, p. 241–42.

38 Merriam-Webster Dictionary Online: *Concept*, at https://www.merriam-webster.com/dictionary/concept.

formed by combining concepts in different ways [and so] concepts ... are the building blocks of law. ... The rule provides the criteria for decision but relies on abstract ideas – concepts – with more or less intuitive appeal. ... Legal concepts come in different levels of abstraction, often nested within one another".[39] For some authors, "concepts are always embedded in a broader theory, so that their essential features may not be observable at all but instead are defined as part of the background theory".[40]

Theory and Doctrine: When we get to these two terms, the lack of clarity in legal discourse soon becomes evident. Comparing *theory* and *doctrine*, Koskenniemi ponders: "It is not obvious where the line between 'theory' and 'doctrine' lies. In general terms, it may be said that where the former asks questions about international law as a whole – as a 'system' or an 'instrument' of policy – doctrine deals with particular, substantive aspects of the law".[41]

From a different perspective, a *theory* can be viewed as "a plausible or scientifically acceptable general principle or body of principles offered to explain phenomena".[42] In Law, a theory may refer to a "set of propositions, assumptions or facts attempting to provide a rational explanation of cause and effect of observed phenomenon";[43] a *legal theory*, to a "principle under which a litigant proceeds, or on which a litigant bases its claims or defenses in a case";[44] and, a *theory of law*, to a "legal premise or set of principles on which a case rests".[45] As a solid legal basis for a decision, a theory of law "helps to explain why a certain law or rule applies to a particular situation ... like the foundation of a building that supports the entire structure".[46]

The term *doctrine* may refer to a widely followed rule (or set of rules), a theory, or a principle in a field of law and which is formed via a string of court decisions applying said doctrine continuously over time.[47] A doctrine,

39 T. Ginsburg & N. Stephanopoulos, *The Concepts of Law*, 84:147 The University of Chicago law Review 147–75 (2017), p. 147, 150–52, at https://lawreview.uchicago.edu/print-archive/concepts-law.

40 *Id*, p. 151.

41 M. Koskenniemi, *International Legal Theory and Doctrine*, *in* Max Planck Encyclopedia of Public International Law (MPEPIL) (online) (Oxford 2007), p. 1.

42 Merriam-Webster Dictionary Online: *Theory*, at https://www.merriam-webster.com/dictionary/theory.

43 Law Dictionary: *Theory*, at https://thelawdictionary.org/theory/.

44 Garner ed, *supra*, p. 979.

45 *Id*, p. 1616.

46 LSD Law: *Theory of Law*, https://www.lsd.law/define/theory-of-law.

47 Merriam-Webster Dictionary Online: *Doctrine*, at https://www.merriam-webster.com/dictionary/doctrine; Wex, Legal Information Institute, Cornell Law School: *Doctrine*, at

whether more or less abstract, binding or nonbinding, can also mean a "synthesis of various rules, principles, norms, interpretive guidelines and values [and which] explains, makes coherent or justifies a segment of the law as part of a larger system of law".[48] In international law, doctrine also represents *scholarship*, a secondary legal source stated in Article 38(1)(d) of the ICJ Statute.[49]

Values, Principles and Rules: *Values* or *ideals* are vague and abstract and, as such, may be reflected in cultural and legal norms in an explicit, implicit, or latent manner. Values underlie other standards as broad expressions of good behavior and social goals; they insert notions of morality prevalent in a given society into legal principles and, through such principles, into rules and policies. Ideals gain concreteness and can be applied only when embedded in principles and rules.[50] From this premise, Verschuuren classifies sustainable development, for example, as an ideal, "a loose, vague, and indeterminate general idea of the perfection we ought to aim at",[51] while knowing we may never fully achieve it, and for whose realization we must resort to tangible legal, economic, and social implementation tools.[52]

Whereas ideals carry moral value, *principles*, whether more or less abstract, hold normative content as legal norms. Principles can guide treaty- or decision-making. Ideals, on their own, cannot. This is at the heart of how to differentiate these two standards from each other.[53]

In the context of international law, *general principles of law* comprise those "derived from national legal systems"[54] and those which "may be formed within the international legal system".[55]

It is the latter category that is of relevance here, but both "may serve, *inter alia*, to interpret and complement other rules of international law".[56] Accord-

https://www.law.cornell.edu/wex/doctrine; Justia Legal Dictionary: *Doctrine*, at https://dictionary.justia.com/doctrine.

48 Oxford Reference: *Doctrine*, at https://www.oxfordreference.com/display/10.1093/oi/authority.20110803095724371.

49 K.D.Z. González, Academic Course: 2020–2021, *Public International Law*, at https://roderic.uv.es/rest/api/core/bitstreams/0e68c009-3a49-4db6-a15b-600f79ac0cc5/content.

50 Verschuuren, *supra*, p. 213–14, 221, 247.

51 *Id*, p. 219.

52 *Id*, p. 220.

53 *Id*, p. 223, 241.

54 *General Principles of Law* ('ILC (2023)'), *in* ILC Report, Ch.IV, 74th Session (24 Apr–2 June & 3 July–4 Aug 2023), UN Doc A/78/10 (3 Nov 2023), p. 14.

55 *Ibid.*

56 *Id*, p. 28

ing to the ILC: "The term '*inter alia*' is used to indicate that the functions referred to are not exhaustive".[57] Embedded with normative content, principles "give guidance to rule-makers [by setting] the goals that have to be reached with (new) rules";[58] and orient the interpretation of rules when those are open-ended, ambiguous or in apparent conflict with one another.[59] Indeed, "we see the relevance of a principle for legal practice especially when applying and interpreting rules in concrete cases or when making (new) rules".[60]

Verschuuren further differentiates between *general principles of law* or *legal principles* – the former being applicable across all legal fields and, the latter, within a specific branch of the law.[61] This categorization of principles seems useful: while the Theory should be viewed within the broader framework of international law, Community-of-Interests originates and operates in the specific context of the law of transboundary basins. In this sense, if one were to qualify the Theory as a principle, it would have to be a *legal principle of international water law*. As such, Community-of-Interests would be anchored in the *basic principle of cooperation*, as captured in the UN Charter and the Friendly Relations Declaration. Per the latter, the basic principles of international law codified thereunder guide all states in their international conduct and mutual relations, and strict observance thereof is required.

Rules are applied in the light of the principles underlying them. Principles gain more concreteness in connection with a specific rule than when standing on their own – such as the Theory in relation to equitable and reasonable use, harm prevention and cooperation. Compared to rules, principles display a higher moral character, originating in the ideals that underpin them. Compared to policies, principles are more long-lasting for having their basis in law and legal culture. Principles form the bridge that interconnects ideals and rules. Principles may evolve into rules and may be codified in treaties,[62] as Community-of-Interests has been, thereby gaining in normative power. In addition, "rules can be more easily directly applied in individual cases, while principles give a general direction for a decision",[63] without imposing determinate outcomes, thus inserting in the law a degree of elasticity. Likewise,

57 *Id*, p. 30.
58 Verschuuren, *supra*, p. 238.
59 *Ibid.*
60 *Id*, p. 239.
61 *Id*, p. 213.
62 *Id*, p. 223, 235, 237, 239, 241.
63 *Id*, p. 237.

flexibility is inherent to Community-of-Interests, which applies where and as appropriate in a given case.

The above functions and characteristics of principles, as the links between ideals and rules, remit us back to the functions and elements of Community-of-Interests, presented in the previous Chapters, and linked to the codification and clarification, application and interpretation and progressive development of international water law.

3 Community-of-Interests Operating as a Legal Principle

The Theory operates as a legal principle framing international water law. Referring to *functions* in our context is intentional, in light of the term's frequent employment in connection to legal principles.[64]

Let us recall the attributes of legal principles, through which they perform their functions. *Principles provide concreteness to values*, whereas *values embed principles with moral content*. Values connected to Community-of-Interests include the already mentioned ideal of *sustainable development* in relation to future generations and to long-term sustainability of the very basins around which communities-of-interests form; *peace*, as regards friendly relations between co-basin states, so that these are maintained even in situations of disagreements and disputes through the residual application of Limited Territorial Sovereignty rules; and *hydrosolidarity*, as an ideal developed for the purpose of progressively embedding ethical values into international water law.

Moreover, principles offer guidance for states and the courts in the codification, clarification, interpretation and application, and development of international law.

On *codification and clarification*, Community-of-Interests inspires the formulations of equitable and reasonable use, harm prevention, and cooperation in the UNWC and the Basin Treaties here examined. Article 16 of the 1995 SADC Protocol requires future Basin Treaties to be in accordance with the Theory. The ECEWC does the same in relation to water agreements or arrangements adopted thereunder. It is reasonable to assume that the Theory has informed the codification and clarification of international water law rules through the multiple watercourse treaties adopted on the basis of the ECEWC and the 1995 SADC Protocol, respectively.

64 R. Wolfrum, *General International Law (Principles, Rules, and Standards)*, *in* Max Planck Encyclopedia of Public International Law (MPEPIL) (online) (Oxford 2010), p. 12.

When serving as interpretative guidance, Community-of-Interests operates as a principle *interconnecting ideals and rules*. Community-of-interests, as viewed by the River Oder Decision,[65] does so by injecting the values of justice and utility into equitable and reasonable utilization – the latter an expression of the rule of equity as applied to transboundary waters. The establishment of these 'values-principle-rule' linkages – from justice and utility to Community-of-Interests and into equitable and reasonable – reinforce the Theory's normative persuasion as a standard underlying a specific rule.

Moreover, specific duties for states to act in accordance with Community-of -Interests, by applying the Theory's elements, may emerge where necessary to ensure compliance with the basic rules of international water law. Principles perform the same function. Through the process of interpretation, principles and rules become entangled;[66] and, "together with more concrete rules …, [principles can] impose duties on the state".[67]

Like a principle, Community-of-Interests inserts flexibility into international water law, providing a direction on the basis of which co-basin states come together to define goals and norms adjusted to the basin's characteristics and to their particular interests and needs. The Theory indicates the general path for the pursuit of common interests, i.e., joint action, for the most part and, at least, where appropriate. But the Theory does not *a priori* specify target common interests, desired results, or joint-action obligations. This specification comes in the form of various standards codified or envisioned in the treaties that reflect Community-of-Interests or captured in jurisprudence applying the Theory. The ECEWC, for example, specifies that joint-action requirements apply in relation to agreements or arrangements and joint bodies. In the Pulp Mills Case, Uruguay mentions the 15 years of monitoring that had been conducted under the umbrella of CARU as part of a dedicated joint program, which points to joint data gathering.[68]

Furthermore, in all decisions examined, Community-of-Interests is captured as an integral and explicit part of their motivation, whether or not they refer to the Theory directly as a principle. In this respect, Verschuuren

65 River Oder Case, *supra*, p. 27.

66 Verschuuren, *supra*, p. 239.

67 *Id*, p. 221.

68 *See* Pulp Mills Case, *supra*, p. 67, referring to the River Uruguay Water Quality and Pollution Control Program ('Programa de Calidad de Aguas y Control de la Contaminación del Río Uruguay').

notes that one of the functions of principles is precisely to "enhance the legitimacy of decision-making".[69]

The Theory's potential influence in *progressive development*, as another function performed by legal principles, may be felt in the incorporation of equitable and reasonable Participation as an autonomous rule into the UNWC; as well as in the requirements under the ECEWC for states to adopt agreements or arrangements and establish joint commissions – broader cooperation tools of which the Basin Treaty and the Basin Body, as elements of Community-of-Interests, are specific manifestations.

The Theory, therefore, *operates as a principle* orienting the codification and clarification, interpretation and application, and possibly the progressive development of international water law.

Further research is required to ascertain if the Theory not only operates as, but actually is, a legal principle of the law of transboundary basins; as well as whether Community-of-Interests is already influencing progressive legal development through state practice and opinion around the Basin Scope, the Basin Treaty, the Basin Body, and Participation, as a manifestation of Close Basin Cooperation. If these concepts could be found to have independent normative status, they would apply beyond specific where-appropriate situations. Automatic applicability would emerge out of a presumption of general necessity, if corroborated by the presence of the requirements that demonstrate the customary nature of a rule. Put differently, if deemed to express binding rules, the Basin Scope, the Basin Treaty, the Basin Body and Participation would require riparian states to act in a certain way not only where appropriate, but as a general rule, even if certain exceptions could still be admitted.

4 Case Studies of Community-of-Interests in State Practice

In order to further assess the status of Community-of-Interests, the next step would be to evaluate its concrete uptake in state practice beyond the treaties currently known to reflect the Theory.[70] To illustrate, we turn to two context-specific agreements as examples, chosen for their value in the context of the book – one, for being adopted under the ECEWC regime; and, the other, to

69 Vershuuren, *supra*, p. 238.

70 For statistics on stakeholder participation and joint action related to climate change in treaties and arrangements and their implementation around the world, *see* UNECE *et al*, *supra*, p. 52, 81–84.

represent Asia in the packet of agreements informing our conclusions. These agreements govern relations among the co-riparian states in the Rhine and Mekong basins, respectively.

4.1 *Environmental Protection of the Rhine Basin*

The *Convention on the Protection of the Rhine* is the framework treaty in place for the overall protection of the Rhine and related ecosystems.[71] As noted in the Preamble, the Rhine Protection Convention is based on the ECEWC, which itself is framed by Community-of-Interests. Is it thus possible to qualify the Rhine Convention as a Basin Treaty? To answer this question, we apply the Theory's normative elements as our analytical framework for reviewing treaty language.

On the *Basin Scope*, the Rhine Protection Convention does not include all states within the basin, but its parties cooperate with the other co-riparians – Austria, Belgium, Liechtenstein, and Italy;[72] and the *International Commission for the Protection of the Rhine* (ICPR) cooperates with the informal body that gathers all basin states.[73] Article 2 determines the Convention's scope *ratione loci*, which includes the river itself, plus connected groundwater (Basin Scope longitudinal and vertical dimensions); aquatic and terrestrial ecosystems interacting, or which could again interact, with the Rhine (horizontal dimension); and the wider basin area, to the extent that pollution by noxious substances therein may harm the Rhine or as appropriate to safeguard riparian areas against floods (horizontal dimension). Reflecting the source-to-sea approach, the Preamble and Article 3 acknowledge the Rhine's restoration and protection as necessary for the conservation and improvement of the North Sea ecosystem.

---

71 *Convention on the Protection of the Rhine*, France-Germany Luxembourg-Netherlands-Switzerland, plus the European Community (Bern, 12 Apr 1999) ('Rhine Protection Convention').

72 International Commission for the Protection of the Rhine (ICPR), About Us, at https://www.iksr.org/en/icpr/about-us.

73 *See Rules of Procedure and Financial Regulations for the Cooperation of the International Commission for the Protection of the Rhine with the Coordinating Committee Rhine* (in force 1 July 2010), at https://www.iksr.org/fileadmin/user_upload/Dokumente_en/IKSR-CC-EN_30.06.10.pdf.

Like the *Basin Treaty*, the Rhine Protection Convention aims to "step up"[74] cooperation, with focus on ecosystem conservation and enhancement and further water quality improvement,[75] following-up on a succession of prior cooperation frameworks.[76]

The Convention sets up ICPR, with legal personality, and which may be deemed to be a *Basin Body* for being placed at the center of Close Basin Cooperation. Article 6(1) of the Convention determines that parties "pursue their cooperation *within* the Commission". Article 8 tasks the Commission, *inter alia*, with preparing international measuring programs; coordinating the parties' warning and alert plans; and evaluating treaty effectiveness based on reports received from parties and the findings of monitoring measures and studies. The ICPR may also take measures to assist parties that submit justified reports about not being able to implement its decisions.

The Commission, moreover, plays a role in the context of harm prevention. In the event of incidents or accidents that might threaten water quality or in the case of imminent flooding, parties are to immediately inform the ICPR and other members that may be affected; and must do so in accordance with the warning and alert plans coordinated by the Commission.

Consistent with *Close Basin Cooperation*, joint action through the Commission is supplemented by the individual undertakings in Article 5, like the gradual reduction of hazardous substances discharges, aiming for complete elimination. These undertakings include individual measures proposed by the ICPR. Per Article 11(2)(b), the Commission may stipulate that parties implement such measures in a coordinated manner. Parties are also in charge of domestic implementation of international measuring programs, as prepared by the Commission, the results of which must be informed to the ICPR. Participation is reflected in the formula for the allocation of contributions by each party to cover the ICPR's annual budget.[77]

On *Coherence*, Article 14(1) foresees cooperation with other intergovernmental organizations, including in the form of recommendations.

On *Social Basin Engagement*, Article 8(4) mandates the ICPR to keep the public informed of its work and of the state of the Rhine, for which purpose

74 Rhine Protection Convention, *supra*, 2nd Preambular Paragraph.

75 *Id*, 2nd and 5th Preambular Paragraphs.

76 *Id*, 4th Preambular Paragraph; International Commission for the Protection of the Rhine, Legal Basis, Convention, at https://www.iksr.org/en/icpr/legal-basis/convention;

77 *See Rules of Procedure and Financial Regulations of the ICPR* (in force 8 July 2022), at https://www.iksr.org/fileadmin/user_upload/DKDM/Dokumente/Rechtliche_Basis/EN/legal_En_RoPaFR_2022.pdf.

the Commission may prepare and publish reports. Article 14 authorizes the ICPR to recognize relevant states, intergovernmental organizations, and NGOs as observers; empowers observers to present the Commission with information and reports; allows the participation, upon invitation, of observers and experts in ICPR meetings, without voting rights; and foresees information exchange and consultations with NGOs before and after relevant decisions are made.

4.2 *Sustainable Development of the Mekong River Basin*

The *Agreement on the Cooperation for the Sustainable Development of the Mekong River Basin* is a partial treaty, as it covers only the lower part of the basin, with the upper riparians, China and Myanmar, not being parties.[78]

The *Basin Scope* is implicitly embraced in Article 3, which formulates the parties' commitment to the protection of "the environment, natural resources, aquatic life and conditions, and ecological balance", in connection with "development plans and uses of water and related resources in the Basin". Tributaries, in particular, are addressed in Article 5, on equitable and reasonable utilization. Article 39 authorizes other riparian states to join the Agreement upon consent of the parties.

Like the *Basin Treaty*, the Mekong Basin Agreement, as stated in its Preamble, builds on the history of cooperation among the four parties, going back to 1957. The Preamble refers to the *community of Mekong nations*, hinting at a preexisting community-of-basin-interests.

The Mekong Basin Agreement establishes what could be a *Basin Body*, the Mekong River Commission (MRC), which enjoys the status of an international organization, and is composed of the *Council*, the *Joint Committee*, and the *Secretariat*. All organs play a role in promoting Close Basin Cooperation. The Council issues policies, decisions, and guidance for joint activities and has rule-making powers. The Joint Committee manages data generation, updating and exchange; conducts studies and assessments; and drafts joint rules. The Secretariat maintains relevant databases. In support of Limited Territorial Sovereignty, the Council and the Joint Committee play a role in addressing and attempting to resolve disagreements and disputes.

On *Close Basin Cooperation*, Article 2 emphasizes and favors joint and/or basin-wide projects and programs, as informed by a basin development plan, to be proposed by the Joint Committee and approved by the Council, identi-

78 *Agreement on the Cooperation for the Sustainable Development of the Mekong River Basin*, Cambodia-Laos-Thailand-Vietnam (Chiang Rai, 5 Apr 1995) ('Mekong Basin Agreement').

fying, categorizing, and prioritizing relevant measures to be financed and implemented.

On *Coherence*, the 7th Preambular Paragraph refers to projects, programs, and activities to be implemented under the Agreement in cooperation and coordination with the international community. In this respect, for example, the Mekong basin countries have endeavored to cooperate under ASEAN, of which all are members, including within the framework of the *Mekong Basin Development Cooperation* (AMBDC). As part of this process, the 2nd *ASEAN-MRC Water Security Dialogue* was held in 2024, under the theme *Sustainable Investment for a Connected, Resilient, and Water-Secure Southeast Asia.*[79]

On *Social Basin Engagement*, the Mekong River Commission "engages a range of stakeholders into its program of work and strategic planning".[80]

5 Conclusions

Looking at the ways in which treaties, jurisprudence, and scholarship have referred to Community-of-Interests is not sufficient to reach a conclusion regarding the Theory's status. We must turn to the definitions of the various standards of international law and policy and consider those definitions in relation to the functions of Community-of-Interests.

Community-of-Interests is not a mere approach, policy or ideal, because the Theory has normative value as evidenced by the numerous primary and secondary sources invoking it. As a multifaceted Theory, Community-of-Interests is not a concept, although the term may apply to its primary and secondary elements studied here.

Like a principle, the Theory has served as a foundation for decision-making and a common yardstick or guidance for the formulation and interpretation of customary and treaty rules. The Theory has had longstanding legal influence, as evidenced by the precedents of its direct application to inform agreements and jurisprudence.

In the sense of a legal precedent or for operating specifically in the context of the law of transboundary basins, Community-of-Interests could be a doctrine. Having appeared in specific treaties, however, Community-of-Interests does not seem well-captured by the term doctrine. The Theory is not a product of judicial precedents. Community-of-Interests is a preexisting Theory,

---

79 MRC, News, Media Releases, *at* https://www.mrcmekong.org/media-releases/2nd-asean-mrc-water-security-dialogue-to-discuss-regional-water-security-challenges/2024/.

80 UN Water (2013), *supra*, p. 20.

founded on the physical reality of the basin and put in practice by states long before the River Oder decision, and which is eventually detected and applied by the courts. As a Theory of international water law, Community-of-Interests serves as a legal lens through which to study the phenomenon of transboundary basin cooperation.

Community-of-Interests already *functions as* a legal principle in treaty and case law when informing the codification and clarification and interpretation and application of the law of transboundary basins and when attempting to further its progressive development through codification. The functions performed by Community-of-Interests corroborate its status as an independent theoretical framework for international water law, as had already been postulated by McCaffrey.

There is yet no evidence that Community-of-Interests is itself a legal principle. With our foundational goal being to unpack the Theory's normative content, the book focuses on the small subset of agreements and cases known to reflect the Theory. To illustrate the applicability of our Legal Analytical Framework, the book offers case studies that suggest Community-of-Interests may have more widely permeated state practice than normally assumed. Yet, we are unable to collate here enough evidence to lead to a solid conclusion that the Theory has indeed attained the status of a legal principle of international water law.

Conclusions

Community-of-Interests is founded upon the natural interdependencies and mutual vulnerabilities that arise in connection with a shared drainage basin, viewed as a unitary whole. From these connections emerge common and potentially conflicting environmental, social, economic, and other interests.

The book presents Community-of-Interests as a Theory framing the norms on the protection, management and use of transboundary catchments and their ecosystems. The focus is on the Theory's normative elements, functions, and status.

Community-of-Interests has the status of an authoritative, accepted, practiced, and distinct theoretical framework for international water law; and gains concrete expression through its primary and secondary elements. It is through these elements that Community-of-Interests operates as a principle underpinning the codification and clarification, interpretation and application, and, possibly, the progressive development of norms in the field. When countries cooperate with the dedicated intent to pursue together common interests in mutually beneficial ways, Community-of-Interests becomes recognizable through its elements. Yet, the Theory stands on its own and exists independently of treaties. We do not reach the conclusion that the Theory is actually a legal principle, only that it has functioned as one such legal standard.

Our core contribution is to move beyond existing literature and its general and abstract conceptualizations of Community-of-Interests towards constructing a more meticulous understanding thereof and demonstrating that actual communities-of-basin-interests exist and operate predominantly around shared concerns, while balancing unilateral interests that might have disruptive effects on the overall cooperation process. In this way, the Theory entails more than simply restricting the rights of riparian countries to develop and use the watercourse but still Limited Territorial Sovereignty represents a facet of Community-of-Interests.

As the world changes and with increasing levels of interdependence among basin states, scenarios calling for cooperation framed by Community-of-Interests are likely to grow ever more frequent and easier to detect. Transboundary water cooperation requirements are expected to respond by growing in detail, scope, relevance, and uptake, with the foundations of international water law possibly advancing faster along a spectrum – from Limited Territorial Sovereignty, focused on unilateral restraint and coexistence, towards Com-

 | HTTPS://DOI.ORG/10.1163/9789004507036-009

munity-of-Interests, prioritizing shared aspirations while retaining norms needed to balance unilateral concerns.

This evolution is likely to unfold in parallel with advancements in general international law towards co-progressiveness, as the common interests between states sharing a basin, a region or the whole world thicken, at the same time that the task of managing potentially conflicting needs at various levels becomes ever more complex.

To anchor the analysis in these developments, the book identifies the elements of Regional Integration Regimes driven by common interests among neighboring countries. These regimes resemble communities-of-basin-interests in that they both emerge from close geographic and related ties among states with important shared priorities to realize. The Regional Integration Regime expresses a commitment to long-term and iterated cooperation, unfolding on the basis of the Founding Charter and the Regional Integration Organization, with the pursuit of regional interests through Close Cooperation at its heart.

Among the Governance Elements of these regimes, the **Founding Charter** is employed to formalize, regulate and institutionalize Close Regional Cooperation. The **Regional Integration Organization** is created and designed to follow and push treaty implementation, support and advise states, engage stakeholders, foster joint action, facilitate the realization of common interests, and maintain stable interstate relations in the long-term. **Close Regional Cooperation** refers to cooperation centered on regional objectives and mostly entailing joint action, while being supplemented by other state engagement modalities and armed with tools to ensure durable coexistence through due attention to domestic needs and peculiarities.

With regard to the institutional relationships of Regional Integration Organizations, **Coherence** of values and overarching goals may be vertical, i.e., with the international community as a whole and with other organizations of global, continental, or subregional scope; or horizontal, with like regional institutions, whether or not sitting under the same mother regime. **Cohesion** may be outward, when members interact as a unified front with the rest of the world; or inward, in the face of external threats or to safeguard regional and national interests. **Solidarity** among members may appear in the Founding Charter explicitly or implicitly, to support countries in special situations, to require mutual assistance when applicable, and to promote cooperation with or between specific state groupings. **Nondiscrimination** may apply between the nationals of different countries and in the field of trade. **Unity** refers to self-sufficiency and efficient circulation and communication across the region. **Social Engagement** reflects how stakeholders may become involved in the cooperation process. Relevant provisions may be in general statements, objectives, and values that acknowledge human rights and nonstate interests; in the form of specific obligations and commitments enabling public participation or targeting the needs of specific groups; or in institutional mandates.

Taking the above elements as starting points, the book searches for comparable concepts within treaty and jurisprudential precedents that unequivocally reflect Community-of-Interests and adjusts them to fit the contexts to which the Theory applies. This informs the construction of the Legal Analytical Framework on the basis of the primary and secondary elements of Community-of-Interests. Getting into the degree of effectiveness of the treaties examined is outside our scope.

The investigation of the primary elements results in the identification of legal concepts with which riparian states are familiar, when taken in their traditional or general meaning. The book explains how such concepts are each reframed under Community-of-Interests.

Among the treaties examined, global and regional frameworks get into less detail when unpacking the Theory than their basin-level counterparts. Still, to varying degrees and taking different approaches, each precedent examined emphasizes the Basin Scope, the Basin Treaty, the Basin Body, and Close Basin Cooperation for common interests. This pattern found in key legal sources leads to the conclusion that such are the primary elements of Community-of-Interests. The secondary elements of the Theory have to do with institutional relationships and consist of Coherence, Solidarity, and Social Basin Engagement.

The **Basin Scope** is the first and most fundamental primary element of Community-of-Interests, and which frames all others, with its three spatial dimensions (with temporal connectivity being implicit therein): *longitudinal,* along the entire length of the watercourse system; *vertical,* between surface and groundwaters; and *horizontal,* across waters, land and biota.

Under the Basin Scope, the drainage basin becomes the central, albeit not exclusive, biogeographic unity for the planning and management of water and related resources. Basins or sub-basins include both surface and underground waters, and both living and nonliving resources, as well as the interconnections between those waters and resources, and the ecological processes and dynamic exchanges across the terrestrial and aquatic environments.

Cooperation premised on basin-level interconnections does not exclude state engagement at other levels but entails that the appropriate tools are in place, at least as appropriate, to allow for a holistic consideration of the entire basin in its long-term planning.

Agreements and other arrangements are widely used tools for transboundary water cooperation, even under Limited Territorial Sovereignty. The **Basin Treaty**, however, displays certain features that tailor it to not only balance unilateral interests but, principally, to meet shared aspirations. The Basin Treaty is informed by the Basin Scope; formalizes *de facto* communities-of-interests into communities-of-law; regulates these regimes by specifying priority common interests and establishing obligations, commitments, procedures, and legal tools required to enable sustained Close Basin Cooperation; and institutionalizes communities-of-basin-interests by establishing the Basin Body, with tailored powers, functions and internal organization.

The **Basin Body** is a treaty-based international organization, endowed with legal personality, and specifically designed to serve the concrete implementation of the Theory. The Basin Body is characterized by its central role in the operationalization of Close Basin Cooperation; the core functions it performs in the service of common interests, including Social Basin Engagement; and its biogeographic scope founded on the Basin Scope.

Close Basin Cooperation is cooperation centered on common interests rather than on coexistence. In the analysis of state engagement modalities within communities-of-basin-interests, the prevalence of joint action in the pursuit of agreed shared aspirations emerges as the identifying trait of Close Basin Cooperation.

Where states so agree, joint action may go as far as to embrace the joint ownership and mutual consent, but these concepts are not intrinsic to Community-of-Interests; they are generally not essential for a community-of-basin-interests to flourish.

Joint action is supplemented by other forms of state engagement, all of which may be employed both in the service of common goals and to balance unilateral interests. Close Basin Cooperation encompasses Participation in the form of mechanisms enabling and requiring states to contribute their fair share to the protection, management and sustainable development of the water resource and related environment.

Principles and tools of Limited Territorial Sovereignty are embedded in the Basin Treaty to reaffirm the exercise of sovereignty when safeguarding common interests and to secure the stability of the cooperation regime through the swift resolution of disagreements and breaches. Well-developed dispute settlement and enforcement systems, while characteristic of a law of coexistence, indicate the members' desire to ensure that implementation challenges are resolved effectively, so that they do not become obstacles to continued cooperation towards common interests.

Among the Theory's secondary elements, **Coherence** applies as between a given community-of-basin-interests and other parallel, broader, or narrower cooperation regimes, related to transboundary waters or broader regional interests. **Solidarity** characterizes relations between the states within a community-of-basin-interests; and may remain as a general abstract idea, be codified as a principle, and/or even underlie concrete rules. **Social Basin Engagement** guides how states interface with nonstate actors within the catchment.

The primary and secondary elements of Community-of-Interests have been usefully employed to guide and govern transboundary water cooperation. Having an appropriate understanding of these elements enables the determination of the Theory's status in international law based on the functions it has played in state practice.

From a broader perspective, Community-of-Interests invites a reflection about the kind of cooperation demanded by a world of rapidly declining aquatic biodiversity, increasing demands for the resource and a changing climate that severely influences water availability and predictability. As a legal Theory, Community-of-Interests prompts the question as to the extent to which current international law – as, presumably, informed by Limited Territorial Sovereignty – may shape and accelerate the broad and deep cooperation processes that are needed going forward.

International water law has evolved before in response to the changing nature of water uses and the needs of watercourse states – from a legal system mainly concerned with navigation to a broader, more complex set of norms dealing with multiple water needs, as well as with matters of protection, management, and stakeholder engagement within the framework of sustainability and human rights. With the water challenge once again going through an unprecedented process of expansion and growing complexity, might we witness another paradigmatic wave of progressive development in this legal field, if it has not started already?

International water law is still largely perceived as being centered on Limited Territorial Sovereignty and its core rules of equitable and reasonable use and harm prevention. But, when we take a closer look at cooperation on the ground, it may be that state practice in many places is already progressing from unilateral restraint to Close Basin Cooperation. Hence the importance of more accurately pinpointing and continually monitoring the stage of current international law and looking for any emerging rules congruent with Community-of-Interests.

An investigation of the adequacy and predominant theoretical framework of current international water law requires an understanding of Community-of-Interests at least as advanced as that existing for Limited Territorial Sovereignty. A well-understood Community-of-Interests Theory offers a framework for informing discussions around international water law and its present and future role, relevance, and evolution for supporting proper levels of transboundary basin cooperation.

It is hoped that this book leads to a more solid understanding of the elements, functions, and status of Community-of-Interests as an enhanced starting point for **further research** on the topic.

The book explores each element but, due to limited space, leaves some questions open. This is the case with catchments where common interests lie hidden behind broader mistrust, lack of dialogue and shared knowledge, ingrained disputes, or higher priorities, and thus overwhelmed by an almost exclusive focus on coexistence and superficial abidance by Limited Territorial Sovereignty, or not even that. In such instances, states are barely, or not at all, prepared to engage in even basic levels of basin cooperation; and it becomes harder to maintain that a community-of-basin-interests exists on the basis of a shared drainage basin, independently of a treaty. The book does not analyze such cases to assess their potential impact on the general conclusion that treaties do not give origin to, but simply formalize, a community-of-interests.

The mere presence of agreements and bodies is not sufficient to qualify a given cooperation regime as a community-of-basin-interests. The Legal Analytical Framework can aid in the analysis of water agreements that neither mention the Theory explicitly, nor have been invoked by a court as a legal precedent in this context. The primary and normative elements may be used to distinguish between a Basin Treaty and other water treaties. With additional Basin Treaties to consider, it would be possible to more accurately detect the actual uptake of Community-of-Interests in state practice and test the general assumption that Limited Territorial Sovereignty remains the dominant theoretical framework in the field.

For doing so, researchers might start with those watercourse agreements that most likely incorporate Community-of-Interests, namely: treaties among parties and nonparties that employ the UNWC as a reference framework by invoking it in their respective preambles; treaties concluded on the basis of the ECEWC; agreements drawing from the 1995 SADC Protocol; treaties adopted among ECEWC nonparties referencing the Convention; and treaties based on the Revised SADC Protocol.

Treaties among parties and nonparties that employ the UNWC as a reference framework are *potential* sources as Article 3(3) allows states not just to apply but also to adjust its provisions to their particular circumstances. This means that some watercourse agreements founded on the Convention might still be inspired principally by Limited Territorial Sovereignty and not Community-of-Interests.

Treaties concluded on the basis of the ECEWC are immediately relevant because, per Article 9(1), agreements or arrangements that parties have or enter into must be compatible with the Convention's basic principles. To the extent that Community-of-Interests is embedded into the Convention as an underlying theoretical framework, the Theory is probably entrenched into all legal instruments in effect among ECEWC parties.

In the case of agreements drawing from the 1995 SADC Protocol, Article 16 of the latter determines that context-specific treaties, including those negotiated with nonmember states, must abide by Article 2 (*general principles*), including Paragraph 2, which codifies Community-of-Interests. In addition to putting forward new Community-of-Interests sources, Article 16 indicates that the Theory has long been informing state practice and treaty law in this region.

Agreements adopted among states that are not parties to the ECEWC, but referencing the Convention, could also *potentially* qualify as Basin Treaties. Yet these agreements should be reviewed with caution: nonparties are not bound by the obligation to respect the Convention's basic principles, within which Community-of-Interests is embedded.

Finally, we recommend reviewing treaties based on the Revised SADC Protocol. As an example, the *Agreement establishing the Orange–Senqu River Commission* (ORASECOM) is the first watercourse agreement adopted in the region following the conclusion of the new Protocol.[1]

Taking the same approach as the ECEWC, the Protocol envisions watercourse agreements that apply its provisions to context-specific situations. This language departs from the text of the equivalent UNWC provision by omitting the verb *adjust*.[2] Considering how the Protocol generally mirrors the UNWC, it is hard to deprive such an omission of legal significance. One may assume that watercourse agreements concluded among Southern African states after the Protocol's entry into force have been drafted, applied, interpreted, and implemented in ways that still reflect Community-of-Interests, even where they lack explicit references thereto. Moreover, Article 6 safeguards the validity of preexisting watercourse agreements, only encouraging harmonization with the new Protocol. Hence, agreements adopted on the basis of the 1995 SADC Protocol, and which remain in force, may incorporate the Theory more explicitly than those succeeding the Revised Protocol.

---

1 Matthews, *supra*, p. 5.

2 *Compare* Revised SADC Protocol, *supra*, Art.6(3), and UNWC, *supra*, Art.3(3).

Going forward, research could further advance knowledge and understanding of Community-of-Interests, along with its elements, functions, and status; as well as the legal content and nature of its elements themselves. In doing so, we might discover that Community-of-Interests is more engrained in state practice then most scholars tend to assume, and certain riparian countries are prepared to admit.

Bibliography

Primary Research Sources

Treaties

General Treaty, Austria-France-Portugal-Prussia-Russias-Spain-Sweden-Norway-UK (Vienna, 9 June 1815) ('Vienna General Act'), reproduced in *Translation of the General Treaty, signed in Congress at Vienna, June 9, 1815, with the Acts thereunto Annexed, Presented to both Houses of Parliament, by Command of His Royal Highness, The Prince Regent* (London Gazette Office 1816).

Annexes, Act XVI – Regulations for the Free Navigation of Rivers, *Articles Concerning the Navigation of the Rhine*.

Boundary Waters Treaty, US-CAN (Washington, 11 Jan 1909) (in force 5 May 1910).

Treaty of Peace with Germany, Allied and Associated Powers-Germany (Versailles, 28 June 1919) (in force 10 Jan 1920) ('Treaty of Versailles').

Treaty Respecting the Utilization of the Waters of the Colorado and Tijuana Rivers and of the Rio Grande, US-Mexico (3 Feb 1944) (in force 8 Nov 1945).

IBWC, *IBWC Signs Minute 331 Focused on Improving Reliability, Predictability of Rio Grande Water Deliveries* (9 Nov 2024) (on file).

United Nations (UN), *Charter of the United Nations and Statute of the International Court of Justice* (San Francisco, 26 June 1945) ('UN Charter').

Convention on the Continental Shelf (Geneva, 29 April 1958) (in force 10 Jun 1964), 499 UNTS 311 (1965) ('Geneva Convention').

Indus Water Treaty (Karachi, 19 Sep 1960), India-Pakistan.

Treaty Concerning the Boundary Constituted by the River Uruguay (Argentina-Uruguay) (Montevideo, 7 Apr 1961).

Convention Relative à l'Aménagement General du Bassin du Fleuve Sénégal (Convention on the General Planning of the Senegal River Basin), Guinea-Mali-Mauritania-Senegal (Bamako, 26 July 1963) ('Senegal River Convention').

Vienna Convention on the Law of Treaties (Vienna, 23 May 1969) (in force 27 Jan 1980), 1155 UNTS 331 ('VCLT').

Treaty of the River Plate Basin (Brasilia, 23 Apr 1969) (in force 14 Aug 1970), Argentina-Bolivia-Brazil-Paraguay-Uruguay, 12550 UNTS 11 (1973) ('Plata Basin Treaty').

Convention Relative au Statut du Fleuve Sénégal (Convention on the International Status of the Senegal River) (Nouakchott, 11 Mar 1972), Guinea-Mali-Mauritania-Senegal ('1972 Status Convention').

Convention portant Création de l'Organisation pour la Mise en Valeur du Fleuve Sénégal (Convention on the Creation of the Organization for the Development of the

Senegal River) (Nouakchott, 11 Mar 1972), Guinea-Mali-Mauritania-Senegal ('1972 OMVS Convention').

Treaty of Amity and Cooperation in Southeast Asia (Denpasar, 24 Feb 1976).

Statute of the River Uruguay (Salto, 26 Feb 1975) (in force 18 Sep 1976), Argentina-Uruguay, 1295 UNTS 340 (1982) ('River Uruguay Statute').

Convention on the Protection of the Rhine against Pollution from Chlorides (as amended with annexes and exchanges of letters constituting an amendment) (Bonn, 3 Dec 1976), France-Germany-Luxembourg-Netherlands-Switzerland, 1404 UNTS 91 (1985) ('Rhine Chlorides Convention').

Additional Protocol to the Rhine Chlorides Convention (Brussels, 25 Sep 1991) (in force 1 Nov 1994), France-Germany-Luxembourg-Netherlands-Switzerland, 1840 UNTS 423 (1994) ('Rhine Chlorides Protocol').

Treaty on the Construction and Operation of the Gabčíkovo-Nagymaros Barrage System (Budapest, 16 Sep 1977) (in force 30 June 1978), Hungary-Czechoslovakia ('1977 Treaty').

Convention relative au Statut Juridique des Ouvrages Communs (Convention on the Legal Status of Common Works and Jointly Owned Infrastructure) (Bamako, 21 Dec 1978), Guinea-Mali-Mauritania-Senegal.

Convention Regarding the Methods of Financing Joint Works (Bamako, 12 May 1982), Guinea-Mali-Mauritania-Senegal.

UN, *Convention on the Law of the Sea* (UNCLOS) (Montego Bay, 10 Dec 1982) (in force 16 Nov 1994).

Charter of the South Asian Association for Regional Cooperation (Dhaka, 8 Dec 1985), Afghanistan-Bangladesh-Bhutan-India-Maldives-Nepal-Pakistan-Sri Lanka ('SAARC Charter').

Agreement on the Action Plan for the Environmentally Sound Management of the Common Zambezi River System, Botswana-Mozambique-Tanzania-Zambia-Zimbabwe (Harare, 28 May 1987).

Treaty Establishing a Common Market (MERCOSUR) (Asuncion, 26 Mar 1991), Argentina-Brazil-Paraguay-Uruguay-Venezuela ('Treaty of Asuncion').

Additional Protocol to the Treaty of Asuncion on the Institutional Structure of the MERCOSUL ('Protocolo Adicional ao Tratado de Assunção sobre a Estrutura Institucional do MERCOSUL') (Ouro Preto, 17 Dec 1994), Argentina-Brazil-Paraguay-Uruguay-Venezuela ('Ouro Preto Protocol').

Treaty Establishing the African Economic Community (Abuja, 3 June 1991) ('AEC Treaty').

UN Economic Commission for Europe (ECE), *Convention on the Protection and Use of Transboundary Watercourses and International Lakes* (Helsinki, 17 Mar 1992) (in force 6 Oct 1996), 31 ILM 1312 ('ECEWC').

Meeting of the Parties (MoP), 3rd Session (Madrid, 26–28 Nov 2003), Decision III/1 (28 Nov 2003) (in force 6 Feb 2013).

MoP, 6th Session (Rome, 28–30 Nov 2012), Decision VI/3 (30 Nov 2012).

ECEWC, *Guide to Implementing the Water Convention*, UN Doc ECE/MP. WAT/39 (UN 2013) ('ECEWC Guide').

MoP, 10th Session (Ljubljana,</misc> 23–25 Oct 2024), *Draft Program of Work for 2025–2027*, UN Doc ECE/MP. WAT/2024/2 (14 Aug 2024), at https://unece.org/sites/default/files/2024-09/ECE_MP.WAT_2024_2_draft_POW_2025-2027_ENG.pdf.

UN, *Status of Treaties*: ECEWC, as of 14 May 2025, Treaty Collection, at https://treaties.un.org/Pages/ViewDetails.aspx?src=TREATY&mtdsg_no=XXVII-5&chapter=27&clang=_en.

ECEWC, *Implementation Committee*, at https://unece.org/environment-policy/water/about-the-convention/convention-bodies/implementation-committee.

UN, *Framework Convention on Climate Change* (New York City, 9 May 1992) (in force 21 Mar 1994), 1771 UNTS 30822 (1992).

UN, *Convention on Biological Diversity* (Rio de Janeiro, 5 June 1992) (in force 29 Dec 1993) 1760 UNTS 30619 (1992) ('CBD').

CBD, 7th Conference of the Parties (COP-7) (Kuala Lumpur, 9–20 & 27 Feb 2004), Decision VII/11: *Ecosystem Approach*, UN Doc UNEP/CBD/COP/DEC/VII/11 (13 Apr 2004).

Special Agreement, Hungary-Slovakia (Brussels, 7 Apr 1993) (in force 28 June 1993).

Tratado sobre Medio Ambiente, Argentina-Bolivia (Buenos Aires, 17 Mar 1994).

Convention on Cooperation for the Protection and Sustainable use of the Danube River (Sofia, 29 June 1994) ('Danube River Protection Convention').

Convention for the establishment of the Lake Victoria Fisheries Organization, Burundi-Uganda-Kenya-Tanzania (Kisumu, 30 June 1994) (in force 24 May 1996).

Lake Victoria Fisheries Organization, *Harmonized Guidelines for Establishment and Management of Fish Breeding and Nursery Areas in Lake Victoria* (Jinja, 2019).

Agreement on the Cooperation for the Sustainable Development of the Mekong River Basin (Chiang Rai, 5 Apr 1995), Cambodia-Laos-Thailand-Vietnam ('Mekong Basin Agreement').

Protocol on Shared Watercourse Systems in the Southern African Development Community (SADC) (Johannesburg, 28 Aug 1995) (in force 29 Sep 1998), Angola-Botswana-Lesotho-Malawi-Mozambique-Namibia-South Africa-Swaziland-Tanzania-Zambia-Zimbabwe ('1995 SADC Protocol').

UN, *Convention on the Law of Non-Navigational Uses of International Watercourses* (New York City, 21 May 1997) (in force 17 Aug 2014), 36 ILM 700 (1997) ('UNWC').

Convention on the Protection of the Rhine (Bern, 12 Apr 1999), France-Germany Luxembourg-Netherlands-Switzerland, plus the European Community ('Rhine Protection Convention').

Rules of Procedure and Financial Regulations for the Cooperation of the International Commission for the Protection of the Rhine with the Coordinating Committee

Rhine (in force 1 July 2010), at https://www.iksr.org/fileadmin/user_upload/Dokumente_en/IKSR-CC-EN_30.06.10.pdf.

Treaty for the Establishment of the East African Community (EAC), as amended (Arusha, 30 Nov 1999) (in force 7 July 2000), Burundi-Kenya-Rwanda, South Sudan-Tanzania-Uganda ('EAC Treaty').

Revised Protocol on Shared Watercourses in the Southern African Development Community (Windhoek, 7 Aug 2000) (in force 22 Sep 2003) ('Revised SADC Protocol').

Agreement on the Establishment of the Orange-Senqu River Commission (Windhoek, 3 Nov 2000), Botswana-Lesotho-Namibia-South Africa.

Assembly of African Heads of State and Government, 36th Ordinary Session (Lomé, 7 Nov 2000), *Constitutive Act of the African Union* (in force 25 May 2001), as amended (Assembly, 1st Extraordinary Session, Addis Ababa, 3 Feb 2003; 2nd Ordinary Session, Maputo, 11 July 2003) ('AU Act').

AU Assembly, 2nd Ordinary Session, *Protocol of the Court of Justice of the African Union* (Maputo, 11 July 2003).

Protocol for the Resolution of Controversies in the MERCOSUL, Argentina-Brazil-Paraguay-Uruguay (Olivos, 18 Feb 2002) ('Olivos Protocol').

Charte des Eaux du Fleuve Sénégal ('Charter of the Senegal River Waters') (Nouakchott, 28 May 2002), Guinea-Mali-Mauritania-Senegal ('Senegal Basin Charter').

Protocol for Sustainable Development of Lake Victoria Basin (Arusha, 29 Nov 2003) (in force 1 Dec 2004), Burundi-Kenya-Rwanda-Tanzania-Uganda ('Lake Victoria Protocol').

Agreement on the Establishment of the Zambezi Watercourse Commission (ZAMCOM) (Kasane, 13 July 2004) (in force June 2011), Angola-Botswana-Malawi-Mozambique-Namibia-Tanzania-Zambia-Zimbabwe ('ZAMCOM Agreement').

ZAMCOM, *Rules and Procedures for Sharing of Data and Information Related to the Management and Development of the Zambezi Watercourse* (25 Feb 2016) (in effect 26 March 2016).

ZAMCOM, *Procedures for Notification of Planned Measures* (2017).

AU *Non-Aggression and Common Defense Pact* (AU Assembly, 4th Ordinary Session, Abuja, 31 Jan 2005).

Traité relatif à l'Adhésion de la République de Guinée à l'Organisation pour la Mise en Valeur du Fleuve Sénégal (Treaty on the Membership of Guinea to the OMVS) (17 Mar 2006), Guinea-Mali-Mauritania-Senegal ('Guinea Membership Treaty').

Charter of the Association of Southeast Asian Nations (ASEAN) (Singapore, 20 Nov 2007) (in force 15 Dec 2008), Brunei-Cambodia-Indonesia-Lao PDR-Malaysia-Myanmar-Philippines-Singapore-Thailand-Viet Nam, *reproduced in* ASEAN Secretariat, The ASEAN Charter (2015) ('ASEAN Charter').

Revised Treaty Establishing the Common Market for Eastern and Southern Africa (COMESA) (2009), Angola-Burundi-Comoros-Djibouti-DRC-Egypt-Eritrea-Ethiopia-Eswatini-Kenya-Libya-Madagascar-Malawi-Mauritius-Rwanda-Seychelles-Somalia-Sudan-Tunisia-Uganda-Zambia-Zimbabwe ('Revised COMESA Treaty').

Agreement on the Nile River Basin Cooperative Framework, Burundi-Ethiopia-Rwanda-South Sudan-Tanzania-Uganda (Entebbe, 14 May 2010) (in force 13 Oct 2024) ('Nile Cooperative Framework').

Guarani Aquifer Agreement (San Juan, 2 Aug 2010) (in force 26 Nov 2020), Argentina-Brazil-Paraguay-Uruguay, International Water Law Project, at https://www.internationalwaterlaw.org/documents/regionaldocs/Guarani_Aquifer_Agreement-Portuguese.pdf.

Summit of Heads of State, *Revised Treaty of the Community of Sahel-Saharan States* (CEN-SAD) (Ndjamena, 16 Feb 2013), Benin-Burkina Faso-Chad-Djibouti-Eritrea-Guinea-Ivory Coast-Mali-Morocco-Niger-Sudan-Senegal-Togo ('Revised CEN-SAD Treaty').

Benguela Current Convention (Benguela, 18 Mar 2013), Angola-Namibia-South Africa.

Treaty on European Union (Maastricht, 7 Feb 1992) (Consolidated Version 2016) (2016/C 202/01), OJ C 202 (7 June 2016) ('EU Treaty').

Treaty on the Functioning of the European Union (Rome, 25 Mar 1957) (Consolidated Version 2016) (2016/C 202/01), OJ C 202 (7 June 2016) ('EU Functioning Treaty').

Acuerdo que Establece la Comisión Binacional para la Gestión Integrada de los Recursos Hídricos de las Cuencas Hidrográficas Transfronterizas, Ecuador-Peru (Trujillo, 20 Oct 2017) ('Ecuador-Peru Agreement').

Regulation of the Binational Commission for the Integrated Management of the Water Resources of the Transboundary Basins between Ecuador and Peru, Ecuador-Peru ('Ecuador-Peru Regulation').

Cases

Permanent Court of International Justice (PCIJ), *Case Concerning the Territorial Jurisdiction of the International Commission of the River Oder* (Denmark-Czechoslovakia-France-Germany-Sweden-UK *v.* Poland), Judgment of 16 Sep 1929 ('River Oder Case').

US Supreme Court (State of New Jersey *v.* State of New York), 283 US 336, 51 S. Ct. 478 (1931).

PCIJ, *The Diversion of Water from the Meuse* (Netherlands *v.* Belgium), Judgment of 28 June 1937, Series A/B, Judgments, Orders and Advisory Opinions, Fascicule 70 (1937) ('Meuse Diversion Case').

International Court of Justice (ICJ), *Corfu Channel Case* (UK *v.* Albania), Judgment of 9 Apr 1949, ICJ Reports 4 (1949).

Reparation for Injuries Suffered in the Service of the United Nations, Advisory Opinion of 11 Apr 1949, ICJ Reports 1949, p. 174.

Arbitral Tribunal, *Affaire du Lac Lanoux* (Spain *v.* France), Award of 16 Nov 1957 ('Lake Lanoux Case').

ICJ, *Cases Concerning the North Sea Continental Shelf* (Germany v Denmark & Germany *v.* Netherlands), Judgment of 20 Feb 1969, ICJ Reports 3 (1969) ('North Sea Continental Shelf' Cases).

ICJ, *Fisheries Jurisdiction* (UK *v.* Iceland), Merits, Judgment of 25 July 1974, ICJ Reports 3 (1974) ('Fisheries Jurisdiction Case').

Fisheries Jurisdiction Case, *Declaration*, Ignacio-Pinto.

ICJ, *Passage through the Great Belt* (Finland *v.* Denmark), Provisional Measures, Order of 29 July 1991, ICJ Reports 12 (1991) ('Great Belt Case').

ICJ, *Legality of the Use by a State of Nuclear Weapons in Armed Conflict*, Advisory Opinion of 8 July 1996, ICJ Reports 66 (1996) ('Nuclear Weapons Use in Armed Conflict AO').

ICJ, *Legality of the Threat or Use of Nuclear Weapons*, Advisory Opinion of 8 July 1996, ICJ Reports 226 (1996) ('Nuclear Weapons Threat or Use AO').

ICJ, *Case Concerning the Gabčíkovo-Nagymaros Project* (Hungary *v.* Slovakia), Judgment of 25 Sep 1997, ICJ Reports 7 (1997) ('Gabčíkovo Case').

Gabčíkovo Case, *Separate Opinion*, M. Bedjaoui.

Permanent Court of Arbitration (PCA), *Case Concerning the Auditing of Accounts between the Kingdom of The Netherlands and the French Republic pursuant to the Additional Protocol of 25 Sep 1991 to the Convention on the Protection of the Rhine Against Pollution by Chlorides of 3 Dec 1976* (Netherlands *v.* France), Arbitral Award of 12 March 2004 ('Chlorides Case').

ICJ, *Case Concerning Pulp Mills on the River Uruguay* (Argentina *v.* Uruguay), Judgment of 20 Apr 2010, ICJ Reports 1 (2010) ('Pulp Mills Case').

Pulp Mills Case, *Request for the Indication of Provisional Measures*, Order of 13 July 2006, ICJ Reports 113 (2006) ('Pulp Mills 2006 Provisional Measures').

ICJ, Kasikili/Sedudu Island (Botswana *v.* Namibia), Judgment (13 Dec 1999), 1999 ICJ Report 1045 ('Kasikili Case').

Kasikili Case, *Separate Opinion*, Judge Kooijmans.

Kasikili Case, *Declaration*, Judge Ranjeva.

ICJ, *Dispute over the Status and Use of the Waters of the Silala* (Chile *v.* Bolivia), Judgment of 1 Dec 2022, ICJ Reports 2022, p. 614 ('Silala Case').

National Statutes

Brazil, *Constitution* (1988) ('*Constituição da República Federativa do Brasil*').

Federal Law 9433/97 (8 Jan 1997) (*Política Nacional de Recursos Hídricos*) ('National Water Resources Policy Act').

National Water Resources Council (*Conselho Nacional de Recursos Hídricos*), Res 22/2002 (24 May 2002).

Colombia, Decreto Ley 2811 (1974) (*Código Nacional de Recursos Naturales Renovables y de Protección al Medio Ambiente*) ('National Environment Code').

France, Interim Executive Council, Decree of 16 Nov 1792.

Senegal, Decree. 2016–1494: *A Bill to Authorize Ratification of the Revised ĊEN-SAD Treaty* (26 Sep 2016).

Secondary Research Sources

UN General Assembly (UNGA) Materials

International Year of Water Cooperation: 2013, Res 65/154 (20 Dec 2010), UN Doc A/RES/65/154 (11 Feb 2011) ('IYWC Res').

Transforming our World: The 2030 Agenda for Sustainable Development, Res 70/1 (25 Sep 2015), UN Doc A/RES/70/1 (21 Oct 2015) ('2030 Agenda').

29th Session, *Charter of Economic Rights and Duties of States*, Res 3281 (XXIX) (12 Dec 1974), resolutions adopted on the Reports of the 2nd Committee.

51st Session, 99th Plenary Meeting (NYC, 21 May 1997), UN Doc A/51/PV.99 ('UNWC Voting Records').

58th Session, Resolution 58/217, *International Decade for Action, Water for Life, 2005–2015* (23 Dec 2003), UN Doc A/RES/58/217 (9 Feb 2004).

71st Session, Res 71/222, *International Decade for Action, 'Water for Sustainable Development', 2018–2028* (21 Dec 2016), UN Doc A/RES/71/222 (7 Feb 2017).

Presidency, 72nd Session, *Letter to Permanent Representatives and Observers, Informal Discussions Summary* (14 Mar 2018), Morning Dialogues 5–7: Multilateralism under Fire? (NYC, 15 & 23 Feb, 9 Mar 2018).

79th Session, *The Pact for the Future*, Res 79/1 (22 Sep 2024), UN Doc A/Res/79/1 (22 Sep 2024) ('Pact for the Future').

International Law Commission (ILC) Materials

Draft Articles on the Law of the Non-Navigational Uses of International Watercourses and Commentaries thereto and Resolution on Transboundary Confined Groundwater ('ILC Draft Articles (1994)'), *in* ILC Report, 46th Session (2 May-22 July 1994), UN Doc A/49/10 ('ILC (1994)').

Draft Articles on Prevention of Transboundary Harm from Hazardous Activities, with Commentaries, 53rd Session, *in* ILC Yearbook (2001), Vol.II, Part Two, UN Doc A/56/10.

Draft Articles on the Law of Transboundary Aquifers, with commentaries (2008) ('ILC Draft Articles (2008)'), *in* ILC Report, 60th Session (5 May-6 June & 7 July-8 Aug 2008), UN Doc A/63/10(SUPP).

Yamada, C. (Special Rapporteur), *2nd Report on Shared Natural Resources: Transboundary Groundwaters*, UN Doc A/CN.4/539 (2004).

Draft Articles on the Protection of Persons in the Event of Disasters, with commentaries (2016) ('ILC Draft Articles (2016)'), *in* ILC Report, 68th Session (2 May-10 June & 4 July-12 Aug 2016), UN Doc A/71/10.

General Principles of Law ('ILC (2023)'), *in* ILC Report, Ch.IV, 74th Session (24 Apr-2 June & 3 July-4 Aug 2023), UN Doc A/78/10 (3 Nov 2023).

Other UN Reports and Publications

Unturbe, J.M., *A 10 Year Story: The Water for Life Decade 2005–2015 and Beyond* (UN Office to Support the International Decade for Action 'Water for Life' (2005–2015) (UN Office) & UN Water Decade Program on Advocacy and Communication (UNW-DPAC) (2015).

UN Water, *Sustainable Development Goal 6 Synthesis Report 2018 on Water and Sanitation* (UN Water 2018) ('UN Water (2018)').

UN Environment Program (UNEP), *Progress on Integrated Water Resources Management: Global Indicator 6.5.1 Updates and Acceleration Needs* (UN 2021).

UN, *Blueprint for Acceleration: Sustainable Development Goal 6: Synthesis Report on Water and Sanitation* (UN 2023).

UNECE, UNESCO, UN-Water, *Progress on Transboundary Water Cooperation: Mid-Term Status of SDG Indicator 6.5.2, with a Special Focus on Climate Change* (UN & UNESCO 2024).

Political Statements and Events' Proceedings, Soft Law Instruments, Strategies and Policy Action Plans

ASEAN, *Declaration* (Bangkok, 8 Aug 1967), Indonesia-Malaysia-Singapore-Philippines-Thailand ('ASEAN Bangkok Declaration').

UN, *Declaration* ('Stockholm Declaration'), *in* Report, UN Conference on the Human Environment (Stockholm, 5–16 June 1972), UN Doc A/CONF.48/14/Rev.1 (UN 1973).

UN, *Mar del Plata Action Plan, in* Report, UN Water Conference (Mar del Plata, 14–25 Mar 1977), UN Doc E/CONF.70/29 (UN 1977), p. 3–65.

Dublin Statement on Water and Sustainable Development (31 Jan 1992) ('Dublin Statement'), *in* ICWE Report ('Dublin Statement'), *in* UN Administrative Committee on Coordination, Inter-Secretariat Group for Water Resources (ACC/ISGWR), Report, *International Conference on Water and the Environment* (ICWE): *Development Issues for the 21st Century* (Dublin, 26–31 Jan 1992) (ICWE Steering Committee 1992) ('ICWE Report').

Report of the UN Conference on Environment and Development ('UNCED Report'), Vol. I, Annex I (Rio de Janeiro, 3–14 June 1992), UN Doc A/CONF.151/26 (12 Aug 1992).

Rio Declaration on Environment and Development, UNCED Report, Vol. I, Annex I.

Agenda 21, Res. 1, *in* UNCED Report, Vol. I, Annex II.

Earth Charter Initiative, *Earth Charter* (Hague, 29 June 2000), at https://earthcharter.org/wp-content/uploads/2020/06/Booklet-Earth-Charter-52-FINAL.pdf.

Earth Charter Initiative, *What is the Charter?*, at http://earthcharter.org/discover/what-is-the-earth-charter/.

Euro-Mediterranean Heads of States and Government, *Joint Declaration of the Paris Summit for the Mediterranean* (Paris, 13 July 2008), at https://ufmsecretariat.org/wp-content/uploads/2012/09/ufm_paris_declaration1.pdf.

World Water Council (WWC), 5th World Water Forum (Istanbul, 16–22 Mar 2009) ('WWC (2009)'), *Istanbul Declaration* (16 Mar 2009).

Ministerial Process, *Istanbul Ministerial Statement* (22 Mar 2009).

UNW-DPAC, International Annual UN-Water Zaragoza Conference 2012/2013: Preparing for the 2013 International Year – Water Cooperation: Making it Happen (Zaragoza, 8–10 Jan 2012), *Conference Report – Water Cooperation in Action: Approaches, Tools and Processes* (UN Water 2013) ('UNW-DPAC').

Government of Tajikistan, High-Level International Conference on Water Cooperation (Dushanbe, Tajikistan, 20–21 Aug 2013), *Declaration* (20–21 Aug 2013).

UfM, Water Ministers Meeting (Malta, 27 Apr 2017), *Declaration on the UfM Water Agenda* (03 April 2017) ('Malta Declaration').

AMCOW, Strategy 2018–2030 (2018).

Bolivia-Brazil-Paraguay, 8th World Water Forum (Brasilia, 18–23 Mar 2018), *Declaração para a Conservação, Desenvolvimento Integral e Sustentável do Pantanal* (Declaration on the Conservation and Integrated and Sustainable Development of the Pantanal) (Brasilia, 22 Mar 2018) ('Pantanal Declaration').

Government of Tajikistan, High Level International Conference on the International Decade for Action, Water for Sustainable Development, 2018–2028 (Dushanbe, 20–22 June 2018) ('2018 Dushanbe Conference').

Final Declaration: Promoting Action and Policy Dialogue ('Dushanbe Declaration'), at https://dushanbewaterprocess.org/wp-content/uploads/2019/11/2018-06-21-final-declaration-clean.pdf.

Co-Chairs' Summary, at https://wsdconf2018.org/wp-content/uploads/2017/05/Dushanbe-Water-Summary-fin.pdf.

Regional Action Plan for the implementation of the Sendai Framework for Disaster Risk Reduction 2015–2030 in the Americas and the Caribbean (3 Nov 2021), VII Regional Platform for Disaster Risk Reduction in the Americas and the Caribbean (RP21): Building Resilient Economies in the Americas and the Caribbean (1–4 Nov 2021, Virtual Event), at https://rp-americas.undrr.org/sites/default/files/inline-files/Regional%20Action%20Plan_EN.pdf?startDownload=true.

Abadi, A., Hurtado, R.M., UfM *Financial Strategy for Water*, v.2 (UfM 2020), at FS-WEB-EN.pdf.

Water, Environment & Blue Economy Division, *UfM Water Policy Framework for Actions 2030: Water Agenda Booklet* (UfM 2022), at PolicyF-2023-EN-Web-2.pdf.

UNGA President, UN Conference on the Midterm Comprehensive Review of the Implementation of the Objectives of the International Decade for Action 'Water for Sustainable Development', 2018–2028 (New York City, 22–24 Mar 2023), *Summary of Proceedings*, at https://digitallibrary.un.org/record/4012972?ln=en&v=pdf ('UNWC 2023 Summary').

Guterres, A., *Secretary-General's Closing Remarks at the United Nations Water Conference* (24 Mar 2023), at https://www.un.org/sg/en/content/sg/speeches/2023-03-24/secretary-generals-closing-remarks-the-united-nations-water-conference.

UNEA, 6th Session (Nairobi, 26 Feb-1 Mar 2024), Res 6/13, Effective and inclusive solutions for strengthening water policies to achieve sustainable development in the context of climate change, biodiversity loss and pollution, UN Doc UNEP/EA.6/Res.13 (5 Mar 2024).

Association of Southeast Asian Nations (ASEAN), *Joint Statement on Biodiversity to the 16th Meeting of Conference of the Parties to the Convention on Biological Diversity*, 44th and 45th ASEAN Summits (Vientiane, 9 Oct 2024), at 19-Final_AJS-on-Biodiversity-to-the-CBD-COP-16.pdf.

Foreign Secretary, *Statement on the Decision of the Cabinet Committee on Security* (23 Apr 2025), Ministry of External Affairs, https://www.mea.gov.in/Speeches-Statements.htm?dtl/39442.

International Expert Association Materials

International Law Association (ILA), *Helsinki Rules on the Uses of the Waters of International Rivers* (1966) ('Helsinki Rules'), *in* ILA Report, 52nd Session (Helsinki, 16 Aug 1966), Uses of Waters of International Rivers, p. 447–533 ('ILA (1966)').

Berlin Rules on Water Resources (2004) ('Berlin Rules'), *in* ILA, Water Resources Committee, 4th Report ('ILA (2004)'), athttps://unece.org/fileadmin/DAM/env/water/meetings/legal_board/2010/annexes_groundwater_paper/Annex_IV_Berlin_Rules_on_Water_Resources_ILA.pdf.

Institut de Droit International (Institute of International Law) (IIL), *International Regulation regarding the Use of International Watercourses for Purposes other than Navigation* ('Madrid Resolution') IIL Session (Madrid, 20 Apr 2011), *in* 24 IIL Yearbook 365 (1911).

IIL, *Resolution on the Use of International Non-Maritime Waters*, IIL Session (Salzburg, 11 Sep 1961), *in* 49 IIL Yearbook 381–4 (1961).

Books

Bogdanović, S., *The International Law Association Helsinki Rules: Contribution to International Water Law* (Brill 2019).

Bruch, C., *et al* eds, *Public Participation in the Governance of International Freshwater Resources* (United Nations University Press 2005).

Bruhács, J., *The Law of Non-Navigational Uses of International Watercourses* (Translation by Zehery, M.) (Martinus Nijhoff 1992).

Caponera, D.A., *Principles of Water Law and Administration: National and International*, 3rd ed, revis ed & updated by Nanni, M. (Taylor & Francis 2019).

de Chazournes, L.B., *Fresh Water in International Law* (Oxford 2013).

Earle, A., Malzbender, D. eds, *Stakeholder Participation in Transboundary Water Management: Selected Case Studies* (African Centre for Water Research 2006).

Elver, H., *Peaceful Uses of International Rivers: The Euphrates and Tigris Rivers Dispute* (Transnational Publishers 2002).

Friedmann, W., *The Changing Structure of International Law* (Stevens & Sons 1964).

Grotius, H., *De Jure Belli ac Pacis, Libri Tres, in Quibus Jus Naturae et Gentium, Item Juris Publici Praecipua Explicantur*, Book 2, Cap. 2–3 (1625).

Henkin, L., *How Nations Behave*, 2nd ed (1979).

Hildering, A., *International Law, Sustainable Development and Water Management* (Eburon 2004).

Hunter, D., Salzman, J., Zaelke, D., *International Environmental Law and Policy*, 5th ed (Foundation Press 2015).

Hunter, D., Salzman, J., Zaelke, D., *International Environmental Law and Policy*, 2nd ed (Foundation Press 2002).

Islam, N., *The Law of Non-Navigational Uses of International Watercourses: Options for Regional Regime-Building in Asia* (Wolters Kluwer 2010).

Kaya, I., *Equitable Utilization: The Law of the Non-Navigational Uses of International Watercourses* (Ashgate 2003),

Kiss, A.C., Shelton, D., *International Environmental Law*, 3rd ed (Foundation Press 2004).

Lammers, J.G., *Pollution of International Watercourses: A Search for Substantive Rules and Principles of Law* (Martinus Nijhoff 1984).

Leb, C., *Cooperation in the Law of Transboundary Water Resources* (Cambridge University 2013).

Magalhães, P., *The Earth Condominium: From Climate Change to a New Legal Concept for the Planet* (Almedina 2007).

Magsig, B.O., *International Water Law and the Quest for Common Security* (Earthscan 2015).

Manner, E.J., Metsälampi, V.M., *The Work of the International Law Association on the Law of International Water Resources* (Finnish Branch of International Law Association 1988).

McCaffrey, S.C., *The Law of International Watercourses*, 3rd ed (Oxford 2019).

McIntyre, O., *Environmental Protection of International Watercourses under International Law* (Ashgate 2007).

Simma, B., *From Bilateralism to Community Interest in International Law*, 250 Recueil des Cours 217 (1994).

Smith, H.A., *The Economic Uses of International Rivers* (P.S. King & Sons 1931).

Tanzi, A., Arcari, M., *The United Nations Convention on the Law of International Watercourses: A Framework for Sharing* (Kluwer 2001).

Teclaff, L.A., Utton, A.E., *International Groundwater Law* (Oceana 1981).

Tignino, M., Sangbana, K. eds, *Public Participation and Water Resources Management: Where Do We Stand in International Law?* (UNESCO 2013).

Verdross, A., *Die Verfassung der Volkerrechtsgemeinschaft* (Springer, 1926).

Vitanyi, B., *The International Regime of River Navigation* (Sijthoff & Noordhoff 1979).

Yee, S., *Towards an International Law of Co-Progressiveness* (Martinus Nijhoff 2004).

Articles in Edited Books

Biswas, A.K., *Water and Regional Development*, *in* Biswas, A.K., Ünver, O., Tortajada, C. eds, Water as a Focus for Regional Development (OUP 2004), p. 1–13.

Blokker, N., *General Introduction*, p. 1–13.

von Bogdandy, A., *Opening Address*, p. 1–2.

de Chazournes, L.B., *The Role of Diplomatic Means of Solving Water Disputes: A Special Emphasis on Institutional Mechanisms*, *in* The International Bureau of the Permanent Court of Arbitration ed, *Resolution of International Water Disputes* (Kluwer Law International 2003), p. 91–110.

de Chazournes, B., *The Rhine Chlorides Arbitration Concerning the Auditing of Accounts (Netherlands-France): Its Contribution to International Law*, *in* McMahon, B. ed, The Rhine Chlorides Arbitration Concerning the Auditing of Accounts (Netherlands-France), Award of 2004 (TMC Asser Press 2008), p. 1–15.

de Chazournes, B., *The Permanent Court of International Justice, The International Court of Justice and International Water Law: Versatility in Consistency*, *in* McCaffrey, S.C., Leb, C., Denoon, R.T. eds, Research Handbook on International Water Law (Edward Elgar 2019), p. 285–300.

Farrajota, M.M., *International Cooperation on Water Resources*, *in* Dellapenna, J.W., Gupta, J. eds, The Evolution of the Law and Politics of Water (Springer 2009), p. 337–352.

Lipper, J., *Equitable Utilization*, *in* Garretson, A.H., Hayton, R.D., Olmstead, C.J. eds, The Law of International Drainage Basins (Oceana 1967), p. 15–88.

Loures, F.R. *et al*, *The Authority and Function of the UN Watercourses Convention, in* Loures, F.R., Rieu-Clarke, A. eds, The UN Watercourses Convention in Force: Strengthening International Law for Transboundary Water Management (Routledge 2013), p. 49–66.

Pellet, A., *Article 38, in* Zimmermann, A., *et al* eds, The Statute of the International Court of Justice: A Commentary, 2nd ed (Oxford 2012), p. 731–870

Runavot, M.C., *The Intergovernmental Organization and the Institutionalization of International Relations: The Modelling of International Organization at Stake*, p. 17–43.

Virzo, R., Ingravallo, I. eds, *Evolutions in the Law of International Organizations, Series 'Legal Aspects of International Organizations*, Vol.54 (Brill Nijhoff 2015).

Wellens, K., *Revisiting Solidarity as a (Re-)Emerging Constitutional Principle: Some Further Reflections*, p. 3–38.

Wolfrum, R., Kojima, C. eds, *Solidarity: A Structural Principle of International Law* (Springer 2010).

Hague Academy General Courses

Caflisch, L., *Règles Générales du Droit des Cours d'Eau Internationaux*, 219 RCADI 9 (1989).

Fitzmaurice, G., *The General Principles of International Law Considered from the Standpoint of the Rule of Law*, 92 RCADI 5 (1957).

Articles

Benvenisti, E., *Collective Action in the Utilization of Shared Freshwater: The Challenges of International Water Resources Law*, 90 Am. J. Int'l L. 384–415 (1996).

Dellapenna, J.W., *Treaties as Instruments for Managing Internationally-Shared Water Resources: Restricted Sovereignty vs. Community of Property*, 26:1 Case W. Res. J. Int'l L 27–56 (1994).

International Water Law in a Climate of Disruption, 17:1 Mich. J. Int'l L 43–94 (2007).

Dellapenna, J.W., Gupta, J., *The Evolution of Water Law Through 4,000 Years*, Villanova University School of Law, Public Law and Legal Theory, Working Paper 2013–3041 (2013).

Denoon, R.T.P. *et al*, *Engaging non-state actors in the negotiation and implementation of international watercourse agreements: Experiences and Lessons Learned from Canada*, 45:4 Water International, 311–328 (2020).

Falkenmark, M., *Forward to the Future: A Conceptual Framework for Water Dependence* (Volvo Environment Prize Lecture 1998), 28:4 Ambio 356–61 (1999).

Finer, M., Jenkins, C.N., *Proliferation of Hydroelectric Dams in the Andean Amazon and Implications for Andes-Amazon Connectivity*, 7:4 PLoS ONE 1–9 (2012).

Gerlak, A.K. *et al*, *Hydrosolidarity and International Water Governance*, 14 International Negotiation 311–28 (2009).

Gerlak, A.K. *et al*, *Hydrosolidarity and Beyond: Can Ethics and Equity Find a Place in Today's Water Resource Management?* 36:3 Water International 251–65 (2011).

Ginsburg, T., Stephanopoulos, N., *The Concepts of Law*, 84:147 The University of Chicago law Review 147–75 (2017), *at* https://lawreview.uchicago.edu/print-archive/concepts-law.

Hestermeyer, H.P., *Reality or Aspiration? Solidarity in International Environmental and World Trade Law*, Outcome Paper 2/2012, Otto-Hahn-Gruppe, Diversität und Homogenität, (Max-Planck-Institut für ausländisches öffentliches Recht und Völkerrecht 2012).

Kgomongoe, M., Meissner, R., *The Revised Protocol on Shared Watercourses and the Management of Water Resources in SADC*, SA Yearbook of International Affairs, 2003104, p. 351–59.

Koskenniemi, M., *International Legal Theory and Doctrine*, *in* Max Planck Encyclopedia of Public International Law (MPEPIL) (online) (Oxford 2007).

Kramer, A. *et al*, *The Key to Managing Conflict and Cooperation over Water*, 11:1 A World of Science 4–12 (Jan-Mar 2013).

Leb, C., *The Right to Water in a Transboundary Context: Emergence of Seminal Trends*, 37:6 Water International 640–653 (2012), DOI: 10.1080/02508060.2012.710950.

Loures, F.R., *The Dragon as Part of Transboundary Basin 'Villages': Community-of-Interests and International Law in China*, 24 Water Law 220–38 (2015).

Matthews, S., *From Source to Sea: Interactions between the Orange-Senqu River Basin and the Benguela Current Large Marine Ecosystem* (Orange-Senqu River Commission 2013).

Mbengue, M.M., *A Model for African Shared Water Resources: The Senegal River Legal System*, 23:1 RECIEL 59–66 (2014).

McCaffrey, S.C., *The Convention Enters into Force*, 44:4 Envtl. Pol'y & L. 351–6 (2014).

Molle, F., *Nirvana Concepts, Narratives and Policy Models: Insights from the Water Sector*, 1:1 Water Alternatives 131–56 (2008).

Rivers as Legal Structures: The Examples of the Jordan and the Nile, 36 Natural Resources Journal 217–250 (1996).

Salman, S.M.A., *The Helsinki Rules, the UN Watercourses Convention and the Berlin Rules: Perspectives on International Water Law*, 23:4 J. Water Resources Dev. 625–40 (2007).

Sievers, E.W., Transboundary Jurisdiction and Watercourse Law: China, Kazakhstan, and the Irtysh, 37 Tex. Int'l L.J. 1 (2002).

Sindico, F., Hirata, R., Manganelli, A., *The Guarani Aquifer System: From a Beacon of Hope to a Question Mark in the Governance of Transboundary Aquifers*, 20 Journal of Hydrology: Regional Studies 49–59 (2018).

Solidarity amongst States: An Emerging Structural Principle of International Law, 49 Indian Journal of International Law 8–20 (2009).

Tarlock, A.D., *Four Challenges for International Water Law*, 23 Tul. Envtl. L.J. 369–408 (2010).

Verschuuren, J., *Sustainable Development and the Nature of Environmental Legal Principles*, 9:1 PER/PELJ 209–61 (2006).

Vöneky, S., *Analogy in International Law*, *in* Max Planck Encyclopedia of Public International Law (MPEPIL) (online) (Oxford 2008).

Wolfrum, R., *General International Law (Principles, Rules, and Standards)*, *in* Max Planck Encyclopedia of Public International Law (MPEPIL) (online) (Oxford 2010).

Yihdego, Z., Rieu-Clarke, A., *An Exploration of Fairness in International Law through the Blue Nile and GERD*, 41:4 Water International 528–549 (2016).

Theses

Howden, J.G., *The Community of Interest Approach in International Water Law: A Legal Framework for Common Management of International Watercourses*, submitted for Degree of Philosophiae Doctor, University of Bergen (2019).

Taylor, J., *Unravelling Cooperation: The Role and Limits of Cooperation in the Governance of International Watercourses in Customary International Law*, ANU College of Law Research Paper 15–05, submitted for Honors Thesis, ANU College of Law, The Australian National University (2014).

Reports, Booklets and Briefs

Agarwal, A. *et al*, *Integrated Water Resources Management*, GWP Technical Advisory Committee (TAC) Background Paper 4 (GWP 2000).

Malzbender, D., Earle, A., *The Impact and Implications of the Adoption of the 1997 UN Watercourse Convention for Countries in Southern Africa* (WWF), International Water Law Project, at https://www.internationalwaterlaw.org/bibliography/WWF/RA_SADC_states.pdf.

Secretariat of the 3rd World Water Forum, Virtual Water Forum, *Final Report* (2003) ('VWF Report').

Stockholm International Water Institute (SIWI): *Water: The Path to Agenda 2030 Implementation*, Policy Brief (2018) ('SIWI (2018a)').

Policy Brief: *Transboundary Waters: Cooperation from Source to Sea* (2018) ('SIWI (2018b)').

SIWI *et al*, *Building a Resilient Future through Water: An Open Letter to the High-Level Political Forum for Sustainable Development from Multistakeholder Representatives of the Water and Development Community* (Apr 2018).

World Bank, *Environmental Protection and Sustainable Development of the Guarani Aquifer System Project: Implementation Completion and Results* (TF-50950 TF-51223), Report ICR00001198 (2009).

World Commission on Dams (WCD), *Dams and Development: A New Framework for Decision-Making Report* (Earthscan 2000) ('WCD Report').

WWF, *Managing Rivers Wisely: Lessons from WWF's work for integrated river basin management* (WWF 2003).

International Institute for Sustainable Development (IISD) Reporting Services

Summary of the 2018 Meeting of the High-level Political Forum on Sustainable Development: 9–18 July 2018, 33:45 Earth Negotiations Bulletin 1–17 (21 July 2018). ('IISD (2018a)').

Summary of the 10th Meeting of the Parties to the UN Water Convention: 23–25 October 2024, Water Convention Bulletin (28 Oct 2024).

Online Resources

Amazon Waters Initiative, *Integrated River Basin Management*, at http://amazonwaters.org/the-initiative/integrated-river-basin-management/.

Annan, K., Two concepts of sovereignty (18 Sep 1999), on United Nations, at https://www.un.org/sg/en/content/sg/articles/1999-09-18/two-concepts-sovereignty.

Bethlehem, S.D., *Project 2100—Is the International Legal Order Fit for Purpose?* (29 Nov 2022), *in* EJIL: Talk!, at https://www.ejiltalk.org/project-2100-is-the-international-legal-order-fit-for-purpose/?utm_source=mailpoet&utm_medium=email&utm_campaign=ejil-talk-newsletter-post-title_2.

Bummel, A., Guest Article: *Let's imagine global citizen participation at the UN*, CIVICUS (undated), at https://www.civicus.org/index.php/re-imagining-democracy/overviews/3335-let-s-imagine-global-citizen-participation-at-the-un.

Dupuy, P.M., *International Law as a Common Heritage of Mankind* (21 Mar 2025), EJIL: Talk!, Blog of the European Journal of International Law, at https://www.ejiltalk.org/international-law-as-a-common-heritage-of-mankind/?utm_source=mailpoet&utm_medium=email&utm_campaign=ejil-talk-newsletter-post-title_2.

ECEWC, *Implementation Committee*, at https://unece.org/environment-policy/water/about-the-convention/convention-bodies/implementation-committee.

European Commission, *EU-MERCOSUR Trade Agreement*, at https://ec.europa.eu/trade/policy/in-focus/eu-mercosur-association-agreement/.

GEF, *Environmental Protection and Sustainable Development of the Guarani Aquifer System Project*, Argentina-Brazil-Paraguay-Uruguay (2003–2009), Project Details, at https://www.thegef.org/project/environmental-protection-and-sustainable-integrated-management-guarani-aquifer.

González, K.D.Z., Academic Course: 2020–2021, *Public International Law*, at https://roderic.uv.es/rest/api/core/bitstreams/0e68c009-3a49-4db6-a15b-600f79ac0cc5/content.

International Commission for the Protection of the Rhine, Legal Basis, Convention, at https://www.iksr.org/en/icpr/legal-basis/convention.

About us, at https://www.iksr.org/en/icpr/about-us.

Istrefi, K., Pasquet, L., *Mind Your Attitude: The Erosion of International Law?* (3 Mar 2025), *in* EJIL: Talk, at https://www.ejiltalk.org/mind-your-attitude-the-erosion-of-international-law/?utm_source=mailpoet&utm_medium=email&utm_campaign=ejil-talk-newsletter-post-title_2.

Justia Legal Dictionary: *Doctrine*, at https://dictionary.justia.com/doctrine.

Kibaroğlu, A., *Water Security and Peace on the Euphrates-Tigris River*, Course on Governance for Transboundary Freshwater Security: 1d. Case study, at https://learning.edx.org/course/course-v1:SDGAcademyX+TBW001+2T2020/block-v1:SDGAcademyX+TBW001+2T2020+type@sequential+block@832541b7e8c14205a836e2f2c45e7234/block-v1:SDGAcademyX+TBW001+2T2020+type@vertical+block@d2fbea28c1fd48bf815667354ea20ed1.

Law Dictionary: *Theory*, at https://thelawdictionary.org/theory/.

List of OAU/AU treaties, conventions, protocols and charters, at https://au.int/en/treaties.

Law, L.: *Theory of Law*, https://www.lsd.law/define/theory-of-law.

McCaffrey, S., *The Entry into Force of the 1997 Watercourses Convention*, International Water Law Project Blog (25 May 2014), at https://www.internationalwaterlaw.org/blog/2014/05/25/dr-stephen-mccaffrey-the-entry-into-force-of-the-1997-water courses-convention/.

Defense, M., *Advanced Modules on Digital Rights and Freedom of Expression Online, Module 6: Litigating Digital Rights Cases in Africa* (Mar 2024), p. 38–39, at https://www.mediadefence.org/ereader/wp-content/uploads/sites/2/2022/12/Module-6-Litigating-digital-rights-in-Africa-2024.pdf.

Merriam-Webster Dictionary Online:

Community, at http://www.merriam-webster.com/dictionary/community.

Concept, at https://www.merriam-webster.com/dictionary/concept.

Doctrine, at https://www.merriam-webster.com/dictionary/doctrine.

Theory, at https://www.merriam-webster.com/dictionary/theory.

Merriam-Webster Legal Dictionary Online: *Community*, at https://www.merriam-webster.com/dictionary/community#legalDictionary.

Moore, S., *How to Solve the Global Water Crisis: The Real Challenges Are Not Technical, but Politica*l (20 Mar 2018), Council on Foreign Relations, Foreign Affairs, at https://www.foreignaffairs.com/articles/world/2018-03-20/how-solve-global-water-crisis.

Movilla, L., *Towards Globalization of Earth Jurisprudence* (23 Apr 2018), UN Harmony with Nature, 8th Interactive Dialogue of the General Assembly on Harmony with Nature, at http://www.harmonywithnatureun.org/dialogue/LYezQHBEJqbu9RK

c9hzp6Kpd28074Qe3L5Z3QdOJjWC8y1fGgRWFbNsjD2pI9uZuVQf9Ctk!buwmSb HIYKd1Sw==.

Nile Basin Initiative (NBI), at https://www.nilebasin.org.

Oxford Learner's Dictionary, at https://www.oxfordlearnersdictionaries.com/us/definition/american_english/approach_2.

Oxford Reference, at https://www.oxfordreference.com/display/10.1093/oi/authority.20110803095724371.

Pearce, F., *Rivers in the Sky: How Deforestation Is Affecting Global Water Cycles* (24 July 2018), Yale Environment 360, at https://e360.yale.edu/features/how-deforestation-affecting-global-water-cycles-climate-change.

Plain Language Legal Dictionary, at https://www.rocketlawyer.com/legal-dictionary.rl.

Regional Strategic Action Program for the Nubian Aquifer System (Vienna, 18 Sep 2013), Egypt-Libya-Sudan-Chad, at https://iwlearn.net/resolveuid/eba4ee45685b4654b5d8a5e278823c49.

Reichert, G., *Entry into Force of the UN Watercourses Convention – Should Europe Care?, on* International Water Law Project Blog (21 July 2014), at https://www.internationalwaterlaw.org/blog/2014/07/21/dr-gotz-reichert-entry-into-force-of-the-un-watercourses-convention-should-europe-care/.

Rieu-Clarke, A., Loures, F.R., *Should we Care whether the UN Watercourses Convention Enters into Force? – Part II* (22 July 2012), International Water Law Project Blog, at https://www.internationalwaterlaw.org/blog/2012/07/22/should-we-care-whether-the-un-watercourses-convention-enters-into-force-part-ii/.

Salman, S.M.A., *Entry into Force of the UN Watercourses Convention – Where are the Nile Basin Countries?* International Water Law Project Blog (2 June 2014), at https://www.internationalwaterlaw.org/blog/2014/06/02/dr-salman-m-a-salman-entry-into-force-of-the-un-watercourses-convention-where-are-the-nile-basin-countries/.

Simpson, E., *There's Nothing Wrong with the Liberal Order that Can't Be Fixed by What's Right With It: Realists need to get a lot more realistic about the global legal system*, Foreign Policy, Voice (7 Aug 2018), athttps://foreignpolicy.com/2018/08/07/theres-nothing-wrong-with-the-liberal-order-that-cant-be-fixed-by-whats-right-with-it/.

Step-by-Step Monitoring Methodology for SDG Indicator 6.5.2 (2020), *at* https://unece.org/DAM/env/water/activities/Reporting_convention/SDG_652_Step-by-step_methodology_2020_ENG.pdf.

Strategic Action Program: Regional Strategy for Integrated Water Resources Management in the Amazon Basin (Brasilia, 2018), athttp://otca.org/en/ctp_otca_projetos/acto-unep-gef-project-integrated-and-sustainable-management-of-transboundary-water-resources-of-the-amazon-river-basin-considering-variability-and-climate-change/.

Strategic Framework for Adaptation to Climate Change in the Dniester River Basin (2015) & *Implementation Plan* (2017), *at* https://dniester-commission.org/en/publications/climate-change/.

Swain, A. Untitled Presentation, Panel IV – Current Transboundary Freshwater Disputes: North Africa, South Asia, and Southeast Asia, International Conference – A Bridge over Troubled Waters: Dispute Resolution in the Law of International Watercourses and the Law of the Sea (Luxembourg, 25–26 Sep 2017), Max Planck Institute Luxembourg for Procedural Law ('Swain (2017'), at https://www.youtube.com/watch?v=d3aafljN60Q&list=PLhELkA58aBZt010iJs_HQU3UQF26dqxJm&index=5&t=2772s.

Swain, A. *Water Cooperation on the Ganges–Brahmaputra River*, Course on Governance for Transboundary Freshwater Security: 1b. Case study, at https://learning.edx.org/course/course-v1:SDGAcademyX+TBW001+2T2020/block-v1:SDGAcademyX+TBW001+2T2020+type@sequential+block@ca04fe41d0e146b3a75695f0a712ac66/block-v1:SDGAcademyX+TBW001+2T2020+type@vertical+block@3ced3eea0f1a4d98af18fa99f7b79d6b.

Traore, A., *Sommet Extraordinaire de la CEN-SAD à N'Djamena: L'Ère du Renouveau* (17 Feb 2013), Lefaso.Net, at http://lefaso.net/spip. php?article52854.

Urrego, M.R., quoted *in* Ramsar Convention Secretariat, *Ramsar Convention at the High-level Political Forum on Sustainable Development* (18 July 2018), Ramsar Convention News, at https://www.ramsar.org/news/ramsar-convention-at-the-high-level-political-forum-on-sustainable-development.

Wex, Legal Information Institute, Cornell Law School: *Doctrine*, at https://www.law.cornell.edu/wex/doctrine.

Wubie, H., Tsegaw, Z., *Legal Personality of the African Union* (29 Feb 2012), *Abyssinia Law*, at https://www.abyssinialaw.com/about-us/item/380-legal-personality-of-the-african-union.

Zarbiyev, F., *Damaged Beyond Repair? International Law after Gaza* (26 Mar 2024), EJIL: Talk!, at https://www.ejiltalk.org/damaged-beyond-repair-international-law-after-gaza/?utm_source=mailpoet&utm_medium=email&utm_campaign=ejil-talk-newsletter-post-title_2.

Wex, Legal Information Institute, Cornell Law School: *Doctrine*, at https://www.law.cornell.edu/wex/doctrine.

Wubie, H., Tsegaw, Z., *Legal Personality of the African Union* (29 Feb 2012), *Abyssinia Law*, at https://www.abyssinialaw.com/about-us/item/380-legal-personality-of-the-african-union.

Zarbiyev, F., *Damaged Beyond Repair? International Law after Gaza* (26 Mar 2024), EJIL: Talk!, at https://www.ejiltalk.org/damaged-beyond-repair-international-law-after-gaza/?utm_source=mailpoet&utm_medium=email&utm_campaign=ejil-talk-newsletter-post-title_2.

Index

www.ingramcontent.com/pod-product-compliance
Lightning Source LLC
LaVergne TN
LVHW020650300926
849161LV00004B/882
* 9 7 8 9 0 0 4 7 4 9 5 2 8 *

www.ingramcontent.com/pod-product-compliance
Lightning Source LLC
LaVergne TN
LVHW020650300926
849161LV00004B/882